Open the door, Fishbait!

That's just what William Miller, who spent 24 years as Democratic Doorkeeper in the House of Representatives, does for you. You look inside at the teeming, scheming, scuffling, and struggling body of men and women known as the Congress, and Fishbait tells you all about them. The drinkers, the philanderers, the big spenders, the sadists. The anecdotes abound:

- how Richard Nixon choked him
- how Eleanor got the VP spot for Harry Truman without FDR's knowledge
- how JFK managed his womanizing—despite his bad back
- how Fishbait made Bella Abzug take off her hat

FISHBAIT

"recounts with earnest sentiment and earthy humor the politics, scandals and foibles of congresspersons, past and present."
—Booklist

"Humorous . . . outlandish . . . fascinating."
Houston Post

FISHBAIT

THE MEMOIRS OF THE CONGRESSIONAL DOORKEEPER

by William "Fishbait" Miller,
as told to Frances Spatz Leighton

WARNER BOOKS

A Warner Communications Company

WARNER BOOKS EDITION

Copyright © 1977 by William Mosely Miller and
Frances Spatz Leighton

Library of Congress Catalog Card Number: 76-58404

ISBN 0-446-81637-X

This Warner Books Edition is published by
arrangement with Prentice-Hall, Inc.

Warner Books, Inc., 75 Rockefeller Plaza, New York, N.Y. 10019

 A Warner Communications Company

Printed in the United States of America

Not associated with Warner Press, Inc. of Anderson, Indiana

First Printing: May, 1978

10 9 8 7 6 5 4 3 2 1

CONTENTS

Introduction   7

Part I.
In Case You Wonder Why They Want to Get
Elected . . .
1. Up the Down Staircase on Capitol Hill   *13*
2. The Making of a Doorkeeper   *39*
3. The High Cost of Health, Welfare and the Good Life on the Hill   *71*
4. The Ladies of Congress—Bless Them All   *88*
5. Every Congressman a King—And the Staff Gets Leftovers   *120*
6. You Can Womanize If You Avoid the Spies   *145*

Part II.
At Work and Play on Capitol Hill/Or Getting Down to Cases
7. The Night I Locked the Whole Damn House In   *169*
8. In the Back Rooms of Congress   *205*
9. The Hot Breath of Scandal/Wayne Hays and Wilbur Mills Are Not Alone   *227*
10. All You've Ever Wanted to Know About the History of the Capitol but Were Afraid to Ask   *267*
11. Profiles in Power   *299*
12. The Jokers Are Wild   *330*

Part III.
Step Lively or Get Your Tail Caught in the Crack . . .
13. Convention Fever   *363*

14. Presidents I Have Known Before They Were Presidents—From Truman to Ford *391*
15. The Other Body *416*
16. Death and Danger on Capitol Hill *444*
17. The Royal Knack *469*
18. For Some Silly Reason, Some Congessmen Insist on Getting the Job Done *496*

Index *516*

✶ ✶ ✶ ✶ ✶ ✶ ✶ ✶ ✶ ✶ ✶ ✶ ✶ ✶ ✶ ✶ ✶ ✶

INTRODUCTION

Who drank? Who didn't? What of Wilbur Mills? Wayne Hays?

Who were the great womanizers?

Who lived like kings on Capitol Hill?

Who were sadistic? Who said words so cruel he caused a congressional colleague to fall dead as he left the floor of the House?

Who were called "the Five Sisters" for their religious ardor? And speaking of sisters, how angelic are the women in Congress?

All will be answered in this ultimate look at life as it is truly lived on Capitol Hill, as seen through the eyes of Fishbait Miller. So well-known is this former Doorkeeper to the general public, who heard him intone, "Mistah Speakah, the President of the United States," that mail addressed simply to "Fishbait, Washington, D.C." had no trouble coming directly to him.

His material is fantastic. Inside stories on the men who run the country. Inside stories on the Presidents he knew before they were Presidents. His stories may not blow the dome off the Capitol, but they should tilt it a little.

Frances Spatz Leighton

* * * * * * * * * * * * * * * * * * * *

THIS BOOK
IS DEDICATED TO
MY FRIENDS AND
ENEMIES IN CONGRESS,
TO THE WINNERS
AND THE LOSERS
. . . BLESS THEM ALL.

* * * * * * * * * * * * * * * * * * *

The Panchatantra is a sort of Aesop's fable of India to teach wisdom by telling stories about animals. Some Hindus were working in a forest one day and they left behind a log they had been splitting, with the wedge still in it. A monkey saw the wedge, wondered what it was and hopped on the log to pull it out. Just as he succeeded, the crack in the log closed on his tail. So ever since, mankind—and congressmen—have been worried about getting their tails caught in a crack.

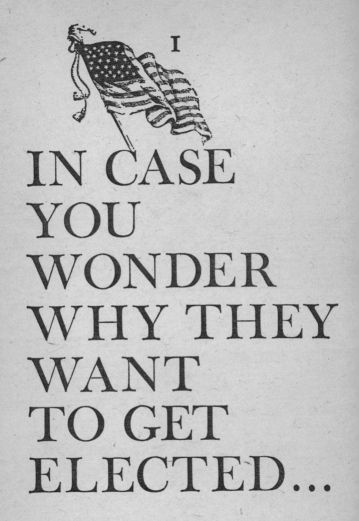

I

IN CASE YOU WONDER WHY THEY WANT TO GET ELECTED...

UP THE DOWN STAIRCASE ON CAPITOL HILL

One Saturday morning, I was standing in front of my Doorkeeper's Office in plaid shirt and stocking feet—I only permitted myself this luxury on the weekend— being friendly and maybe showing off a bit. A ramrod- like figure came by and I thought I'd warm him up, maybe make a friend.

I pointed to the sign on the door and said proudly, "That's me."

The man stopped, gave me a haughty look, reached into his pocket and pulled out a Heath candy bar. "That's me," he said, and kept on walking.

It was an unnerving moment. I suddenly realized that my head had started to swell a little. I'd been around congressmen and senators—or, as we on the Hill liked to call them, "535 high-school class presi- dents with a few prom queens thrown in"—for too long. The egos on Capitol Hill are incredible. I had been warned when I came to the Capitol, direct from Pascagoula, Mississippi, to take my first job as messen- ger to the House postmaster—salary $1,740—"The rule around this place is 'Every man a king'—and don't you forget it!"

I didn't forget. I thrived as I made my home among the mighty. I was like a pilot fish. Or maybe the little fish that swims along with the biggies, grooming them, keeping the little pests and blood suckers away. I studied the big fish. I learned their every need and habit.

Even the telephone operators on the Hill were told, "If you run into anything you can't answer, just switch the call to the Doorkeeper's Office. Tell them to ask for

13

Fishbait. He'll give them an answer that they'll be satisfied with. Because if he's not sure, he will make them believe it's true anyway."

Well, I'm out now, retired, kicked out or voted out, if you please, after forty-two years on Capitol Hill, twenty-eight of them as the doorkeeper. And while it is all vividly clear in my mind, I'm ready to give you the true, unvarnished picture of life as it is lived on Capitol Hill. It's not the same as the sweet little newsletter that gets mailed to constituents back home. And it is the truth, so help me God, to the best of my ability.

Incidentally, I want you to know that Mr. Heath of Heath candy bars and I eventually became good friends.

I suppose the first thing you are asking is what the devil does Congress need a Doorkeeper for? Can't these guys who earn $44,600 open their own doors? They can and they do. The doors referred to here are those that bar the way to the floor of the House of Representatives. So important are those doors that it takes a full-time Doorkeeper and twenty-six Assistant Doorkeepers to keep out the unwanted, the unauthorized, the dangerous.

The job of Doorkeeper is more than that of a doorman. Sometimes I thought it was part footman, part chauffeur, part courtier, and part royal clown or hatchet man. By the time I left office, my salary had advanced to the $40,000 level. I didn't get it for standing idle. My domain included the House press galleries, the House cloakrooms, the House rest rooms and even the House Prayer Room, besides the House floor.

Messengers, pages, cloakroom employees, the barbers of five barbershops, the attendants of eight ladies' rest rooms and five men's lounges, and janitors came under my auspices, as well as the House Document Room employees and the Publication Distribution Service employees who perform duties required by various members of the House. Employees manning twenty-eight very important telephones came under my special attention—these phones are especially important because they are used for incoming and outgoing messages for members of Congress when the House is in session and legislation is up for debate.

It was an incident in one of the barbershops that almost caused a chunk of my powers to be chopped away—if not my head. The time was August 1973, and a congressman came out bitching that instead of the usual dollar, the barber had dared to charge him $2.50. (Thanks to a generous public, congressmen paid only $1 for a haircut up until that time and the taxpayer made up the difference.)

Straight to Wayne Hays he went—Wayne Hays, one of the toughest, short-tempered men on the Hill, chairman of the House Administration Committee. Immediately, Wayne Hays called me to his office, roaring mad. "Mister Potato Head [one of Hays' favorite epithets], I'll tell you what I'm going to do to you. I'm appointing a committee on nonessential personnel and I'm going to take away about forty percent of your work and cut your salary so much you'll be skinny as a rail!"

"Mable, my wife, will thank you," I said. "Can we get rid of about fifty pounds like my doctor ordered?"

Hays had a way of terrifying just about everybody on Capitol Hill. Still, I had been trained by Speaker of the House Sam Rayburn to "be humble but never let a bully get the upper hand." I told Hays I would look into the matter and report back. I returned soon, explaining, "Mr. Chairman, the barber says he had to take three times as much time as normally—he had to do a complete restyling. He says he should have charged $3 at least. He says the guy's hair was long—awful long."

Congressman Hays sputtered, but by now he had calmed down considerably. "Well," he said, "I'm going to keep the barbers on your payroll. But from now on we're going to have a new system of rates. I want signs printed up and I am raising the price from $1 to $2 for everybody. And I want you to print 'no tipping' at the bottom of the signs. And I want the signs posted in every damn barbershop. And, oh yes, I'm hereby raising the cost of a shave from 50 cents to $1."

So now, instead of one man bitching, the whole House was bitching. But Brother Hays laughed. He had triumphed as usual—they did it *his* way.

In all, I had to supervise over 300 permanent employees. Just recognizing all of my gang was job enough. But much more important was recognizing the 535 members of Congress on sight and from the first day they appeared as congressmen-elect. It was not me, I assure you, who made the famous *faux pas* of taking the scrawny John F. Kennedy for a page when he first came to Congress as a representative. It was an elevator man who thought JFK should get off the members-only elevator.

I developed such a knack for memorizing names and faces and matching them together that soon members were inviting me to their big formal parties just to have me stand at their elbows on the receiving line, helping them with the names of their guests.

Almost anyone who watches television has seen me in my big moment, just before the President's appearance before a Joint Session. The door is flung open and I bellow: "Mistah Speakah, the President of the United States." In fact, if you saw the movie *All the President's Men*, you may remember me in the film clip which is the opening scene: Nixon gets out of a helicopter and is next seen entering the House Chamber, with me ushering him in and doing my thing—my famous bellow. But that is the only moment of glory. A lot of work goes in ahead of time, for which I, as the Doorkeeper, was responsible: security to make the presidential appearance safe; issuance of special tickets required for all who attend; split-second timing.

When it is a foreign chief-of-state who addresses the House and Senate, there are complicated details to be

16

worked out with the State Department. But many of my big announcements were heard only by members of the House and whatever reporters, tourists and other visitors happened to be in the galleries that day. That's when I, as Doorkeeper, announced to the House, during normal business days, the arrival of messages from the White House or the Senate—which we deigned only to refer to as "the Other Body," when speaking on the floor.

I seldom had a dull moment. Whenever the House was adjourned, I was off doing something with the members who wanted me, needed me, or just hated to be alone. I went campaigning, helped celebrate with the living and helped bury the fallen leaders. I was at every Democratic nominating convention during my span and saw the making of the President from the smoke-filled rooms of the winners to the tear-filled rooms of the losers.

I remember well how deals were made to push one good man aside for another man—maybe better, maybe not. I know, because I was on the platforms or nearby, doing the bidding of such leaders as Sam Rayburn.

Rayburn. The very name brings back the sound and the smell of a convention hall. He had a trick of rewarding a good party worker—or turning him *into* a good party worker—that made the man a friend for life. For this trick, he needed me.

Before a convention, Rayburn would say, "Fish, don't forget to pick up about four dozen extra gavels. You hear me?"

"Yeah, boss," I would say.

At the convention, I would show up each day in my special jacket, which I had made especially large around the middle and saved only for wear at the conventions. Whenever I wore it, I looked like a walrus. The reason was that I had six gavels stuck into my belt. And if you think that's easy, try it.

Every once in a while, when the moment was ripe,

Rayburn would send for a man—which automatically made the chosen one feel like the most important man in the convention hall. Rayburn would then make a little presentation in his most serious voice: "I want you, Joe, to take my gavel back to your home town for your museum or school. And tell 'em, this gavel was used to bring the presidential convention to order." The party worker would leave the platform walking on air and be sure of immortality back home.

Then Sam would grin at me and say gruffly, "Hey Fish, fish me out another one of those gavels, will ya?"

Sam Rayburn was a prince of a man, even if he did single-handedly set the cause of women's lib back at least ten years. He was a man's man and the women of the Hill were safe around him, no matter how pretty or tempting they were. I loved him like a brother and we used to sit on a bench at the end of the day while he gave me bits of his philosophy—"When two men agree on everything, you can be sure *one* of them is doing all the thinking."

Or, when he didn't like the way the opposition had skunked a bill of his, he would say, "A jackass can kick a barn down, but it takes a carpenter to build one."

As he talked, Sam would glance curiously at any good-looking girl, many of whom made a play for him. But he was not a chaser. Fortunately or unfortunately, other members more than made up for him. One congressman, as a matter of pride, made it a point to sleep with a different girl every night. When he had to repeat, he was vexed indeed. But I think it's only fair to say the men of the Senate were not too different.

One story comes to mind. There was and is a particular senator, whom I first knew as a congressman, who prides himself on his prowess with women. It came to pass that a certain committee, of which he was a high-ranking member, was worried that material was being leaked to lobbyists. So a certain room in which

18

the leakage was suspected to occur was bugged by some of the staff. "We'll catch that peckerwood," they said.

The next day, as the tape was played, instead of skullduggery involving lobbyists, a different story unfolded. The senator's voice was heard as he arrived, and it was established that he was alone with the secretary on duty, working overtime, alone, to get a report out. The senator's voice was heard explaining how he had been watching her and yearning to get her undivided attention, if only for a moment. How he'd like her to work for him.

Things went on from there, and soon the senator's voice was heard promising the girl the greatest thrill she had ever experienced. Eventually, her voice was heard asking, "What does that scar mean?"

"It's the result of a youthful indiscretion, my dear," the senator replied. Things went on from there and eventually came the girl's solemn admission that the senator was indeed one of the greatest lovers of the Western world.

It should have ended there, but the aide could not resist sharing his good luck and the tape was heard by a few close friends on the Senate side and then a few close friends on the House side. Eventually, it was copied by friends who had friends, and it became the talk of the Hill, which is like a small town. As a matter of fact, everyone heard the tape except the very important senator who sat in great dignity while aides all around him smiled and asked each other *sotto voce* if this or that was "the result of a youthful indiscretion."

As I said, the senator is still there, dignity and all, but the girl soon transferred away from the Hill to a government agency. It was just easier that way.

I suppose few men knew as much as I did about what went on behind the closed doors of the Capitol. I was the keeper of countless secrets and the dispenser of advice—some of it good. I never let on what I knew. You might say I played a role that was part clown, part confidant—and always one of eager helpfulness. It was not a painful role.

I loved the game and played it to the hilt, even once standing by until a particular congressman, Ray Madden, finished eating a popsicle at the back of the House Chamber. He then handed the stick to me and I tiptoed out to get rid of it, having to take a little teasing for slavish devotion along the way.

It was true. I was slavishly devoted to all my friends on the Hill, and that friendship once almost cost me my life. Whenever my friends needed me, I would drive them around and help them get reelected just as I had done for others back in Pascagoula, Mississippi —and I was scheduled to go on an ill-fated trip to Alaska with Congressman Hale Boggs of Louisiana and Nick Begich of Alaska. But fate stepped in, in the form of a greater loyalty—my wife, Mable, suddenly insisted I go with her to Atlanta to visit our daughter, Sarah Patsy. So Begich took a man from his office instead of me. All those aboard disappeared with their plane.

I soon learned you could hardly move around Capitol Hill without running into a lobbyist. And at parties you knew where they were because they laughed the loudest at the congressmen's jokes. They were always around the favorite eating spots just off the Capitol grounds, too—the Monocle and the Rotunda, to name just two—and they always tried to pick up the tabs of various senators and congressmen, sometimes even when they hadn't been eating at the same table.

Lobbyists were great at trouble-shooting if a congressman had a problem. If the problem involved making some extra money, they could easily arrange for him to be invited to make a speech for a nice fee, or "honorarium," as it's called on the Hill.

The best lobbyists, I was told, were former congressmen, because they knew the ropes and less would be thought of the fact that a legislator would be having lunch with an old crony. With the help of old friends, one ex-congressman once did so well in getting a certain bill passed through the House that he had to drag out his work when he went over to the Senate side, for fear his bosses would think lobbying was too easy. Since a bill has to be passed by both houses, he didn't push for its passage through the second House until the end of the session.

Speaking of the end of the session reminds me that lobbyists really get busy at that time and it's then that any number of little amendments and riders are sneaked onto a bill that everyone wants passed. The Hill is still talking about the worst case of this that ever happened, a bill that was so overloaded that they called it the "Christmas Tree Bill of 1966."

It started as a legislation that would help the elderly, but ended up with every kind of amendment—including a higher depletion allowance on aluminum ore, a depletion allowance for oyster shells and on and on, adding up to forty-nine riders.

Sometimes—but thank goodness not often—lobbyists on opposite sides of the fence get together to strike a deal. That was the inside story on the Hill of why it took so long to get warnings put on cigarette packs that smoking is dangerous to health.

When the surgeon general's report was about to be released, proving that cigarettes produce cancer, the tobacco lobby struck a deal with the American Medical Association in a way that helped both of them. According to word on the Hill, the tobacco companies came up with a $10 million grant for a new study on the hazards of cigarettes, which automatically made it seem that something must have been wrong with the government's study—thus enabling cigarette companies and tobacco farmers to continue making their usual profits.

21

In return, by getting southern Congressmen to vote against the Medicare bill, tobacco lobbyists helped the AMA fight legislation which, it was feared, would cut down on doctors' earnings by establishing "socialized medicine."

The irony of this story is that both lobbyist groups needn't have worried. Doctors earn more than ever because of Medicare, and cigarettes are as popular as ever—no matter what warning they carry.

It's a real eye-opener to take a look at the list of lobbyists, all of whom must register with Congress so that their connections are known. There is even a frozen pizza lobby. It has the name of National Frozen Pizza Institute.

In case you are wondering why pizza parlors would need lobbyists—just as you may have wondered why able-bodied congressmen need a Doorkeeper—I can give you several reasons. One is to try to keep down the cost of equipment. And even more importantly, to try to get a higher quota of imported cheese because the price of domestic cheese increased for them by about forty percent in the course of one year. The higher the price of pizza goes, the harder it is for pizza makers to compete with other food producers.

And that's just one tiny story behind the three thousand registered lobbyists on the Hill, who are unofficially called "the fourth branch of government."

Sometimes humor used by a small lobbyist can defeat the bigger expenditure of the bigger lobbyist. An important lobbyist for the big trunk airlines was spending a lot of money wining and dining Senate aides in a series of "nonpartisan" meetings—cocktails, dinner and propaganda.

It was reasoned that the aides would in turn influence their bosses to protect the subsidies of the big trunk airlines and scuttle independent competition. Unable to compete and pick up similar tabs, the lobbyist for the small companies who were trying to get a cor-

22

ner of the business came up with a gag, a supposed menu which had been served. Printed first in a newsletter, it was picked up quickly by the news media.

So devastating was the menu that it killed the series of fancy dinners and propaganda meetings scheduled for the future by the big trunk airlines, who decided they couldn't afford the bad publicity.

I saved the menu:

Purée Monopoly
Prime Ribs of Mailpay, Rich Gravy
Potatoes à la Treasury ☆ Dollared Greens
Lettuce, Inter-Island Dressing
Sparkling Franchise, 1938
Chocolate Profiterole ☆ Big-Four Cookies
Demitasse (for Local Service Lines)
Corona Pan Am
Empire Brandy

Every now and then something mighty funny happens involving lobbyists. Let me tell you about one case. In Washington, a $100-a-person fund-raising reception is standard procedure when a man is up for reelection, and it's almost mandatory that all lobbyists and other friends show up, or else. It's the equivalent of an invitation from the White House—it's a must. In this case, a particular lobbyist got a call from a congressman's aide, telling him there was going to be one of these $100-a-plate fund-raisers for his boss, who had been working on an amendment to a bill with the lobbyist.

Even though the lobbyist could not attend, he forked over the C note. Then, when the congressman sold him down the river on the amendment, the lobbyist called the aide and said, "I have a message I want you to deliver verbatim to the candidate. Tell the son of a bitch I'd like to know the name of his opponent so I can give *him* a hundred dollars."

23

I remember the case of a Republican congressman from Georgia who held one of these fund-raising receptions in the Rayburn House Office Building. But he made the mistake of receiving cash and checks right *inside* the building proper. The rules are such that no cash or checks may be received for campaign purposes within the confines of any of the buildings used by the House members for their offices, or in the Capitol itself.

The Georgia newspapers had an alert reporter at the party, and he described how the money changed hands, though the congressman denied it. But not for long. This was one time Wayne Hays came in like thunder on the side of right. He threatened to expose the congressman completely and even go so far as to take it up with the U.S. Department of Justice.

Wayne called in the reporter and got more eyewitness details. The congressman decided it wouldn't be necessary to call in the Justice Department. He said he hadn't realized the rule and it would never happen again. And it didn't because he was defeated in the next election.

It's amazing what a person can learn just by taking notes as the congressional gang relaxes in the back rooms, out of sight of the galleries. Especially on the Democratic side.

I recall how much fun the gang had with a thing called "The Sterling Bulletin," which explained how to know whether one was dealing with a Democrat or a Republican. The first way was the fish method. Democrats eat the fish they catch, Republicans hang theirs on the wall.

Then there was the bug method. Republicans phone for exterminators, Democrats step on them.

And, of course, the bedroom method. Republicans sleep in twin beds, some even in separate rooms. That's why there are more Democrats.

And when they ran out of definitions and comparisons that made the other side look more ridiculous than they did, they would try to remember who was the last congressman to wear a certain garment. They seemed to agree that the last man to hang on to the politician's string tie was Robert Alexis Green of Bradford County, Florida, who came to the Hill in 1925 and served until 1944.

When they got to the discussion of how you could recognize potential political talent or who was fated to become a politician, my home state congressman, Bill Colmer of Mississippi was the expert with his story.

"My neighbor had a young boy about seventeen or eighteen years old and he was concerned, wondering what his son was going to be when he grew up," Colmer would begin. "The lad was already full of vim, vigor and vitality. So the father got three objects and placed them on the table and hid behind the door.

"The boy came in whistling as he always did, stepped lively to the table, picked up the cards, opened them, counted and found the count was right, so he put them in his pocket. And his daddy thought to himself, 'Oh my God, he's going to be a gambler.'

"Then the son picked up the second item, the bottle of whiskey. He shook it to see if he could get a good bead at the top of the bottle. He seemed satisfied and stuck that under his arm. The father groaned to himself, 'Oh, my son is going to be a drunkard.'

"Then the son picked up the Bible and thumbed through it. He turned to the Twenty-third Psalm, wherein the first line reads, 'The Lord is my shepherd, I shall not want . . .' and started reading aloud. The father scratched his head in perplexity and then came the revelation, 'Oh my God, he's going to be a politician.' "

Visitors to the Hill, looking down at the serious men on the floor, sometimes come back and ask me whether congressmen ever notice pretty faces in an audience and whether they are influenced. I do not tell them how often a pretty girl, aware of the eye of a congress-

25

man, eventually finds her way to his office on the pretext of asking an important question.

The story comes back to me of the time Jennings Randolph, when still a congressman, was the speaker at an aviation meeting in Louisville, Kentucky, just before World War II. His hosts had placed his chair at the edge of the platform, which fortunately was rather low, because when he saw a beautiful face in the audience and hitched his chair to get a better look at her, the chair leg went off the platform and so did he.

Down he tumbled and came up unhurt. Still undaunted, he tried to get acquainted with the beauty after the speech, but she preferred the guy she was with. The story was met with high glee on the Hill.

I've known seven Presidents—Roosevelt, Truman, Eisenhower, Kennedy, Johnson, Nixon and Ford—and, to me, LBJ was the most interesting. That's because he was the hardest to figure out—was he dumb or foxy?

Remember when LBJ showed everyone the scar from his gallbladder operation? No one could figure out why he was so anxious to have it shown. It was crude, everyone said, exposing his body to have the ugly thing photographed. On the Hill, we had the inside story, told by a doctor. Lyndon had asked him, "Could this scar be anything but for gallbladder? If people thought you had an exploratory operation for cancer, could they think this was a cancer operation scar?"

"Hardly," the doctor had replied. "It is a classic gallbladder scar." So LBJ just wanted to have everyone know it wasn't cancer that had sent him to the hospital.

How's that for foxy?

As for whether Lyndon Johnson was emotional, I can assure you he certainly was. I remember when Lyndon lost the presidential nomination to Jack Kennedy in Los Angeles. At the time, I was standing with Sam Rayburn and Lyndon, and they were both crying. That was before LBJ was offered the vice-presidency, and I can tell you the tears were real.

I remember that little Luci Johnson who didn't quite understand ins and outs of conventions, asked, "How come everyone is so mean to us?" Lady Bird answered, "Well, you'll have to get used to that."

And what do you suppose was Lyndon's first move when he got the phone call that JFK was offering him the vice-presidency? He came running to Rayburn. It was Rayburn's administrative assistant—John Holton —who called Bobby Kennedy, Jack's brother, to see if there was any truth in it or whether it was a hoax.

I'm asked so many questions about the Hill. Are the members all alike? Or are they vastly different from each other? All I can say is, whatever type you can think of, we've got at least one.

Unusual names?

Davey Crockett. Is that unusual enough? Or "son of Davey Crockett"—John Wesley Crockett.

Or how about Philemon Herbert, born in Pine Apple, Alabama? Phil was a *lemon* all right, and maybe even a pineapple, and he proved it one day when he was eating in the elegant Willard Hotel in downtown Washington. The service wasn't fast enough to suit him, so he simply took out his gun and shot the waiter dead. That was in the 1850s, when he was a congressman from California.

Has any congressman worn a gun in recent years? Yep. A few years back, Eugene Snyder, a Republican from Kentucky, admitted to carrying a concealed weapon. Fortunately, he never used it to my knowledge, though Washington has become a dangerous town.

Embarrassing moments?

Well, you really have to feel sorry for Bob Edgar, a Democrat from Pennsylvania, who thought he was being a man of the people by riding his bicycle on his first invitation to the White House. He wondered why so many people, including the President, looked at him strangely. There was nothing wrong with his fly. When he got out of the White House and was walking to his bike, he realized he'd been wearing his pant legs rolled up all the time!

Everyone knows about snuff-sniffers on the floor of the House, but has anyone ever been into hard drugs? One of the most brilliant men the House has ever known took opium. It was long before my time, but old John Randolph was supposed to be a descendant of both Jefferson and Pocahontas and opium only seemed to stimulate his mind and make him more cantankerous. When high on the drug, he would insult people —and the insult most quoted on the Hill is what he said of Henry Clay while accusing him of corruption: "Like rotten mackerel in the moonlight, he shines and he stinks." What Clay called Randolph, I do not know.

Huey Long, the political boss of Louisiana, was a most disruptive force in the Senate. But he was a fantastically colorful talker, using all kinds of southern expressions. When he was going to make a speech, the word would be flashed up and down the halls, and anyone who had time would rush to the galleries of the Other Body just to listen to him. Secretaries on the Hill adored him as he railed against FDR or bankers rich enough to "burn a wet mule."

One person who didn't adore him was Carter Glass, the famed senator from Virginia and the Hill's top banking expert, who was always being attacked by the Louisiana Kingfish until he fought fire with fire. Being a Virginia gentleman, Senator Glass bit his tongue until he eventually could take no more. He made a beeline for Huey after adjournment on a day that Huey had made one of his floor attacks, shouting that Glass was a "tool of the house of Morgan."

Trying to head Glass off, Majority Leader Joe Robinson walked over and took Glass by the arm, saying "Come here, Carter, I want to talk to you." Glass whirled out of his grasp, turned and faced Huey about fifteen feet away, and said, "Yes, but I'm tired of this man making a personal issue with me, you damned thieving son of a bitch." As I say, it was the last time Huey attacked Glass.

Huey Long had an unfortunate way of expressing himself when displeased or in his cups—like a dog, he would point and urinate. Once, in the members' men's room, he pretended to miss his mark in the urinal and hit another senator with whom he'd been having words a short time before. The victim tried to slug him, but Huey fended off his blow with one hand and walked out laughing.

Another time, Huey did not make it to the rest room. He was at the bar of a nightclub and he proceeded to cast a spray which did not hit the man it was probably aimed at but struck a lady's leg instead. Her escort promptly slugged him.

We never knew what to expect next when Huey was around the Hill. I was told that he was the only member of Congress to have ever lighted a firecracker in a legislative chamber. He had wanted to be provocative and he certainly was.

Once I was in the Senate trolley, which goes between the Senate and the Capitol Building, when Huey sat down beside me and proceeded to tell me the power of the vine and how he had learned to use the power of grape juice even as a boy.

I had some people with me whom I was showing around the Capitol and Huey kept us all riveted until he had finished his story, long after the underground trolley had deposited us and gone back for more passengers. He had a roundabout way of telling things, and after talking about his home state, his philosophy of life and whatnot, he finally got down to it:

"You know, down in Cajun country we have a whole lot of Catholics who appreciate the vine, and a whole lot of Baptists who don't. Well, this is a story about how one group in life can learn from another group.

This is a Baptist story about this reverend I knew when I was a little tadpole.

"Well this reverend wanted to raise some money and it was communion time so he discussed his problem with me and he decided that maybe instead of his using that old grape juice he would send me shopping and if I made a mistake and got something red and a little stronger than that old plain grape juice, well, that was an honest mistake that the church would be making.

"I went out and got a couple of bottles of good strong wine. The next thing I heard, he had not only raised the amount that he wanted but he had a $750 surplus for the first time in history. So, you see, I learned early in life the value of the vine in doing good works."

When Huey was shot dead at the Louisiana statehouse, the Hill people were suddenly full of compassion and no longer called him "that scoundrel" or "the wild man of the Hill." Instead, they started talking about how he could have been President if only he had lived.

My favorite memories of Huey Long are in his role as champion of the poor, thundering how he wanted "to share the wealth" and standing in the Senate filibustering by reading cook books, letters and his favorite reading, the encyclopedia.

But famous as he was for his encyclopedia readings, Huey couldn't hold a candle to Strom Thurmond, who gave the longest filibuster of them all—twenty-four hours, nineteen minutes. That's how long Strom talked on during a particularly bitter session, filibustering against, not for, something, naturally. The subject? The Civil Rights Bill, of course.

The Hill is its own world.

Congressmen even have their own spiritual guide. One of the top jobs a man of the cloth can aspire to is that of chaplain of the House. It pays $19,770, has many side benefits for retirement and, since not too many congressmen come rushing in for spiritual help, lots of free time. Members used to go instead to Senator Harold Hughes, who was one of them and who didn't mind saying he was a reformed drunk. He started saving people on the Hill and recently left the political life to devote his full time to spiritual matters.

There is a little-known room on the Hill. The Prayer Room. If a congressman is deeply upset or even just in need of guidance from his own heart and mind, he may go there and sit in silent meditation. As a joke, Elizabeth Ray has said that she thought of using the room for other purposes. I'm almost sure she would not have been caught.

I think I spent more time than most in the Prayer Room. That's because whenever there was an honored group of churchmen visiting Speaker Sam or his successors, I would be called in and instructed to take them to this room. I would explain to them, tongue in cheek, how members would come here when deeply troubled and in need of spiritual guidance.

It's a beautiful room, dark and colorful, with a fine altar suitable for Christians and Jews alike. Or Moslems and Hindus for that matter, I suppose.

The Prayer Room was used most often by a little group of religious zealots who were nicknamed "the Five Sisters." I remember how the Five Sisters—all Republicans—would ask me to have the Prayer Room open for them early every Monday morning—about 7:30—and daily during Lent.

The leader of the group was Jerry Ford, the minority leader. The others were John Rhodes of Arizona, who would succeed Ford as minority leader; Les Arends of Illinois; Charles Goodell of New York; and Albert Quie of Minnesota.

They would not have the House chaplain present. They would hold their own prayer meeting, and when one of them got his tail caught in a legislative crack,

31

they would have an extra talk session with God to see how to get the tail out.

But the men who pray together stay together on the Hill and seem to have less troubles in life and less bad publicity than other congressmen.

One Democrat, Senator Robert Byrd of West Virginia, had his own way of expressing his religious fervor. Instead of going to the Prayer Room, he held a prayer meeting in his office with his staff every day before they set to work. They had Bible readings, and each person had a chance to speak. They even went over the hometown newspapers together.

Prayer has certainly not hurt the senator's career. Bob was the whip of the Senate when I left and was in line for the majority leadership. He had come to the House in 1953, already filled with religious fervor.

Bob had started out as a poor boy with a flair for teaching Sunday school. In fact, when he was in college he had started a Sunday school class in the hills of West Virginia with only five people in it. Before he got through, he had built his little Bible class to a crowd of 525 members, some of whom drove twenty miles every Sunday to attend.

Some of our religious congressional members had a way of making their calling less stuffy. I remember our Presbyterian minister, Congressman Bill Hudnut of Indianapolis, would say he had come to Congress from the "hatch, match and dispatch profession"—in other words, he had performed baptisms, marriages and funerals.

Joan and Walter Mondale both had ministers for fathers. But on the Hill they were fun people as well as being serious. In fact, I have been told there is a big painting in their home over the fireplace which shows Joan as Cleopatra and Fritz Mondale as Caesar with the caption, "All Hail, Mondale."

There have always been a few fancy dressers on the Hill. When I first came there, the strangest outfit was worn by Congressman Loring Black, a Democrat from Brooklyn, New York, who had once worked for William Jennings Bryan and wanted the world to know it. He tried to look exactly as Bryan had many years before. He wore his hair down on his shoulders and the same kind of swallowtail coat Bryan had worn in the 1880s or 1890s or early part of this century. Among today's youth, Black would have looked very in. Those days he looked very out.

And when I left, it was "Dapper Dan," Democratic Congressman Dan Flood of Wilkes-Barre, Pennsylvania, who was known for his sartorial pace-setting. He wore fancy waistcoats, two-color shoes, and fancy ties. Not only that, but each day when he went to lunch at the Rotunda restaurant, a block from the office buildings on the House side, his special table was reserved for him in a dark alcove and a tall candle would be lighted on his table. He ate alone. Also on the table would be a vase containing a lone rose. We called him the Salvador Dali of the House of Representatives because his waxed, pencil-line thin mustache was almost exactly like that of the great artist.

Flood, a very able congressman incidentally, was all of forty-six when he married his very charming wife, Catherine, in 1949. For all the quarter century that I would see her, I would tease her about being a bride. At first she wanted desperately to have a child and told me she even consulted psychics to see if she would have one, but she didn't. She was one of my favorite congressional wives, always sweet and good-natured.

And at the bottom of the list of people who cared about clothes and niceties was Fiorello La Guardia. Most people think La Guardia was just the mayor of New York, but he was a congressman from 1923 to 1933 before becoming mayor in 1934.

What he was famous for was his complete and total dedication to work. He'd look like an unmade bed. As long as the House was in session, he would not leave the chamber and would have a pocket full of peanuts to eat if he got hungry.

Though he was supposed to be a Republican, he thought Democrat, worked for federal aid to workers and once picketed in New York City with the clothing workers who were out on strike. But what I'm leading up to is that only once did Fiorello get dressed up and go to the White House.

As I have said, a White House invitation is considered a command performance—and was even more so in his day. The fiery congressman got to the door of the East Room where the reception was being held and stood looking inside at all the men and ladies in their finery. "This is not for me," he said and turned around and walked out, thus making history as important to the Hill crowd as the Gann-Longworth precedence fight over who sits higher above the salt, described later.

But back to Dapper Dan Flood, the congressman proved long ago that nobody had better get the notion that he was a homosexual. One guy, seeing him in strange spangled garb up on the platform in Wilkes-Barre, made the mistake of calling him a "pansy," and Flood came down and gave him one quick right that sent him sprawling back into the next row.

At times, Flood wears a cape that makes him look like the ringmaster of a circus—which some congressmen say really makes sense on the Hill—and when Flood and his wife are driven home to Wilkes-Barre in their white limousine, the townfolks are delighted that in the car with them are a bird, some goldfish and a noisy chihuahua.

For unusual characters who have come to the Hill, I give my vote to "Front-Porch Harmon." I well recall when Brother Randall Harmon, a new Democrat from Indiana, sailed in on the 1958 tide. This time he had embarked in a Democratic craft. Four or five times previously he had floundered in a Republican boat.

Right from the start, as I got acquainted with Randall, everything he had to say was most interesting—for example, this time he had been elected after spending only $162. About the first thing he did was to install a time clock in his office. And the second thing he did was to find out from the House administration that you were allowed $100 a month for office space back in your hometown if you couldn't find anything suitable to your needs in Washington or nearby.

"So what I've gone and done," he told me, "is I've taken down the screens of my front porch back in Muncie and replaced them with glass. And I'm renting the porch to the government for $100 a month as my office." Then he sent his wife home to take care of the porch while he was away.

The other congressmen meowed him—they were mighty catty about it. But Front-Porch Harmon made himself even more famous by letting the newspaper people in Washington know that he didn't care what they wrote about him because he didn't read anything they wrote anyway. "All I read," he said, "are the funnies and the *Saturday Evening Post*."

The philosophy of the House is "live and let live," but Brother Harmon went too far when he made a nuisance of himself to Speaker Rayburn. Rayburn would be hurrying into the chamber to get the day's session gaveled into order and he would almost fall over Front-Porch Harmon, who had stationed himself in the Speaker's Lobby.

What Harmon wanted was just to say hello and shake hands with Speaker Sam, but the Speaker was not in the mood for distraction and hadn't the heart to tell him to cut it out. Seeing Sam's discomfort when he had to go through this routine, the members joked that now the Speaker had a house like down South—he had to pass the veranda to get in.

When I arrived on the Hill, the first oddball I became aware of was George Tinkham, a bachelor con-

35

gressman from Boston. He was about the only one sporting a beard, but that wasn't the only strange thing about him. He was a real scrooge about money, not buying any clothes for himself unless he could get an odd lot at a bargain price. But he did allow himself one luxury—big-game hunting in Africa. He had brought back every head of any beast he'd ever shot and hung them all on his walls in his hotel room.

A congressman who had been there once came back saying, "Never again," and talked about how eerie it was at Tinkham's place, sitting with the lights low and all the animals glaring at the two of them from the walls.

Along the same line, Sam Steiger, a Republican from Arizona, didn't like *live* animals staring at him and killed two burros with his trusty gun on an Arizona highway. "It looked like they were going to stampede me," said Steiger, by way of explanation, "but the owner claimed he was raising them for kiddie rides." The last I heard, a civil case had been filed against Steiger by the owner of the animals.

Steiger was a most unusual man around the Capitol House, frequently wearing boots that had not been cleaned of the manure from his Virginia farm into the House Chamber. When he announced he was running for the Senate, the House wags said they hoped the Senate could teach him big-city ways and discussed getting him a box of shoe polish.

With the voters' ax always poised over their heads, the Hill crowd is obsessed with elections.

LBJ's favorite stories were about illegal voting. He would tell about a man who had come to see him for a favor and who had pointed out that he deserved the favor because he had voted time after time for Lyndon's terms in the House and then the Senate.

As LBJ told the story, "So naturally, Ah thanked

the man foh his fine support and Ah said, 'Mah friend, what can Ah do for you?'

"Mah visitor said, 'Well, Senator, after I've done all Ah did to help you, Ah wonder if you could help me become a citizen?' "

LBJ had another story about two fellows busily at work copying the names on the tombstones in a graveyard just before a Texas election. They were doing very well, going up and down the aisles and not missing a single cemetery resident, when they finally came to one tombstone that was so old and worn down that they couldn't make out the name. One of the fellows was all for giving up and skipping that particular person, but the other would not leave and kept struggling to read the name as if his own life depended on it.

"What's the matter with you?" the impatient one said. "Why are you staying here?"

"Well, Ah care," said the other one in Lyndon's rich Texas accent. "This man's got every bit as much right to vote as all the rest of these fellows here."

It's not easy to be a congressman who must sometimes buck every other state in order to get what he wants for his own state. Sometimes it's like trying to stop the tide or like trying to walk up the down staircase when the herd is thundering at you.

To express that feeling and the sometimes bitter, sometimes gentle competition between states, the Hill gang has this little exchange of toasts:

> Here's to the American Eagle
> That noble bird of prey
> He flies on high
> O'er Illinois
> And poops on I-oway.

The reply to the toast is unvarying and immediate:

> Here's to the state of I-oway

37

With its fields so fertile and rich.
We need no turd
From your God damn bird,
You Illinois son of a bitch.

THE MAKING OF
A DOORKEEPER

Sol Bloom, the New York congressman, used to say, "Fish, some day, someone's going to do a musical about you and your life here on the Hill. The only trouble is that Gilbert and Sullivan may have already written the theme song when they wrote *H.M.S. Pinafore*. It goes something like this: 'I washed the windows and I swept the floor and I polished up the handle of the big front door. I polished up the handle so carefully that now I am the ruler of the Queen's navee.'"

I'll admit it was some kind of miracle that a character everyone dimisses with a nickname of Fishbait from a town named Pascagoula ever got to Washington, let alone rose to the important post of Doorkeeper of the House of Representatives of the United States, with a salary that topped $40,000 and an empire of 357 employees with a $3 million budget.

Bloom said someone like Jerry Lewis would be perfect in the role and I say it could be Woody Allen. Bloom said the scenario writes itself—you take this dirt-poor, seventy-five-pound, scrawny soda-jerk kid who works at the Palace Pharmacy and whose idea of success is being able to hold nineteen ice cream cones in one hand and whose idea of trying to get out of playing at a piano recital with a bunch of girls is to dye his hair orange with mercurochrome so his mother won't let him go.

You take that kid and you bring on the scene a perfectly sane legal officer—the district attorney for five counties—who becomes obsessed by this strange kid with all the big talk and high energy. The legal eagle comes in to drink a soda and smoke a cigar as he talks and studies the little weirdo. Well, the district attorney is somehow so taken with the kid that he hears his own voice suggesting that he will give the kid a scholarship of $15 a month to send him to junior college.

Now comes an act of unparalleled political stupidity that's guaranteed to keep a kid out of Washington forever. The dumb kid, to make a little extra money, takes a small job, driving a candidate for sheriff around the county and drumming up votes for him, not realizing or bothering to find out that the candidate for sheriff is the enemy and bitter competitor of the very man who was kind enough to be sending the kid to college on the small scholarship. And to make matters worse, the man he is driving wins, thanks to the kid's inspired campaigning.

And would you believe the improbable ending to the story is that the kid does indeed make it to Washington? In fact, he becomes something called the Doorkeeper of the House with a big salary like I just said and a $3 million budget empire.

And what happens to the kindly benefactor—the scholarship man? Well, when he gets over his anger, he grudgingly lets the kid drive *him* around in his own bid for a political office—a congressional seat—and he ends up a congressman and eventually with the chairmanship of the important House Rules Committee.

It's true. It's all true. So help me.

I'm not going to make myself out an angel. I'm going to tell it like it was. I'm the little devil who made good. I'd have been a bigger devil, but I didn't have time. I was too busy getting ahead.

People ask me if I shoot pool. I had a misspent youth, so of course I play pool. But I've reformed some. I'm the Howdy Doody man at church. I shake hands with everyone who comes to the Baptist church, whether I know him or not. And I have learned how to practice a verse of scripture from the Bible that comes from 1st Peter, chapter 5, the last part of verse 14: "Greet ye one another with a kiss of charity."

I also tithe, giving 10 percent of all I earn to the Baptist church. This makes me feel a little easier about the run of luck I've had since I was eight years old and on my first job—the one at the Palace Pharmacy. I was in training to be a soda-fountain cowboy. My boss, T. T. Justice, was trying to drum up business by offering curb service, and I was it. Most townspeople wanted to come inside and pick up the latest gossip, but the curb service was a car-owner's way of showing off a little for out-of-town visitors who weren't that interested in the inner workings of Pascagoula. I would play it big for out-of-town visitors, suggest showing them the local sights—the big pile of oyster shells, the new boat at the wharf—and would put a little extra ice cream in their sundaes, with an extra cherry or two and plenty of nuts.

A few years rolled along like that, then dang it, suddenly I was hooked. Every time a parent that visited the drugstore would have a female visitor from upstate Mississippi, I would have to meet the chick. Consequently, for the duration of the visit, I had dates every night.

The parents thought I was kind of cute and safe. I wasn't, of course, but I certainly looked harmless.

By the time I reached age fifteen, I still weighed only seventy-five pounds. The surprise is that I reached it at all. My mother had a working agreement with God. Every time I had been pulled through some childhood ailment, God would approach Mother and say, "Mrs. Miller, we have a new childhood disease we'd like to try out on your little son, William Moseley. Would you mind?"

Mother would say, "I know he's only here on loan. He's your child. And he's already beat three others, so go right ahead."

And so He did and I did—I beat the string of childhood diseases. But when the dear Lord was through with me, I was such a scarecrow that everyone took turns finding new nicknames for me—shrimp bait, gar bait, crab bait, alligator bait. But when they got to plain "fish bait," something clicked and suddenly I was Fishbait to everyone.

The exact words that set me up for life was what the captain of the baseball team said when I tried to join. "You little shrimp. Fall out of my hair. You ain't even big enough for fish bait."

Scrawny as I was, I knew no fear. In order to make still more money than the 75 cents a day I was earning at the Palace Pharmacy, I took a side job for Sundays at the competing J. K. Drug Company that paid all of $1 for the day and all I could eat.

Postal Telegraph and Western Union both accepted my services at age thirteen, giving me four jobs in that town of 3,903 living creatures, counting the individual dogs and cats. Now I had status, a bicycle—there were only ten in town. When I worked I put on the proper cap, while carrying the other with me at all times, so people would know which I was delivering.

I had carried so many telegrams down to our ship-yard, Blodgett's, that I was almost a regular there. In fact, they would yell, "Fishbait, will you hand me that wrench over there?" So as I grew a little older, but not much bigger, I went to work doing odd jobs for Blodgett's after hours and on holidays for 50 cents a day.

Then I hit a real bonanza and added a sixth job to my repertoire—for a whole dollar a day. And it could be done before and after school. What I did was push a 250-pound man in a wheelchair about three-fourth of a mile twice a day from his home to work and back. He was A. B. Crane, a jeweler, and from him I learned that nothing need break your spirit. Even though he had no use of his legs and was overweight, he had a keen mind, a good pair of eyes, a fine-looking face, and was married and had children. This was an important thing to know for a kid who had been jousting with death all his life.

Now fortune really smiled on me when at age fourteen the local banker, Mr. Robert Farnsworth, came up with the idea of giving me what were considered uncollectable coal bills to track down. It was strictly commission work, but the beautiful part was that I got half of all I could collect. I got so persuasive in collecting that I made as much as $5 on some of my deals and my mother was even able to pay up some of our own old bills.

I haven't mentioned it before, because it's still painful, but my father left us when I was twelve years old. He left not only me but two older brothers and three younger sisters. Until she died in 1948, I think my mother was still waiting for him to come back.

For a kid though, I had a good life—even with being the third son who ran around all summer with a shaved head. I saved out a dollar of my earnings for myself—which was more allowance than the rich kids had—before giving the rest to my mother.

My father, incidentally, was the captain of a schooner hauling supplies around the Gulf ports and the Caribbean. His life was not easy. Once he was lost at sea for a half year during World War I and was presumed dead. But he showed up that time. During World War II, he was held as a prisoner of war by the Japanese.

When I had just gotten my head shaved for the summer, my father arrived home after one of his lengthy absences and was talking to a neighbor out in the yard as I walked by. My dad said, "Tom, who is that youngster going there?"

The neighbor said, "Captain Albert, don't you know your own son Mosely?"

I heard my father say, "I must not. With those ears, from the back he looks like one of our local pickup trucks with both doors open. I'm afraid to look at the front."

So that's my memory of my father. Years later, when I got acquainted with Congressman Gerald Ford, who

43

came for his first term in 1948, I felt a real bond with him because he too had been deserted by his father in the same way.

I had still another early morning job when school was out and that was working at the Mallett Bakery Shop. We would go to work at 4:30 A.M., making the first loaves of bread for the day. My job was to hand-wrap every loaf that came out of the oven except for the French bread, which was baked on the hearth. And on Sundays, I sometimes made as much as $4 selling newspapers—the *New Orleans Times-Picayune* and the *Mobile Register*—at the train station.

Just because I was busy with jobs doesn't mean I didn't have time to be a boy. I hung around the base-ball team in free moments, hoping against hope they would eventually let me in, but they didn't. So I made a name for myself as team water boy, forecaster and a good judge of new talent.

But I wasn't very lucky when my mother insisted that I take part in a piano recital. As soon as I found out I was going to be the only boy among a gaggle of girls, there was no way she was going to get me cleaned up and sitting on a piano bench. My mother, in a bow to culture, had insisted that I learn to play piano, and I had suffered through lessons week after week. I think she was afraid that I was going to be too puny to earn a living doing "tough man's work," and she hoped that maybe her little tyke could grow up to be a piano teacher. If worst came to worst, she figured, with my penchant for making friends, I could always be some kind of entertainer if I could develop my voice in the Presbyterian choir.

The day of the recital dawned and my mother had still not relented. On a sudden impulse, I studied the medicine cabinet and used the bottle of bright orange Mercurochrome to dye my hair. Instead of hiding me out of sight, she grimly washed my hair as best she

44

could and sent me off in all my shame. It was a lesson for life—don't tilt with windmills.

I liked pleasing the women who came to one of my favorite establishments in town, the Huntsburger–Perry Grocery store. Two partners ran it. I liked their place so much—the fruit counter had me bug-eyed—that I offered to work for them. The first week, they said, "You can have anything you want, as long as you eat it on the premises." In three days, I got so tired of cold cuts and fruit that I didn't want any more for a long time. And it was here that I learned there is a cut-off point at which you no longer try to please. It concerned my bout with the old-time coffee grinder.

A particularly crusty lady always came in for our hand-ground coffee and was always suspicious that she was being short-changed and not getting her complete sixteen ounces. I had tried everything to please her, but she still showed no signs of liking me or my service. The next time she came, I tried even harder to please and stuck my finger up into the coffee grinder to make sure every last grain was out. But coming to my senses in a flash, I pulled my hand out faster than I had put it in.

I wasn't fast enough. Fortunately, the drugstore was next door. Mr. Perry went with me and Dr. McIlwain was able to wash all the coffee and blood off my finger, push it together, and put collodion on it—known at that time as "new skin." He gently wrapped it and slipped on a cotton finger, and Mr. Perry thanked him for me.

Dr. McIlwain said, "Take him back to work. We can't have him losing a day's pay." But he never sent the bill; he was that kind of man.

The best thing about my working for a grocery store was the food I was able to taste for the first time in my life. The second best thing was finally getting to see the inside of the grand Henry Wadsworth Longfellow house which was in our town. I saw it when I went to work

45

one day a week for the rival grocery—owned by Francis Frederic. I drove the delivery wagon, which was horse-drawn, and sometimes we had as many as twenty-five orders to deliver on Saturday. One of the persons we delivered to was the president of one of the shipyards, whose Italian name fascinated me— Piaggio. Mr. Piaggio lived at the Henry Wadsworth Longfellow house, and being acquainted with the poem we all learned in our town, "The Building of a Ship," I was thrilled to bring the groceries into the house even though Piaggio would scold me.

"Whatsa matter, you not bring enough cheese," he exclaimed. "Looka here, I order more tomatoes than this. How you expect me to live without spagmatenna?"

I had occasion several times to be invited to partake of what he called "spagmatenna," and I just wish I could find some more of it. All I can say is that it was made with very thin spaghetti, lots of mushrooms and tomatoes, and great chunks of chicken. The sauce smelled heavenly with garlic. I wondered if Longfellow's ghost was there to smell it and to see me eat.

I loved the Longfellow house with its old oak trees— hundreds of years old—draped with Spanish moss hanging from the bows. The walls were very thick, and indoors it would be cool in summer and warm in winter.

I had a stubborn streak a mile long. During my high-school days, I got a job at the Ford Motor Company in town as a mechanic on Model-A Fords. Just to show you how hardheaded I was, I refused to pay attention to the number one mechanic who, trying to break me in, said, "Fishbait, if you're going to reline the brakes, you must put a rag on each side of the drum to keep the nuts and bolts from falling down into the bottom of the pan." But I wouldn't listen. I was sure I could handle it. And each time, I guess for ten different times, I had to take the pan off to collect the bolts. But I learned my lesson and still made my 20 cents an hour. I worked five hours for one dollar a day—not bad for someone sixteen, going on seventeen.

In my array of jobs, I finally hit on something that would bring some return on my mother's investment of 50 cents a piano lesson. Pascagoula probably had the first open-air movie theater—even in the days of silent films. There I was up front, pushing the pedal of the player piano so the piano roll would come through easily. Naturally, when the action on the screen would speed up, I would push a little harder and make the piano play faster. When it was tragic and the heroine was spouting bitter tears, I would slow it down to a crawl.

I learned early that when you apply for a job, you'd better talk only of what the other guy needs and not what *you* need. It's one of the most important things I ever learned. One summer I decided I wanted to be a carpenter. After I had snooped around, I got dressed in a carpenter's apron with nails in it and a hammer sticking out, and went to the boss on the crew who were building the new sea wall and said, "Boss, you need a carpenter's helper today?"

"How the hell did you know we need a helper today?" he asked.

I answered, "A little bird told me."

"You're hired," he said. "Can you drive a nail without getting it in crooked?"

My carpenter's gear had sold me. I said, "Yes, sir," though I had never hit a nail before. However, in defense of eager amateurs let me say that I had much to do with building the forms and getting them ready to lay the structural steel for the sea wall at Pascagoula, Mississippi. They laid the steel in the forms, poured concrete over it and nothing can break it up. Not only did I work every day without hitting my finger, but I and the old man I was assigned to help were the only two workers who could stand the heat that sent fifteen

47

others home with heat prostration and three to the hospital.

It was 145°F. and everyone was amazed that the youngest and oldest of the crew could stand it. The secret was that my buddy had taught me to wear heavy underwear in spite of the heat and to pour water on my wrists instead of drinking it. Then he and I would chew gum to keep our mouths wet. The others who drank water by the quart upset their bodies' salt balance. I made $1.25 an hour, and the whole family ate good that summer.

In another phase of work on the sea wall, I was permitted to drive an old truck with a sixty-foot trailer behind it. Believe it or not, I learned to drive backwards in a straight line with the trailer loaded with structural steel to the point where the building of the new bridge had left off. There were no protective railings on either side. I guess they thought the truck was insured. But I made it somehow.

On another summer job, I learned to concentrate with great intensity after a disastrous mistake. The local postman, Carl Rohr, was breaking me in by letting me help deliver mail. On the first day, he sent me into a business establishment with a COD package and I felt very adult and responsible as I made them sign for it. For an hour thereafter, Rohr kept looking at me funny but not saying anything. Finally, he said, "Fishbait, I think you're in a heap of trouble."

I said, "What have I done wrong?"

He said, "Well, I let this go purposely in order to teach you a lesson. You did not collect for that COD package and now I am going to wait in the car going a little slower than usual along the route while you walk back and get the money and run back here as fast as you can." Even in the halls of Congress, when I was tempted to rush through a job and get it over with, I remembered my blisters and used my head instead.

In between jobs and chores, I chummed around

with a schoolmate, Bud Pelham, and I would go along with him as he worked his muskrat traps in the marshes around Pascagoula. He wouldn't let me share in his earnings from muskrat skins, but we did make a little money roping the big logs that had broken loose from the heavy tow on their way to the mill. It was the tradition of finders, keepers. We would drive a hook into the log and hitch the log with a rope to our skiff, and we would pull it two or three miles to the mill where we could sell it. It would take two of us working hard to row the skiff, one on each side.

Not only did I become a log jockey, but I also became an auto jockey. With no driver's license, I would be trusted to go to Mobile, Alabama, forty miles away, and drive back a new Dodge car. About that time, I was also working as a helper on a truck for Barq's Bottling Company which sold root beer, grape and orange drinks, cream soda—but no colas.

Once a week, we would cross the county line and I was always getting in trouble. I wanted the people in Grand Bay, Alabama, to know that Fishbait was coming to town—no ego problem, even then—because I had taken piano lessons there for five years and made a lot of friends. I would pull the cord on the exhaust whistle—a horrible noise. The sheriff seemed to know we were coming, and would give us a citation.

The citation would say, "You are reprimanded and reminded to come to the Court House when you have finished your route to pay your fine." The company would have to pay two dollars each time, but I never could break the habit.

I had been doing a lot of bragging about how I was going to go to college when I graduated—to the biggie, Mississippi A & M. But it was time to go to college and obviously I wasn't there—instead, I was back working at the Palace Pharmacy. One of my "friends" at the drugstore, a frequent visitor, was William M. Colmer, district attorney for the Gulf Coast area. He seemed to get a kick out of sparring with me verbally, and he would come in and have a soda as he smoked his cigar and kind of studied me.

I'd try out some of my best jokes and bits of philosophy on him, and he would chuckle a little to himself. But now it was his turn to josh me, because I was not going to college like I'd been talking about. I didn't tell him that what little money I had saved had been used a couple of years earlier to help send one of my brothers to college.

But maybe Mr. Colmer knew, or at least suspected. At any rate, he said, "Bait, if you can't go to the big college, would you be willing to go to Perkinston Junior College?"

Would I! I said I would, but asked how such a thing could be possible.

Almost as if he were surprised at his own words, Mr. Colmer gruffly started offering me a $15-a-month scholarship which, as he explained, would be enough for "your tuition, your entire room, board, medical fees and laundry. I don't know what you will do with the other 50 cents, but your set expenses are going to be $14.50."

As it turned out, that 50 cents stretched a long way and I had a supreme thrill one day of lending 5 cents to a kid in worse shape than me. I lent it, and he paid it back.

Somewhere along the line, one of the boys who had a sweeping job quit, and I was able to earn a little money sweeping the boys' dormitories, serving tables and even delivering mail, permitting me to cut down by a trifle the amount I required from Mr. Colmer.

Which brings me to my introduction to politics. It was my first summer back from college, 1931, and a man who was going to run for sheriff, J. Guy Krebs, asked me if I'd like to drive around with him—me at the wheel, of course—and help him drum up votes. Everyone in town said he hadn't a chance, but I thought it would be fun. I *had* bothered to check out his chances, but I hadn't bothered to find out anything about the other candidates and who was sponsoring them. So off I went with the underdog.

Every morning we would start at 4:30 or 5 A.M. and hit every backroad and general store in the county. I took my campaigning seriously. I spoke sincerely about the fine qualities of the candidate and gave out handbills with his name and his picture on it. I always managed to be at the court house close to noon when court would be in recess so I could pass out campaign literature there.

One day a dignified gentleman came out and I said, "Sir, may I have a minute of your time?"

"Can't stop now. I'm a busy man," he said brusquely, starting to pass.

Quickly I called to his back, "Will you give me thirty seconds of your time?"

He turned around with a broad grin.

I said, "I have a friend who is running for sheriff. I'm from his hometown, Pascagoula. I would like you to take time to read this card and support my candidate if you could."

He looked at the card and then at me and said, "Son, you seem like a fine honest fellow, but I can see you are not schooled in the game of politics. I can't vote for your friend because I am a candidate myself."

So I went back to tacking up posters on sides of trees and simply handing out the cards. I learned that low-key sell was best. What I would do was stop in a community and play checkers at the crossroads store and maybe throw in a word or two about the candidate, drinking gallons of coffee and soft drinks.

The checkers were made out of bottle tops from soft drinks. The checkerboard, if it was "store-boughten," was old and ragged, or it might be drawn on a piece of cardboard. Whichever it was, I treated all men with equal respect and was grateful for the chance

51

to share their lives and their humor. I learned from them and I learned a little from a sign that was on the side of an old grocery store: Trading with Us Is Like Making Love to an Old Maid. It Is Appreciated and It Can't Be Overdone.

To everyone's amazement, including the candidate's, he won. The margin was a mere 165 votes.

I thought everyone would be very pleased with me. But it came to pass that my benefactor, Mr. Colmer, came to my school to make a speech. There had been a rumor that he was getting ready to run for the Congress of the United States and so I went up to him afterwards and said, "Boss, I hear you're running for Congress. You'll have to have someone to drive you around this seventeen-county district—and I'm your boy."

Colmer looked at me as if I'd taken leave of my senses. "Bait," he said, "I haven't told you before, but I'm going to tell you now. You embarrassed me to no end last year in that sheriff's race. You beat my sheriff by 165 votes. Fie and shame upon you."

I was thunderstruck. I had never realized that this man might have anything to do with local politics. But having gotten all that off his chest, the smoke had stopped snorting out of his nostrils. I wasn't going to beg, but I told him again how much *he* needed me because I had saved every voter's name and knew where everything was. "I can do the same thing for you that I did for Sheriff Krebs. I'd really like to drive for you. I think you need me."

Colmer was still not happy. "Well, I don't know," he said. "I'm going to be back this way in three days and I'll be thinking about it. And if I need you, I'll stop by and pick you up."

When three days had rolled around, I was packed and ready and waiting at the front office as his car ground to a halt. "Get in, Bait," he said.

Again I was on the pop-top, checkerboard trail. And this time, when the campaign was over—24,500 miles and 27 flat tires later—I made two vows to myself. One, that I would never run for political office myself, and two, that I would never drink another cup of coffee.

Colmer won by 1,500 votes against the nearest of five competitors. Again I didn't want to beg, but I wanted him to know that I wouldn't mind going to Washington to work and to be near him.

I said, "Will you call me if there is anything I can do in Washington?"

He said he would, and such promises are usually easily given and easily forgotten. But Colmer is a rare, completely sincere man. He did call, and I arrived in Washington on the first train out. I was going to make use of my post-office training and began working in the House of Representatives post office.

The year was 1933 when I came to Washington. The place to be was the new Shoreham Hotel. It had opened with great fanfare about that time. Crooner Rudy Vallee was flown down from New York with his megaphone and band in a specially chartered Amelia Earhart tri-motored plane. But the Amelia Earhart hex was working even then. The plane got caught in a snowstorm and was delayed half the night. Still, the crowd waited for him until he finally showed up at four o'clock in the morning.

But the exciting thing in my life—in my first job on Capitol Hill—was that I would finally get to see that creature I had been reading about in school all these years—a strange breed of *Homo sapiens*, sometimes gentle but definitely not to be trusted. In other words, a *Republican*.

Strangely enough, with all the cultural advantages of Pascagoula, we had no great art galleries and no Republicans. When I learned that there were no Republicans on my particular mail route in the House of

53

Representatives, I gave another carrier 50 cents to let me carry his mail into a Republican's office so I could take a look at him. It was a great disappointment.

Hoping for something a little more exciting, I gave the carrier another 50 cents to let me service the mail in the office of the delegate from Alaska, and again I was disappointed. From then on, it was free looks or nothing. Sophistication was just too expensive to buy by the piece.

One thing that comes to mind these days when Wilbur Mills is cited for his misadventure with Fanne Foxe is that I knew Wilbur well when I was the mail-delivery man. We got so friendly that when he would bring his children in to keep him company while he worked on Saturday, he would turn them over to me. I have memories of them piled on my truck as I rode my mail loads down the hall.

From $15 a month in Mississippi to $145 a month —all of $1,740 a year—was a mighty jump. I didn't know what to do with so much money. Then came a chance to be something that paid even better—a messenger to the Doorkeeper. That was the job that Lyndon Baines Johnson first had in his early days in Washington. I had earned it by service beyond the call of duty—always getting the mail delivered correctly and on time, and even getting a single copy of a hometown newspaper delivered at a quarter of six in the morning to a cranky congressman.

As messenger to the Doorkeeper, I got to see everything that was going on in and out of the House chambers. I started to learn how bills were passed. It is a long and cumbersome ordeal, and for every bill that is passed perhaps five hundred fall by the wayside. I was amazed to learn the importance of a man's name to his ego. Even congressmen who have been acclaimed by thousands of voters love to hear their names—and pronounced right.

I remembered it being said of Julius Caesar that he

was popular with his armies because he could remember the names of every officer and man with whom he had come in contact. In my own humble way, I too have learned the secret of remembering names—a secret that keeps me much in demand, even now that I have retired, by congressmen giving parties for large groups. The secret of remembering names is really a trick, and connecting the name with the face is part of the trick.

When I meet a new person, I really look at his face, and I tell myself a story that connects his face with his name. Take, for example, the name "Andy," as in "Andy Jacobs." When I met Congressman Andy Jacobs, I looked at his forehead and saw a big A and a Raggedy Andy doll sitting on his head. With that in mind, I can never forget my good friend Andy Jacobs whenever I see his face. Of course, you have to do a little homework in this name business. I had already fitted the Andy and the Jacobs together, so I only needed the A to remind me of the "Raggedy Andy Jacobs."

Sometimes I would use a rhyming word to help me with my homework, like "Bender the blender" or "Bayh won't lie." Or sometimes just a funny twist or play on the man's name helps you remember it.

When Estes Kefauver first came to the Hill I remembered his name by telling myself, "Keep off the grass." The very corniness helps you remember it. Whenever I saw him I'd picture his hair as grass, and the admonition would fly through my mind as if a man was stuttering, "Keef-off-'er."

If you really think about a person's name, and play games with it and get the sound of it and the feel of it and see it with his face in your mind's eye, you are going to discover you can really remember names.

If I forget a name—and I do, now and then—I don't worry about it. I just make a fuss about introducing the person whom I do know. One out of two names is

55

fine. The other name might already be known to the person and if not, in the world of politics, the one who's been left out is not bashful. He rushes forth with, "Hi, I'm so and so." I never want to embarrass people, so I'm never bashful about saying, "Hi, I'm Fishbait," and nine times out of ten they say, "I know. I'm so and so. Don't you remember when we met at Lindy Boggs' party?" or some such.

I've had people tell me, "If I could remember names the way you do, I'd have run for Congress." And I tell them, "That's the dumbest reason I've ever heard for not running for office. Remember, you can always hire a flunkey like me to help you with names. You just worry about the legislation and the promises and let someone like me help you."

I had been working at the House Post Office for about six months back in 1933 when a letter arrived from Mississippi with a three-cent postage stamp thereon. It was addressed as follows: "Fish Bait, Washington, D.C." No return address and no other markings were on the outside of the envelope. I hurriedly opened the letter and to my amazement I found a note and another envelope, smaller than the one my note came in. It was addressed, "TO MY CONGRESSMAN Courtesy FISH BAIT." The note to me read, "Dear Fish Bait, You see I did remember your name, but I could not remember my congressman's name. Will you see that he gets the enclosed letter. Thank you."

I asked my boss, the postmaster, if I might personally deliver the unopened envelope to Congressman William M. Colmer. Colmer looked at the note to me and the envelope to him and said, "Bait, when I sent you to school, I thought that you were going to be a drain on my resources for the full two years. But to my surprise, you got a bunch of jobs and you were an asset. Now I brought you to Washington, thinking you might be a drain on my reputation in some way, but again from all I hear you are an unusual asset."

As a matter of fact, getting back to names, it was because I had become so adept at memorizing names and faces, using my tricks, that Colmer recommended, after six and a half years in my Post Office job, that I put that talent to use as messenger to the Doorkeeper. After watching the flow of congressmen in and out of the House Chamber, I became so good at it that I was placed at the East Lobby door, where the press came to interview congressmen. Actually, I worked for a while at the West door where we were asked to get Republican members, and then was shifted to the East.

Through the years, I noticed that nicknames were also very important in helping a man get ahead on the Hill—and in campaigning. Jackson was "Scoop" much more than he was Henry. Everyone loved that nickname. He had gotten the scoop as a newspaper reporter and has been coasting on it ever since. And look how far Humphrey got on "HHH"—which is just the use of his initials—and "the Humph." And even "Gabby" —but he didn't like that one.

Those who liked Javits called him "Jake" and liked him more for the intimacy. That's what's good about a nickname. It makes the voter or other outsiders feel more intimate with those in the seat of power. Also, it keeps them from having to mess around with the "Mister" and the "Senator" and the other fancy titles that make the outsider feel a little inferior and a little below the level of the big man.

The fact that James Carter wasn't known as "James" but as "Jimmy" and that he smiled when they called him "Mr. Peanut," helped him immensely when he was running around in every state of the union trying to make friends before each primary. How much warmer it sounds. Dignity is great to have on state occasions, but isn't it nice to be homey!

But much more important than a nickname to be called by is the thrill the politician hands the voter by using his or her first name, even if the name has just

57

been fed to him by me, standing at his elbow in a receiving line. In which case, the voter isn't fooled.

Before every new Congress came in, I memorized a whole list of names and all the photographs of new faces. I mentioned how I tricked myself into remembering Congressman Andrew Jacobs, using his first name, but say that I was meeting Andy Jacobs for the first time and I didn't know he was a congressman and all I had to remember was to call him "Mr. Jacobs." What I would do then is place Jacob's ladder up his forehead and whenever I saw him I would think of Jacob's ladder. I would somehow connect in my mind the line of his eyebrows and hairline with the rungs of the ladder.

But just remembering names isn't enough to get you promoted. Extra services never hurt. Though I didn't smoke, I carried a cigarette lighter that I whipped out at the first sign of a congressman's cigarette. And I became much in demand for rounding up babysitters for congressmen's wives, and if none were available I went myself.

All of this had given me no time to find a wife of my own. If I hadn't needed a hernia operation, I might still be a bachelor. But, as it was, I needed the operation, and I went back to Mississippi to have it.

It was summer 1936 and Dr. Thomas R. Ramsay, a good friend in Laurel General Hospital, did the honors. When the operation was over and I had returned to my own private room from the recovery room, I was feeling very poorly indeed. I opened my eyes and saw this tall nurse standing at the foot of my bed and heard her voice saying crisply, "Mr. Miller, is there anything I can do before I leave?"

"Yes, ma'am, please take your foot off the bed and quit shaking it."

She flounced out of there, and as I heard the story later, returned to the nurses' house where she ran into her landlady, Carrie Mitchell, who asked, "Mable, how do you like that big shot from Washington?"

"Big shot, my hind foot!" exclaimed Mable. "He's nothing but a little kid and he comes from Pascagoula, Mississippi, which is on the Gulf Coast where all they have is shrimp, crabs, oysters and an old stinking, rotten papermill." Then, still hot under the collar, she added, "Carrie, do you know what he dared say to me? He told me to take my foot off the bed and quit shaking it. I hate him. I hate him. I hate him, and I'm not going back till he's out of there."

I stayed on and on in the hospital so there was little she could do to avoid me. While I was recuperating, I would ride around with Dr. Ramsay as he made his rounds. One day he invited me to come along with him to the Rotary Club. I said I would like to but I had to go sit in the clinic. "Well," he said, "then you may as well go ahead and have your tonsils out, too."

While I was recovering from the tonsilectomy, Mable and her nurse buddies brought me a present almost as soon as I had opened my eyes—a bag of salted peanuts, the meanest thing they could think of.

I knew that Mable was getting used to my sense of humor by now, so I started borrowing a car to ride her around. It was much nicer than riding with the doctor, much as I appreciated Tom Ramsay's views on Tulane's football team. As a matter of fact, it was in Ramsay's car, which I had borrowed while he went to the Tulane–LSU football game, that I proposed to Mable. The moon had risen before I got my nerve up, and hearing the hit song "Stardust" gave me the final shove. We agreed to disagree for the rest of our lives.

So, on February 14 of the following winter, 1937, I sent both an engagement and a wedding ring to her, with instructions to put one on and wait until I got home to put the other one on properly. That's the way it happened. We were married September 2, 1937, and every day since then I've kept her informed of how long she has been in control of my life, adding a junior

59

comptroller on January 17, 1943, named Sarah Patsy. As of this writing, we have been married thirty-eight years, nine months and twenty-six days. And Mable is still fighting her status as housewife. When she leaves a note that she has gone to the store, she invariably signs it, "the maid."

After my stint as messenger to the Doorkeeper, I had a chance to improve myself by becoming special officer to the Capitol Police, which meant that I was still on duty in the Capitol Building. But within a few months I was made special assistant to the sergeant-at-arms, with a raise—I was now making $2,400 annually.

I really thought I had it made with that beneficent salary, but toward the end of 1945 the chairman of the Accounts Committee, Congressman John J. Cochran of St. Louis, snapped his fingers loudly and said, "Fishbait, come here."

I asked, "Yes, sir, what can I do for you?"

He said, "I want you to know I've been watching you and your operation—how you work around here. You're a fine employee, you're loyal, faithful and always on the job early. When they get cantankerous, you keep the members in line in a very pleasant way, as is your job."

He really had me worried. Cochran was in a wheelchair—both legs were gone—but he was a very powerful man around the Hill. All that praise had to be leading up to some disaster. "I hope I haven't done anything wrong."

"Do you know my clerk, Frank Karsten?"

I said, "Yes, he's a mighty fine gentleman. I know him real well."

He said, "I didn't ask for any personal testimony about him. But he's my clerk. You call him at the Accounts Committee Room and tell him to get the hell up here."

60

I said, "Yes, sir." I hurriedly called Karsten on the inside telephone.

When Frank arrived, Chairman Cochran asked him, "Do you know Fishbait Miller?"

"Yes I do, Mr. Chairman," he said. "He's one of our best workers here—and we can always depend on him. He's never too busy to help someone."

Cochran sputtered, "Well, damn it, I didn't ask for any testimonial about him. What's the matter, are you two conniving against me?"

With that, he directed Frank to go downstairs and "fix a resolution for me, ready to have adopted in the House when it meets tomorrow. Word it so that the job Fishbait is now holding will have a salary increase of $600, and also state in there that as long as he holds that particular job he is to have an additional salary raise of $600."

I was amazed. Of course, I had to admit to myself I really had done a pretty good job in my position as Assistant to the Sergeant at Arms. I had even kept an altercation from turning into a full-fledged fistfight. I had run between two congressmen with the Mace, the symbol of authority in the House of Representatives. It is a long and impressive standard that stays near the Speaker of the House until it is needed to bring excited members back to their senses. According to the rule, when the Mace has been presented in front of a member, he is not permitted to speak on the floor any more that day. In this case, since both had behaved in an undignified way, neither could speak for the rest of the day.

I had my raise to $3,600 but, showing that things don't generally last long on the Hill, the next year brought a change in control of the House, and with the Republicans in power, I was in danger of having no job at all. Fortunately, I was able to become Minority Doorkeeper and survive the change-over of January 1947.

Even though I was only Minority Doorkeeper, I was determined to be so helpful and efficient that if ever the Democrats came back in power I would stand a chance of becoming Majority Doorkeeper. One of the first things I could do to be helpful was to get the best possible officers for the new Democrats coming in, as well as for members who were dissatisfied with the offices they were presently occupying. The beginning of every session is a frantic game of musical chairs, everyone trying to get the best possible rooms and view of the Capitol dome. The first year, I arrived at 4:30 on the afternoon of December 4, 1946, in order to be ready for the best choices when the office opened at nine o'clock the next morning.

I brought with me a sandwich and some orange juice to hold me through the night and eventually some office aides, representing individual congressmen, showed up and they had brought along cards. We played hearts until a fourth came along, an office secretary, and then we switched to bridge.

All the others were just interested in one office. I had brought letters of authority from a couple dozen congressmen—I had even sent letters to all new Democratic electees—so when the door opened, I was pretty busy. So busy that I didn't realize that the female among us was getting furious.

She raised such a stink about my usurping all the good officers for my gang that two years later, when it again came time for the selection of new offices, the rules had been changed. Metal discs were going to be placed in a bowl, and we would draw for the order in which we would be permitted to pick an office.

They were trying to circumvent me and I was still trying to get around them. I arrived with my fingertips filed down to the underskin and they were so sensitive that it may have helped me feel around and come up with the lowest numbers. All I can say is that my batting average was so good that two years later, when the new Congress came in, they had again tightened the rules. This time the discs were encased in plastic. Still, let me say, that kind of dedication to your group gets the word around that you're a loyal team player.

Two things stand out in my mind from those adventures with the musical chairs. One was that two new members were such good friends that they had only one request—to have offices next to each other. In the noble drawing of 1948, I was able to get the Honorable Peter W. Rodino, Jr., and the Honorable Hugh Joseph Addonizio adjoining offices, and they continued to enjoy each other's company through the years.

The other incident concerns a relatively young congressman named Richard M. Nixon who happened to come rushing by when I was sitting waiting in the corridor about one or two o'clock that December night of 1948. He seemed in very high spirits and said, "You are working very late—or early—aren't you?"

I said, "Yes, sir. We have to select offices for new members in the morning. What about you, Mr. Nixon, are you just ending your day or beginning your day?"

I could see he was on needles to get away, but he was so delighted with something that he had to share it. He said, "I'm going to get on a steamship and you will be reading about it. I am going out to sea and they are going to send for me. You will understand when I get back, Fishbait." He looked very elated and keyed up, as if he were dancing on wires. Even his eyes were dancing.

I said to myself, "What the hell is he talking about?" But by then the congressman was half-way down the hall and I had learned better than to push for more information than someone wanted to give me.

I called "Thank you very much, Mr. Nixon," at his rapidly receding back. "Have a good trip." Later, when Nixon was called back because of the discovery of the "Pumpkin Papers," I realized that I had been in on the beginning of something most peculiar, but I didn't know what at the time.

All I knew, as I watched Nixon hurry down the hall, was that the young congressman was getting pretty important around the Hill for his astute questioning of witnesses as a member of the House Un-American Activities Committee which was trying to determine whether Alger Hiss or Whittaker Chambers was telling the truth.

Hiss had been a State Department official who was accused by Chambers of being a communist. In fact, Chambers, who had been a senior editor on *Time* magazine, was accusing Hiss of passing State Department secrets to him, when Chambers was an admitted communist spy in the 1930s.

Imagine my surprise, after having forgotten all about my midnight encounter with Nixon, when on December 5, 1948, I saw by the headlines that the House Committee on Un-American Activities was being "called back to Washington today for hastily arranged hearings to bring into the open new documentary evidence" that would prove Hiss had given documents to Chambers. And what they said had been found were microfilm reels "concealed in a pumpkin in a garden patch behind a barn" at Chambers' Maryland farm.

On the next day, December 6, the *New York Times* carried a dramatic front-page picture of Nixon, coat slung over his shoulder like a good soldier, getting out of a Coast Guard plane that was sent to rush him back to Washington. The caption read, "Representative Richard M. Nixon hopping from Coast Guard plane to boat to land at Miami on way back to Washington for Un-American Activities Committee meeting."

The accompanying article entitled "Nixon Gets Sea-Air Lift," datelined Miami, told the story. The lead said, "Representative Richard M. Nixon, Republican of California, was removed from a ship in the Caribbean Sea today to rush to Washington for new spy hearings which he said were of 'top importance.' "

He had been interviewed aboard a "speeding crash boat" that was taking him ashore from the seaplane, and he said, "For the first time we have documentary evidence—it is no longer just one man's word against another's."

And now finally I knew what he meant about the trip. The story said he had been aboard the steamship *Panama* with a congressional group *en route* to Panama when the call came to return to Washington. I thought to myself, "That clever guy—he knew all the time."

There was great rejoicing when the Democrats won control of the House again in the 1948 election, and I knew it was my big chance to come riding in on the crest of the wave as Doorkeeper. *The* Doorkeeper. All other doormen and the clerks who work around the Speaker's stand are under the Doorkeeper. I went to John W. McCormack, who was to be the Majority Leader of the new Congress coming in in January, and I showed him a list.

"I have it all worked out, sir," I said. "I think these men will support me. Bill Colmer of Mississippi, who brought me here, can put up my name, and I have the names of others I'm sure will second him."

McCormack grabbed my list and looked at it. "Colmer," he said. "Out and out Dixiecrat. F. Edward Hébert. New Orleans. Another Dixiecrat. Joe Bates, Kentucky—how did he get in here?"

"Well, he's a friend," I said.

McCormack tore up my list and said, "Now here's what you do. You get Wilbur Mills of Arkansas to nominate you. Get William T. Byrne from upstate New York to second your nomination and the Honorable Harry R. Sheppard of California also to second you. And then you get three non-Dixiecrat freshmen members from across the country to second your nomination."

"Yes, sir," I said.

But McCormack wasn't through with me yet. "And if I were you," he said, poking a finger at my chest, "I would get this new Italian boy from New Jersey, Hugh J. Addonizio, and Wayne L. Hays of Ohio—a tough cookie, he's going to be a fighter. And then you get "Porky" (Harold A.) Patten of Arizona to get up and say, 'I like Fishbait because . . .' and give them each one minute's time."

And that's all they had when the time came in January 1949. Later in the year, an old-timer, Compton R. White, congressman from Idaho, came to me and said, "Fishbait, where in the hell did you get all your political savvy?"

I said, "If I tell you, that would be telling—and I don't think you want to know because you're one of the best politicians I ever knew." His head sort of popped back. "I just quit," he said.

I never told anyone the story of how I got to be Doorkeeper. Until this writing, only John McCormack and I knew our strategy or the names he had torn up. I didn't even tell Mable. One thing I heard over and over on the Hill was, "A smart politician never tells his wife the full story." I'm sure the same advice is given to congresswomen with husbands. Every now and then someone would be talking about some poor colleague who had told his wife something in strictest confidence only to have her blurt it out at some party.

I kept such a close guard over my own tongue that *my* wife often accused me of loving the Congress of the United States more than I loved her. And of loving Speaker Sam Rayburn more than I loved her. But she never dared say I loved anything more than the apple of my eye, the one and only Sarah Patsy, born in 1943.

Now that I'm retired, Mable says I have transferred all my Capitol Hill affection to my car—known to one and all on the Hill as "The Car"—and that I love *it* more than I do her. That's her story. The Car, like my marriage, has a lot of mileage.

All my loyalties have a lot of mileage. In forty-four years, I have continued to use my Pascagoula banker, Willie Herring—a good name for a Gulf town man. But loyal as I am to my bank, Pascagoula-Moss Point Bank, I am more loyal to The Car. I bought it back in 1946 when there were no cars to buy and World War II shortages were very severe. It had only three hundred miles on it. It wasn't owned by a sweet old lady who only used it to drive to church. It had been owned by a sweet old man who only had a heart attack and was warned by his doctor to quit driving.

At first, since he was a friend and I had no car, I simply chauffeured him around for the fun of it. I liked the way his mind worked. He had founded the Curtis Furniture Company in the outlying Anacostia section of Washington, and his idea of advertising was to walk in front of the furniture and department stores on F Street in downtown Washington, mingling with the shoppers and dropping a lot of pencils on the sidewalk, as if there were a hole in his pocket. The pencils said, "Curtis Bros. Furniture, Anacostia." Then some of his seven sons took over the store, and suddenly pencils had given way to big, fat newspaper ads.

But back then, in 1946, he said, "I can only make enemies with this car. If one of my relatives gets it, the others will never speak to me." It was one of the new 1947 Dodges, a custom-built sedan, and though he had paid $2,400 for it, he had been offered $3,000.

I came by one evening and he said, "Fish, you got any money?"

I said, "Yes," and reached in my pockets to fish out 37 cents.

"I mean have you got any folding money?"

"Pop, [everyone called him Pop Curtis]" I said, "I think I have seven dollars. Will that be all right?"

He said, "Man, let's get down to business. I don't

want to start a riot in my family. So you've got to take this car and hide it and it's yours for $2,000 cold cash on the barrelhead." At that time I was making $200 a month and was supporting a wife and three-year-old child. But I called my banker, Willie Herring, cashed in my government savings bonds, and was in business.

For five years, The Car purred like a kitten. Then, in 1951, The Car ran into trouble. My family and I were headed for Mississippi and we were going to stop at Bristol, Virginia, at the Tennessee line to buy two quarts of oil at a bargain price of 60 cents. I knew I was running short. Just when I saw a sign that said, Rural Retreat, Virginia, Population 737, I heard a little ping, ping, ping, and I stopped. One of the townspeople at the filling station phoned Rural Retreat's best mechanic, B. L. Musser, who sent his son with a wrecker.

The son arrived, jacked us up, hooked us to the wrecker and started to get into the cab without a word. I yelled, "Now, son, what am I supposed to do?"

He looked back and called, "Well, damn it, you can't do but one thing. Sit still and I'll get you there."

His father, one mile up the pike, was just as testy, but a positive genius at diagnosis. He had me turn the motor on for just a second before he motioned me to quickly turn it off.

He said, "Sounds to me like you've scorched the connecting rod bearing and you'll have to have a ring job. Costs $80. No credit."

So it was back to the telephone and to Pascagoula-Moss Point Bank's Willie Herring. Since then, Mr. Musser has made me come back to him every 6,000 miles or every 6 months—whichever comes first. The Car now has 291,558.3 miles. In other words, it's just getting nicely broken in. True to my notion of loyalty, The Car has never been serviced by any other mechanic. Since I had found the right man—I call him

Dr. Musser, because as I see it he is a doctor of mechanics—I see no reason to change.

But I must say that certainly was an expensive two quarts of oil back in 1951. It's not easy to get back to Rural Retreat, Virginia. It's 310 miles from Washington and I have to stay four days. But there are advantages in loyalty. From being the laughing stock on the Hill, The Car has matured gradually to vintage age and I was asked by the Capitol Hill police to park it in the front of the Capitol so that tourists could crowd around and enjoy it.

The Car has given me so many memories that I could never part with it. Speaker Rayburn once didn't want to wait for his chauffeur, who was off somewhere, going to the men's room no doubt, so he hopped in The Car and said, "Fish, we are going to do my Christmas shopping." He filled up the backseat with toys and things for friends' and relatives' children and happily sat in front with me talking about how anxious he was to get to Bonham, Texas, and hear some *real* Christmas caroling with the right accent: "They just don't know how to handle the English language up here, do they, Fish?"

The Car and I also hauled Congressman John W. McCormack to his home in the most convenient place in town—the Washington Hotel—one block from the White House and across the street from the most expensive store his wife could shop at, Garfinkel's. And the list goes on.

But perhaps The Car was most proud—and so was I—when it was invited to be the get-away car at a very fancy modern wedding. It was to drive the bride and groom from the church to a country club and on to parts unknown. The Car was proudly parked outside the church, all spit and polish, until the crowd descended throwing rice. The bride and groom jumped into the backseat and off they drove in Fishbait style.

And speaking of weddings reminds me of how really

involved I became in the lives of the Hill people. Not only was I all things to all congressmen—supervisor of their patronage workers, guardian of the doors, babysitter and escorter of dignitaries—but I even was there to help in important moments of their private lives.

When Congressman Bill Colmer's secretary, LaNora, was getting married, I was there at the church to help seat people and assist in any other way possible. After all, her boss had brought me to Washington. Suddenly, in the middle of the wedding ceremony, the minister turned white and acted as if he was going to faint. I sidled up to him, took his book, and continued reading the wedding ceremony as he sat down, having a heart attack, as it turned out. Fortunately, just as I got to the place where somebody was going to have to pronounce them man and wife, the minister recovered enough to say the final words. Happily, the wedding ceremony was not fatal to any of us—including the minister.

It was just your average day in the making of a Doorkeeper.

THE HIGH COST OF HEALTH, WELFARE AND THE GOOD LIFE ON THE HILL

The public cannot imagine the secrecy that revolves around the health problems of the nation's legislators. There is a standing order at the military hospitals—Bethesda Naval Hospital and Walter Reed, where they go for V.I.P. treatment at bargain rates—to clamp complete security when a member of Congress is brought there. Congressmen are afraid constituents and even colleagues might get the idea they are not coming back or are not in good enough shape to handle their offices.

It's hard to believe how much stress is put on health on the Hill. Congressmen have the best medical care money will buy and all the free medicines and vitamin pills they care to indulge in. They have a heart specialist standing by at all times. Every expensive medical gadget is available to them in the Hill medical office, including an electric thermometer.

Everything is free. There is a station wagon standing by which twice a day speeds blood and other specimens to government laboratories to get the best diagnoses.

What does all this cost the taxpayer? Plenty. Still, some Congressmen feel they are not getting enough and try to get supplies to take home for the family as well. One congressman made so much of the good deal that he would send his aide to the medical office to "pick up a package that will be waiting for you." The aide thought it was some kind of medical stuff. Fish-

71

bait knew better—it was tissues the congressman's wife had phoned him to get.

Health with its high cost to the taxpayer is only one phase of the good life congressmen lead. Capitol Hill life is awash with special funds—travel funds, stationery funds, a jillion freebies. Fringe benefits are called "perks" on the Hill, short for perquisites.

Among the minor freebies are free plants and flowers. Congressmen were getting so generous, wanting so many plants for friends and relatives, that it was finally decreed that each congressman could choose only two plants every other week. But it's still an expensive item—for the taxpayer. Free goldfish and the experts who would come around to take care of them also used to be available but were discontinued. Some congressmen felt deprived.

Just recently it was discovered that one of the greatest critics of government spending, former Representative H. R. Gross of Iowa, withdrew $23,611 from the stationery fund in the Ninety-fourth Congress rather than let it go back to the general fund—even though he retired in the Ninety-third Congress.

Incidentally, Gross is not alone, though his slush fund withdrawal by a former congressman was the largest on the 1975 list. In all, some seventy-seven representatives withdrew a total of $193,000 for the year. The next largest was $9,726, made by Congressman William Widnall, Republican of New Jersey. Others who took the last penny they could get from Uncle Samuel from their unused stationery funds were George Goodling, Republican of Pennsylvania; Thaddeus Dulski, Democrat of New York; John Rooney, Democrat of New York; Leslie Arends, Republican of Illinois; and William Minshall, Republican of Ohio.

The unused portion of the $6,500 annual allowance to Congress for stationery and office supplies would be built up year after year and withdrawn at the end of their service. Gross, who was always complaining about government spending, had an answer for those who registered shock at his action. He pointed out that if he had taken his $23,000 out in small amounts now and then, as others did, it wouldn't have looked like such a big figure. And besides, it was legally his if he wanted it.

After this assault on the stationery fund by ex-congressmen, however, the rule has just been changed and from now on money not used within the year will not be redeemable later.

I know that compared with the national debt, this sum sounds like a drop in the bucket—and it is. But it does show the kind of thing that has made the overall cost of keeping Congress five times more expensive than it was in 1960. It's not my figure. It was a non-profit research outfit—the Tax Foundation—that recently figured out that it now costs almost a billion dollars a year to keep Congress in business—$925 million in the last fiscal year and still rising.

Since 1970, the cost of operating Congress has tripled. As for the tax money spent on each of the 535 members of Congress, the figure is creeping up toward $1.7 million.

When I came to Washington to work for Congress, a congressman's salary was $10,000. In the 1960s, it went to $22,500, and when I left it was $42,500. As I write this book, it is $44,600.

Chairmen of committees receive extra funds, and the leadership gets extra money that does not have to be accounted for.

When I was there, the Majority Leader had a $3,000 slush-fund expense account. The Speaker of the House did even better and got $10,000 to handle all social requirements—or anything else he thought was important.

When Carl Albert retired at the end of the Ninety-fourth Congress, he was entitled to the highest retirement salary anyone had ever had on the Hill—about

73

$51,000 a year. His Hill salary as Speaker of the House was $65,000, and he had had a military career as well.

The retirement pensions for other members leaving at the end of 1976 ranged from $11,000 to about $34,500. A few special men like Minority Leader Hugh Scott, Republican of Pennsylvania, and Majority Leader Mike Mansfield, Democrat of Montana, can receive about $40,000.

The rule is that no member can get more than eighty percent of his top three-year average salary.

The basic salary is only part of what a congressman really makes. There is a $3,000 tax deduction as a consolation prize for living away from one's home district.

Then there are travel costs. I used to ask friends who wondered what it would be like to be a congressman, how would you like to get 12 cents a mile for 18 trips home each year, or a lump sum of $4,500? You dog-gone betcha, some took the money and ran. It really pays to run for Congress from a state close to Washington, D.C.

There are only a very few who don't take every penny just because it's there for picking or plucking. The black delegate from the District of Columbia, Walter Fauntroy, set a good example. And so did Gilbert Gude, who lived across the line in Maryland.

You need a vacation? How about a junket? If you are a congressman, you may be able to get the chairman of the committee you are on to make you a delegate on a fact-finding mission. It has to be approved by the chairman, but many are flexible. In fact, they are so flexible, they may go along. If you're the chairman, you assign yourself.

Members go free and the wife and family travel at cost. I don't know what the ladies of Congress called it when they went to retrace the steps of the Presidents —Ford and Nixon—and take a look at the Great Wall of China. There are all kinds of names given for junkets

—an inspection trip, an information-gathering trip, a study mission.

Wherever you go, a congressional person is automatically a VIP, dined and wined. The embassy of each country you are visiting will be alerted to roll out the red carpet.

Also, there is that $75 a day expense account wherever the congressman is. Seldom is the unused portion returned to the government. Once, an embassy wanted a group that was with Senator Ted Kennedy to return some unused funds, and the non-congressional study group was most annoyed and refused to do it. They had been around congressmen long enough to know that they didn't have to.

On a junket, the congressmen usually take along a staff person or two to give a work-like appearance. From what I hear, the real work is done by the staff on return. Maybe a little report is written. It used to be *de rigueur* to write a report. But it was so expensive to print the damn thing at government expense that the congressmen changed the rule. Now, if they want to, the junketeers can file a report of what they learned with the committee of Congress which approved the trip but may or may not care two hoots in hell about what they saw.

Top junketeer in the good old days was Adam Clayton Powell, who took trips as chairman of the House Labor Committee that lasted so long some thought Powell had forgotten the way back. He took a beauty-queen staffer along to help him with his homework.

It's hard to know what junkets cost the taxpayer. In the old days, there would be a report filed every year in the *Congressional Record* giving a complete rundown on what junkets each committee had approved and who had traveled and where and, most important, what it had cost.

But Wayne Hays of Ohio changed that in 1974, slipping through a bill that said such information would only have to be given if requested. Hays justified it by saying it was a waste of the taxpayers' money to print the reports in the *Congressional Record*.

Such bad publicity resulted that Congress passed a new rule that the junket facts and money costs would be available for viewing in the office of the clerk of the House.

In the old days, H. R. Gross, Republican of Iowa, would fight to keep more committees from being authorized to start taking junkets at public expense. Once it was the House District Affairs Committee that had decided it needed to visit foreign capitals of the world to see how they handled their local government.

Gross was furious, but following the rules of protocol, he started out very politely, asking that the gentleman from Missouri, Democrat Richard Bolling, yield the floor for a few minutes. Bolling was the man who had gotten the resolution, making it possible for the district committee to take the trip, through the Rules Committee. But as the questioning by Gross of the chairman of the district committee, Congressman Charles C. Diggs, heated up, other Republican members yielded Gross minutes of their time.

"I think that it is a full-time job, both on the part of the present District Government and on the part of this committee," said Gross. "That is one of the reasons why I oppose this resolution, because I think the committee ought to spend its time here, and not in some foreign fleshpot some place."

Diggs kept explaining that he hoped seeing what other capitals of the world did would help his committee "find some way out of the quagmire that has existed for so long in this District." But then Gross discovered that the junketing group was planning to go to Birmingham, England.

"Why does the gentleman wish to go to Birmingham?"

Mr. Diggs: "Because one of the greatest experts on

the whole subject of the relationship between a nation's capital and the local interests is located in Birmingham, England."

Mr. Gross: "He must be a real expert if he can draw any real comparison between Washington, D.C., and Birmingham, England. I went through there one time a good many years ago on the way to France. It is an industrial city. The biggest industry in Washington, D.C., is shuffling papers. Why in the world do you want an expert from Birmingham, England, to tell you what you should do in the District of Columbia?"

As the chairman ventured the information that the group was also going to this foreign point and that, Gross sneered, "The next thing we know the committee members will want to travel to Ouagadougou."

But the *coup de grâce* was administered by Minority Leader Gerald R. Ford, Republican of Michigan, who pointed out that the committee already had a study on committee problems and solutions that was written "in great depth and breadth" and which it hadn't studied yet, a report by the Nelsen Commission.

Another potential junketeer jumped into the fray to point out that the committee wasn't trying to avoid work and in fact the trip would be very exhausting. This was all my friend Gross needed to really set him off.

Mr. Gross: "I hear that story all the time about how hard Members work on these junkets. It is a common summer complaint that they are overworked on these foreign junkets. Some of the stories that come back to us, however, dispute the fact that everyone works like hell when they go on a foreign trip.

"Did the gentleman say there is someone in some foreign capital somewhere who is dissatisfied with the way the Government of Washington, D.C., is being run?"

Gross rested his case with the comment, "If we now have to send them off to some foreign capital to get answers on how to run the District Government, then we are in a whole hell of a lot worse shape than I thought we were."

After Jerry Ford took the floor again to point out that "the Nelsen Commission's recommendations total better than 450," the House voted to kill the district's junket-taking authority—at least for the time being.

But Chairman Diggs more than made up for the loss with other junkets a little later as chairman of the House International Affairs Subcommittee on International Resources, Food and Energy. In June and July 1975, and January and February of the Bicentennial year, he studied such things as food deficits in India and Africa and petroleum resources in Indonesia, to name just a few. Helping with his studies was a female aide, Herschelle Challoner, listed as his consultant on the committee.

Diggs was only one weary traveler. Wayne Hays of Ohio, whom some called the "Marco Polo" of the House when they were not calling him other, less flattering things, traveled many thousands of miles before his problems with Elizabeth Ray brought his whole financial structure on the Hill, including his junkets, under FBI investigation.

When he was flying high, Hays was one of the luckiest men on the Hill, because as chairman of the North Atlantic Assembly he had charge of $25,000 a year in travel funds for which he did not have to make a public accounting. And this was besides his regular travel-fund drawing potential for his other committees.

Other happy junketeers were a group led by Majority Leader Tip O'Neill, who managed to see the pyramids in Egypt during the Easter holiday of 1975, and Congressman Daniel Flood, Democrat of Pennsylvania, who took his wife along on a tour of Europe that was so impressive that they even had a military escort.

If the trip to Europe was all work, the congressman

78

certainly worked late because the records on Flood's auto rentals showed the cars he had used stayed with him until two or three in the morning. The return trip was not made by plane but on the luxurious ship *Queen Elizabeth II*, which cost Uncle Sam $1,500 in British pounds.

The work schedule of a congressman would be viewed with envy by the average nine to five worker—and rightly so, I think. The average employee—and by that I mean even a Hill employee—gets three-day holidays at best. Congress gets ten-day recesses at the drop of a mention of Columbus Day or the Fourth of July.

I kept track after I left the Hill and found that in the first five months of 1975, Congress had already taken twenty days off and was getting ready for a third ten-dayer.

While some are going home to rest and take care of side business or make speeches before potential voters, others go off on those quick ten-day junkets—government-paid, of course. Committees are good to their members, dreaming up reasons why members should go to sunny places like Jamaica, San Juan and Aruba as the States fight the snow in December. I know men, never farther away from home than their state capital before they were elected, who have become great world travellers at government expense.

Of course, one reason they can do it is that they have so much office help. In 1954, one congresswoman reported the budget for operating the Congress was only $42 million. But today Congress appropriates $328 million for its own operations. As for the number of people on congressional staffs, that number has risen from 4,500 to over 16,000. That's a lot of bodies around the Hill and a lot of flunkies falling over each other in their effort to be helpful to the boss and ingratiate themselves to him. It amounts to 16,000 people hovering over 535 superstars.

79

At this writing, each individual congressman gets up to eighteen helpers, if he wants them all. He has a $238,500 staff allowance and decides what he will pay each employee. If he wanted to, he could divide the money evenly and give each of the eighteen staffers $13,250—but I don't think that's ever been done.

Usually, the Congressman pays his A.A. and L.A.— Administrative Assistant and Legislative Assistant— very well and others at any figure that suits his fancy.

Nor does he waste his time, or theirs, jotting down what's going on during the day on the floor.

Congressmen don't have to take notes on the floor. They'll get the whole thing the next morning in the *Congressional Record.* It costs the government over $80,000 a day for that little service.

If a congressman stays long enough to rate a top spot on a committee, this gives him many more perks —perquisites or special fringe benefits—extra money to run that office, extra secretaries, extra aides, greater consideration at the Library of Congress for quick research jobs.

Even in the matter of the photos that congressmen send to their constituents on request, or use for campaigning, the Hill gang is lucky, due to a most unusual circumstance. Dev O'Neill, the official photographer of Congress, is a man of means who takes the photos free, just because he loves Congress.

Dev, a very dear friend of mine, is a jet pilot and sometimes flies a plane back to his hometown of Cleveland, where he still maintains a residence. Some of his wonderful pictures will show up in a book on Congress that he has been working on for some time, just as some show up in this book.

Even ex-congressmen get so many benefits for having been in the Congress that one of them actually complained, "It is becoming scandalous."

That was former Representative Hastings Keith, a straight arrow from Massachusetts who came back to testify before the House Post Office and Civil Service, Retirement and Employee Benefits subcommittee that his pension from the Hill had increased in two years from $1,560 to $2,095 a month.

Being a reasonable man, he warned that if Congress didn't eliminate its generous cost-of-living increases, he personally would be getting $6,000 per month by 1990.

Keith said that getting rid of the so-called "kicker" provision of retirement, which has been in effect since 1969, would save the taxpayers over $10 billion.

The Republican congressman, who is only about sixty years old and served for fourteen years in Congress after several years in the military service, is one of the few who is truly alarmed that, by being too good to itself, Congress can add to the inflation troubles of the nation.

There is even a $45,000 life-insurance policy waiting for a congressman, no matter what the state of his health may be. If he fears he is dying, he at least is comforted by the fact that his widow will be voted a full year of his pay.

In memory, how it all comes flooding back as I lean back in my comfortable retirement chair. I remember a few years back when Congress was crying for a backdoor pay raise—to increase the $3,000 annual limit on income-tax deduction by at least another $3,000 for having to maintain a home in Washington, D.C.

And I remember when congressmen voted themselves a $2,300 per member increase in expense allowances to permit themselves more trips home or other trappings of the good life.

I remember and I say again, as I have so many times, "When H. L. Mencken described democracy as 'a milk cow with 125 million teats' he must have been thinking about Congress."

After the sex scandals of 1976 started to break, the

public suddenly became very interested in the hideaway rooms on the Hill. The most important hideaway on the House side is called the "Board of Education Room," belonging, as a perk, to whoever is Speaker of the House. When newspapers hinted that there might be drinking and sexual dalliance going on there, recent Speaker Carl Albert hurriedly called in all the keys he had passed out to those he permitted to share his hideaway.

The man who was known to have made the best use of that room was former Speaker John Nance Garner, one of the most determined boozers the Capitol has ever known. His routine, I was told, was to motion for certain cronies on the floor to come up to the Speaker's stand near adjournment almost every day, and he would say this:

"Boys, it's almost five o'clock. Let's get this House adjourned so you fellows can lead me down the steps [he was known also to take a snifter to help him through the day]. And on the way, after the first landing, let me stick my finger in the mouth of my pet snake and see if he'll bite me this afternoon. Because if he does, as he has in the past, I will be in need of the cure and we will have to go to the Board of Education Room and take care of that situation pronto."

The four bells would ring and the valiant little crew would go to the hideaway for the Speaker's favorite cure—Bourbon and branch water.

The Hill hierarchy thought it was a terrible waste when the Honorable Joseph W. Martin, Jr., Republican of Attleboro, Massachusetts, became Speaker—on the two occasions that the Democrats were out—because he broke with all tradition. He did not need a hideaway. He was an angel. He did not drink. "He didn't *anything*," they said.

The room, which has no number or marking to show its importance, is on the first floor of the House wing of the U.S. Capitol, near the office of the sergeant-at-arms. Actually, it has several uses. It is the room where the leaders invite a few recalcitrants or obstreperous members of the Democratic party for a private lunch and arm-twisting session.

About twenty-four people can eat there. It is also the place where a Speaker can go for a little snooze if things get too much for him or his lunch hasn't sat well. "I'm going to rest my eyes," a Speaker would say. "You know the signal."

If I close my eyes, I can see it now—the black leather couch with the red pillow, the two windows and window seats—you can sit on a cushion and glance out. The room has two black chairs, very comfortable leather. One desk, one telephone, one well-stocked icebox, one closet with the key kept only by the Speaker or one of his close aides.

For private luncheons, they would get the former headwaiter of the Speaker's Dining Room, Carl E. Sommers, who worked for me as my clerk. It was truthfully said about Carl that if you gave him a thousand-dollar bill, he would still not tell what went on there or what was said.

Many times, when I had to find a Speaker, I would go to that door and knock gently two times or ask a page to do it. That would be the signal that the Speaker was needed on the floor.

This room, incidentally, is historic in the career of Harry Truman, because that is where he first learned that the White House was hunting for him. He was on his way there to hoist a few—"strike a blow for liberty" is the way he put it—with Speaker Sam. He was Vice President at the time but he still kept in close touch with his old friends.

In fact, it was Rayburn who actually took the call from Eleanor Roosevelt, which was merely that Truman was needed right away at the White House. Truman didn't know it, but he arrived at the Board of Education Room as a Vice President and left as a

83

President, because FDR had died at his own little hideaway at Warm Springs, Georgia.

But the Board of Education Room and other Hill hideaways are only part of the special facilities on the Hill. There are also special restaurants. There is the Speaker's Dining Room, used by the top man of the House and loaned out by him for special occasions when a committee chairman is honoring someone.

There is the Joseph W. Martin, Jr., Dining Room that was used for ten years by Jerry Ford when he was Minority Leader. So far, that room is the only Hill tribute to Joe Martin. He lived to see it named for him. As yet, nothing on the Hill has been named for Gerald Ford, even though he ascended to the presidency.

For breakfast and lunch only—though it is sometimes used for a meeting—there is the Members' Private Dining Room, which is strictly private. Then there is the Main Dining Room for members and guests.

Some members cannot bear to wait a minute to be served and there is something even for them: special large tables where they never have to wait more than a minute for service. The only problem is that they might have to sit beside someone they don't like—but now and then even a congressman has to put up with a little hardship.

One of the hardships they don't have to put up with is deciding how to vote. There is always leadership to tell them—the Democratic leadership tells the Democrats how to vote, and the Republican leadership tells the Republicans how to vote. And the go-along guy even gets praised for not kicking over the traces.

One guy who carried this principle to extremes, however, was Congressman Luther Patrick, Democrat of Alabama. Someone once asked Brother Luther how he had voted on something that day, and he said with all sincerity, "I won't know until the Alabama papers get here tomorrow. I just vote whatever my delegation tells me."

84

Almost anything a congressman's heart desires is taken care of, somehow. We had a Republican congressman named Robert Rich who used to spend all his spare time sitting around the Republican cloakroom and worrying about the money situation of the nation. He wanted all his colleagues to worry about it too, and so he ordered a Treasury Report to go to every member of the House every day of the week. We would have to get hundreds of copies and distribute them around even though you could count on two thumbs the members who ever looked at it.

It was with a sigh of relief that the House met the news that the good Congressman Rich was retiring. The first request they made was to please, for Christ's sake, stop giving us the damn daily Treasury Report.

Another daily headache for me in my early days was that two old codgers had to have their hometown newspapers before they could do another thing. They had to have them at 6 A.M. and I got a call immediately if they weren't ready. Carl Vinson had to have his Millidgeville, Georgia, newspaper and Cliff W. Woodrun had to have his Roanoke, Virginia, newspaper at the same time. Carl Vinson was known as "the Admiral" so there was no question that he got first service. But when they both left to retire, we decided that was it.

The Speaker's Lobby was the scene of a small competition—a race to see who would get to read the *Wall Street Journal* first. Two stern gentlemen, Merlin Hull, Republican of Wisconsin, and George M. Grant, Democrat of Alabama, had transferred any thought of searching for a pretty chick to searching for hot stock-market tips. The Republican would usually get the paper first because it was closer to the Republican side of the lobby, and he would purposely dawdle over it and worry it to pieces as the Democrat paced, waiting. It was the conclusion of their colleagues that both men were too tight to buy the paper even to see how their stocks were doing.

I think we might have ordered two copies of the *Journal*, but it was more fun to see them fight over it.

Still another fringe benefit came to Capitol Hill in the form of instructions in karate in the Senate gym, where congressmen and senators alike met twice a week to get instruction from an expert, Jhoon Rhee, a Korean who has his own chain of karate schools, but who volunteered to help shape up the solons.

Becoming so adept that they all could break two boards were Representatives Jimmy Symington, Floyd Spence, and Richard Ichord, all of Missouri and Democrats; Ed Roybal, a California Democrat; Tom Bevil, an Alabama Democrat; Senators Ted Stevens, Republican from Alaska, and Quentin Burdick, a Democrat from North Dakota. The latter is sixty-eight, but in the pink of condition.

The men claim they don't do it just to protect themselves in the streets of Washington, though they admit it would help. "I do it because it keeps the blood moving and clears the head," said Symington.

What it has done for Rhee is make him a very famous man around Washington. To be known as the man who helps congressmen is worth more than a million dollars of paid advertising.

Unknown to the public, the congressmen even have a secret place to strip and sunbathe if they wish. It's a portico or porch on the south side of the House wing, on the second-floor level there. When the weather is right, they duck out, strip to the waist usually, and get a good dose of sun while they relax and read the newspapers from home. We have even been able to supply them with dark green lounge chairs. Here they are out of sight of the public, reporters and their own staff.

I had to teach the pages and my doormen always to check the porch to be certain that a member was not overlooked when he was having a phone call or when

86

some excited reporter out in the Speaker's Lobby was trying to get hold of him to find out what his vote was going to be.

It was Speaker Sam who came up with all these great little ideas—the sun porch and others. And I must say no one on the Senate side looked after the senators the way Sam Rayburn looked after his "good ole boys" in the House.

One night Speaker Sam went home and just as he was falling asleep he had a great revelation. He saw a beautiful room—a sort of magnificent living room—where constituents who came to Washington could greet their congressmen and sit and talk with them in the hallowed halls of the Capitol itself. The friendliness of their congressmen would be most impressive in such an atmosphere—worth many votes.

Upon arrival at the Capitol the next morning, Sam met with the four architects who were moving the east front of the Capitol outward 32½ feet to keep the dome from falling through and he told them what he was thinking about.

To design it, they used a portion of the east front and labelled it H207. The four architects then went to the leadership of the Senate and told what Rayburn had dreamed up.

A similar room was quickly copied for the Senate side, on the second floor, called the S207, or the Senators' Conference Room. They named it that because they had no hero like the House did. We called ours the Rayburn Room.

THE LADIES
OF CONGRESS—
BLESS THEM ALL

In the whole history of Congress, up through my own years on the Hill, there have been only eighty-four female congressmen and eleven female senators. Some I knew, some I never knew. Some I wish I had known better. Some I wish I had never known. No, I take that back and say, they're the ladies of Congress—bless them all!

But I've had my moments. I'll never forget the day a committee of three irate congresswomen came storming into my Doorkeeper's office and demanded, "Get that blasted girl out of our washroom!"

I studied the faces of Edith Nourse Rogers, Frances Bolton and Jessie Sumner and quaked. "What seems to be the trouble?" I asked innocently.

With all of them talking at once, like a Greek chorus, I finally got the story that Congressman Albert Thomas of Texas, annoyed at the puny office space that had been allotted him, was showing his displeasure by sending one of his secretaries into the ladies' room to do her typing.

It wasn't easy to do—I really felt sorry for the girl when I saw her working in there, after I timidly opened the door. She confirmed that the ladies were definitely right. It was their rest room. But she had her orders.

By the time I got back to my office, Speaker Rayburn had sent for me, and when I hurried to his office, he in turn spewed his wrath at me, telling me, "Fish, get that girl out by tomorrow morning or you are going to be smelling the south end of a northbound mule."

When it came to playing the heavy or doing the dirty work, the leadership always made Fish do it.

I've know a lot of the women of Capitol Hill and have admired many of them for their accomplishments: Senator Margaret Chase Smith, who dared run for President and fight like a tiger against opposing senators in spite of that gentle rose in her lapel; Shirley Chisholm, the first black woman to be elected to Congress and the other black women who followed her; and, of course, Jeannette Rankin, the first woman ever elected to Congress, the one who voted "No" to going to war in World War I.

I wasn't there when Congresswoman Rankin cast that historic vote in 1917. But she told me about it years later when she was elected back to the House in 1940.

Again there were war clouds over Europe and the world. Like a horrible dream, Jeanette found herself again in that same chamber with the vote coming up once more to declare war, this time against "the Japanese Empire."

The date was December 8, 1941, the day after Pearl Harbor. Our ships lay at the bottom of the harbor and no one knew what to expect. The Senate had already acted 82 to 0 without a dissenting vote on President Franklin Delano Roosevelt's request to "declare that since the unprovoked and dastardly attack" a state of war already existed.

FDR had himself personally come to the Joint Session at 12:12 P.M. to make his impassioned plea.

It seemed pretty cut and dry. All that remained was for the House to echo the Senate. Speaker Sam was in charge and Majority Leader John McCormack moved to pass the resolution. For a few minutes, there was a little confusion as Miss Rankin tried to speak on a point of order, but someone else was demanding a roll call. Rayburn ignored the lady and ordered the roll-call vote. When her name was called, she shouted a firm, "No."

The chamber seemed thunderstruck. Suddenly, top members of her own party—like Everett Dirksen, who was still in the House—descended on her and tried to talk her into changing her vote. But they got nowhere with her.

After war was declared with the one dissenting vote, Miss Rankin required police-escort service across the street to her office in the old Cannon House Office Building and even people in her home state of Montana sent wires demanding that she redeem the honor of Montana.

Eventually, she released a statement and I couldn't believe my ears. It was that, first of all, the stories about what had gone on in Pearl Harbor were only radio stories as yet. And though they were probably true, one should still wait for "more authentic evidence" than radio reports. And second, that "sending our boys to the Orient will not protect this country." She said that sending our men there was not under the heading of "protecting our shores"—and protecting our own shores was the only reason for fighting.

It took a lot of years before she was at least partially vindicated on many points—especially on evidence that FDR helped bring about the aggression of Japan by first ignoring the "Neutrality Act of 1936," which would have stopped shipments of war supplies to Japan, and then suddenly, after the Atlantic Conference, cutting off the Japanese lifeline of civilian supplies, causing great hardship there.

Whatever history will show in the future, I don't know, but I know that Miss Rankin was a lonely woman forever trying to justify what she had done. On her "No" vote on World War I, she was a little bitter that she was the only one whom history remembered for her vote, whereas there had been others who had voted the same way.

Everything about Miss Rankin's career was ironic. She was elected to the House by men before women even had the vote—that happened with the passage of the Nineteenth Amendment in 1920. She had promised male voters she was going to Congress to take care of the things they couldn't do as well as a woman—"look after the nation's greatest asset—its children."

Well, in voting against war, maybe she was doing just that.

Jeannette told me she had tried the "feminine occupations" before she ran for office at age thirty-six. The daughter of a wealthy lumberman, she tried teaching and quickly gave that up, tried sewing and quickly gave that up and studied the designing of furniture, but did not ever finish. She got interested in the suffrage movement and travelled around the country as a lobbyist from then on.

In a way, the family was like the Kennedy family. Even that far back, it was a family affair, with her brother Wellington handling her campaign and all the members of the family—three sisters and even her timid mother—going out on the campaign trail, holding teas for neighbors, trying to explain why a woman was needed in the House.

Women who are scorned and ridiculed—women like Rankin and Eleanor Roosevelt—if they live long enough, are idolized and revered in a far greater share than others who were not so controversial. I was glad to see it happen to Jeannette Rankin when she was practically idolized for her dove stand on the Vietnam war, even leading a peace march to the foot of the Capitol at age eighty-eight.

She was really supposed to bring her people onto the House floor—at least she had threatened she would—but Speaker McCormack had caught wind of it. It used to be that a former member of the House was permitted to go on the floor, as a courtesy, and bring a guest with him. But when McCormack heard that Jeannette Rankin was threatening to bring five thousand women and to march in with them right down the aisle, he changed the rule immediately so that only the former member could have the courtesy of the floor. Members were no longer permitted to bring a guest with them.

But Rankin made out very well on the Capitol steps. And she was cheered as she said, "The world must finally understand that we cannot settle disputes by eliminating human beings." She was still preaching the same thing from a wheelchair two years later, when breaking a hip at ninety didn't slow her down.

How did she do on legislation? Well, it wasn't easy for a lone female to get anything through Congress, but she did manage to get passed the first maternity bill that provided free hygiene lessons, and she was proud that she had been the first to fight for the eight-hour workday for women and had singlehandedly forced the government to cut down its twelve-hour workday for women who labored at making paper money at the Bureau of Engraving.

Some think that Hattie Caraway of Arkansas, who was appointed to fill the unexpired term of her husband in 1931, was the first woman in the Senate. That's wrong. The first lady senator arrived in 1922 and she was eighty-seven years old and not too steady on her feet. The poor soul was being used for the political benefit of her governor of the state of Georgia, who had made the mistake of voting against the Nineteenth Amendment giving franchise to women. The ladies were very much up in arms against Governor Thomas W. Hardwick and, as they say on the Hill, "He had some fences to mend before the opposition wolves bored through and ate him up."

So to curry a little favor, but not too much since he himself was planning eventually to run for the office, Hardwick appointed "Mother Felton"—Mrs. Rebecca Latimer Felton—known as "the grand old dame of

Georgia," to fill the unexpired term of Senator Thomas Watson.

Fortunately, the dead man's term was about up because the gentlemen of the Senate were not generally in favor of having their freedom curtailed by the appearance of any lady, especially a tiny, gray-haired, grandmotherly lady in floor-length black gowns. What they called it, however, was "a waste of public funds" to bring her up for such a short time.

But Mother Felton packed her bag anyway and showed up at the Senate door. They kept her waiting in the chamber quite a while before a gallery packed with a group of irate women watchdogs helped them decide to melt the opposition. And suddenly the President pro tempore was calling for the reading of Mrs. Felton's credentials, and she was sworn in to applause led by the gallery and followed by the senators.

It cost the taxpayers only a little over $500 for both travel costs and service pay for her swearing-in, well worth the cost, I'd say, to break down another barrier.

Hattie Caraway was a different matter. When I arrived in 1933, she was the talk of the Hill. She didn't care what the other senators thought. She shocked them by having a bottle of—would you believe—not booze, but milk delivered to her office door. And she put the empties back out. Nor did she follow her Democratic party's leadership. She sat knitting and listening to her colleagues, and then voted her own mind.

She voted against permitting retail sales taxes. And lost. And she voted for forcing airlines to provide a parachute for every passenger. And lost. One of her staunch supporters was the publisher of the *Fayetteville Daily Journal*, Roberta Fulbright. And it was the publisher's son, J. William Fulbright, who, at age thirty-nine, unseated the lady in 1944 in her sixty-sixth year and fourth time up.

Hattie may have been her own woman, defying the wolfpack of men, but she followed the pack in one thing—she refused to leave Washington after her defeat. Truman kindly appointed her to the Employee's Compensation Commission and she stayed around the Capitol until she died in 1950.

When Huey Long of Louisiana was shot by a man described in the press as a jealous husband in the State House in Baton Rouge, his widow, Rose, was appointed to his Senate seat in January 1936.

Knowing what an all-round wild man, boozer and womanizer Huey had been, the whole Hill was waiting to see what the long-suffering Rose would say and do on the Hill. What she said was that her husband had been such a great and virtuous man that no one else could ever interest her. The Hill crowd couldn't believe its ears.

Rose Long didn't try for reelection. After the Seventy-fourth Congress ended, she just packed up. She hadn't done anything, but she hadn't caused any trouble either. She had kept the seat warm, and fairly soon, in 1948, she would be sending another Long to Washington—her son, Russell B., whom I grew to admire for his quiet hard-working ways, so unlike his father's boisterous harangues on the floor.

Hill dynasties interest me. The Long one is the only father-mother-son combination in history, and I knew all three. But there have been various other combinations: the Kennedy brothers—three; and the father-son teams of Senator Barry and Congressman Barry Goldwater, Jr., and Senator Stuart and Congressman James Symington. In recent years, there has also been a mother-son team—Congressman Frances Bolton of Ohio and her congressman son, Oliver.

Both served at the same time, but the mother's staying power far outweighed her son's. Oliver lasted but one term and Frances continued on from 1940 to 1969. I knew Congresswoman Bolton very well. Good-natured, matronly and the richest woman on Capitol Hill, the multimillionairess was still about the loneliest woman in town. I used to talk to her chauffeur and he would tell me how both of them killed time riding around, just talking because she didn't want to go home.

After all, though she was one of the hardest-working people on the Hill, she couldn't stay in her office and work all the time. Sometimes I would keep her company, and though she was a Republican, I really grew very fond of her. She would talk to me about yoga and how she stood on her head to relax and gain serenity. Seeing how fat I was getting, she would advise me to stand on my head, as she did, to improve my mind and my circulation.

Nobody knew the tragedies she had sustained. Her only daughter lived just one day—she never mentioned her in her *Congressional Directory* biography, only her three sons. Another child broke his neck in a diving stunt. And her husband, Chester, had died suddenly in 1939 when he was at the height of his congressional career.

Since I had known her husband, too, this gave us a special bond, especially as the years went by and fewer and fewer people remained who had known Congressman Chester Bolton. He had been one of my first buddies on the Hill, and in fact, it used to amuse everyone that he would give his coat and hat to me, a Democratic employee, rather than hand it to an employee of his own party.

Mrs. Bolton never seemed to consider anything but widowhood. But she was tough. She got angry if I called her a congresswoman. "I'm a congressman," she said. "A poet is not a poetess and an author is not an authoress. It's degrading to call her that."

I felt particularly sorry for good old Frances when her son, Oliver, ran for Congress in another Ohio district—hers was the 22nd, and his, the 11th—and made it without her. I think she wanted to be more of a team with him, but he wanted to go it alone. And you could hardly blame either one of them. But I remember what she told me once: "He said if I wanted to help him I could stay the hell out of his district." And she laughed, but not convincingly. "He's afraid I'll try to control him."

I felt sorry for her again when her son developed heart trouble and didn't run for reelection. At least for his term of office she had enjoyed knowing that her grandchildren were nearby.

The trouble was there was really nobody she could control or who needed her desperately. She had all the money in the world—more than she could ever use—and no one to really feel close to. But she did great things—she was one of the most generous people on the Hill. She met a strikingly brainy girl in Kenya and brought her over and sent her to medical school. She gave Uncle Sam her $10,000 congressional widow's pension. She used her own money to make a survey of conditions in Africa, and I'm told it's a good one.

Her money had come from shipping, coal, iron and oil. Not only had her father and other relatives handed her a fabulous fortune, but she was related to a signer of the Declaration of Independence, Robert Paine.

As a teen-ager, she had sneaked out of the family mansion in Cleveland to go into the slums and help the public health nurse. What she saw influenced almost everything she did in Congress, she told me. Because of it, she fought through the bill that set up the U.S. Cadet Corps. And using her own money, she established a school of nursing at Western Reserve University—cost, $1.5 million.

And she even worried about men not having the chance to be nurses, so she got an equal rights for men bill passed for the express purpose of letting the Army and Navy commission male nurses.

There was only one time we argued—and that was when she needled me about drafting women. Was I for it, she asked?

"No, indeed," I said. "I'm still for men protecting women and letting women stay home."

"Fishbait, that kind of gallantry is silly. Plain silly. It's as out of date as the dodo. You wait and see. In the next war, women will be out with guns defending their homes. They ought to be drafted so they'll know how to defend their men and their children."

I wanted to say she'd been standing on her head too long, but that wouldn't have been chivalrous, so I just shut up. Besides, even though she didn't have a gun, she outranked me in the House.

There have been all kinds of family combinations on the Hill. And women will be proud to know there was one time when a wife preceded her husband into Congress. She was the liberal Democrat Emily Taft Douglas, who came to the House of Representatives in 1944, putting her one up on her guy, Paul Douglas, an economics professor at the University of Chicago. He had run for the Senate in 1942 and failed.

Just to show how fickle the public is, Mrs. Douglas had come in with more votes in her district than FDR got, but after working night and day, going to Europe to study the plight of the children raised under Nazi and fascist regimes and working out plans to rehabilitate them, and after working on legislation that would control armaments and the proliferation of the atomic bomb, even though she had done all that, she was swept out of office in the 1946 election which gave the GOP control of the House.

But life—and politics—goes on. Two years later, she was out campaigning again—this time for her husband, who tried again for the Senate and made it.

The gentlemen of Congress were not all pleased when the House was more and more invaded by female members. They especially resented it when one of them acted "uppity," as if she had just as much a right, if not more, to be there, than they. For many years these gentlemen felt that the women were there on sufferance.

Therefore they were very much upset when the famous Clare Boothe Luce swept into their midst and walked around with her nose in the air. As one of the members kept describing it, "If it had been raining, she'd have drowned."

But that was nothing compared to what was said about another lady of the House. One day I was sitting on the Democratic side of the House when a West Coast congressman said to me, pointing to a congressional woman from the Midwest, "She's a bitchy bitch, ain't she?"

He was pointing across the aisle to the Republican side. I said, "Well, she's still one of my bosses. I don't know what to say."

"Well, I'll tell you what I say," he said irritably and a touch bitterly. "If her pants were on fire I wouldn't even shoot my water pistol to put the fire out. I'd let her burn up."

I remember once we were having a quorum call in midafternoon on a very important bill and trying to get through rather early so the entire Congress could go to the White House. Congresswoman Iris Blitch of Georgia had come in dressed fit to kill and ready to go to the White House.

I went over to her and said, "Iris, do you love me just a little bit, honey?"

Her reply was, "Fishbait, what are you trying to tell me that I'm not going to like?"

It seemed that I was always the bearer of bad news and I always tried to soften the blow. I said, "Well, it ain't good, because in the rush to leave your office to get to the floor and answer the roll call, you have stockings on that don't match. One has a seam and one is seamless."

She said, "The hell I have. Fishbait, go phone my secretary and tell her to get me a pair that match and for her to bring them over to me so I can go to the retiring room and put them on."

When I returned from delivering the message, she said, "I'm so glad there's one man here who walks where others fear to tread. Thank you so much. I really do love you and I appreciate this very much."

Probably Clare Boothe Luce was the most beautiful woman to come to Congress. I think most of the congressmen were half in love with her and I'm afraid I was no different. She was beautiful, elegant, dainty, well-dressed. She had a tongue like a dragon's and could cut down anybody she didn't like or who crossed her.

Congressman William Fulbright, who had been a Rhodes scholar and was one of the top debaters on the Hill, was her first victim. It was her maiden speech and she had called Henry Wallace's freedom of the skies theory "globaloney." The House was shocked. You just don't insult the administration on the floor that way, no matter how pretty you are. So Fulbright was chosen by the leadership to refute her.

Rising, he said that the congresswoman had "inferred that Wallace's plan for free skies would endanger the security of the United States." Jauntily, Clare Luce corrected him, and I can still see his face getting red. "I inferred nothing," she snapped. "I *implied* and the gentleman from Arkansas did the *inferring*."

She didn't make friends on the Hill that day, but meanwhile the word "globaloney" was spun around the world and so was her picture. And she had made Republican brownie points. Others in the FDR administration fared no better. Harold L. Ickes, she said, had "the soul of a meat ax." She said FDR had lied us into a war he hadn't the guts to lead us into.

Anytime she wanted publicity, she took another swat at FDR—claiming in her "G.I. Jim and G.I. Joe" speech at the Republican Convention of 1944 that President Roosevelt had broken his 1940 promise not to send American men to fight foreign wars. She said G.I. Jim was the soldier who never complained but who now was very dead because the government was bungling the war.

After that one, someone said she was well-named—Boothe—because she was trying to assassinate the President verbally.

I think she learned her fighting technique from her poor childhood. It was said around the Capitol that she wanted the Hill crowd to think she was to the manner born, but she was really a little ole poor gal who made good. Her father was a down-on-his-luck traveling musician who deserted the family when she was just a little thing. Her mother did the best she could, dancing and singing and clerking to earn a living.

As a child, Clare was so cute that David Belasco saw her and made her Mary Pickford's understudy in a play. Unfortunately, the star never missed a performance, and that might have made Clare bitter at an early age. I do think she told me she got a few small kid roles in movies, if I remember correctly. But her first real job as a teen-ager was beneath her talents—making paper decorations for some company.

Fortunately, her mother remarried to a successful doctor and Clare knew security for the first time. Eventually, Clare married a man more than twenty years older than herself, George Brokaw, and they had a daughter before she divorced him.

When she came to the Hill in 1942 and I met her, the daughter, Ann Brokaw, was about ready for or already in college at Stanford, and Clare was married to *Time* and *Life* publisher Henry Luce, with all the power that implied.

I'll never forget my first run-in with her. She had arrived for the opening-day session dressed to the teeth and wearing what a member called "her fanny freezer"—a short fur jacket. She was making an entrance by being late and I said, in greeting, "I'm Fishbait Miller. I want to be your friend and I want you to be my friend."

100

Then I looked around to be sure there were no reporters in the Speaker's Lobby, where we were standing, and I said, "I am going to show you that I am your friend and tell you something that I hope won't hurt your feelings, but your slip is showing this much." I made a motion measuring about two inches with my fingers.

The famous Luce chin went up more than two inches and she thanked me coldly and proceeded to the other side to the Republican entrance and took a seat in the chamber.

Reporters were soon on the phone demanding to know what that was all about and what I had said to the new beauty queen of the Hill. I said, "I didn't tell her anything except words of friendship." But obviously she herself must have told somebody because that night, it was told to me later, she had an overseas call from her daughter who was in England at the time. There were tears in the daughter's voice as she said, "Mother, after we worked so hard to get you elected to Congress, you didn't even take time to completely dress and some little old page boy had to tell you that your slip was showing."

Mrs. Luce didn't speak to me for months afterward, but when her daughter had the terrible accident in California, in which she lost her life when her car was wrecked on the freeway, Mrs. Luce came to me.

"Fishbait," she said, with tears in her eyes, "I've been a bad person, but you have been very sweet about it. I want to apologize for being such a heel, and I *do* want you to be my friend, and I want to be yours."

Clare seemed to change before my eyes. She started taking an interest in Catholicism. She decided not to run again in 1946. Under Ike, she did come out of retirement to be Ambassador to Italy. But even that became controversial when it looked like someone was trying to poison her. Then it turned out that arsenate of lead paint falling from the ceiling in the study off

101

her bedroom was making her sick. Well, if it weren't dramatic, it wouldn't have been Clare, bless her.

I had occasion to see her when the President of Italy was invited to come to America and, while here, he spoke to a Joint Meeting of Congress. Naturally, it was fitting for Ambassador Luce to fly over and be present on the floor of the House when he spoke. Just before the program started, one of my bosses directed me wordlessly to look where his eyes were looking. Naturally, I was the one who always had to do the necessary. I walked over to the good lady and she took one look at me and said, "Fishbait, what am I doing wrong? It can't be my slip."

"No, ma'am." I still just looked at her. Suddenly she said, "Oh, my God, I'm wearing my hat and I know it's against the rules."

I remember Helen Gahagan Douglas as the other glamor gal who arrived at the same time as La Luce. She didn't try to compete—either in high fashion or in spiced wit. They had a ladies' agreement not to go for each other's jugular. They had even shaken hands on it in front of Hill witnesses.

Poor Helen became the victim of another ambitious political person, Richard Nixon, who was after her scalp in the senatorial race of 1950.

She had said in a speech that "communism is no real threat to the Democratic institutions of our country," which gave Nixon the opening for a red smear of Helen.

As Mrs. Douglas tried to explain over and over again, the speech had also said, "Communism has no place in our society. We have something better."

What she also said on the Hill was that *fear* of communism had grown to "an irrational" degree and was being used as a smoke screen to hide other things. Nixon won handily against Helen in that California race, and for years you hardly dared mention her name on the Hill for fear you would be accused of being soft on communism.

But I think Helen got the last word. I thought of her the day that President Nixon resigned. In the 1972 presidential campaign for Nixon's reelection, she had said, "There is no new Nixon. How could there be? He can't change."

My happiest memory of Mrs. Douglas is when she once told me how she had gotten into politics in the dust-bowl days, when she couldn't stand to see the Okies, like in the movies, moving on from place to place to get migrant farm work. Had she been able to stay in Congress, who knows what good things she could have done for the poor?

If you saw a row of pictures of all the women who served in the House, you wouldn't call many of them "sex objects." Still, once in a while there was a little fireworks that made one of them suddenly seem most attractive to us around the Hill.

It happened when a wife of one of the men on Edith Nourse Rogers' staff publicly accused the congresswoman of winning away the affections of her husband. Edith looked soft and cuddly but not really like a sex object for a man that much younger than herself.

Another congresswoman who seemed to excite some of our members was Jessie Sumner, a Republican from Illinois whom God had endowed with ample hips and other feminine attributes. There was frequently some talk, especially during the winter, of how nice it would be to be able to go home with a gal like that who could really keep a man warm—"Man, if you lived with that you would never get cold at night."

Perhaps Congresswoman Sumner heard some of the comments on the floor, because she bent over backwards to show how prim and proper she was and opposed to females flaunting their virtues—and this was in the casual attire days of World War II and immediately thereafter.

I remember when she wanted Speaker Joseph Martin, Jr., to check the rule books to see if he could issue a ruling that everyone female had to be properly dressed to come into the galleries and that not even school girls could be in shorts. Poor bachelor Joseph Martin, who was very timid with women of all ages, but did enjoy looking, sweated that out. He kept putting her off, but she was making an issue of it. Then he was saved by the sudden appearance of a whole high-school group of girls all neat and presentable, scrubbed and well-combed—but all wearing shorts.

Martin had his solution. He pointed out this group to the prim congresswoman and commented on how unfair it would be, and even unthinkable, to bar such an attractive, dignified group of young ladies. Jessie sputtered but gave up, and then her term expired in January 1947. Leggy teen-agers were safe again for a while.

I would say that the ladies of Congress had much less interest in extra-marital affairs than their masculine counterparts. And when they did have an affair, on rare occasions, they were much more discreet. There was one congresswoman who had a standing arrangement with a particular delivery man who worked on the Hill. Every afternoon at a particular hour he would come to her office with a delivery of packages and she had a standing order that he be permitted to come to her private office with just a knock on the door.

Once inside, she locked the door for a happy half-hour with him, except for one thing. The poor fellow said it was most awkward because she preferred to stand up rather than use the couch—but who was he to argue, especially since she was sure the standing position kept her from getting pregnant.

But getting back to Edith Nourse Rogers, she was one of my favorites. She took a special interest in veterans.

Her interest had begun in World War I, when her husband, Congressman John Jacob Rogers, and she had gone to Europe to see the war conditions and she had spent her time caring for the wounded as a Red Cross worker. After that, even in Washington, she spent all her spare time in military hospitals helping the disabled.

When her husband died in 1925, she became the Republican candidate in a special election and beat her opponent, a governor.

All through her career on the Hill, the Massachusetts congresswoman made veterans her special concern, and in 1944 she introduced the blockbuster G.I. Bill of Rights Act that made it possible for those who had served their country in wartime to go to college and prepare for a different kind of career. She also fought through legislation that resulted in the building of various veterans' hospitals.

It is amazing how much legislation having to do with our military personnel came from this one little woman with the fluffy hair. Turning her attention to women, and solving a military problem of finding needed personnel to do paper work, she pushed legislation through Congress that set up the WAAC—Women's Auxiliary Army Corps.

Mrs. Rogers was one of the first to speak out against Nazi mistreatment of the Jews, and as the war clouds gathered, she was a hawk rather than a dove.

Gallant to the end, Edith kept her final illness secret. She was busy running for reelection—she had been unopposed for the 1960 primary and she had to let no one know that she was in the hospital. As usual, she didn't want to disturb or be a burden to anyone.

I didn't finish telling the story of the ladies' rest room, or "retiring room," as it was delicately called on the Hill. It was Edith Rogers who had led those irate congresswomen to my office—not that she wasn't more than a little irate herself. But the thing that was turned up on further investigation was that the Texas congressman who had sent the girl to type in the rest room had simply gotten carried away with power. What had happened was that he had suddenly received a plum by way of patronage and was permitted to choose a ladies' room attendant on his patronage. He thought it would be very nice to let her work as a secretary as well as taking care of that rest room, and he was making the most use of her talents.

Things were more casual in those days and Speaker Rayburn simply suggested to Albert Thomas, in a mild voice, that the congressman find some corner of his own office where his patronage rest-room attendant could type and then let her go into the rest room for the strict business of taking care of it every now and then.

As I recall, being a bouncing ball did not suit the young lady and she gave up both Hill careers soon after.

Even more startling was what happened to Coya Knutson, a good-looking blonde lawmaker from Oklee, Minnesota, who will probably be best remembered long after she is dead for the "Come Home, Coya" letter her husband wrote, which cost her an election.

Even President Kennedy got involved in this one. What happened is that Coya beat Harold C. Hagen, who had been around the Hill more than a decade, and was spending her time in Washington while her husband managed the family business back home in Oklee.

She was reelected in 1956, but when she announced she would try for a third term, her husband, Andrew, made public his grievances against Coya, accusing her of having an affair with one of her young male aides and saying he would sue him for $200,000.

Part of the story seized on by an eager press was a letter in which he begged her to come back to her hearth and home and give up politics.

106

Coya was defeated as a direct result. Then her husband admitted in a public apology that Coya's political enemies had talked him into writing the letter. And, in fact, he admitted that the press release he had issued had been written by the campaign staff of the man who won Coya's seat away from her.

Sorry wasn't good enough. Coya got a divorce and now lives far from Washington (Bemidji, Minnesota) with her son.

But back in 1960, after the smoke had cleared, she ran again, campaigning more for Kennedy than for herself. It was her district that was credited with helping him win Minnesota. Though Coya lost, as she knew she would, Kennedy, in appreciation, gave her a job with the Office of Civilian Defense.

It was a logical job for her. She had authored Title II of the National Defense Education Act, the bill which created the student-loan fund so that even youngsters who can't afford college can go now and pay Uncle Sam back later.

Yes, she was a gallant lady.

About the most beautiful love story I knew on Capitol Hill belonged to another gallant lady, this one of the Senate—Margaret Chase Smith.

It is a love story that reads like the pages of a Brontë sisters novel and that continued after Mrs. Smith left the Hill following her defeat in 1972, after trying for a fifth term in the Senate.

Bill Lewis was an Air Force officer of World War II whose father was a general and a wealthy descendant of an Oklahoma oil-Indian family.

General Lewis reorganized the Air Reserve Association after the war and his son met Margaret when she was serving in the House as the widow of Republican Representative Clyde Harold Smith. (Congressman Clyde Smith, incidentally, was a dear friend of mine, and to show how he felt about me, he also would give me his hat and coat and insist that I, the Democratic

107

employee, take care of it instead of someone on his own Republican side.)

Young Bill Lewis' experience in promoting the association was an asset when Margaret ran for the Senate in 1948 using the slogan, "The can-do candidate with the can-did record." She became the first woman to win a first-term election to the Senate rather than get there by appointment, as Caraway had.

And she was reelected to three more six-year terms.

Not only did Reserve Lieutenant-Colonel Lewis act as Margaret's very able administrative aide throughout all her career in the Senate, but eventually he built a house for both of them to share—he on one floor and she on another—two lovely, separate apartments.

Even today they share the same house arrangement. She lives in her apartment, joins Lewis—he is now a general of the Air Force Reserve—for lunch and to discuss the news of the day, just as in the Hill days. They travel, the former congresswoman making speeches and keeping in touch with campuses to help the youth of America.

But every now and then, even after Mrs. Smith left office in 1973, the *cause célèbre* is brought up again of the time she single-handedly held up a list of Air Force promotions until justice was done to her A. A., Bill Lewis. Mrs. Smith was on the Armed Services Committee and was a powerful force in legislation concerning the Air Force Reserve, in which Bill had risen through the years. After he had become a full colonel and completed all requirements, time went on and he was not nominated for brigadier general. However, the Air Force had the effrontery to send up to the committee a list of colonels recommended for a general's star which included movie-star Jimmy Stewart but not plain, hard-working Bill Lewis.

What had happened was that President Eisenhower had nominated his good friend Colonel Jimmy Stewart. In committee, Senator Smith asked why the actor had been promoted over others when he hadn't put in the required flying time. Lieutenant-Colonel "Rosie" (Emmett) O'Donnell, chief of personnel of the Air Force, justified the special treatment of Stewart because he had made a great contribution to the Air Force during the war.

But Mrs. Smith pointed out with cool dignity that Stewart was not qualified to fly the current military planes and had spent only nine days on active reserve duty in ten or eleven years. She recommended that Stewart's promotion be turned down. After he *did* comply with regulations, she withdrew her objection.

Bill Lewis' name also appeared on the list, and he continued to rise in the ranks, retiring as a major general.

Not only was Margaret Chase Smith a tiger in fighting until right was done, but she was one of the women I knew who could tell a good story. I particularly remember this one she told on herself which helped the men on the Hill feel that she was one of them, in spite of being a woman.

"When I was first campaigning for the Senate in 1948," she said, "I stopped to introduce myself in a small town to a grocery-store owner and all his customers clustered around him.

"The grocery-store owner listened to me for a little while as I stood there telling him why I'd appreciate his vote and his support, and then he said, 'What are you running for, Madam?'

" 'The United States Senate,' I replied.

" 'From where?' he asked.

" 'Maine, of course,' I answered, annoyed.

" 'Well, lady,' he said, as all the customers looked at each other, 'you are in New Hampshire. Maine is over that way.' "

In 1964, Margaret Chase Smith became the first woman to be nominated for President at a major convention—that of the Republicans. She entered two primaries and received twenty-seven delegate votes at the convention—more than any contender but Goldwater.

Four years before, when the Senate dared censure Joseph R. McCarthy for his badgering tactics and his witchhunts for communists in government, Senator Smith was the first to have the courage to speak out against him and his "inquisitorial investigative methods" which would later become known by his own name—McCarthyism.

The Hill remembers Mrs. Smith for many things: for her fearless stand against McCarthyism, for her noble run for President and even for her frugality in running for office. She spent only $4,500 in running for her fourth term. As I knew from conversations with her husband in the old days, Margaret truly knew the value of money. As the eldest of six children, she had helped support her family, even clerking Saturdays at the local five-and-ten-cent store for a big dime an hour.

She also helped her husband when he became congressman, serving as his secretary at $15 a week. It makes one wonder whether nepotism is all bad. As Mrs. Chase said, "I'm the product of nepotism. I wouldn't be in Congress if I hadn't gotten experience on my husband's staff."

Another dear Republican friend among the ladies of Congress was Mrs. Katherine St. George of Tuxedo Park, New York, who was very dedicated to looking after folks back home and was a member of the Senate Rules Committee. One of her greatest loves was a solid-gold elephant pin that she always wore on her dress, just as Margaret Chase Smith was known for the fresh rose in her lapel every day.

Mrs. St. George managed to lose the pin; her office was in an uproar and so was she. Everyone hunted everywhere. Finally, she appealed to me to help her, admitting it was probably hopeless.

I combed the House Chamber. No luck. Since she walked, as was her habit, on the grass instead of the sidewalk on her way from the Cannon House Office Building to the Capitol, I had a feeling that if I could retrace her steps, I might spot it. Four times I walked her usual path back and forth.

Then I decided she must have taken a shortcut. I kicked the leaves as I walked, and suddenly there it was —the priceless gold elephant shining up at me.

I told a Democratic friend about it afterwards and he grunted, unimpressed, "Well, Fish, just remember it's the donkey and not the elephant that's feeding your face and keeping you up here."

Even as a "male chauvinist pig" coming from the Deep South, I must admire Shirley Chisholm, the first black congresswoman to come to the Hill. I've never had a bad moment with her. Who knows, she may someday be my President and yours. No less a man than Hubert Humphrey, the wizard of politics himself, once said in reminiscing about the 1972 election to a group of us, "With a little bit of money and an organization behind her, she might have made it at the convention and beaten McGovern and all of us."

What happened was that at the 1972 Miami Beach Democratic National Convention, Shirley got herself nominated, and surprised the whole Democratic party by receiving some 150 delegate votes for the presidency in one of the convention ballots.

I was there and was amazed. I liked her spunk and her self-confidence, and when I talked to her about it she was not modest. She said she was a candidate who had more qualifications than anyone. "I've got more of everything than the other candidates—more brains, more education," she said, "I've got four degrees and I'm a few credits from a Ph.D. And I'm the only candidate who can speak Spanish. Now tell me, what other candidate can qualify with *me*?"

And Shirley Chisholm does something few women

111

do—she lets women have top positions in her office. She has a female legislative assistant—a rarity on the Hill where men write the laws, men introduce the laws, and men pass the laws.

Members don't usually complain about their assignments, thinking the leadership is all-wise and all-knowing. Usually new members visit with me and learn the ropes on getting assigned to something they have particular interest in.

However, Shirley Chisholm made history on the Hill by going on strike when she learned of her committee assignment. Chisholm, a representative of a ghetto area in New York, found herself on the Agriculture Committee. She was one of the few newcomers who hadn't come to visit with me or she'd have known how to avoid such a *revolting* development.

Not talking to me was her first mistake. I would have told her the way to get on a committee she liked is by polite hinting. I would have told her to write a nice letter to the chairman of the committee on which she wanted to serve. And another nice note to the chairman of the Ways and Means Committee, because that's the one that until recently made the committee assignments. And a nice note to the Speaker of the House, because he, too, carries weight. And a nice little letter to the head of the delegation of her state.

That was her second mistake, not writing notes—and her third was that she went over the head of Wilbur Mills, chairman of the Ways and Means Committee, to make her complaint directly to Speaker McCormack, saying, "I will not serve on that committee."

Not only did this make her a powerful enemy in the form of the top committee chairman, but it didn't help her with the leader of her party either, the Speaker.

Shirley was then switched to the Veterans Committee, which she also wasn't happy about, but she knew when to quiet down. Then she got smart and made a deal with Hale Boggs after she got reelected in 1970.

She supported him for the leadership and he helped her get on the Education and Labor Committee, which she really wanted.

I sometimes wonder what would have happened if McGovern had chosen Shirley Chisholm as his vice-presidential running mate instead of first Tom Eagleton, and then Sargent Shriver, after Eagleton was found to have had emotional problems in the past that had caused him to be hospitalized for psychiatric help. I'll bet McGovern has pondered it too and wondered if he wouldn't have won more states with Shirley than the one lone state—Massachusetts—and the District of Columbia, that he won with Shriver.

Mrs. Chisholm told me it cost about $50,000 in left-over debts for her own presidential caper.

Usually such a bid for the presidency is a hint that the person would accept the vice-presidency and this was taken to have that meaning by the Hill crowd.

What especially interested me was how a woman like that handles her marriage, and I was amazed to find out how really liberated Shirley is. She not only talks liberated woman, Shirley *is* liberated woman. She frankly says, in private conversations, "When I'm home, my husband does the cooking. I'm the politician, he's the cook. It suits us—it might not suit you, but it suits us."

And no one can call Conrad Chisholm a sissy. He's a big, tough private investigator. "He just happens to be a gourmet chef," his wife says.

About the toughest female I've had to contend with was not Shirley Chisholm, but Bella Abzug, the Manhattan bombshell. In my first confrontation with her, she told me forthright, "Go fuck yourself." She really did. She said it sharp and clear and she not only told about it later, but she mentioned it in her own book about herself.

Maybe I should say, "She suggested I perform an impossible act," but we'll tell it like it is.

Bella Abzug came to the Ninety-second Congress that convened in January 1971. But in November 1970, after the election, Democrats were already having the usual seminar and all the freshman congressmen were meeting in the Rayburn House Office Building, with lunch brought in to them.

On the second night, they had a reception for the new members. A group of incumbents from New York were talking to Bella. One said, "Bella, you think you're a complete character in your own right, don't you?"

She said, "You're damn right I am."

Another in the group said, "Now we have a fellow on the House floor that will set you back on your heels and make a lady out of you."

Bella said, "How the hell is he going to do that?"

"We'll tell you." They said, "He'll make you take your hat off so quick it will make your head spin like a top."

Bella answered, "Well, if that guy tries to bother me, I'll just tell him to go fuck himself."

So when she came to the House floor on January 21, she was met at the door of the chamber where the Doorkeeper barred the way. "Bella," I said softly, "you'll have to take your hat off, honey."

She said, "Didn't you get my message?"

I said innocently, "If I did, I don't recall. What was it you were going to tell me?"

She said, "I told some of my colleagues from New York, who were telling me about you last November, that if this thing happened, I'd just tell you to go fuck yourself." She looked me right in the eyes as she said it, as if waiting for me to blush.

I just stood there looking at her and she reached up and took off her hat sort of meekly and handed it to me. She said, "Here, dammit, you take care of it."

Several years later, in the spring of 1974, I was invited to a meeting of 350 Jewish civic leaders at the

114

Shoreham Hotel. Not only did I introduce Bella, but I gave the opening prayer. Just as Bella finished her speech, the president of the group reminded those present that the congresswoman had a book to sell and she would be happy to autograph copies for anybody who wanted one.

Some, who had brought their copies from home and knew that I was on page 29, rushed at me and before I was through, I had autographed about fifty page 29s "For History."

So you can see that in spite of our dramatic first encounter, we became good friends. In fact, I could understand that encounter much better as soon as I learned about her background—she was used to street language. She was collecting pennies on New York street corners to help Zionism when she was only a child. And she was hanging around her father's store, the Live and Let Live Meat Market, which was on Ninth Avenue.

In her memoirs, she says, "They call me Battling Bella, Mother Courage, and a Jewish Mother with more complaints than Portnoy. There are those who say I'm impatient, impetuous, uppity, rude, profane, brash and overbearing. . . . But whatever I am . . . I am a very serious woman."

She was the first member of Congress who said openly, "Nixon should be impeached." Everyone thought she had lost her marbles to suggest such a thing. It turned out she knew what she was doing.

And she did, right from the start, have a flair for getting attention in the newspapers. For example, the very day she was sworn in in the Ninety-second Congress, she had a grandstanding second swearing in on the steps of the Capitol, with Shirley Chisholm administering the oath. Some of the members stopped me and said, "Fishbait, you shouldn't allow that out on the steps. It's a travesty of Congress—the steps are for things like accepting messages from the President."

I said, "I don't own the steps. I just work here. Why don't you pass a law on what the steps can be used for? I can't just chase her away from the steps like she's a dog."

The first day Bella was in office, she also annoyed the old guard by introducing a bill right off the bat. It was an order calling for the withdrawal of American troops from Vietnam. Even congressmen who agreed with her view were shocked. "It's bad taste and goes against all tradition," said one. "She should wait till she's been in Congress a respectable length of time before throwing her weight around and introducing anything. This is downright disrespectful."

But Bella Abzug didn't worry about tradition, she just went her way—flinging off her hat before she went on the floor and flinging it back on when she left. She even wore hats to cocktail parties—and usually was the only woman in the room with one on after six.

I wondered how Bella's home life matched up with Shirley Chisholm's—did she also have a husband who cooked? "No," said Martin Abzug, her stockbroker husband, laughing. "I can't remember when I had my last home-cooked meal. Oh, yes I can—it was just before the housekeeper left."

Well, I wondered, how did Martin shape up as a helpmate. After all, think of all the congressional wives who have helped their husbands in a million and one ways, including becoming their secretaries on the Hill until nepotism was outlawed.

"Oh, I qualified," Martin happily assured a group who had gotten together to see movies he had made of Bella and her female colleagues at the Great Wall of China. "Some people think it's just sex, but I can type."

Bella then confessed that she cannot type and that her husband typed all of her papers at Columbia Law School.

I knew the congressmen were waiting to catch her at some point and rock her back on her heels. They

116

finally got their chance when she introduced a bill called the "Abzug Abortion Rights Bill." To support her position she ordered about 150 pages of material inserted in the *Congressional Record* which is delivered to every congressman first thing in the early morning. Immediately, the Joint Committee on Printing pointedly made a rule that anyone wanting to insert more than a few pages had to include a cost estimate. Abzug was insulted and said so, but there was little she could do to make a fuss because, though she claimed to be for economy, her little insert message to her colleagues had cost the American public $150 a page, or something like $22,500.

But before Bella decided to run for the Senate against James Buckley, she softened a bit. She was even seen once at an evening event without a hat.

Bella may become the example of the old saying that yesterday's radical is today's moderate and tomorrow's conservative. Without changing her views, I saw her gain acceptance as the times caught up with her.

During her first term, she had shocked her colleagues by extreme statements such as President Nixon should be impeached and his Vietnam war was proof that he was "motivated by insane priorities." By her next term, many of her colleagues were agreeing with her on both points.

Looking back at the array of women I've seen in Congress, I realize that bitchiness, as the girls call it, didn't just take place in recent years. I remember when Congresswoman Mary Elizabeth Farrington of Hawaii, who had replaced her late husband, Joseph R. Farrington, was so annoyed at the appearance of Delegate John A. Burns, who had arrived ahead of time to replace her in the Eighty-fifth Congress, that she would not even give him sitting room in her office.

I had to take that poor man to my office and give him a desk and a corner to work in to be ready for January 3, 1957.

Barbara Jordan is another woman to watch. Somebody said recently that Congresswoman Jordan is exactly the way God looks if God is black and a woman. She really is. Seeing her walk into the House Chamber with her tall, stately figure and fierce dignity makes you kind of rise up in fear and respect and admiration. She has a presence about her. And she takes herself seriously.

Well, she should; she's strung up a list of firsts that would stagger a mule—to name only two, first black state senator in Texas, first black congresswoman from the South.

And when she came to the Hill in 1972 she was only thirty-six years old, yet she had already helped Texas get its first minimum-wage laws. On the Hill, however, most people became aware of her when she was one of the most articulate members of the Judiciary subcommittee which drew up the impeachment articles on Nixon.

The new breed of lady legislators are not shrinking violets. Congresswoman Pat Schroeder, Democrat of Colorado, was furious when an amendment to a defense bill that she had written was defeated 25 to 1 in her House Armed Services Committee. She got up and sputtered, "I know the only reason my amendment failed is that I've got a vagina."

Chairman F. Edward Hébert, who had led the opposition, did not help her disposition any when he smugly retorted, "Well, my dear, if you'd been using your vagina instead of your mouth, maybe you'd have gotten a few more votes."

My good friend Liz Carpenter, who used to be Lady Bird Johnson's chief aide and who helped found ERAmerica, also told an anecdote involving Pat Schroeder's feminine anatomy.

As Liz told the story to Judy Flanders of the *Washington Star*, "The day she came to Congress, some old codger said to her, 'How can you be the mother of two

118

small children and a member of Congress at the same time?' " According to Liz, Pat Schroeder looked at him and said, "Because I have a brain and a uterus—and I use both."

EVERY CONGRESSMAN A KING—AND THE STAFF GETS LEFTOVERS

Ever wonder what it's really like to work in the offices of various congressmen? I can tell you. Some were and *are* angels, some devils. Some are so tight they drive their staffs to save every penny on allowances they can pocket. One congressman went so far as to wash paper clips to make them look like new for reuse. If you are that kind of penny pincher, try dipping paper clips in water with ammonia and soap. It makes them shine like new.

Then there are the demands congressmen make on their staffs, the little extra jobs they must do to keep their bosses feeling like kings. Staff must work until the boss goes home, get up in the middle of the night to drive the boss to or from the airport, or fly off with the boss if he so decrees at a moment's notice.

The wife of a congressman's aide can count even less on her husband than a congressional wife can count on hers.

As for secretaries, some of them are treated as chattels or secondary wives or harem girls. One congressman got so possessive about the secretary who served as his "office wife" that when she said she had to stay late to catch up on work, he decided to check up on her to see if she was "cheating" on him. He pretended to be going on a trip and doubled back, using a ladder to look over the transom to see what she was doing. She was sitting at her typewriter. She looked up casually, after hearing the scratching of the ladder, and said, "Oh, there you are. Do you want carbons on this report?"

In my own job, I was also engaged full-time in making all the congressmen feel like kings, and some—the leadership—more kingly than others. In this pursuit, I cooperated and worked with members of the congressmen's staffs and their committee staffs every day.

Three or four times, important leaders tried to steal me away from Rayburn and McCormack to work for them. Secretary of the Senate Les Biffle, who was invaluable at political conventions and even on the Hill because he could talk without moving his lips, liked my work at the conventions and tried to switch me to his office. And the Republican side made informal inquiries on whether I would like to work for them. ˙

The toughest moment for me came when Lyndon Johnson, as Majority Leader, told Rayburn, "I want you to let me have Fishbait. I need him because he's the only one who knows how to get things done around here and hang on like a Mississippi mule until he does."

Speaker Sam said, "Now Lyndon, just this once I'm going to have to say no to you. It's taken years of training over here to get him just the way we like him and we can't give him up now."

I was certainly glad to hear that, because I had no desire to work for the Other Body.

Working for some individual congressmen has its drawbacks, but aides do get all kinds of fringe benefits like junkets and leftover gifts that come to the office.

Of course, sometimes taking leftovers isn't too bad either when it's a cutie leftover from the congressmen. On one trip to China, a couple of aides were lucky in having a selection of exotic feminine company that the congressman had declined for the evening.

In the middle of the night—actually at 3 A.M., as one of the aides told me on his return—the other congressional aide called his hotel room, waking him up. "Hey fellah, how about trading girls for the rest of the night?" he wanted to know.

Not only congressmen but staff people have gotten their tail caught in the crack. Half the time when they get into trouble, it's because of what they learn from their bosses and not the other way around, and you'd better believe it. Congressmen seldom get led astray by their assistants.

And when you are feeling sorry for the congressmen caught in the whirlpool, save a little sympathy for their secretaries and the other office help.

I'm thinking of a Wayne Hays committee P.R. aide, Carol Clawson, for one. When Wayne Hays got into trouble over Liz Ray, it was Carol Clawson who was taking the heat as much as he was, though it was not her problem. But most aides are very loyal and noble people and stick by their bosses through thick and thin.

In Carol's case, she and her $28,950 job on Hays' House Administration Committee were the family mainstay in supporting herself, her husband and the three children he brought with him into their marriage. Her husband had also gone through a tragic job situation and had later suffered, as Pat Nixon did, a stroke. He was Ken Clawson, director of communications for Richard Nixon in the latter days of Watergate.

Ken had been loyal to Nixon, and Carol was loyal to Hays. She stayed at his side at all times, even making trips to Ohio with him to do his talking for him and to keep him from making things worse with his sharp tongue.

"I didn't let him out of my sight except to go to the bathroom or to bed," Carol said. Nevertheless, Hays somehow took an overdose of sleeping pills, which made her job even harder.

But even while her boss lay recuperating, she was still the buffer zone between Hays and the new chairman of the House Administration Committee, Frank Thompson, Jr., of New Jersey, who set about checking through Hays' records by ordering an audit. Involved was the matter of many of Hays' trips abroad and the expenses involved for himself and his entourage, and the cost of the souvenirs brought back from the trip— for example, what money had been spent for paintings.

Carol Clawson, as spokesman, stoutly maintained that the congressman's personal checks would show that anything he brought back did not come out of the public trough. And it was Carol Clawson who took on the onerous job of explaining why Hays had at first denied that he had had an affair with Elizabeth Ray and then had made a dramatic confession of guilt on the floor of the House.

"Quite frankly," she said, "Hays did have a relationship with Liz Ray prior to his marriage," but she explained that at first he was trying to protect his bride of six weeks—who was, incidentally, another Hays staffer, Pat Peak.

Being the buffer zone between a congressman and the public—especially reporters—is not easy.

But I must say, Elizabeth Ray was not your usual Hill staffer playgirl. Those who play while on the public payroll don't usually brag to the world as she did, but keep it between themselves and just a few close staff friends.

Some congressmen treat their staff as equals and even take them to lunch occasionally. But on the other hand, some congressmen I have known were so tight they would hardly buy lunch for themselves.

One congressman would go to the Hill dining room and order a bowl of soup and a hard roll. Then he would ask for any old lettuce leaves that hadn't been used and he would cut them up and make himself a salad so he didn't have to pay for it. Salad dressing was free. It was already on the table. Did he tip? It was not known whether he had ever heard of the word.

In the old days, the food cost a little less in the employees' lunchroom so a few of the congressmen would duck down there to save about 35 cents.

Word of what a congressman or senator is like gets around very fast on the Hill. Even though Lyndon Johnson's temper was testy at best, everyone wanted to work for him because he really was warm-hearted in spite of it. And when he wasn't mad at you, he might give you a big bear hug and tell you what a great job you were doing.

For the aide who's willing to put himself out, all kinds of good things can lie in his future. Some aides have become congressmen with an assist from their old bosses. In my own career, I rose from the lowest level on the Hill to the top administrative job for services rendered, not only doing my job as best I could, but also doing anything else that I have ever been asked to do short of shoot a man—and I guess I've never been asked to do that, or perform sexual favors.

But I *was* once asked to wipe the boo-boo from a congressman's rear end, and I did. That's how helpful I was willing to be. He was John J. Cochran, Democrat of St. Louis. He is the man who had put in a resolution to get me a $1,200 raise, which I sorely needed and which brought my salary up to all of $3,600 per annum. At the time, when I had thanked him with all my heart, he had told me he didn't want any thanks and added, "Just always be yourself and let me give you this bit of advice. Don't be bowing to anyone up here, because if you do admit you think you're not as good as they are, then when you bow they will turn their backs and you will get all that shit on your neck. So I'm going to tell you this once more—don't get any of that shit on your neck."

So time passed and I tried to take his advice and act proud and still do all the favors I could for everyone. But one day I got a call to come to his office immediately because it was in the nature of an emergency. I hurried to Congressman Cochran's office and his secretary pointed that he was in his private rest room, to go right in.

I went in, and he was sitting on his private john. Inasmuch as he had lost both legs, he could not raise himself to clean himself—and his regular aide was out. So I got the toilet paper and did the necessary and helped him back into his wheelchair. And got his pants up. He thanked me graciously and asked me if I had ever done anything like that before.

I said, "No sir, but I guess back there you were accusing me of being an ass-kisser when you gave me that advice. Now I guess in this instance it wouldn't count because I was just getting your boo-boo clean."

He said, "You're right. There's a big difference. Just be the kind of dependable bastard you are."

Again I thanked him for the advice.

Sometimes being too helpful and too dependable got some of the employees in trouble. This was the case with one of our messengers to the Doorkeeper, who tried to help the congressman too much during the Korean War, when good Bourbon and good Scotch were hard to get. This eager fellow made some good contacts throughout the city of Washington, D.C., and was able to get the best brands.

Then he tried to be still more helpful and knew somebody else who could place a bet on a hot horse. This lasted about six months, and the fellow really thought he was on his way to becoming the next Doorkeeper or who knows what.

But he made the mistake of trying to find more people who needed his services and ran right into the top do-gooders on the Hill—Edward Rees, of Kansas and H. R. Gross of Iowa, both Republicans. They wrote letters to the members of Congress objecting to what was going on and the word quickly got to Speaker Rayburn. Unknown to me, they had a conference with Rayburn and Rayburn sent for me. "Now Fish," said Speaker Sam sternly, "I have a report here on one of your messengers to the Doorkeeper. Do you know what he's up to?"

I said, "Well, I've heard about it and I don't know if it's true."

Rayburn said, "These two gentlemen *do* know about it and do know it's true, and therefore I want you to go get him and bring him to my office so we can have a meeting."

I went to get him and his tenure in office didn't last longer than that proverbial snowball in hell. He barely had time to say good-bye before they had him packing.

"I was just trying to be helpful," he muttered as he left. Which brings me to a thought: Right or wrong, there was no one to whom this fellow could appeal his case.

My slogan was "yours for service," and I really meant it. In my early days as Doorkeeper and the years leading up to my election as Doorkeeper by the majority of the Democratic members, there was very little I wasn't called on to do to prove the slogan.

I babysat for Frank Karsten's baby boy, Frank, Jr. He later became one of my pages and today he is a lawyer. I babysat for members who had little girls and those little girls taught me to play jacks and croquet, not exactly my idea of an exciting afternoon. Nor was hopscotch and jump-rope, which they also inflicted on me.

I would get calls from members wanting me to drive a carful of constituents to see Gettysburg battlefield, the U.S. Naval Academy, Jefferson's home at Monticello, and even over to Harper's Ferry, where they would want a complete fill-in on the facts about John Brown's raid. I would consider it a lucky break when all they wanted was to go to Mount Vernon and I would bless George Washington for having the good sense to live near Washington.

While I'm confessing, I once had to take a congressman's son on a boat trip down the Potomac River to Mount Vernon because a popular author and lecturer of that period, Dale Carnegie, was going to be on the riverboat. I will never forget how cleverly Carnegie handled the fourteen-year-old boy who had brought along a copy of Carnegie's best-selling book, *How to Win Friends and Influence People*, to be autographed.

"Sir," said the boy timidly, "will you honor me by autographing this for me?" Dale Carnegie looked at the boy and then at me and said, "Young man, I don't honor you by autographing this book, but on the contrary to what you think, *you* honor *me* by asking me to do it."

I remember when Dale Carnegie was must reading for every congressional candidate—and still should be. The message he gives is that the little services pay off, favors are usually returned.

How do congressmen and senators treat staff? Every which way!

Senator Philip Hart, married to one of the richest women among the Hill wives—Briggs Stadium was named for her father, who owned the Detroit Tigers at one point as well as being the largest manufacturer of auto parts—and himself wealthy, was nevertheless one of the nicest men on the Hill to his staff. He never let any staffer do anything for him—like drive him to the airport, or carry his briefcase.

At the other extreme was Wayne Hays, who came from Ohio and was so poor that, as he bragged to his colleagues, "I didn't have a pot to piss in." He was a slave driver with his staff and would invent picayune little things for them to do that hadn't even been invented yet.

Bella Abzug had trouble keeping some of her staff more than a few months at a time, because she would scream at them and roundly insult them. They would cry on my shoulder. Fortunately, it was not held against them that they could not get along with Bella, and they would find jobs at other offices.

With Hays, his bark was really worse than his bite. Though he would threaten constantly to fire his staff members, he usually never did.

A different kind of boss was Jim Haley of Sarasota, Florida, who once managed the Ringling Brothers Circus and kept one of the happiest staffs on the Hill. He was so kind-hearted that he would bring back to the office handfuls of candy bars and other goodies every time he went to the House Restaurant. He would even suggest that a staffer take a little longer lunch period if that person had a friend in town—an almost unheard-of suggestion up on the Hill.

It is common for leadship to have an aide walk along and serve as a sort of escort, litter bearer and notetaker wherever he goes. But F. Edward Hébert went them one better by surrounding himself—like a military general on the march—with committee personnel as well as members of his own office for any short walk from his office to the committee room, or his office to the floor. It goes without saying that someone else would be carrying his papers or briefcase.

Ted Kennedy is known to stay in a committee meeting only as long as the TV cameras are there. And as they pack up, so does he, disappearing and leaving his legislative aide behind to do the follow-up work. Kennedy strides ahead of his aides as he rushes out—a hard man to keep up with.

Most congressmen and senators hate to see an aide get a bit of publicity unless it is in an article in which all the guy does is talk about the congressman. Members have such egos that aides have been fired for getting publicity for themselves.

Even popular Fritz Mondale has been reported as telling an aide that if he wanted personal publicity he ought to get out and run for office. Those who knew about it were amused when Mondale, as a newly-an-

128

nounced vice-presidential candidate, suddenly got very retiring and stayed in the background, in Carter's shadow, as his own aides have done for him.

Having to keep from getting personal publicity isn't the worst thing that can happen to an aide on the Hill. Some young male aides have been propositioned by the congressman or senator who likes sex with boys. Some congressmen pay, some just use the power and glamor of the job to entice the staffers.

Some male staffers have gone ahead and done what was expected of them, some have changed jobs or left the Hill. Some, who were already gay, came to the Hill hoping to find a rich, powerful congressman or senator to get next to for the same reason pretty girls seek out the rich and powerful politicians.

You learn on the Hill not to ridicule anyone and to be courteous to everyone. Seeing Speaker Sam Rayburn's sister, you wouldn't think she had a bit of pull or power on the Hill, but ignore Lucinda or do something that hurt her and you'd really get your tail in the crack.

One young elevator boy thought he could act superior with a little man who got on, calling him "Shortstuff." The little man turned out to be Senator John Tower of Texas, and the elevator boy turned out to be jobless.

Because every congressman is king and all the aides are conscious of it every minute, it is a great relief to have occasionally a congressman like Leo O'Brien of Albany, New York. Jack Botzum, who publishes a newsletter, and several other press guys were sitting around with me reminiscing about old Leo.

Brother O'Brien was home during a winter recess and they had a snowstorm. One of his constituents phoned him and said, "Can't you do something about getting my street cleaned, Congressman? They haven't come to plow the snow on my street yet."

"Why don't you call the street and garbage people?" suggested Leo. "You can call the Commissioner of Public Works."

"Well," said the constituent, "I thought of that before I called you, but I didn't want to go that high."

There were 357 people I could hire and fire. But I did as little firing as possible. Most of the employees are on patronage. However, every now and then firing did take place, usually at the suggestion of the leadership.

Once it was a top man of the Capitol Hill police force who almost got canned for a memory lapse. He was supposed to walk the senators and the distinguished guests up to the door of the House Chamber on the important occasion of a Joint Meeting.

For some reason, the high-ranking police officer didn't stop at the door and came marching right in ahead of the honored guest. So as soon as the meeting was over, the man was put on suspension for thirty days, and they put the police force in my charge while he was gone.

Before the month was out, I had to fire two sergeants and one lieutenant. One had gone to sleep on the job. That was serious. But the other had done something even more serious. He had tried to be funny with his gun. On one hand, the words "Pay me" were tattoed and on the other was "Thank you." So when he was fooling around and the gun accidentally went off, he almost ruined his "Thank you." He also ruined his job.

The third man fired had deserted his post altogether and had chosen the most comfortable private office of a congressman that he could find in order to take a nap for three or four hours.

One of the men who worked for me was a regular sex machine. And good-looking to boot. He was so much in demand that he would not pick up a phone to

130

call a girl. They had to call him and make an appointment—or date, call it what you will.

He had been rendered sterile for medical reasons and this made him even more popular.

Eventually he married, but he couldn't refuse a woman in need and he was very busy after hours, arriving home late and tired. He was the wonder and talk of the Hill.

His wife, furious at how her husband was being "overworked," called and demanded a few days off for him so that he could recover. He got the time off. It was time he had coming, anyway.

When he came back, he still kept a busy calendar. The other day I saw him and I asked if he was still at it and he said, "Of course, but they still have to call me, man. I'm still going out on consignment only."

Why didn't I fire him? Because I was not his keeper. As long as a man got his work done, what else he did was his own business.

Many a girl settled for him instead of a man with more rank—a senator or congressman. At least this boy played it straight. He did not pretend he was going to get a divorce to marry any of them. And many's the time it was he who comforted a girl who had been left in the lurch by a congressman or senator, and saw her over the pain of her unhappy romance.

I have always been lucky in the secretaries that I had on the Hill. I inherited the first one with the job of Doorkeeper. She was Ann Vincyard, and she was the niece of Congressman Dewey Short, who later became secretary of the army under Eisenhower.

She was followed by Miss Katheryn Dumphries of Massachusetts. Then I inherited Mrs. Shelva Rota, whose husband became postmaster of the House of Representatives.

Next came Pemmie Lee Embry. And when she got married, I inherited Carolyn West of South Carolina.

131

Miss West had worked for a congressman, a senator and Postmaster General Edward Day. I remember how amazed Carolyn was at our busy office.

One day she said to me, "Mr. Miller, do you want to know something?"

"I want to know everything if it's about the Hill, Miss West."

"Do you know," she continued, "you are more powerful than a member of Congress, more powerful than a senator, more powerful than the clerk of a committee?" She thought a moment, and continued, "And it seems to me I could also include the postmaster general, because as long as I have worked for you, I have never known anyone to refuse any requests you have made."

After Dan Cupid shot his arrow in Pemmie Lee's heart, Miss West stayed with me for six and a half years. As I said, I was always very lucky.

Things were always happening to displease the various Speakers of the House. Once John McCormack motioned me over and said, "There's a woman wet-nursing her baby in Gallery Five. Go up and see what you can do with her." I was known as the man who walked in boldly where angels feared to tread. I ended up taking the woman and baby—which I carried—to my office so that the infant could finish its meal in privacy.

When McCormack was stepping down from the speakership and Carl Albert was taking over, I was elected by the staff around the Speaker's table to find out whether Albert intended to follow McCormack's precedent of passing out greenbacks at Christmastime.

Speaker John had been extremely generous, and all the men jumped to do his bidding as a result. But with his usual modesty, McCormack would always say, "This is just a little remembrance from Mrs. McCormack and me."

I told Speaker Carl what had gone before and said

132

that some of the boys were wondering if they could count on this continuing under his speakership. Carl Albert was a little annoyed as he said, "I don't know whether I should, Fishbait, because John McCormack was a different man than I am." But eventually he did grudgingly pass out $20 bills one time only—less than half of what McCormack had given.

Through the years, some congressmen have shown remarkable originality in finding ways to save money on the cost of housing.

In the recent Ninety-fourth Congress, Representative David Emery, a Republican from Maine, came up with the idea of continuing to live as he had campaigned throughout his district—in a mobile home.

Not only that but, as he told a group of us, he had heard how members of Congress were wined and dined starting with Prayer Breakfasts, fancy luncheons and lobbyists' receptions and parties with buffet tables groaning with food in the committee rooms at the end of the day. He said he was sure the combination of living in his mobile home and this partying would help him pay off his campaign debts in short order.

I didn't tell him that one congressman, Allard Kenneth Lowenstein of New York, had gone him one better. When Lowenstein came to Washington in 1969 with the Ninety-first Congress, he was so busy in his office that he never did find a place to sleep. He was a bachelor. As he explained his living conditions to me, "I work out in the House gym and get a good sweat before I take a nice shower down there. And the old couch in the office is good enough for me."

But it wasn't good enough for the big three on the House Office Building Commission, who were shocked to the core when they heard what Al was doing. The commissioners who were in charge of maintaining the standards of the House—Speaker John McCormack; the congressman with the longest tenure, in this case, Manny Celler; and the top Republican, Minority

133

Leader Jerry Ford—sent word that they disapproved. They would have disapproved more had they heard his secretary telling me how during her lunch hour she had to take his shirts to the Chinese laundry three blocks away.

"Why can't I send a page with his shirts over to Second Street?" she demanded. "I can't take my time for such things." I had to explain to her that under the House rules a page is not permitted to "leave the Hill." Pages can only go to the three House office buildings, the two Senate office buildings, the Library of Congress and the Supreme Court. Most of the time they are on the floors of the House and Senate answering the page calls which are activated by buttons at each member's seat.

Lowenstein, being a congressman—and therefore a king among kings—did not have to pay attention to what the commission officers said, no matter how powerful they were in the hierarchy. He continued to sleep in his office. But just to keep out of sight for a while, he said to me, "Now Fishbait, do you mind if I come rest in your office for a few hours some nights just to keep the 'big three' off-balance?" The disposition of that case had best remain a mystery.

Congressional staff and congressional wives are natural enemies. Sometimes, but usually when the staffer is already looking for or has landed another job, he might tell the wife off.

Bethine Church once was told by an angry staffer that there are only two senators from Idaho and she wasn't one of them. Church might have had a better chance at the vice-presidential post if he didn't have a wife who considered herself an equal partner.

The same goes for Birch Bayh, who, unlike Church, wasn't even on Carter's list of potential Vice Presidents. He might have been, but around the Senate his wife has a powerful reputation of running the show when

134

her husband isn't there. In effect, she has told the staff that she is the senator when the senator isn't there. There were rumors about staffers getting fired if they didn't do what she directed. And sometimes Bayh himself would have to soothe hurt staffers and say he understood and just to let it go as a favor to him. He inspired such devotion and trust from his staff that it made up for other things.

The 1968 campaign and Senator Eugene McCarthy's desperate effort to get the Democratic nomination wrecked Gene's political career and his marriage as well.

Abigail McCarthy tried to protect her husband from the staff that kept him working so hard to get the 1968 presidential nomination. As a result, *she* isn't there at his side any more. Candidates don't appreciate all that protection. The couple ended up divorced after McCarthy spent a lot of his time with the girls of the press who weren't trying to protect the candidate from anything.

I'm sure Jimmy Carter was carefully looking over the wives as well as the husbands when he decided that Senator Mondale was the guy for him. Mondale's wife has never interfered and is known for two things— eternal optimism and a good, clean, shiny house.

There is apt to be a little jealousy toward aides who are the constant companions of the king. I am referring to the L.A. or A.A. who is permitted to stay ever close to his congressman or senator and who acts too proud as he struts down the hall in lock-step with the man of power. When other staffers from his own office or elsewhere around the Hill could stand it no longer, they would give him an "Attaboy" award.

It was an actual certificate, very handsome, and at first the recipient's face would light up until he read it through to the end. Bordered with a lovely design and decorated with flowers, the certificate read:

135

☆ ☆ ☆

For Your Very

*OUTSTANDING
PERFORMANCE*

*You are
AWARDED*

*ONE
"ATTABOY"*

1,000 "Attaboys" qualifies you to be a leader of men

☆ *Explain assorted and sundry problems
   to bosses*
☆ *Work overtime with a smile*
☆ *Be looked upon as a local HERO*

**One "AWSHIT" wipes the board clean and you have
to start all over again.**

☆ ☆ ☆

It isn't all hard knocks and hard work for the aides.
They have clubs to lighten the load.

People coming to work on the Hill would ask me if
you had to actually write poetry to join POETS Club
or if you could just be someone who appreciates it. I
had to fill them in that poetry had nothing to do with
it. The spelled-out name of the club was *Piss on Everything, Tomorrow's Saturday*. It was the excuse for
a Friday night party in the Rayburn House Office
Building for unattached—or mentally or morally unattached—staffers.

The younger, livelier congressional staff belong to
POETS. The more mature Hill helpers have the Secretaries Club. It, too, is for male and female staffers of
either political party.

For those dedicated male staffers who want to argue politics and strategy in their off-hours and make good contacts, there are two popular Hill clubs—the Bull Elephants Club for Republican male staffers, and the Burros Club for Democratic aides.

Their bosses, the congressmen and senators, do even better for themselves and have two luxurious private clubs. The more elegant of the two is the Capitol Hill Club, a whole building which has been taken over for Republican V.I.P.s to relax and play after hours, as well as for eating at any hour of the day.

It has a chandelier and circular staircase that are famous. However, the club is so dignified that some of the GOPers go sneaking over to the National Capital Democratic Club in the old Congressional Hotel across the street from the House office building, where things are always jumping and the members tend to be more playful and given to the telling of tall tales.

Congressman Barry Goldwater, Jr., is not the man to cross on the Hill. I wouldn't be surprised if he follows in his daddy's footsteps and runs for President someday. I remember when Barry wanted a partition put up in one of his office rooms to give some aides more privacy. He called the Clerk's Office and was told they would put him on a list but it would take about six months to get to him.

That very weekend he went to a hardware store, bought some lumber and nails at his own expense, pressed his two aides—Ken Black, his legislative assistant, and Bill McLean, his administrative assistant— into service and got to work.

By Monday, Barry was really proud of his job. All he wanted now—since it hadn't cost the taxpayers a cent—was to have a new paint job for his office to get rid of the dull color and a change of rug from the drab one there.

It was back to the Clerk's Office, and this time he

137

was told that the color of the rug in his office was what was considered appropriate for all offices and that he would have to wait for the paint job, which, however, would have to be another coat of the same.

"Well, damn it, then I'll get my own," he said.

"But you can't. It's against the regulations," he was warned.

Young Goldwater went his merry way, impressed his same crew into duty, and before the week was over the office didn't match anyone else's. It was painted and it even had new carpeting. The congressman had gotten down on his hands and knees and laid it out himself.

Nobody ever dared say a word about it once the deed was done, for congressmen are a law unto themselves. I had a laugh about it with Ken Black after he had succeeded Bill Mclean to the top spot of AA, and I asked him what other adventures Barry Goldwater had had lately.

Ken commented that life was still moving onward with its many surprises in the life of the congressman. The latest that had happened was that Barry had been on a plane, sitting by accident beside George Bush, the new CIA chief. Both men had briefcases, and when Barry got back to his hotel and was anxious to get his razor to shave before going out to make a speech, he quickly opened his briefcase and made a grab.

But all he had in his hand was a bunch of dirty underwear. He tried to locate the headmaster of the spies to no avail, nor did the spy master seem to be able to locate Barry. It was days before the CIA chief got his underwear back.

"But did the congressman learn any great secrets in that briefcase?" I asked.

"No," said Ken. "Only that Bush can afford much more expensive underwear than a congressman can."

It shows that it's a good thing aides usually hand-deliver their bosses to wherever they are going. The incident would never have happened if Barry had had his aide along.

On the subject of offices, I remember when Ronald V. Dellums, the suave and elegantly dressed black congressman from California, wanted one pink wall in his office and the Clerk's Office expressed its shock. Ron and his wife became do-it-yourselfers too, and the Clerk's Office never recovered.

Nor did they dare touch it.

The Library of Congress has an army of experts of every kind in its Legislative Reference Service, ready, willing and able to turn out any report or written work a congressman could ask for. Though some subjects are very complicated, some congressmen are very unreasonable in demanding that the report be turned in on very short notice. Lyndon Johnson and Wayne Hays both were exceptionally unreasonable, even threatening to get the person in trouble or fired if the job wasn't done by the next morning.

But what hurts the library people most is knowing that sometimes the work isn't for a congressman at all, but for a constituent.

I was talking about this to Don Curry the other day at the National Press Building, where he now has his public relations office. Don used to be one of those burners of midnight oil in the Legislative Reference Service.

"I don't know how many college and high-school theses I've written," he said, "but it used to burn me up. During the Suez crisis of 1957, we'd spend a week or ten days researching and writing twenty or thirty pages on it and send it to the congressman who had requested it. He'd send it on to the constituent, who gave it to his son to turn in at college as his term paper. The Legislative Reference Service is not dumb. It knows when the subject matter requested is not what the congressman is interested in."

Don Curry told how he was frequently pressed into service to write speeches for congressmen that should have been written in their offices by their own staff with just basic material furnished by the library.

"Former Congressman Leonard Farbstein of New York was especially bad about calling on us to write his speeches," Don said. "I once wrote a speech for Farbstein on the Middle East. I did a very balanced view of the Arab-Israeli conflict. He sent it back angrily to Roger Hilsman, who was my boss. With it came a note from his office that said, 'The Congressman is speaking before a group of rabbis in Brooklyn. We certainly don't want a middle-of-the-road approach.'"

At no moment does a congressman feel more like a feudal king than when he snaps his fingers and finds a page immediately at his side. Many prefer the fun of finger snapping to pushing the button at their seat which would also summon a page. I think if ever they change the system and have older persons running the errands, the congressmen will miss the feeling of power it gives them to have this remnant of medieval times.

The only trouble with the page system is that it is impossible to supervise the kids during the time they are not at work. While some study, others are making the rounds of every bar on the Hill that will serve to minors, picking up a few girls as they go. Some are robbed. One was mugged and ended up in the hospital.

Some pages were found to be filling up on hot dogs and hadn't seen a vegetable for weeks. To try to get some order into their lives, a minister on Capitol Hill, James P. Archibald of the Capitol Hill Methodist Church, was brought in.

The Jaycees—Junior Chamber of Commerce—took an interest for a while and got the YWCA—Young Women's Christian Association—to permit pages to live in their home for young women between the ages of eighteen and thirty-four. This seemed like a good solution because the YWCA was close to the Senate Office Building. The home said it would take the young men in if the Jaycees would pay for doors to separate the women from the little pages, some of whom were not so little—fourteen to eighteen.

The Jaycees even took up a collection and hired a student to act as house father for them at $50 a month. But the home informed Congress it would throw out the pages unless they appropriated $7,000 to make the pages' quarters soundproof. They raised the roof with noise. The congressmen said a flat no and the male pages had to move out.

Still, as I have said, I feel the page system has been very good for those who knew how to make the most of the experience. Of the six pages who later became congressmen, one flashed to stardom at the 1976 Democratic Convention when he seconded the nomination of Jimmy Carter for President. That was Governor David H. Pryor of Arkansas, whom I've known for a long time.

The other pages who became congressmen were William Franklin of Oklahoma; Bill Gunter of Florida; Compton I. White of Idaho; Jed Johnson, Jr., of Oklahoma; and John D. Dingell, Jr., of Michigan. Dingell's daddy, Congressman John, Sr., was the father of early social security legislation, and a dear friend of mine. Other jobs on the Hill, though sounding very menial, have also been a springboard into Congress for brainy young men. An elevator operator who was elected to Congress was Angelo Roncallo, Republican of New York. Two doormen were later elected to Congress—Mendel J. Davis of South Carolina and Lyndon Baines Johnson, who went on to become a senator, Vice President, and then President.

Even a Capitol policeman was once elected to Congress—Robert O. Tiernan of Rhode Island.

I hardly know where to begin when I talk about pages. Some have been good and some so bad. Some have gone far since being a page. Bobby Baker started as a page. Later, he got in headline-making trouble.

Ulysses S. Auger, Jr., now runs one of the top restaurant chains in Washington, Blackie's House of Beef. I remember him when he was just a kid on the verge of trouble and his father, Ulysses, Sr., a multimillionaire who came up the hard way, was worried about him because he wouldn't cut his hair, wouldn't take direction, wouldn't stay home.

"What can I do with him?" the father asked me.

"Would you like me to see if I can get him a sponsor to be a page?" I asked. "Then he'll have some discipline." He did become a page and he greets me happily now, even though there was a time he did not appreciate the little talks I held with him on getting along in the world.

It is not exactly known when the practice of using pages to run errands began, but the first time they are mentioned is in the Twentieth Congress when it is recorded that three boys—Charles B. Chalmers, John C. Burch and Edward Dunn—were employed as "runners" to the 227 members and 4 delegates of the House.

Now there are 435 members of the House. And there are fifty-one pages. For years, all pages had to be *boys* aged fourteen to eighteen. But little by little attrition began. Back in 1939, Edward Eugene Cox of Georgia got permission to permit his daughter Gene to serve just one day—opening day—of the Seventy-sixth Congress so that she could go down in history. She did make history and received $4 for her time. I hope she framed it.

When I left, there were eight girl and forty-three boy pages.

A number of pages have stayed on to do other jobs on the Hill. Donn Anderson, a former page, is now manager of the Democratic Cloakroom, a very responsible job at age thirty-three.

Of course, some pages have gotten into trouble as

well. Some have been arrested for disturbing the peace, for drunkenness and for theft. Such things would happen with any group of teen-agers, and these youngsters are no exception. But I think for the few who are baddies, the rest of them more than make up for it by being superior students and superior boys and girls in every way.

Somehow the congressmen who sponsor and bring these kids to Washington will have to find a better way of protecting them from bad influences when they are through for the day. One girl, through ignorance, found herself a place to live in a red-light district in Washington, and she was snatched away from there as soon as our people on the Hill found out about it. And one boy, as I recall, was found sharing his room with a woman older and wiser than he. The trouble is that congressmen who sponsor the fourteen-to-eighteen-year-old boys and girls make the parents sign a paper saying that the congressman is not legally responsible for the page.

Though pages were under my Doorkeeper's jurisdiction, other than scolding some a little and encouraging others to keep trying and do their best and not be hurt at the angry words that harassed congressmen sometimes direct at them, there was very little I could do. With over three hundred people to supervise, I had my hands too full to concentrate on pages.

Still, I feel it would be a terrible mistake to change the page system and permit only college students to become pages, as some members of Congress tried to do in 1973. In fact, in that year, the Other Body saw fit to pass a bill making it mandatory that pages be at least first- or second-year college students.

The bill came over to the House and went to the Rules Committee. I went to see Ray Madden of Indiana, the chairman of the committee, and told him that if that bill passed, the dream of thousands of children all over the country would be gone forever. Kids need

Horatio Alger dreams even today. The work of a page is beneath the dignity of a college student. A fourteen- or fifteen-year-old page is proud to be sent on errands around Capitol Hill and on the floors of both chambers, but a second-year nuclear physics major would be insulted to be turned into a go-fer, doing menial chores with some congressman snapping his fingers at him to call him over.

I told Ray to please "sit on that bill, put it in a pigeonhole and let the spiders spin their webs around it no matter what happens." He did just that, even though he was coerced, cursed and beaten over the head. So the bill did not get to the floor and the page system remains safe a little longer.

On the plus side, pages have a wonderful start in life —earnings of $7,215 per year, their own school with excellent teachers, fine health care and contacts with men of power that might help them through all the rest of their lives.

To show you how some youngsters yearn to become pages on Capitol Hill, one young man mowed lawns, cut hedges and trimmed trees until he had saved $500 to use for becoming a page. He thought that if he could advertise in the Washington, D.C., newspapers, saying that he was available for duty, some member of the House or Senate would write to him and tell him to come for an interview.

The ads cost $540, but it didn't work. Then he wrote me and I had to tell him that he should try to interest his *own* congressman in sponsoring him because all pages are under the patronage system. He wrote back again to tell me sadly that he had done that but had gotten nowhere because his member was only a freshman, not entitled yet to choose a page.

Though that boy didn't make it, I predict he will be on the Hill one day in some other capacity, because he has the right spirit.

Now all he needs is to read Dale Carnegie.

144

YOU CAN WOMANIZE IF YOU AVOID THE SPIES

The spies are, of course, the press. But not all the press. Some members of the press are like members of the congressmen's own staffs—and even their lovers—and keep their secrets very well.

Through the years, various congressmen have managed to combine "B and F"—boozing and floozying—as it is called in the back rooms of Congress, without a speck of dust on their public reputations. But the staffers know what is going on and don't mind sharing the details with their friends in other Hill offices.

Girls in various offices are given various labels—a "grass monkey," for example, is a girl who will oblige a congressman or senator behind any bush or nice spot where they can find a bit of privacy.

The powerful have hideaways in little-known rooms of the Capitol or office buildings. Three congressmen have an apartment they share for daytime use, near the U.S. Capitol. When I was a beginner on the Hill and a bachelor, a certain man would send me to a movie several times a week and demand my apartment key. Even now, when we meet, the guy says, "Hey Fish, have you seen any good movies lately?"

One of the greatest womanizers in history on Capitol Hill was Speaker Nicholas Longworth, who is best-remembered today for having married the daughter of President Teddy Roosevelt. Up on the Hill, they are still telling Nicholas Longworth's adventures as a lady's man.

The story goes that the Speaker was sitting in the House floor library, right off the floor, reading a Cincinnati, Ohio, newspaper from back home, when a brash congressman thought he'd make a splash by putting down the Speaker on his womanizing.

"Mr. Speaker," he said, "I've always wanted to say something to you but I've never caught you when you were not busy. Your pretty bald head reminds me of my wife's behind. Is it all right if I rub my hand across it? Then I'll be sure."

Without waiting for an answer, he went ahead and rubbed his hand all the way across Longworth's bald head and said, "Yes, it does feel just like my wife's behind."

He looked around at his audience a bit smugly as he waited for Longworth to explode. But he didn't. Instead, Longworth lifted his own hand and ran it across his own head thoughtfully. "I'll be damned if it doesn't," he said.

The brash congressman went slinking out of there and stayed out of sight for some time.

Alice Roosevelt Longworth was catty about her distant cousin Eleanor Roosevelt when the story broke that FDR had had an affair with Lucy Mercer, Eleanor's social secretary, and that, unknown to Eleanor, Miss Mercer had been at his side when he died in the little hideaway house in Warm Springs, Georgia. The truth eventually came out that Eleanor and FDR did not have sex together for many years.

Alice had said, "Well, Franklin was entitled to a little fun. After all, he was married to Eleanor."

But Alice's own husband, Nicholas, was one of the early swingers. And he was, as they used to say of the battery, "ever ready." One day a man was waiting to see him, sitting in his office, and he picked up what he thought was a cigarette from a cigarette box on Longworth's desk.

Longworth's secretary said, with a perfectly straight face, "Oh, I don't think you are going to like that cigarette." He looked at it, and it was a rubber condom disguised as a cigarette.

146

Nick and Alice pretty much went their own ways. They would go to parties together, but came home separately and Nick might not go directly home. It was one of the original open marriages.

Frank Boykin, a Democrat from Alabama and one of the richest men ever to walk the halls of Congress, is now dead. But if money can do it, he is still probably casing Capitol Hill for pretty girls from some convenient heavenly cloud. Frank, a veritable giant of a man in several ways, drove us all crazy for years going around the Capitol booming, "Everything is made for love!"

Well, he certainly seemed to think *he* was. His specialty was to have two pretty girls in bed with him at the same time. Once, he thought he had nicely shipped off a close relative to his home state with a kiss and a wave, but the plane was grounded and she returned to the hotel where they were staying—walking in upon a rare scene of nudity and lewdity.

Savoir faire reached a new high as all persons involved, including the naked girls, carried off the situation with great dignity and politeness, discussing everything but what was going on—which by this time was that they were scrambling into their clothes. Frank told me about his wild adventure and laughed at being caught.

But the friendly giant, who weighed in at about 275 pounds, dismissed it all with his "Everything is made for love!" And as he pointed proudly to his favorite decoration, a dried elephant penis which hung from a wire on his office wall, he added, "Anything goes, Fishbait. Just as long as some mean old newsman doesn't get a hold of it, there's no harm done."

Brother Boykin was the most sensuous man in the House. He was always grabbing and touching and hugging—and he wanted to be touched in return. He'd go to the barbershop for a haircut and he would stay for practically hours. And a particular barber knew what

147

to do. He'd pet him and pat him after the haircut, all over his body seemed like, short of getting into his pants.

The barber would reach into his shirt and massage him up and down and crosswise, I'd say all the way from the neck to the belly button. Some who were in the barbershop at the same time and observed it said it was a sickening sight, but if that was what the "everything is made for love" man wanted, he could have it, of course. And they weren't going to object, because, after all, on the Hill every congressman is king.

Boykin was known for another little habit. He would leave the floor or the committee meeting suddenly and go across the street to the Congressional Hotel. Then he'd come back happy as a lark and not care who heard him say "a sex break beats a coffee break any time." Some of the other men envied old Frank a little.

It is not too unusual that sex is used on Capitol Hill to get damaging material on a congressman from one of his female aides who is sleping with him. In one case, a pretty secretary on a congressman's committee was "friendly" both with the congressman and one of his male aides. In this case, the male aide was playing along with a certain columnist who wanted to get a story involving the congressman's financial records. The male aide made a date with the young lady and enlisted her help in "nailing the bastard so he won't dare run again."

But the girl was coy and said she'd need a little time to get the files. She went to the congressman and told him what was going on. He said, "Well, let's give him another date and this time let's have a recording machine in your purse." It went on from there to a great confrontation scene in the congressman's office that taught the aide a bit about loyalty—if he was able to get another job on the Hill, that is!

Everyone around the Hill wondered how John F. Kennedy could be a swinger when he hobbled around on crutches much of the time because of that back trouble dating from the old P.T. boat days of World War II. In his office, when his back was bad but his passion was worse, Congressman Kennedy and then Senator Kennedy was known to use the hard surface of the floor with just the padding of the rug under him, rather than the couch.

And as some of his buddies put it, "He lets the girl do all the work."

Every congressman and senator I can think of has a leather couch in the inner-sanctum office. Some are used for sitting. Of other couches in other rooms, it was said that they had never experienced a body that was not in a horizontal position.

Wayne Hays was another acknowledged girl-chaser, always talking about his great goal—to be shot at, but missed, at age ninety, by a jealous husband. He would greet pretty young things around the Hill with a big hello and a handshake. He would say, "Hi, I'm Dr. Wayne Hays, D.D.—Doctor of the Divan."

Some girls thought that was pretty cute.

I'd say there must be at least a hundred divorced or separated people on the Hill now. Some are actually living with people other than their own spouses. Even with kids in the house. One ex-wife is doing that while her congressman husband plays the field on Capitol Hill. It sounds like Hollywood, doesn't it?

In 1973, Congressman Bill Hudnut of Indiana—Republican, of course—was preaching a sermon in the East Room of the White House at the invitation of President Nixon, just before he got another invitation to be in court, because his wife was suing him for divorce.

In this case, since he had been a practicing clergyman in Indiana and was a man of the cloth, I think the divorce case hurt him politically. At any rate, he didn't make it back in 1974 but, ironically, was defeated by Andy Jacobs, another divorced man.

I remember Bill had told us he was through with both careers—Congress and the church. When I last heard, he had married a real-estate woman and had become the mayor of Indianapolis.

Sonny Montgomery, a handsome bachelor of Meridian, Mississippi, had high ratings as a playboy and swinger on Capitol Hill, and the word was that "for every lady you see him with, he has five stashed away in the wings."

Any bachelor, even Sam Rayburn, bald and short, was much in demand. So the ladies could be forgiven for making a fuss over a handsome devil like Sonny. Sonny would come into the chamber after a night on the town looking as if he were on his last leg.

Congresswoman Martha Griffiths of Michigan got a big kick out of watching Sonny. Every day, it seemed, she would observe Sonny's entrance and converse with her seat mate about it. In fact, they would have a running commentary in which Martha would say, "Where the devil is Sonny? He's not here yet." And he would reply, "I don't know where he is now, but I know he was in deep trouble last night. If you put a needle in his finger you wouldn't get a drop of blood."

About that time, Sonny would come dragging in, looking very pale.

Another lady-killer on the Hill was Ross Bass of Pulaski, Tennessee. "Lover boy" was the nickname given him by his colleagues, who were well aware that one of my employees was giving him the signal that he had a girl waiting for him. They would time him to see how long it took for him to return to the floor. The sad thing about Ross is that he had a beautiful wife who had been a Powers model. She divorced him and went to work for Senator Lloyd Bentsen of Texas. She told me she had come within a hairbreadth of applying for a job in my office.

Some lives on the Hill would make good soap operas. Representative Robert Leggett, a Democrat from California, admitted after the heat of disclosure that he was actually supporting two families in two houses—his legitimate family and his illegitimate family.

On a daytime serial it might be called, "Congressman Bob Faces Life," or, "Can Life Be Endured on Capitol Hill?" Taking it from the top, as the story would unfold, Bob Leggett comes to Washington in the midterm election of the Kennedy administration. He is young, handsome. He has a lovely, understanding wife, Barbara, who doesn't make waves when he decides to give up a lucrative law practice—in the neighborhood of $85,000—to be a part of the New Frontier. He gets a seat on the House Armed Services Committee and is starting his rise in power. But almost immediately it happens. He meets a beautiful, sophisticated Capitol Hill secretary and starts dating her.

She becomes pregnant and wants him to marry her. He is Catholic and can't get a divorce. The sophisticated young girl is not *that* sophisticated. She is Catholic too and doesn't want an abortion.

The compromise, in true soap-opera style, is that he buys her a house and sets her up as his back-street wife. More plot comes with the second pregnancy.

Meanwhile, knowing nothing of the reason her husband is overworked and overtired, Congressman Bob's wife continues to raise their three children.

After more than ten years of this situation, there is a traumatic moment. Barbara finds out about her husband's other family. She is shocked and grief-stricken. She also finds out that her husband has forged her name to something, a signature he needed when buying the house for his mistress.

Now it all comes out. Shocking as it is, it hasn't been easy for the poor congressman either. How he has suffered making ends meet with two families on a salary of $42,500, which was mercifully raised to $44,600 eventually. He has had to cash in a small retirement plan and give speeches on the lecture circuit

151

to try to meet that $20,000-a-year cost of a second family.

The inconveniences and humilities he has suffered are endless—even being forced to get advances on his salary. And then there is that matter of the bogus signature. In order to get his wife's true signature, he must sign something in return—a $15,000 note due upon divorce or separation.

As if that weren't complicated enough, in soap-opera fashion, it turns out that a new girl has entered the picture several years ago, Suzi Park Thomson, the exotic Korean-born assistant to Leggett's top-leadership boss, Speaker of the House Carl Albert. Leggett's position as a member of the House Armed Services Committee, with access to classified military information, makes the situation even more sensitive. His colleagues are disappointed when he changes his position and starts supporting the government of South Korean President Park Chung Hee.

As I've said, it would make one hell of a good soap opera, but how would it all end?

In winter 1975, it was reported on the Hill that the FBI was investigating charges that the congressman might have benefited financially from the South Korean government.

In July 1976, as the story was unfolding in the press, Bob Leggett continued to write his own best lines. While not denying his complicated love life, he did deny that he had benefited financially from his position on Korea. "I will state that I have egg on my face, but not gravy," he said.

When Myra McPherson was getting ready to write her book on congressional marriage, she asked me for help, but I had to turn her down. I said I needed the material for my own book. Myra has always been a good reporter, and she then asked me to tell her at least the names and states of all the eccentric congressmen.

As I recall, I said, "Honey, all you've got to do is put down the names of 435 members plus the three delegates and the resident commissioner of Puerto Rico. And if you want to go a step further, you can take all the humility in Washington and fit it into John Wayne's navel and still have room for Carl Albert."

That's not original with me. It was said first by Mark Russel who for years was the top standup comic in Washington, performing at the Carroll Arms and then the Americana Shoreham every night. But he's about right.

I had to do the opening for him once on a tape they were making. I was asked to do for Mark what I do for the President of the United States, bellowing out with my southern accent, "Mistah Speakah, the one and only, the great Mark Russell," which I did, and gladly. They used it for commercial purposes. No payment was made to me. It's what we call friendship.

I was happy to do it for the many laughs he had given me, as when he told me, "They're always talking about which candidate has the most personal magnetism up here. The way to prove which candidate has the most magnetism is to have them walk by a line of hookers—whichever man gets solicited the most times wins."

The ones who know what is going on up on the Hill are the night staffers, the parking-garage people, the guards, and the elevator operators. They see which congressman has doubled back to the office with a pretty girl at about midnight. This usually means the girl has a roommate and the congressman is too cheap, or afraid, to get a motel room.

Usually what they say is, "I have to pick up some papers. I'll be right back." They may be back in an hour or they may not. The employees never bat an eye. They say, "Yes, sir."

Once a congressional wife told me her husband had asked her for a divorce. She said, "He admitted he wants to marry this hooker in his office. I said, 'Why can't you be like that nice young Riegle?' " I almost laughed out loud but kept my mouth shut. That nice young Riegle she was referring to was Donald W. Riegle, Jr., Republican of Michigan, turned Democrat of Michigan, who was also about to get a divorce and marry a girl from his office.

In fact, Riegle even wrote a book about his divorce and remarriage and all the rest of his life as a congressman. I like the name of his book and only wish I had thought of it first—*O Congress*.

Quite frankly, the press is viewed by some as the snake in the Garden of Eden. So the clever congressmen frequently use their wiles to capture the snake and defang it. Maybe it is not surprising, maybe it is, that quite a few girl reporters have gotten involved with congressmen and senators.

I have heard congressmen talk about how much safer they feel dating a reporter. "I know she isn't going to write anything damaging about me now," was one remark. And another who had captivated a reporter crowed, "Damn it, that's one story she won't write." Not only that, but some have felt that having a female reporter as a bed-partner gives them a playgirl who could actually do them some good.

Sometimes, on the campaign trail, male reporters have actually gotten jealous because of this alliance between some pretty female reporter and the candidate. LBJ was only one of many known to give a female reporter an inside track.

Of course, fair is fair—some male reporters have made time with the female side of the Hill, especially top female aides to both congressmen and congresswomen. But the simple truth is that congresswomen as a class have been much more virtuous than their male colleagues—and much more discreet.

The trouble with Hill marriages is that congressmen, after the election brings them to Washington, can't remember how and don't have time to be good husbands —they don't have time to be good lovers to their outside cuties either. Congressman Hays, for example, used to brag that he had a gal he liked to lean over the desk at noon time and "have for lunch" every day. I have no idea who he meant.

Some congressmen need constant change. Girls were always asking me to explain why they had been dropped—"I was making such progress with him and I think he was happy with me. At least he said he was. He was even talking about getting a divorce. And now he is having me transferred to another committee."

In this case, I knew the congressman was playing around with another girl who had just arrived on the Hill. You have to give credit to the old boys for at least one thing—they have the conscience to feel bad about seeing their old sweeties mooning around. They at least put them out of sight in someone else's office.

Some of the men really do love their wives. They just need to feel young. One told me, "You're as young as last night's piece of ass."

I remember what Barbara Howar said about romance in Washington and I think it should be put on a card and given to every new girl on the Hill who thinks the whirl she is getting from her boss or some other congressman is for real. "Sex in Washington is Henry Kissinger slowing down to thirty-five miles per hour to drop you off from a date." Believe it!

One female who didn't mind telling what senators were like was the glamorous reporter Sally Quinn. The sharp-tongued Sally made a stir throughout the Hill when she told exactly what had happened after a senator offered her a ride home as they were both leaving a party.

On the way home he started pawing her and she said, "I thought you were offering a *ride* home."

The annoyed senator shot back, "What do you think I am, a taxi service?"

I can believe it. I certainly can.

Some senators who play actually prefer call girls. "No muss, no fuss," they say, "and they don't want to hang around for the rest of your life." But others, as the aides tell me, "will only settle for free ass. They want to think that she loves him for himself."

Some say the staff of the Senate does the fooling around for the boss. Not true. But truth is that since a senator is so much easier to recognize, he needs a lot more help from some aide to cover for him. It looks like the girl is with the senator's assistant. But she's with the senator. Some staffers have to scout for dates for the boss.

Sometimes the aides get their tails in the crack too. But unless they cause the boss to have bad publicity, nothing comes of it. Usually the senator is engaged in something of the same kind, so the buddy system works. In one well-known case around the Hill, an aide managed to have two children out of wedlock and the unmarried woman went around using his name as if she were married. He did not marry her. He divorced one gal and married another, but she wasn't it.

Senate wives worry about their marriages just as much as the congressmen's wives. Some wives are worrying themselves needlessly. They have husbands who really are faithful. But it's a jungle up there. When some senators are in heat, they can be animals.

I ran into one aide who looked really harassed and I asked him what the matter was. He said, "The boss has got to have his balls cracked, and if I don't find him somebody, I'm going to be stuck on the Hill tonight working till midnight. He's not leaving or letting me leave until he's been serviced, the damn stud. I know his tricks."

I said, "Well, I wish you'd stay over on your side and not come over here to the House side to hunt for your grass monkeys."

One famous senator I know has a beautiful wife but still is not in a rush to get home to her. Instead, he always has something going with a staffer and the funny thing is he seems to find someone to work for him who greatly resembles his own wife. It is a source of amusement for his staff, and many male staffers have made a fervent wish they could go comfort the wife.

Senator Javits leads a very strange life by normal standards. He commutes home to New York City for weekends, but before he gets there he stops off at some nightclub and sees all his political friends and cronies.

In spite of how wives are mistreated, nothing happens. But when one is *well-treated* by her husband, there is the devil to pay. I'm thinking of poor Jane Muskie. When her husband was running for the presidential nomination during the 1972 primaries, he rose to her defense and probably lost his chance to be President by crying with frustration.

What happened is that he was campaigning in New Hampshire where William Loeb, owner of the Manchester Union Leader, a right-winger, printed an editorial accusing Jane Muskie of sneaking smokes, using off-color language and drinking on the press bus.

Senator Edmund Muskie did what no good politician should. Instead of attacking Loeb on the tube, he went right to the paper to defend her. Standing outside in the snow, he actually shed tears—a great political novelty when it is tears for someone else—and he called Loeb a "gutless coward." Had he gone to a TV station, taped a show and shown only anger, he might have won the primary—but he had the bad taste to cry. I should say the lack of control did him in.

Even Democrats on the Hill laughed among themselves and said if he had a crisis in the White House, he would just sit down and cry. Also, they said this showed that maybe Jane wasn't the kind of girl who belonged in the White House. Of course, that was a lot

157

of hogwash. Mrs. Muskie was a terrific woman. As for drinking, I can't think of a President I've known who didn't drink and so why shouldn't the potential First Lady have a drink, too, if she wants it.

I remember a congressman who had no particular excuse except the thrill of the chase. He had his eye on a certain girl who in this case worked in someone else's office. He tried to get the girl to go out with him, but the girl just didn't play around. She was fairly new on the Hill and really serious about her career.

This congressman trusted one of his female aides—there is usually one girl who is the keeper of the congressman's secrets and who isn't involved with him—and he got her to strike up a friendship with the girl.

It took months of casual friendship and lunches and shared laughs over this and that before the friendship had progressed enough for the congressman's trusted aide to invite the girl to her home outside of Washington for a weekend. The girl went, thinking they would be alone and would just rest and go hiking.

But when she got there, as if by accident, the congressman showed up and said he might as well stay the night. Well, it was worse than stories of the farmer's daughter. She carefully took no liquor, encouraged him in no way and felt secure because she went to sleep on the couch after he had gone to bed.

However, in the night, she awoke in the midst of being molested and ended up giving in. Was it rape? I don't know, but she was furious and told me she was sure the so-called friend had been in on it from the beginning. Incidentally, having had her once, the congressman was content never to take her even to lunch after that. Did she report it? Of course not. Who would listen? And besides, most people go by the code on the Hill—*silence!*

I asked her why she didn't call aloud to her friend to come help her. She said even her explanation of that made her angry at herself thinking of it now. At the time, all she could think of was that she didn't want her friend to hear them and this was one of the reasons she had given in rather than continue to struggle.

Sometimes the girls that are preferred by the top leaders seem drab in comparison to the cute chicks they pass by in their offices. One top senator prefers a fattish, sluttish-looking girl. All the other girls are so neat and trim, and his own wife is far more attractive than the stout one who has only youth and a fun way of saying insulting things to him. His male aides figure that's what he likes. He has been praised so much, he just adores the way Miss Slob says, "You dumb cluck, let me alone," or "Come on numb nuts, I've got the answer you wanted, now tell me how to answer this bastard's letter."

I don't know how many wives of straying husbands have cried on my shoulder, but I'd say dozens over the years. Some have begged me to spy on their husbands for them.

I would try to comfort them, tell them they were not the only wives who hated the Washington life and suggest that they concentrate on the good things of Washington—the schools, the good salary, the things they could do for their children. I suggested they get out more and join clubs and spend time at the Congressional Club, which is the club for Hill wives and has the mannequins of First Ladies that are smaller than life size but are dressed in exactly the same clothes as each First Lady wore. It's sort of a replica of the Smithsonian display.

There really is nothing that can be done unless you are going to change human nature. These men are so petted and pampered and have such a choice of women —some of whom work for them and some of whom just stop by to see if they can get close to the congressman or senator on any excuse—that it's amazing they ever get home.

Usually it's just the husband who plays and strays. But now a new thing has happened. They used to call it swinging or playing around, but now they call it open marriage. Some wives have come back to tell me that they are no longer waiting around for their husbands to get back to them. They are playing the game too, having their own flings with men and saving the weekends for home life.

Some formerly straitlaced wives have gotten very cynical and are getting their sex where they can—going along on campaigns and dating a fellow at one hotel while their husbands are "busy" with a staff girl in another hotel—or a girl reporter or a movie star.

Some of the best Hill marriages—on the outside—have the most rotten cores on the inside. I know of two congressional couples who are the dearest friends possible. They get together several times a week and they sit around and talk and play cards and just relax together. The wives are best friends and do everything together during the day while the husbands are on the Hill.

But the truth of the matter is that Wife X, a beauty, is in love with the husband of Plain Jane Wife Y and only tolerates her so she can know exactly where her true love is. She encourages Y to talk about her husband constantly and Wife Y is very happy with such a friend who shares her interest in everything.

The funny thing is the husband of Wife X is much better looking than the man who is beating his time. But somehow Wife X prefers his brand of love making and his sense of humor. I must say Husband X is not much on conversation—very serious.

Wife X bragged to me that even under her own husband's eye and Plain Jane's eye, she gives her lover a kiss of greeting that reminds him of what they mean to each other—"I put my tongue right in his mouth and I've never been caught yet."

One of these days there is going to be a terrible explosion. But for now Wife X is getting away with it. Listening to Plain Jane give all her schedule of the week, she knows just when she can call Congressman Y at their regular spot.

When I came to the Hill, divorce was something whispered about. Though she might threaten, a Hill wife didn't get a divorce. She just sat it out because, as the Hill men would say, "She's eating out of the same trough he is. She better not cause a scandal."

What the husband did didn't count until the wife complained. If she was sweet in public and didn't make waves, it was assumed she was perfectly happy and didn't know that her husband was a chaser. Or didn't care.

In recent years, Alice Longworth has been interviewed on her marriage and she has said herself that it wasn't the big thing in her life and that when the time in life arrived to get married, she had simply picked the best politician she knew because she liked politics.

But as for having any passion for her husband, the dowager who is known for her acid tongue and brutal honesty insisted she had no particular feelings about her husband—"None. Absolutely none!"

She could be brutal in her treatment of other guests at parties as well. I've heard the story of how she put down Senator Joe McCarthy at the height of his power. He had been her dinner partner at a party so the next time he saw her, Old Joe greeted her in a friendly manner saying that now he was going to call her "Alice."

Drawing herself up regally, she retorted, "No, you are not. The trash man can call me Alice, and so may the clerk in the store and the policeman on the beat, but *you* may *not* call me Alice."

By the time I was leaving the Capitol, divorce was getting so common that the Hill wags were calling the Prayer Room, "Little Las Vegas." That's because so many congressmen were getting married there for a

161

second time around. The most famous of these was Al Ullman of Oregon, who had been married a quarter century or more before he got divorced and married a gal from his own office.

Ullman, incidentally, is the man who became head of the powerful Ways and Means Committee after Wilbur Mills mishandled an affair with a stripper so badly that he stepped down from the chairmanship.

Sometimes there are touching moments in dealing with congressmen and their ex-wives. I would wish I could make them both happy, but my duty lay with my bosses. I did not work for their wives. I am thinking of the former wife of Al Ullman, Anita Ullman, who came to see me. She hadn't remarried. He had, to a girl in the office. Anita asked for a pass so that she could watch her ex-husband from the gallery.

I gave her the pass and she did come at least three times a week to watch him. Al looked up one day and saw her there. He sent word to me not to admit her to the family gallery anymore.

For a view of love Capitol-Hill style, the story of Representative Martha Keys, Democrat of Kansas, and Congressman Andy Jacobs, Jr., Democrat of Indiana, is pretty good.

Andy Jacobs had been divorced for a long time and I knew him as a happy bachelor. He was friendly, frivolous and funny. His special love was Great Danes. He bred them and he kept a kennel on a friend's estate in Clifton, Virginia. But his favorite dog was always in his office. The huge dog—weight 156 pounds—would lounge beside the congressman wherever he sat. The only time C-5—the Great Dane was named after an airplane—sprang to life with a growl was when Congressman Jimmy Symington of Missouri was around.

Since Jimmy was a Democrat like Jacobs, it couldn't have been his politics that C-5 was objecting to. No, it was something else that made the hair on the back of C-5's neck stand on end when Jimmy visited the office.

162

Andy always took C-5 along with him to the after-hours parties in the House office building, so Jimmy and dog were bound to meet. Once when dog confronted man and man tried to extend a friendly greeting, C-5 bit him instead. Jimmy Symington was very gracious about it, because his former training as protocol chief of the State Department had prepared him for graciousness under all conditions—including seven punctures on the hand from canine teeth.

That was several years ago, and when time had healed the wounds—mental and physical—Andy had another party in March 1975 in honor of the fact the C-5 had become a father. Of course Andy invited Jimmy Symington, his old friend.

Congressman Symington arrived with a present for C-5—several slices of cheese, gift-wrapped. He also had a little speech of forgiveness ready to deliver, but he never got a chance. Oh, C-5 accepted the cheese all right, but then he suddenly changed. The hair on the back of his neck stood up and he lunged at the outstretched hand.

Again it was toothmarks and a bandage and blood on the floor. Full of apologies, Andy assured his friend Jim that he was the only person against whom his Great Dane had a vendetta. "Well," said the former protocol chief, still trying to hang on to his dignity as Andy applied a bandage for the second time, "I believe it might be the time to find a shrink for your dog."

So that's the kind of dog that was in the picture, sharing Andy Jacobs, Jr.'s life when the new Congress was voted in in November 1974. Among the new ladies was Martha Keys, a Democrat of Kansas, and it was practically love at first sight.

Never had Martha laughed and been so amused at anyone who could at the same time challenge her mind. Of course, Andy had a reputation as a man about town. He was known to attend some of the receptions

163

"just to fatten out my list of phone numbers," as he put it.

Then there was the matter of Andy's casual attitude toward time. He might show up and again he might not. He might come alone, he might bring five friends. And once, he had the Hill clucking when he invited fellow Indianan Congressman Lee Hamilton and his wife to his home for dinner and never showed up himself.

But then, Martha was intrigued by the other stories about Andy—how, in 1969, he had gone and sat on the Capitol steps to help the Quakers with their sit-in. And how, in a lighter moment, he had taken pen in hand to write to Batman on the TV series to tell him to wear a seat belt.

Martha Keys had arrived as a married woman, but she and her husband, Dr. Samuel Robert Keys, a dean of Kansas State University, obtained a friendly divorce after the papers were filed in midyear 1975.

I was well aware of the heavy romance going on between Congresswoman Martha and Congressman Andrew long before their announcement that they would make history by marrying in January of the Bicentennial year, 1976, and becoming the first couple to serve together in Congress.

These days, any candidate for federal office stands a much better chance of election if he is married, even if it is for the second time. It used to be just the opposite, especially for a presidential candidate.

We would hear the question raised now and then about whether Adlai Stevenson was interested in women or not. His wife may have shared a lot of the blame for his not becoming President when she cast aspersions on his manliness.

If Adlai had remarried immediately, would it have helped him get the presidency? That's a good question and I wonder. But in those days the accepted theory was that if a man had divorced, that was somehow acceptable to the American public, just as long as he didn't remarry.

Now the theory in congressional marriages, held by many, is that it's all right to get divorced just as long as the man marries again so that he can present a pretty picture of a homebody to the public.

Some congressmen as well as some wives have hired detectives to get pictures of the other's misconduct to use for getting a better divorce settlement—from their own standpoint. One congressman claimed to have taken his own picture of his wife with the man she was later to marry. That was Gene Snyder, a Republican from Kentucky, who also tried to gain custody of his teen-age son. It was one of the smellier Hill divorces, with charges and countercharges, and with even the ex-wife, Louise, announcing, when her ex-husband married his home office manager, that she was going to run against him in the 1974 election. She called in the press, made many headlines. Eventually she backed out and he won his election, though it's hard to say any more if one had any effect on the other.

I thought of Gene Snyder and his new wife, Pat Robertson Snyder, when Wayne Hays divorced his wife of many years standing and married his home office manager. But in the case of Wayne Hays, it was his girl friend, Elizabeth Ray, and not his ex-wife or his new wife, who made waves. A sort of third girl theme.

One of the biggest surprises on the Hill was the sudden divorce of Senator Robert Dole and his wife, whom he gave so much credit to in the past for helping him regain use of his arm and hand after World War II. His hand had been shattered and he had married his therapist, a lovely looking gal named Phyllis Holden. I liked her.

I knew Dole for many years when he was in the House, before he went to the Senate, before Nixon picked him to be Republican national chairman, or before Ford picked him as his vice-presidential running mate. I would feel sorry for him because he always had to shake hands with his left hand and he would hold something in his right hand so that no one would grab it.

Though a Republican, he had come in with the Democrats and Kennedy in 1960. His life story was an inspiration on the Hill. He had been a combat infantry officer in Italy with the 10th Mountain Division and had been wounded twice and had spent more than three years in military hospitals getting his body—especially his arm—put back together. It took years of operations to transplant bones and muscles. He had a bronze star with cluster for heroism. And he was even a fellow Mason, as was Harry Truman and many top politicians.

Anyway, in 1971, after twenty-three years, Dole made a public statement that he was ending his marriage because he simply did not have time for both marriage and a career.

Dole was so tall, dark and handsome that he was called the Cary Grant of the Hill and he did resemble the star. Everyone wondered who he was getting ready to marry. The answer was nobody. He remained unmarried from 1971 to December 1975, when he got hitched to another self-reliant gal—a good-looking commissioner of the Federal Trade Commission—Elizabeth Hanford.

On the Hill, they call that "a marriage of honorables." She was entitled to be addressed as the Honorable Elizabeth Dole just as he was the Honorable Robert Dole.

II

AT WORK
& PLAY ON
CAPITOL
HILL/OR
GETTING
DOWN TO
CASES

THE NIGHT I LOCKED THE WHOLE DAMN HOUSE IN

The Senate has filibusters. Over there, in the Other Body, as we call it, men strap on a contrivance to relieve their bladders as they stand talking and they go on for five and six hours without sitting down. They are filibustering. But in the House, we have only dilatory tactics.

You don't say "filibuster" in the House. It is a dirty word. Instead, you have dilatory tactics which can get as tricky as a chess game. You have sneaky suggestions that the House adjourn. And calls for the reading of the *Journal*—the proceedings of the day before—and the endless droning of the reading of the *Journal*. And you have quorum calls. Did I say quorum calls? Before day merged into night and night merged into day on this particular session, there were quorums coming out of our ears.

For this was the night of high drama and low comedy, the historic night, the precedent-making night, the night I locked the whole damn House in. Yes, locked the doors. Locked in Gerald Ford, the Minority Leader from Michigan who was destined to become a President. Locked in Bob Dole, destined to be chosen as Ford's running mate in 1976. Locked in poor Republican member G. Robert Watkins, who had kidney trouble and wet his pants twice. Locked in Democrats, too. Locked in the whole damn House on the night of October 8, 1968, and kept everyone captive until a vote was reached.

No, I'll never forget the night when the House stayed in session almost around the clock and managed never to mention what the hell the question was before the House. I mean the legislation they were sneakily fighting over never surfaced until 6:30 A.M., when the night was over and the members were so groggy they hardly knew what was happening.

Had a man come down from Mars, he would have been hard-pressed to know what the question was that was being so well suppressed. The Martian might even get the notion that the problem being discussed was, what is a "dilatory tactic"?

What it was all about was the upcoming 1968 election. Hubert Humphrey needed TV exposure like a trapped whale needs air. But there was a pesky "equal time" provision that was part of the FCC law. The Humphrey friends in the Other Body had already passed a resolution suspending Section 315 of the Communications Act of 1934, getting rid of that pesky equal time clause for the duration of the Nixon-Humphrey campaign of 1968.

The Humphrey forces were desperate for Brother Hubert to participate in what were being planned and billed as "The Great Debates." But Nixon was agin 'em and hiding behind the television networks' refusal to give free time for such debates if they also have to give equal time to every other candidate—Wallace and his American Party, a Prohibition party candidate, and the socialist and communist candidates, and perhaps even that famous barnyard pig candidate.

Wallace had nothing to lose. He was going strong and every time he appeared on TV, getting equal time under the Communications Act of 1934, he was grabbing potential votes away from both candidates—but especially from Nixon, since both appealed to the ultra-conservative voters.

The Republicans in the House were determined to keep the bill from coming up for a vote, and that was the word that was given them by the Nixon forces—kill that bill.

170

Some Wallace backers in the House had already weakened the suspension of the equal-time resolution in committee by rewording it so that it would be possible for Wallace to be included in the Great Debates. The way they worded it was that only the candidates who had qualified in some thirty-odd states were eligible for the special treatment and could have equal time without going to other, minor candidates. In other words, some would be more equal than others.

Even this was quite agreeable to Humphrey and his supporters, as long as he could get some air time to refute Nixon and get his own message across.

Nixon was afraid of debates and with good reason, as he himself told college audiences, milking a laugh out of his well-remembered disastrous encounter with Jack Kennedy in 1960, "I am a dropout—from the electoral college. I flunked debating."

So Nixon's signal to the House GOP had been stop that bill, and Humphrey's signal to the House Dems had been pass that bill at all cost—we need it.

At this exciting moment in history, I am going to take you onto the floor of the House and show you democracy in action and let you really feel that you are there.

As you follow me into the hallowed chamber of the House on this historic day of Tuesday, October 8, 1968, let me give you a word of warning. Whatever you do, don't laugh. The members take themselves and their political game very seriously.

So enter and take your seat. It is high noon and prayer is offered as usual by Chaplain Edward G. Latch. He's a great guy. His prayer this day has just the right prophetic note for the day ahead—if anyone has been listening. "We come to Thee now facing tasks that tower above our ability to handle well and living through days that disturb us with their demanding duties . . ."

Dr. Latch was a minister for fifty years before he came to the Hill. A couple of congressmen had been in his vineyard over at the Metropolitan Memorial Methodist Church on Nebraska Avenue in Washington —Carl Albert, George Mahon, Leslie Arends, Wilbur Mills, Tom Abernathy and William Springer—some Democrats and some Republicans. Chaplains are chosen by the Congress itself.

Speaker John McCormack has just hit his desk a mighty blow with his gavel. That always means he's much perturbed. He knows something's up, but he's proceeding as usual, directing the reading clerk to report the *Journal* of the preceding session.

Aha, trouble already. That's Durward Hall, Republican of Missouri, jumping up from his seat and making a point of order that a quorum is not present. I've been around long enough to know that looks like the beginning of dilatory tactics. As a matter of utter truth, there never is a quorum in the House at twelve noon unless the Queen of England has arrived, or, as one of our chaplains once said, "Unless there is a rumor that Racquel Welch is coming into the gallery."

The Republican strategy, I see, is to delay even the reading of the *Journal* of the day before. So there we are in the House, running on borrowed time—it's less than four weeks to the general election. Congress is anxious to adjourn to get to its campaigning. This is D-day.

Roll has to be called orally, which consumes anywhere from twenty-seven to thirty minutes to establish a quorum. Once started, even though a quorum has been reached, the roll must be continued to the end.

So there is the call of the House—three bells for quorum—and the Speaker eventually announces that 276 have answered to their names—a quorum of 218 being needed.

A word about the bells. They ring very loudly in every congressman's office, all committee rooms, all dining areas, even down in the House gymnasium. I have often been asked why the devil they have to be

172

so loud that tourists jump as if they've been struck by a bolt of lightning. I say that if you realize the age of most members—averaging close to sixty-five—it's a miracle they hear it at all and a further miracle that some make it. They come huffing and puffing into the chamber so much out of breath that they can hardly say "Present" when their names are called.

Donald Rumsfeld is a lively, young exception. Age thirty-six. Born in 1932. The Republican congressman from Illinois, who is later destined to become chief assistant to President Gerald Ford and then secretary of defense, rears up on his hind feet and demands that the *Journal* "be read in full."

Testily, McCormack snaps back, "The Chair assumes that the *Journal* is always read in full." *Assumes* is the right word for it, because, of course, it never is or there would be no time for anything else.

The clerk, Hackney, starts to read but has hardly begun when Rumsfeld again hops to his feet: "Mr. Speaker, I make a point of order that a quorum is not present."

McCormack grits his teeth and says, "The gentleman from Illinois makes the point of order that a quorum is not present. Evidently a quorum is not present."

Let me digress a moment, friend, to explain about the reading of the *Journal* as it is done in this year of 1968. The *Journal* is not the same as the *Congressional Record*, but it is a publication in its own right, compiled by the clerk of the House. It is the deadly dull technical report of every bill and action taken up the day before.

The tradition of the reading of the *Journal* involves the reading clerk rapidly reading only the heading of each subject matter in the order in which it has taken place the previous day—a fast shuffle through, taking only a few minutes.

This day, however, there is an underlying excitement in the House. Little clusters of congressmen on each side of the House are talking in soft voices in some places, not so soft in others. The voice of John Dingell, Jr., is always heard, and you can always hear Congressmen Bill Hungate of Missouri. Both are Democrats. That handsome young John Tunney of California, destined for the Senate, is even louder. Others are giving them a dirty look which does not seem to bother them at all.

The bill is scheduled to be the first order of business after the reading of the *Journal* of the preceding day.

Carl Albert, the Majority Leader, must follow parliamentary procedure since the Republicans have called for a quorum count. He moves a "call of the House" —meaning that the bells be made to ring, and again McCormack directs the clerk to call the roll.

The clerk is not the man, however, who makes the bells toll. It is one of my two pages, sitting at the documentarian desk, who gets his key out of his pocket, unlocks the little door below the Speaker's chair and twists the knob to Number 3. It is electronic, and while the bells are ringing in the Speaker's Lobby, right off the House floor, the clerk is already busy starting the roll call.

As I've said, it takes 27 to 33 minutes to read the whole roll of the House of Representatives. On this roll call, 255 answer—218 being a quorum.

Now Brother Albert gets up on his hind legs and asks unanimous consent that further proceedings on the *Journal* be dispensed with. But the gentleman from Ohio, Robert Taft, Jr., says, "Mr. Speaker, I object." Speaker McCormack directs a second clerk—Mr. Bartlett—to continue to read the *Journal* of the day before.

Albert, being Majority Leader, wants to get the bill on the floor and quit the shilly-shallying and dilatory tactics. But he's stuck on how to do it.

Taft has been too fast for him. So far not as sharp as his father, who had tried to run for President, he nevertheless is trying to build himself up with people back

174

home so that he can run for the Senate—which he is destined to do in 1970.

After a few minutes of listening to Bartlett drone away on the *Journal*, the word-for-word playback of every piece of legislation from the day before, Congressman Silvio Conte from Massachusetts, a Republican, offers a motion to the effect that the House now adjourn. The Speaker puts the question on the motion, and, after a division vote, demanded by Mr. Conte, the Speaker counts sixty-one yeas and ninety nays. So we are not adjourned.

Conte is a thorn in McCormack's side because he comes from the same state—Massachusetts—but he is a most loyal Republican. Again Conte hops to his feet, addressing the Speaker and saying, "I demand tellers." Tellers are ordered and Speaker McCormack appoints Mr. Conte and Mr. Albert as tellers. So Conte stands on the right side and Albert on the left side of the center aisle. The entire membership must get up and go to the center part of the well and proceed to march up the aisle in order to be counted by the tellers.

A teller vote is one of the procedures used in the House to find out exactly how many vote for and against. Each teller touches the member on the shoulder as he goes by, counting aloud. Only a teller vote is done this way. The usual way is a voice vote—the ones who make the most noise win.

The result of the teller vote is 67 yeas and 110 nays. So the motion to adjourn is again rejected.

Now Speaker McCormack directs the clerk to continue reading the *Journal*. Within a period of sixty to ninety seconds, the gentleman from New Hampshire, Republican James Cleveland, pops, "I make a point of order, quorum not present."

The Speaker replies, "Evidently, quorum is not present." Majority Leader Carl Albert moves a call of the House. Bells again. Quorum call—250 show up.

Majority Leader Albert is getting annoyed. He asks

175

for unanimous consent to dispense with further reading of the *Journal*. Speaker McCormack says, "Is there objection to the request?"

Bill Steiger of Wisconsin, a swashbuckling Republican, springs to his feet and says, "Mr. Speaker, I object." Then a Southerner, Democrat George Andrews of Alabama, asks the Speaker's permission for a parliamentary inquiry. It is his fancy way of saying he wants to ask a question.

McCormack replies: "The gentleman will state it."

Andrews: "I would like to know how many pages have been read and how many remain."

McCormack: "That is a very proper inquiry."

Andrews: "I am most interested in the reading of the *Journal*." At this point, I'm thinking a sarcastic "I'll bet!"

The Speaker, all honey, drawls that there are sixty-eight pages and the clerk has read thirty-eight.

Now it's the turn of L. Mendel Rivers, a powerful Democrat from South Carolina, of whom it has been said, "If ol' Mendel gets any more installations built down there, it's gonna sink his whole Carolina coastline." He rises up, with dignity, to try to help his leader.

Rivers: "Mr. Speaker, a parliamentary inquiry."

McCormack: "The gentleman from South Carolina will state his parliamentary inquiry."

Rivers: "Will the Chair please define the term 'dilatory tactics?' "

Before the Chair can answer, Gary Brown, a Republican from Michigan, calls out, "Mr. Speaker, I demand regular order." That means he wanted no shortcuts in the reading of the *Journal*. But the Speaker replies, "The Chair will ask the gentleman from South Carolina to elaborate upon what he means by 'dilatory tactics.' "

Before Mendel Rivers can answer, the gentleman from Washington state, Tom Pelly, Republican and also a heavyweight champion wrestler, rolls to his feet to demand, "Regular order."

Speaker McCormack: "The Chair might understand them, but the Chair wanted to get the gentleman's understanding."

Rivers: "I have asked the Chair if he will define dilatory tactics."

As the floor bursts into laughter, McCormack says with a poker face, "Well, the Chair can state that there has been a lot of dilatory action that has been going on under the rules of the House."

To get back on the track, a new tactic is brought up by John Dingell, a loyal Democrat, who asks for a parliamentary inquiry, and then says, "Mr. Speaker, I wonder if the distinguished gentleman from Illinois [Mr. Arends, the Minority Whip] will tell us why the Republicans are so afraid of having Mr. Nixon debate Mr. Wallace."

McCormack says, "The Chair does not hear the gentleman's parliamentary inquiry. There is too much noise in the Chamber."

(I had long ago learned that McCormack had one dead ear and one ear that functions better than some people's two ears put together. I would always talk into his right ear, the good one, unless I didn't want him to hear something, and then I would talk to someone on McCormack's left side.)

Dingell replies like this: "I wonder if the distinguished gentleman from Illinois, the Minority Whip, will tell us why the Republicans are so scared of having their tiger debate George Wallace."

Speaker McCormack has served enough time in the House to know he doesn't have to honor that question, so he directs the clerk to continue reading the *Journal*. Dingell has made his point and there is no need to belabor it. He has cleverly laid a little blame on Arends and succeeded in implying that the Republicans have a cowardly candidate.

177

Donald Rumsfeld, switching the attention from Nixon, calls for a quorum call.

Poor Carl Albert gets up and moves a call of the House.

Again my little pages have to get the key to open the small door and twist the electronic device to make the bells ring three times. This time, 249 show up. The number is shrinking but it is well over the necessary 218.

Now Majority Leader Albert gets up, trying to look taller than his five foot two, or five foot four—depending on whose eye is measuring him—and says, "Mr. Speaker, I ask unanimous consent that further reading of the *Journal* be dispensed with."

Naturally, the Speaker asks if there is any objection. Bill Steiger is on his feet, calling in a shrill voice, "Mr. Speaker, I object."

McCormack sighs and says, "The objection is heard. The Clerk will continue to read the *Journal*."

Tired of sitting, I slip behind the rail in the rear of the chamber and listen to two Democrat members talking about "the damn dilatory tactics of that bastard Nixon gang."

The other says, "I'd like to know what they're going to do next. They've asked such silly assed questions already. It's getting on toward 10 P.M."

"Well," I say, "dilatory tactics is the art of asking silly assed questions. Why don't *you* tell them? Call it what it is."

"No, *you* tell them, Fishbait." They laugh and sit down.

I laugh and go back to my seat at the Speaker's table. The Speaker's table in the well of the House has three levels. At the top is the chair for the Speaker. He sits alone. Below, on the second level, are four clerks: the *Journal* clerk, the bill clerk, and the two reading clerks. On the first level, elevated about six inches, is the minority journal clerk, the pair clerk and usually the

178

doorkeeper—if he gets to sit down for a few minutes. And next to him are the necessary clerks that help get out the *Congressional Record*—plus a few seats for the shorthand reporters, who take down every word spoken by hand in order not to make a bit of noise with the new-fangled court reporters' machine. The only noise the Congress permits is the noise it makes itself—with its mouth.

On Steiger's quorum call, we lose 10 more members who fail to answer "Present" and now we only have 239. Mr. Albert asks unanimous consent to offer a privileged motion to suspend the rule and provide for the suspension of the reading of the *Journal* at this time. Taft loudly objects.

Speaker McCormack glumly directs the reading of the *Journal* to continue.

The clerk continues to read.

Charles Joelson, a New Jersey Democrat, calls for a parliamentary inquiry and says, "Mr. Speaker, would it be possible to terminate these quorum calls by agreeing to substitute Mr. Agnew for Mr. Nixon in the TV debates?"

A rumble of laughter.

McCormack, in a no-fun mood, shoots back, "The Chair doubts if that qualifies as a parliamentary inquiry."

Mr. Joelson: "Well, then, Mr. Speaker, how about an old Ronald Reagan?"

McCormack ignores him and directs the clerk to continue to read the *Journal*.

I sit there thinking that it has been such a long time since we've had a quorum call that I am about ready to believe a miracle has happened, and maybe we'll soon be able to get down to business. Taft must have read my mind, for he hops up again and says, "Mr. Speaker, I make the point of order that a quorum is not present."

Again the rigmarole of my pages and their key and

the opening of the little glass door. Bells ring and the number answering the roll call this time totals 234—we have lost another five.

Again Carl Albert asks for unanimous consent to dispense with the *Journal* reading and Bill Steiger objects. Back to the *Journal*.

By now it is getting toward midnight and not a lick of the nation's work has been done. Not even has the *Journal* of the day before been finished.

Now Brother Roman Pucinski, a loyal Democrat of Illinois, pops up with a parliamentary inquiry.

McCormack: "The gentleman will state his parliamentary inquiry."

Pucinski: "Mr. Speaker, we have had in the last twelve hours twenty-three quorum calls. My parliamentary inquiry is this: In the event that a quorum does not respond on one of these quorum calls, is it then in order to make a motion to arrest the absent members and bring them down here?"

I hold my breath wondering what the answer will be.

"Yes," says McCormack, "such a motion would be in order if a quorum is not present."

Brother Pucinski thanks McCormack and sits down, and the clerk proceeds with the reading of the *Journal*.

Although no one seems to pay attention to McCormack's shocking pronouncement, a seed has been planted.

While Hackney and Bartlett take turns droning on, the members sit around in little knots talking with each other about legislation that pertains to their districts—trying to work out deals with committees that are not their own, trying to get promises of votes. Some are arguing about whether Eddie Hébert of Louisiana or Mendel Rivers of South Carolina will sink his coastline first with special projects. A laugh bursts out as someone reminds the group that New Orleans is already below the water level, and they'll have to build the levees higher to avoid a flood.

The two reading clerks, who take turns reading aloud, try to help their respective political parties. Charles W. Hackney, Jr., as a loyal Democrat, is reading as fast as possible, and Joe Bartlett, as a Republican, is helping the dilatory tactic as best he can by dragging out every word.

I listen in on the strategy boys talking and realize even more the significance of this effort to get the FCC rule changed so we can have those two-way or three-way Great Debates. If, as a result of the TV debates, Wallace can steal a few votes from Nixon and Humphrey can steal a few votes from Nixon, then no one will have a majority of the electoral college votes—and in that case, the election will be thrown into the House. And it doesn't take a soothsayer to know who the Democratic House would choose.

No wonder the Republicans are fighting for dear life. But my Democratic friends are confident they will win in the long run, if they have to stay up all night.

I look round the chamber. Early in the show, the mood is lighthearted, and one Democrat, my good friend George Andrews of Alabama, refers to the fact that Nixon doesn't want to participate in any Great Debates by calling out facetiously on a point of parliamentary inquiry, "Mr. Speaker, if I could assure my Republican friends that Mr. Wallace would be easy on Vice President Nixon, would that bring this thing to an end?"—meaning, would the Republicans then quit their dilatory tactics and let this matter be brought to the floor for a vote.

The Speaker pro tempore—who at this moment is Wilbur Mills—does not even bother to dignify the gambit with a reply. He ignores Andrews and says, "The Clerk will read."

Even the man who will one day be touched by destiny and lead his country as President is irritably brushed aside and treated in a cavalier fashion by the Speaker pro tempore, as if to say don't ask dumb questions.

181

Gerald R. Ford: "Mr. Speaker, if there are 257 Members in one part of the House, and if they keep 218 Members on the floor, there is a quorum present, is there not?"

Speaker pro tempore Mills: "The Chair will state that the gentleman has answered his own parliamentary inquiry."

Now it's Brother Pucinski who takes a gentle poke at Minority Leader Ford, the guardian of the Republican party.

Pucinski: "Mr. Speaker, is it in order to inquire whether it is fair to assume that the Republican leadership . . ."

Gerald Ford: "Regular order, Mr. Speaker." (Meaning, no interruptions.)

Speaker pro tempore Mills: "The gentleman from Illinois asks the Chair to recognize him to state a parliamentary inquiry. The gentleman will state it."

Pucinski: "Mr. Speaker, I wonder whether the Republican party has lost control of the kiddie car?"

Wilbur Mills does not scold. He says: "That is not a parliamentary inquiry. The Clerk will read."

Now Jim Wright, a popular Texas Democrat interested in highway safety, tries to stop the Republican tactics, referring to a precedent of many years back in which an opposition party has been stopped from using the tactics now being used. "Mr. Speaker," he says, "my inquiry is this: Under that rule and under the precedent, would it not be in order, particularly in view of the very obvious dilatory tactics being employed on the part of certain Members of this body on the other side of the aisle to prevent the transaction of business, for the Chair to recognize a member of the Committee on Rules as the spokesman of the Committee on Rules to call up a rule in order that the business of the House may be transacted and the will of the majority of the Members of the House may be worked?"

Speaker pro tempore Mills: "Did the gentleman from Texas put his inquiry in the form of a parliamentary inquiry?"

Wright: "Yes, Mr. Speaker. At the end of the statement was a question mark. The question is, would it be in order under the circumstances and in view of this precedent for the Chair forthwith to recognize the gentleman from Indiana, Mr. Madden, who acts at the direction of the Committee on Rules to call up a special order for consideration of the bill and permit the House to work its will?"

After much consultation and scratching of heads and shuffling of reference books, and time wasted again, Speaker pro tempore Wilbur Mills comes up with this:

"In Cannon's Precedents, Volume 6, of the 1936 edition, Section 630, the ruling pointed to by the gentleman from Texas has been superseded by a subsequent ruling of the Chair. It reads, 'On January 23, 1913, immediately after prayer by the Chaplain and before the *Journal* had been read, Mr. James R. Mann of Illinois made the point of order that a quorum was not present. A call of the House was ordered, and a quorum having appeared, Mr. Augustus P. Gardner of Massachusetts proposed to present a conference report . . . The Speaker ruled that no business was in order until the *Journal* had been read and approved.' "

So it is back to dilatory tactics.

Quorum call. Quorum call. Over and over, various Republicans ask for a quorum call. The number showing up slides downward from 236 to 230.

At 2 A.M., when Jim Cleveland, a three-term Republican from New Hampshire, makes his point of order, the roll call shows only 229 present. We are getting dangerously close to no quorum. Just eleven over.

I look across the chamber. There has been a little flurry of activity over Brock Adams' way. He's on his way up in the Democratic party and I know something

183

special is about to happen. Brock starts out low key:

"I have a privileged motion, Mr. Speaker, which is that I rise to ask unanimous consent that it may be in order for a motion to suspend the rule on the reading of the *Journal* and that under the suspension of the rules, the *Journal* be dispensed with."

Speaker McCormack: "Is there objection?"

The ambitious gentleman from Ohio, Taft, objects loudly.

Adams shifts now and asks a question in parliamentary language: "Mr. Speaker, in the event that quorum is not present, is it the situation on Rule 15 of the House that the first alternate that applies is that the Speaker of the House may sit during such period of time as a Sergeant-at-Arms shall search the premises in the nearby areas on the request of the Speaker in order to provide a quorum. Is that the first situation that applies in the event a quorum is not present?"

Speaker McCormack: "The statement, as generally made by the gentleman, is correct."

Adams: "Now, Mr. Speaker, the second alternative is this. In the event that a quorum is not present, after the efforts of the Speaker to obtain Members from nearby areas and through whatever means he wishes to pursue while he is sitting in his chair and the call is proceeding, the next alternative then is a motion supported by fifteen Members of the House to have a warrant issued and after that warrant is issued and this motion is passed and the doors are locked and Members are brought to the floor, then under the instructions of the Speaker, they may be detained on the floor throughout the quorum and remain present for the transaction of business? Is that the second alternative, Mr. Speaker?"

McCormack answers this way: "The Chair does not wish to take this matter into consideration in the nature of an alternative, but the Chair would state that such procedures are carried out requiring the presence of

184

Members. Is that what the gentleman has in mind?"

Adams: "Would it be in order at this time for a motion of that type to be made?"

McCormack: "That would depend upon the action of the House."

Adams: "I am asking, Mr. Speaker, if such a motion by fifteen Members would be in order at that time?"

McCormack: "The Chair has difficulty in following the gentleman when he says, 'a motion by fifteen Members.'"

Adams: "I refer the Speaker to Part II of Rule 15 which reads as follows, 'In the absence of the quorum, fifteen Members, including the Speaker, if there is one—'"

McCormack interrupts: "There is one now."

A further word about Brother Brock Adams. He is relatively young—forty-one—small in stature but gutsy. Great talker and doer. Already he has written a book, *Estate and Gift Taxation*. Before going to Harvard Law School, he studied economics and graduated *summa cum laude* at the University of Washington. He's been in office only since 1965, but this is the night he shows his fire and makes brownie points with the Democratic leadership. He doesn't know it now, in 1968, but he is destined to become chariman of the important Budget Committee and eventually Carter's secretary of transportation.

I am watching my buddy, Brock, now, as he is saying, "I appreciate that fact, Mr. Speaker. But in the event that you wished . . ."

He then proceeds to read what could happen. ". . . shall be authorized to compel the attendance of absent Members, and in all calls of the House the doors shall be closed, the names of the Members shall be called by the Clerk, and the absences noted; and those for whom no sufficient excuse is made may, by order of the majority of those present, be sent for and arrested, wherever they may be found, by officers to be appointed by the Sergeant-at-Arms for that purpose, and their attendance secured and retained; and the House shall determine upon what condition they shall be discharged."

Adams looks up: "Mr. Speaker, that is my inquiry in the event that this should continue and a quorum should not be present, if that is important."

Adams and McCormack continue a long back-and-forth discussion in parliamentary lingo of how such a thing could come about; followed by a call to dispense with the reading of the *Journal*, followed by another quorum call.

McCormack: "The Chair will count."

He picks the gavel up by its head and, using the handle as a pointer, he proceeds to count. This is one of Mr. McCormack's idiosyncrasies when tired. When we get to the report of the timekeeper who is at the Speaker's left with pencil in hand, McCormack advises the timekeeper that the count is 159 present (218 needed—not a quorum).

Majority Leader Albert: "Mr. Speaker, I move a call of the House."

Call ordered.

My poor little old sleepy-headed boys, the pages, hunt up the key to open that little door to twist the knob to the third number which rings three bells. When the last names answer, the Speaker announces there are 226—now only eight over the necessary number.

Roll call.

Roll call.

Roll call.

In between, Mr. Bartlett drones on from the *Journal:* "Commercial fishing vessel means a vessel engaged in the business of taking of fish, mollusks, or crustaceans for subsequent sale . . ."

Philip Burton, a great guy and a Democratic liberal from San Francisco (we have two Burtons at this time;

the other being from Utah—a Mormon and a Republican), rises and calls: "Mr. Speaker."

McCormack: "For what purpose does the gentleman from California rise?"

Burton: "To merely bring the attention of the House to the hour of 5 A.M. having arrived. I was going to raise the point of order that the House was asleep, but I shall not make it."

McCormack: "The Clerk will continue the reading of the *Journal*."

Poor Brother Conable—Barber Benjamin Conable, Jr.—a Republican from New York, innocently decides to join the party and is startled at what he's getting into: "Mr. Speaker, I make a point of order that a quorum is not present."

Jim Wright: "Mr. Speaker, a point of order."

McCormack: "The gentleman will state his point of order."

Wright: "Mr. Speaker I make a point of order against the gentleman's point of order on the ground that the gentleman's point of order is a dilatory motion, prescribed by the rules, wherein it is clearly set forth that no dilatory motion shall be entertained by the Speaker."

Conable looks alarmed, realizing that somehow *he* is the straw that broke the camel's back.

Now suddenly Brock Adams plays his trump card, calling out, "Mr. Speaker," and demanding that as part of the motion of a call of the House, the missing members be "found and returned here on condition that they shall not be allowed to leave the Chamber until such time as the pending business before this Chamber on this legislative day shall have been completed."

That amounts to House arrest. There is a stir in the House—some of sheer fury and some of delight.

My own shocked reaction is, "What now?" I haven't long to wait. The motion is agreed to and the clerk is starting to read the roll when Lester Wolff, a Democrat from Kensington, New York, rises to make a point of order.

Annoyed, McCormack says: "The Chair will state to the gentleman from New York that there is a quorum call underway and it cannot be interfered with."

Two years later, in 1970, Wolff will distinguish himself by becoming the only member of Congress to walk out on a foreign dignitary during a Joint Meeting of the House and Senate, walking out on the French visiting chief of state, Georges Pompidou. Now Wolff's action makes history in another way.

Wolff: "Mr. Speaker, I make a point of order on the quorum call."

McCormack: "The gentleman makes a point of order?"

Mr. Wolff: "Yes, Mr. Speaker. The doors are not locked."

It is my shining moment. As it would later be told in Deschler's *Procedure*, the official book of precedence of the House, page 190:

> The Chair personally instructed the Doorkeeper to lock all exits from the House Chamber and to prohibit Members from leaving during the call of the House. Doors leading from the Chamber to the Speaker's Lobby, as well as those opening from the cloakrooms were locked.

Actually, I lock seven doors—I take the master key that locks all the doors on the House floor—the east door, the main door that leads to the Senate, and the west door—and I also hand-lock from the inside the four doors leading out to the Speaker's Lobby.

As I finish the "lockup" I recall with a shudder what happened to another fellow in my shoes on the Senate side back in 1943 and hope it won't happen to me. A sergeant-at-arms over there—they have no title of "Doorkeeper"—was told to go get the senators and

188

bring them on the floor to make a quorum. He literally did—in effect, arresting them and escorting them back. The next think he knew, he was fired. You don't tell a congressman or senator what to do.

When the dust has cleared and the roll has been finished, a quorum of 222 are in the room—we have four bodies to spare.

A polite pandemonium is taking place as members realize they are locked in, sealed in, stuck for the duration of the reading of the ghastly *Journal*. First, Republican Bill Brock of Tennessee—not to be confused with Brother Brock Adams, the Democrat—tries to use a little humor to appeal to the Chair, kiddingly calling it a sticky situation.

"I can tell it's a sticky situation shaping up," he says, "because we have a candy factory down my way in Chattanooga and if we aren't careful, this candy is liable to get too sticky to handle. So I'd like to make a parliamentary inquiry, Mr. Speaker. Am I to understand if further proceedings under the call have been dispensed with, according to the last motion, it is correct that the doors of the House are now open?"

Almost gleefully, the Speaker says he was "awfully glad the gentleman made that parliamentary inquiry" because, as a matter of fact, the doors certainly were not open and wouldn't be opened again until the "pending business before this Chamber on this legislative day shall have been completed."

Now half the Republicans are on their feet, buzzing angrily like a swarm of disturbed hornets.

Minority Leader Gerald Ford is recognized and tries to argue that the ones who have been in the chamber before it was sealed should have their freedom to come and go, and only those who had to be sent for should have to be locked in.

In a long speech with flowery language which pays tribute to "the distinguished Minority Leader," Speaker McCormack nevertheless ends up saying, "The doors

189

will remain locked until the present business is disposed of."

I could have predicted it. When they start sounding sweet to each other, that means they are getting ready to put the knife in just a little bit deeper and twist a little bit harder.

Now the Speaker recognizes Congressman Taft, who is furious and makes a long speech about freedom of movement, ending with this comment: "If the House attempts in any other circumstances, circumstances not necessary to the business of the House, to restrict the freedom of the Members to pass in or out of the Chamber or anywhere else that they care to pass, do they not under the Constitution and the laws of the United States constitute a violation of the civil liberties of the Members?"

He, too, has a good point I think, but obviously the Speaker doesn't agree.

Speaker McCormack: "The Chair could observe that there are civil liberties of other involved. The House has acted. A majority of the House has spoken for this motion and, without getting into any long discussion, the motion on the pending business which is before the House is binding on the Speaker and the Members of the House."

Taft is not willing to give up. He tries one more thing, asking again for a parliamentary inquiry.

Speaker McCormack is getting annoyed: "The Chair is not going to prolong these parliamentary inquiries too much, because we want to proceed with the finishing of the reading of the *Journal*."

There is no one on the floor who cares two beans to listen to any more of that droning.

Taft: "Mr. Speaker, my further parliamentary inquiry would be this: Is the statement of the Speaker meant to imply that the majority of this House may restrict the liberty of the minority Members of this House?"

Speaker McCormack: "The Chair does not so construe the motion."

Of course that is exactly what is going on. Both the majority and minority members are restricted. And only I have the key. Now the Speaker shows that he has a compassionate heart by recognizing the distressed-looking Republican gentleman from Michigan, Elford Cederberg, who tells his sad story:

"Mr. Speaker, yesterday my wife underwent major surgery and she is in the hospital at the present time. I have been going back and forth to the hospital to see her. I have missed several quorum calls during this period of time.

"Do I have to get unanimous consent from this body to return back to the hospital when I would probably be going back within the next hour or two?"

Speaker McCormack: "The Chair will state to the gentleman from Michigan that if the gentleman will consult with the Speaker, certainly, we are all sorry to hear about the condition of the gentleman's dear wife and the Speaker will recognize that first things come first and that one belongs with his loved ones."

Cederberg: "I thank the Speaker."

Now Mendel Rivers is getting up. He can afford to take his sweet time because he and John McCormack have a mutual admiration club going, the McCormack–Rivers Club, and they are the only two members allowed in it.

Rivers: "Mr. Speaker, a parliamentary inquiry."

Speaker McCormack: "The gentleman from South Carolina will state his parliamentary inquiry."

Rivers: "Mr. Speaker, we have taken the unusual step of sending for absent Members. Even though a quorum is present, my parliamentary inquiry is this: In construing the motion pursuant to the rules of the House, will the absent Members be merely notified or will they be sent for by a Marshal or will they be placed under arrest or how will they be returned?"

191

Speaker McCormack: "The Chair will state to the gentleman from South Carolina that they will be notified by the Sergeant-at-Arms."

Rivers: "Will they come in on their own or will someone in authority bring them in?"

Speaker McCormack:. "The Chair has announced that they will be notified by the Sergeant-at-Arms. Certainly, there is no wording contained in the motion to bring about the attempted custody of any Member."

At this point the progressive Republican Jim Fulton of Pittsburgh, God's gift to Washington hostesses needing a single man, very cautiously gets up and addresses the Chair.

He is just trying to get a little rise out of Speaker McCormack and he has a parliamentary inquiry that makes everyone laugh.

Fulton: "Mr. Speaker, in our Pennsylvania delegation we have one member, Mr. John Saylor, who has leave of absence from this Chamber for two days and who is at the present time on board a naval ship. Does this motion apply to a person with such a leave of absence?"

McCormack, annoyed, says it does not, and gavels down the laughter.

But determined to get a real rise out of the Speaker, Fulton tries again: "One further parliamentary inquiry on the enforcement of the motion: Is it not within the full discretion of the Chair as to what methods and means shall be used to notify or to arrest or to bring in Members and that that full discretion still lies within the Chair? So, unless there is an order by the Chair as to the method, the motion simply represents a notification to the Members to return because insofar as I know the Chair has made no ruling as to the arrest or as to bringing the Members back in custody."

Now the Speaker is really mad.

Speaker McCormack: "The gentleman is the only one who has used the word 'arrest.' The Chair used the word 'custody.' The Chair does not construe that that is a part of the motion, and the Chair has construed that motion to mean that it is the sense of the majority of the House that the Sergeant-at-Arms come up with the Members that are not present and do everything he can within the limitation of the motion to assure their presence.

"The Clerk will continue with the reading of the *Journal* of the proceedings of yesterday."

McCormack is looking at Fulton with fire in his eye, and now Jim boy is happy.

The clerk, Charlie Hackney, Jr., hastily wipes the sleep from his eyes, takes a swallow of water, puts a cough drop in his mouth and forcefully continues to read the *Journal* from yesterday. Both Hackney and Bartlett are tall and thin and always look half-starved or exhausted or both due to the nature of their work. It is getting on toward 7 A.M. Hackney tries to speed up his reading, but he's too beat.

Now Robert Dole takes over. The "daring darling from Kansas," we call him. Bob hastily jumps to his feet demanding to be heard and calls for a parliamentary inquiry.

But even before Brother Dole can get his feet well-planted, the Speaker, still angry from his words with Jim Fulton, cuts him off: "The Chair will not entertain any more parliamentary inquiries at this particular time."

The Chair is the boss. If he doesn't choose to recognize a man, tough turkey. Dole is a thorn in McCormack's side, too, being such a Mr. Republican that he will later in Nixon's term end up as chairman of the National Republican Committee.

Majority Leader Albert hastens to pour oil on troubled waters and to test whether the House is finally ready to settle down to the legislative business of the day. In a sweet, placating voice, he says: "Mr. Speaker,

I ask that the further reading of the *Journal* be dispensed with."

McCormack relaxes visibly and asks with a note of hope: "Is there objection to the request of the gentleman from Oklahoma?"

Taft, the Republican jack-in-the-box, jumps to his feet again and objects with vitriol in his voice.

McCormack, looking and sounding grim again, orders the clerk to keep reading. And in so doing, it is time for Joe Bartlett, the Republican reading clerk, to have his turn, reading with great articulation to drag it out as long as possible and help his side.

Mr. Taft is still burning not only mentally but physically. His face is flushed. He raises his voice. "Mr. Speaker, I object."

Speaker McCormack: "For what purpose does the gentleman from Ohio rise?"

Not even waiting for the Speaker to reply, the virile-looking Democrat Sidney Yates of Chicago hastily calls out, "A point of order, Mr. Speaker. That is not in order until the reading of the *Journal* has been completed."

Sidney Yates has been in Congress about a quarter of a century starting in January 1949. He was the guinea pig—a congressman picked by the Democrats to run against Dirksen. He didn't make it, but he gave a good race and he was reelected to Congress the following term. He's a Navy man—tough, a lawyer, black-haired, holding a Bachelor of Philosophy from the University of Chicago. Yates is a good committee man, right down the line with the Democratic main line leadership, but that is as far as he gets in trying to protect the Speaker because Taft is still on his feet. Still, Yates keeps standing, too.

Speaker McCormack says: "Will the gentleman from Ohio state his privileged motion?"

Taft: "Mr. Speaker, my motion is on a point of personal privilege."

194

Speaker McCormack: "Will the gentleman from Ohio state whether it is a point of personal privilege or a privileged motion?"

Taft: "It is a privileged motion, and a motion of personal privilege. Under Rule 9, questions of a personal privilege are privileged motions, ahead of the reading of the *Journal*."

Speaker McCormack: "The Chair will advise the gentleman that a question of personal privilege should be made later, after the *Journal* has been disposed of. If the gentleman has a matter of privilege of the House, that is an entirely different situation."

Taft: "I believe, Mr. Speaker, this involves not only personal privilege as an individual, but also as a Member of the House and also the privileges of the House."

Speaker McCormack: "The Chair does not recognize the gentleman at this time on a matter of personal privilege. But the Chair will, after the pending matter, the reading of the *Journal*, has been disposed of, recognize the gentleman if the gentleman seeks recognition."

By now poor Yates is sitting down. He knows it is hopeless. And Taft is still rambunctious about being recognized. He is still on his feet addressing the Chair.

Taft: "Mr. Speaker, a parliamentary inquiry."

Speaker McCormack: "The gentleman will state the parliamentary inquiry." Taft is carrying on the fight for the Republicans.

Taft: "Mr. Speaker, is it not true in Rule 9 relating to questions of privilege it is stated that such questions shall have precedence over all other questions except motions to adjourn?"

Speaker McCormack: "Will the gentleman state the question of privilege?"

Taft: "Mr. Speaker, my motion is that I and all other Members in the Chamber who were here at the time of the last quorum call and answered 'present' be permitted to leave the Chamber at their desire.

195

Mr. Speaker, this is a matter of privilege of the Members of the House because there is no right under the rules of the House or under the statutes, or the Constitution of the United States to interfere with the liberty of a Member to leave the House under these circumstances."

Underneath all the fancy language, Taft is quite angry and standing on several copies of the Constitution so he can be seen and heard. I look up. The poor reporters in the gallery are straining their ears and eyes and scribbling like crazy.

Speaker McCormack: "The Chair will state in response to the parliamentary inquiry that the action of the House has deprived—has caused—the doors to be closed and has deprived temporarily the privilege that the gentleman refers to. That has been done by the action of the House."

Taft: "Mr. Speaker, I was recognized to make a privileged motion and it was not a matter of a parliamentary inquiry. I have made that motion and I ask that the Chair rule on the motion."

McCormack, looking perfectly innocent, asks, "What is the motion?"

Taft, kind of confused himself, mutters, "I request that I be given time to discuss the motion as a matter of privilege." The Republican caper has backfired and the GOP members are indignant.

McCormack, realizing he has an advantage, says loftily, "The gentleman will state his motion."

Taft: "Mr. Speaker, my motion is that I and all other Members present on the floor who answered 'present' at the time of the last quorum call shall be permitted to leave the House freely at their own desire. The basis of my motion is under the rules of the House and the Constitution and statutes of the United States there is no basis for restricting the freedom of Members who were here at the time there is a quorum call, regardless of the action of the House."

196

By this time Taft has grabbed a copy of the Constitution and is waving it at McCormack.

McCormack says haughtily, "The Chair does not recognize the gentleman for the purpose of making such a motion because the Chair has already clearly indicated the House has already taken action and it is within the power of the House to take the action that it did. Therefore, the Chair does not recognize the gentleman to make such a motion."

Now the big man from Michigan, Minority Leader Gerald R. Ford, is on his feet demanding recognition.

Brother Ford has a reputation for trying to look out for his little gang. Some call Taft Ford's puppet. "Ford pulls the strings and Taft jumps," it is said.

Gerald R. Ford: "Mr. Speaker, it was my understanding that the gentleman from Ohio had been recognized for the purpose of offering a motion."

Speaker McCormack: "The gentleman from Michigan is well aware of the fact that the question of recognition rests with the Chair. The gentleman did not make a motion which was in order by reason of the action heretofore taken by the House. The Clerk will continue to read the *Journal*."

McCormack is reminding Ford who is boss.

Charlie Hackney gets to his feet, opens his mouth, reads about two sentences as fast as he can, but Taft is again on his feet addressing the Chair.

The early morning drones on. The Republican team of Jerry Ford, Les Arends, Bob Taft, Don Rumsfeld, Craig Hosmer, Bill Brock and Bill Steiger try everything —calls to adjourn, calls to table motions, and calls for more tabling and calls to permit employees of the House to have access in and out. McCormack replies that the doors are locked only to members, not to the staff.

My head is spinning and half the captive audience is "resting its eyes." But what it all adds up to is that McCormack is a strong leader and is still in charge.

197

Now and then I have been running escort service for male and female members whose kidneys are giving way—not fast enough, however, for one Republican, sixty-six-year-old G. Robert Watkins of Pennsylvania, who has not one but two accidents. At one point I become aware that he is furiously kicking the door as if that will open it. "I'm very sorry," I tell him, meaning it, "but that seems to be one of the hazards of the job of congressmen tonight." He is not amused.

At one point, Republican Craig Hosmer gets so groggy he votes on the Democratic side by mistake and has to ask permission to change his vote. His colleagues rag him and that helps wake them all up for awhile.

Again the order to read the *Journal*. I can hardly believe my ears when Mr. Hackney drones off the remaining paragraph and announces that the reading is concluded.

Speaker McCormack: "Without objection, the *Journal* as read will stand approved."

There is no objection.

The members look at each other in shock for a moment.

I look up at the clock above the Speaker on the north wall of the chamber in Gallery 7 and note that it is 6:30 A.M. Now, at last, comes the business of the day—or more accurately, the day before.

Congressman Ray Madden's big moment has come. Madden says, "Mr. Speaker, by direction of the Committee on Rules, I call up House Resolution 1315 and ask for its immediate consideration.

"This will enable the House to approve the Senate Joint Resolution 175, suspension of Equal Opportunities Provisions of Section 315, Communications Act of 1934, for the 1968 Presidential and Vice-Pres.dential campaigns."

And with that language read into the record, the Speaker directs the clerk to read the resolution, providing that the equal time rule be suspended for the

198

1968 presidential and vice-presidential campaigns for all candidates not qualified to be on the ballots of the thirty-four states.

Brother Madden, the number two man on the Rules Committee, and not its chairman, Brother Bill Colmer, of my hometown, who brought me to Washington, is introducing the rule for good reason. Colmer—a conservative, to the nth degree—is anti-Humphrey. Madden, a liberal from Gary, Indiana, is for the rule and for Brother Humphrey.

Speaker McCormack: "The gentleman from Indiana is recognized for one hour."

But before Brother Madden can start, here comes that Gerald R. Ford again, addressing the Chair. "Mr. Speaker, a parliamentary inquiry."

Speaker McCormack: "Does the gentleman from Indiana yield to the gentleman from Michigan?"

Gerald R. Ford: "Mr. Speaker, a parliamentary inquiry."

Madden: "I do not yield."

Speaker McCormack: "The Chair is asking the gentleman from Indiana if he yields to the gentleman from Michigan for the purpose of making a parliamentary inquiry."

Madden stomps his foot and yells, "No!"

But the Minority Leader is not intimidated.

Mr. Ford, displaying the same stubbornness he would have as a President years later, says, "Mr. Speaker, I demand the right to make a parliamentary inquiry."

Madden: "I yield."

Gerald Ford: "Mr. Speaker, I make a demand of personal privilege."

Speaker McCormack: "Just a minute. The gentleman from Indiana has yielded to the gentleman from Michigan for the purpose of making a parliamentary inquiry."

Gerald Ford: "I appreciate the delayed recognition by the gentleman from Indiana."

Speaker McCormack: "The gentleman will state his parliamentary inquiry."

At this point the clock says 7:10 A.M.

Gerald Ford: "Mr. Speaker, I ask the parliamentary inquiry: Are the doors to the Chamber now unlocked?"

Speaker McCormack: "As the Chair stated previously in response to a parliamentary inquiry, the pending business was the reading and approval of the *Journal* of the House. And the Chair, in response to the parliamentary inquiry, reiterates that reply, that the business before the House at that time which was pending was the *Journal* of the preceding session. Accordingly, the doors will be opened."

The Speaker directs the Doorkeeper—me—to open the doors. All of them, he tells me. I rush around with my key. I unlock the West, the East, and the Main doors, and then I manually unlock the four doors leading from the chamber to the Speaker's Lobby, that had been hand locked.

Score one for Jerry Ford.

About 150 frantic members rush out. One yells at me, "Fish, damn you, I'm going to pee. One minute more, I'd have used the spittoon."

Gerald R. Ford: "I thank the distinguished Speaker."

Ray Madden: "Mr. Speaker, House Resolution—"

Delbert Latta: "Mr. Speaker—"

Speaker McCormack: "The gentleman from Indiana [Mr. Madden] has been recognized for one hour. Does the gentleman from Indiana yield?"

Madden: "I will yield to the gentleman from Ohio [Mr. Latta] thirty minutes for debate only," and he adds, "Mr. Speaker, I yield myself as much time as I may require."

There is an old tradition that when the member of the Rules Committee is recognized to bring up a resolution, he is recognized for one hour with the understanding that he will yield thirty minutes of that time to the ranking member on the opposing side, who, in this instance, happens to be the Republican gentleman from Ohio, Delbert Latta.

Though a member may say he's yielding to another member, he can sometimes keep the other waiting until he's good and ready. This now happens.

In a scolding voice, like a schoolteacher, Ray Madden reproaches the Republicans for their dilatory tactics that included 34 quorum calls "and 19½ hours of the time of the House." He says the resolution "merely gives an opportunity for the three presidential candidates to partake of a discussion of their platforms before the American people," and also "to clear up some of the extraordinary confusion in the minds of the millions of voters in this country."

But it remains for the Republican spokesman Latta to put it on the line when he finally gets the floor, and really tell why the Democrats need the bill passed:

". . . the only emergency that exists is the fact that Hubert Humphrey is way down in the polls. It is an emergency for Hubert Humphrey. He is even running third. You know it and I know it. Let us lay our cards on the table. Let us stop kidding ourselves. We are not kidding the people. Nobody in this Chamber is being kidded. We are not, as I say, kidding the American people. You can read those polls. They know, you know, and I know why this legislation is on the floor. You are going to try to get HHH before the American people with the two other candidates so he can possibly confuse and befuddle the American people into believing they should vote for him. You know, I really believe the best way to amend this legislation is to give Mr. Humphrey all of the time and let him debate himself.

"He has been on all different sides of the Vietnam question since the convention. So give him all of the time and let him debate himself."

Then Latta, who years later will make news by defending President Nixon against impeachment, points

201

out that the resolution is still unfair because it really does not provide for George Wallace equal time on the *same* program at the *same* time with the others. And he adds, "There are people in this Chamber from the South who want to see Mr. Wallace have equal time on the *same* program at the *same* time"—not "equivalent" time but "joint" time.

It is almost time to vote, but first Minority Leader Ford rambles on and on about "erasing that black mark from the record which Brock Adams' 'antiliberty amendment' [locking the doors] has put on the House" but nobody pays him a bit of attention. Even when he calls it what it was, "a house arrest," and calls it a very serious matter.

Eventually, with Hackney so exhausted that he is unable to continue reading roll calls and with Republican Reading Clerk Joe Bartlett finishing the job, the vote on the Senate joint resolution is taken and passed—280 voting yea, 35 nay and 3 answering present.

So that is the story of the day.

The Democrats are elated and show it to the best of their ability, considering the condition they are in. They congratulate each other as the Republicans scowl glumly—especially Jerry Ford.

How does it all end? The story is not over.

The next day, October 10, 1968, everyone is still talking about it and my friend Lester Wolff of New York, a Democrat, rises to give the bad news that Senator Everett Dirksen, the Minority Leader of the Other Body, has just said, in effect, that hell will freeze over before he will let the resolution become law.

And then Wolff—true to the oft-proven theory that you can only find out the truth about what is going on in one political party from what the opposition party is saying—tells it like it is:

"I think this is a very definite indication of the fact

that Mr. Nixon is afraid to meet with Mr. Humphrey and Mr. Wallace. It is a sad commentary for the American people that they will be denied their right to see all candidates in direct confrontation and that the Republicans in Congress will go to any length to see to it that this denial will be enforced."

So after all that work, all that 27½-hour House floor debate and dilatory tactic, there were no Great Debates and the rest is history.

Nixon proved he was a mighty smart cookie when he gave the word he didn't want the resolution passed and he didn't want to debate anyone. Poor old HHH was left out in the cold, unable to make full use of his gift of gab. He lost by a narrow margin. Humphrey has told me and others that had he had just a little more exposure and a little more time—just several weeks—he is sure he could have made it. He was just starting to really come into his own, to have gotten his second wind, when the fight was over and he had received a knockout punch.

I thought of this night when Humphrey sadly decided in 1976 not to try to run again, saying, "I don't want to be another Harold Stassen."

I thought of this wild night, too, when the U.S. Court of Appeals, in April 1976—early in the 1976 presidential campaign—gave the equal-time rule a knockout punch. It would never be the same. And, ironically, now it was the Democrats who were on the side of equal time and fighting for their lives to keep the equal-time clause.

What had happened was that, in 1975, the Federal Communications Commission had reversed its stand on political equal-time requirements that had been the rule. As they said on the Hill, Dick Wiley, chairman of the FCC, "gave Ford the best present he could have." The commission had ruled that President Ford could go ahead and have his press conferences on the air without having to provide equal time for his opponents.

"Anything he wants to say," they explained, "the President can say in a press conference." Now the Democratic National Committee had objected and taken the matter to court, arguing that it was unfair that an incumbent President, like Jerry Ford, could use his press conferences as a forum for political campaign speeches, and pleading that his opponents should have equal time to state their side of the argument.

But the U:S. Court of Appeals ruled that the broadcast stations had the right to decide what newsworthy speeches to give time to, just as long as the station wasn't trying to push a particular man's candidacy. The court ruled, "The judgment of the newsworthiness of an event is left to the reasonable news judgment of professionals." So again the Republicans were laughing.

I guess the main thing that can be said is that the more things change, the more they are alike.

IN THE BACK
ROOMS OF CONGRESS

The public is lucky. Unless a congressman jumps into the drink after a pretty girl—à la Mills—or lands a punch on a fellow lawmaker in full sight of everyone —which has also happened—nobody knows except the intimates on the Hill and public illusions remain safe.

The insults and race baiting, the fistfights, the complaining, the whining, the drinking in the back rooms of Congress, away from the sight of the public, generally stay out of the newspapers.

There have been some memorable physical confrontations just off the floor of the House. And it's nine chances out of ten that the poor old codgers are so out of condition that they couldn't land one on a standing lamp post.

More often, feuds just kind of drone along with the exchange of verbal insults, which are nonetheless deplored by the more peaceful members of Congress. The public does not know that during sessions, when there is danger of members coming close to blows, the sergeant-at-arms is ordered to walk between them with the Mace of the House of Representatives, the symbol of authority.

When I was special assistant to the sergeant-at-arms, I was the one who, at the order of the Speaker of the House, jumped between two angry men, waving the Mace and "presenting" it before the guilty one who had started the ruckus. For some reason, this has a magical effect in stopping fights on the actual floor—but in the back rooms there is no Mace to stop the squabblers.

The time I intervened could have been called a "sitting violation." That was when Congressman Will Rogers, Jr., son of the famous humorist, got into an argument with the poker-playing, traditional-Southern-gentleman type of congressman, Edward Eugene Cox of Georgia.

The debate on the floor had been gathering up steam, but what made this confrontation remarkable was that there was disunity between fellow Democrats. Sometimes the bitterest fights are those within your own family.

Cox was six feet tall and very impressive and so was Will Rogers. But Cox had the added dignity of gray hair, and so when Cox terminated the argument by ordering Rogers to sit down, Rogers' first reaction was to do so. But Rogers got furious immediately thereafter and jumped up and started to pull Cox's hair.

At a signal from the Chair, I ran and got the Mace and held it between them. Since the protocol is that once you get the Mace, the guilty person is "floored" for the rest of the day—which means that he cannot say a word, cannot rise to speak again—both Cox and Rogers were floored.

I'll tell you more about the Mace and its many adventures on the floor in the chapter on the history of the Capitol. But just another word or two might be of interest here.

Under the rules of the Mace, sometimes it doesn't even matter who gets hurt, it's the one who strikes the first blow who is guilty. In one case, Martin L. Sweeney, Democrat of Ohio, and his opponent would not quit arguing even when the Speaker had rapped the gavel to order. Arms flailed and Sweeney ended up with a bloody nose. But the Mace still ended up in front of Sweeney because he had swung the first blow. He was dripping blood and unable to say another word for the day.

In general, however, I have noticed that Democrats are much worse at controlling their tempers than Republicans.

The House has tried many ways to keep members

from coming to blows or holding up proceedings indefinitely by harping on one subject. It tried the gag rule on May 26, 1836, on the subject of slavery, hoping the problem would go away.

As adopted, the rule said that whereas it was impossible to come to an agreement to stop further dissension, not a single word more would be said on the subject. One war later, the problem of slavery was solved—which explains why gag rules don't work.

They used to ask a riddle on the Hill, "What's the difference between a discussion and a fight?" The answer was, "Six Bourbons."

The Hill crowd merely laughs about drinking problems. Mendel Rivers was fair game for the jokesters. One would say, "I never knew Mendel Rivers drank until I saw him sober."

The other would reply, "Yeah, he has sober spells."

Once one of the Hill personalities was telling how a congressional wife had come to him to get advice on her husband who was home drunk at that very minute. She had asked what she could do.

"What advice did you give her?" another congressman broke in. "What could she do?"

"What do you think I told her?" the first congressman said. "I said to be sure he gets a clean glass."

One of the first things I learned when I moved into the Doorkeeper's Office was that a long, long storeroom leading off it had been the hideaway during Prohibition days—with sawdust on the floor, spittoons in each corner and a bar forty feet long, with a railing to rest a foot on.

These old boys couldn't wait for a 4:30 P.M. cocktail hour; they opened the bar before the House went into session at noon and reopened immediately upon adjournment at the end of the day, no matter how early or late.

In keeping with the tradition of the speakeasy, they

also feasted as they drank—hard-boiled eggs, pickled pigs' feet, hot smoked sausages and pretzels.

Possibly the greatest boozer of them all on the Hill was Democratic Congressman Marion Zioncheck from the state of Washington. He was swept in on FDR's Democratic landslide election of 1932. To Zioncheck, the whole congressional experience was a lark. He had run for office as a gag with a friend. Eight other friends had put up the filing fees. The two fellows had drawn straws for which offices to run for and Zioncheck had lucked into Congress.

The other fellow picked governor of the state of Washington, or some other high state office. Whatever it was, I seem to recall Zioncheck telling me that both came riding in on FDR's shirt-tail.

On the Hill, Zioncheck set new records in drinking that were hard to beat. He would drink anything liquid but his favorite was absinthe, which set him wild.

The police did not catch up with him until he drove on the sidewalk in front of a prominent Washington hotel. When they helped him out of his car, many beer cans and other potables tumbled out with him.

It is impossible to say whether he would have settled down into the kind of congressman who is a credit to Capitol Hill, because in August 1936, during his second term of office, he died quite suddenly while back home in Seattle. But while he lived, Zioncheck made a concerted effort to live life to the fullest.

In comparison Zioncheck would make Wilbur Mills' escapade in which his girlfriend jumped into the Tidal Basin look tame. Zioncheck would ride around in his big white Cadillac with a carful of wild women, whooping and drinking and yelling out of the window at passersby. Once they stopped to take a shower at an open fire hydrant. Other times Brother "Z" would stop his car, tear off his pants, and jump into one of the many fountains around Washington. The Cadillac, Marion told me, was the first thing he had bought when he came to town, and he considered the investment not wasted.

He would hold open house at his office and make a lot of friends that way—especially with girls. And he was always trying to make more, especially when he was in his cups.

I remembered once when he was just loaded enough to try to be helpful to a pretty girl in front of the Capitol, who was obviously a beginning driver. He stood there a half hour giving her instructions—now turn right, now left, turn, turn, turn.

This went on and on and she was jerking back and forth in the parking space. Finally her car lurched out. She was furious, but Congressman Zioncheck didn't notice. He acted pretty proud of himself.

"Okay, my dear, you're on your own," he said with a sweeping bow of gallantry.

"Are you crazy?" she snarled. "I was trying to *park* this car."

Good old Marion bowed again and said, "Sorry, dear. Come see me at room such and such." And he went wandering off, listing a little, in the general direction of his office building.

Another congressman—Carl Albert of Oklahoma—seemed to have a little trouble with fires which burned up his apartment. It was understandable that he was asked to move, not once but several times. When he moved to a particular apartment house in Virginia, the unfortunate Hill employee who happened to find out who the new man above him was called his own insurance agent immediately and said, as he repeated to me, "Double my insurance and call the police and tell them to get the ambulance ready. Then notify the fire department and tell them to be on the lookout for a call from down this way. And get it on the record that *I* have never had any trouble!"

Once Speaker Carl Albert's car collided with another after he had spent a relaxed evening in the Zebra

Room, a favorite hang-out of the young crowd, adjoining the Georgetown area. What made it particularly bad was that the other car had been standing still. It made the news but was soon forgotten.

Not so lucky was Representative Frank Horton, Republican of New York, who had the misfortune of being caught by police while driving over 100 m.p.h. on the New York State Thruway near Batavia.

Brother Horton was charged with reckless driving, drunk driving, and trying to outdistance police by driving up to 105 m.p.h. during a six-mile chase. With him were two women, whom he said he had taken to dinner.

That was what the police had to say and for his part, Horton had a few things to say, too. "I'm a private citizen and I have a private life. I'm also a public citizen and I have a public life. What's involved here is my private life."

The judge did not distinguish between the private and the public life, and both the private and public Horton landed in the pokey with a sentence of eleven days. He was out in less than a week—for good behavior.

A Speaker who had an on-again, off-again drinking problem was the famous Champ Clark, who became Speaker way back in 1911. But to show how stories go down through history by word of mouth, Rexford G. Barry, a man who now leads the International Discussion Club of Washington, was once a housemate of the retired Wallace D. Bassford, who had been secretary to Champ Clark for many years.

"Speaker Clark," Rex said, "could go for years without taking a drink, but when he did drink he would go on a binge. Once Clark was obviously drunk and he was scheduled to make a speech in another city. The staff was frantic because if they let him make his speech, the bad publicity could ruin him politically.

"So they hit upon the bright idea of turning out the

210

lights so that he could not see to read his speech. It stopped him from giving his speech, all right, but the *Detroit Free Press* printed the story.

"Again drastic measures were necessary. When the copies of the *Free Press* arrived in Washington by train, Wallace Bassford himself seized all copies of the newspaper before they could be delivered on Capitol Hill, knowing that if the story could be delayed for twenty-four hours, no other newspaper would print it."

Champ Clark—whose real name was James Beauchamp Clark—was just one of a long line of hearty drinkers on the Hill. We called those who might on occasion show up on the Hill already a bit swizzled, even before the day's session started, "stinkers." And I must say that Harry Truman, as a senator, would occasionally be a "stinker" when he came in.

We had a Republican member from the New York silk-stocking district, who could hardly wait for his committee's meeting to be over at about 11 A.M. so that he could have his first drink. He would come trekking onto the floor just in time to catch the prayer that opened the day's session and he would, at the same time, learn what the business of the day was to be.

Then he would leave his name with the telephone switchboard, telling where he would be—at one of the watering troughs in Independence Avenue. If he was still in a functioning condition when he got the call that his vote was needed, he would come rolling back. Otherwise, he would say, "The combined brains of the greatest deliberative body of the world will just have to do."

Another congressman now dead, Herman P. Eberharter, Democrat of Pittsburgh, was one of several who used to be called "the bottle baby." He would drink until he was thick-tongued, and four or five times a week one of the doormen of the House would drive him home.

In those days I was not yet the Doorkeeper and if the

regular doorman could not drive "the bottle baby" home, I would be assigned to do it.

Eberharter would be very sweet and easy to handle but we had another representative, William E. Minshall, Republican of Ohio, who would have to be helped off the floor of the House when he was in his cups. He was what we called an angry drunk, always giving us a lot of lip as soon as the firewater made him feel powerful.

I remember the last time I had trouble with him was when he was seeking me out to demand his tickets for a joint session at which President Nixon would be coming to the Hill. Even at a distance I heard his voice demanding, "Where's that goddamn Doorkeeper?" I was involved in security matters concerning the President's arrival and the coordination involved. But I decided I'd better quiet Minshall down first.

I said, "Now, Bill, what in hell's the matter with you? Your eyes are red and you don't look so good." I neglected to say that he also smelled like a beer bottle.

He said he wanted his tickets and he wanted them immediately and he let loose a string of abusive language on what he would do if I didn't hand them over to him.

I said, "Your damn tickets are over in your office, Bill."

He said, "If they're not, I'll come and beat the hell out of you and I'm going to take it up with Gerald Ford, the Minority Leader."

I said, "Why don't you take it up with Speaker Albert? He's more in charge of this Joint Session."

He said, "Oh that little bastard won't do anything. I'm just a Republican."

But by then he was laughing and when he got to his office, sure enough his tickets were there. But my secretary was terrified of him and his language.

There would be times when I would be making frequent trips to Bethesda Naval Hospital to see our various members who were drying out. Mendel Rivers was one who would be in and out of the hospital, though for a time Sam Rayburn and John McCormack tried to keep an eye on him and keep him sober for good stretches of time. Pat McCarran of Nevada would also be at the naval hospital.

I remember the time I went there and old Senator George Norris came to see Rivers. It was a touching scene, the obvious concern that Norris had and the display of friendship between the two men. Tom Hennings of Missouri, whom I had known as both a congressman and senator, also would be at the hospital and the nurses got to know me pretty well. In fact, they would be happy to see me because I could take over in looking after Hennings or Rivers for a while so that the nurses could run and do some errands of their own.

Rivers especially gave the nurses a hard time, and so they liked having me there as a buffer zone to straighten him out. There used to be a saying on the Hill that Mendel Rivers was neither a Democrat nor a Republican but he belonged to the McCormack–Rivers–McCormack party. He and John McCormack were a close team and they would always keep each other voting properly.

When I would help a soused member out of the Capitol, his buddies would ask me how it had all turned out and I would always say, "Well, I peed him, put him in a cab and pointed him home."

His pals would nod their heads, satisfied.

A magazine, *New Times*, once carried a senator's picture on the cover with the heading, "The dumbest Congressman of them all: Sen. William Scott." When he decided against suing the magazine for libel, Scott told reporters, "I don't want to bring a suit and not win. Then people will think it's true. There are people who believe what they see in print."

As I've noted a thousand times, the only people really feared on the Hill are reporters. Even Lyndon Johnson, after he was President, was afraid of reporters, especially Mary McGrory. His aide, Joe Califano, once quoted President Johnson as saying, "Mary McGrory is the best writer in Washington, and she keeps getting better and better at my expense."

But when it comes to fear, I kid you not, the person the Congress is most afraid of is not the President of the United States, it is Jack Anderson.

They really do feel he is everywhere. Once Senator Barry Goldwater said, "The other day I phoned the White House and told the President my best joke and the only one who laughed was Jack Anderson."

People don't realize how privileged the press is in the Capitol. They are the only ones permitted to take notes in the galleries. Note-taking is forbidden by anyone else. Rayburn said it was so the reputation of the Hill would not be tarnished by people getting a story wrong. Only the press, who were used to it, could understand what was going on. And if a congressman had second thoughts, he could change the transcript of what he had said on the floor before the *Congressioinal Record* was printed the next day.

Historians were very angry about these changes. They would come to me and say they had to take notes for history because they were doing a book and I would say they would have to take it up with the press galleries and see if they could make out an application form and qualify as a reporter.

Usually they couldn't, and they were furious and said it was not a democracy on the Hill. "It's more like a fiefdom, a duchy or a kingdom."

They have a point. It is also not a democracy in how the members get to ride elevators that take them to where they are going immediately, leaving plain citizens to wait. In some places, the press have their own elevators too. Some are marked, For Members and Press.

Congressmen usually consider it a must to attend women's and men's press club functions that they are invited to and they even have their best speech writers turn out a good speech if they are honored by being asked to speak.

In fact, it's a kind of love fest between the congressmen and the reporters until a mean story is written. Then that reporter may not be welcome at the member's office—but the congressman can't get him barred from the press gallery.

There are two cloakrooms, the Democratic and the Republican, each with its phone set-up. In each cloakroom—which incidentally, has no cloaks—there is a crew composed of manager, assistant manager, and a telephone clerk to handle incoming and outgoing calls. On the side of the desk where the manager sits, there are four pigeonholes where instructions are kept and congressmen who hurry by can say "Pair me for" or "Pair me against." Or else the congressman can tell where he can be reached if he wants to be called to the floor to vote.

In the good old days, before the miracle of electronic voting made it possible to complete a vote in fifteen minutes, congressmen used to have a half hour to get back from a local hideaway. Some would be visiting a girl friend. Some would be at a restaurant—with or without a girl friend. They would get the phone call, grab a cab and make it safely back to the House floor before the completion of the second reading of the roll.

I remember when Brock Adams, Democrat of Washington, had a great system. He would usually be at the Washington Hotel, where there were no bell hook-ups, as there were in some of the restaurant hideaways on the Hill, for members to know, by the number of bells rung, what was going on on the floor.

Since no bells rang, Brock's secretary would phone to alert him to an upcoming vote, jump into her car, pick him up in front of the hotel and get him back to the floor with several minutes to spare. She'd wait in the car while he voted and hurried back out. Then she would drive him back to the hotel and to his luncheon, meeting or whatever.

Senator Joe McCarthy, the Senate demagogue, was quite a drinker—especially after the Senate censured him. After the collapse of his red-baiting activities, he would hang around the Hill bars even in the middle of the day.

My friend Don Curry, who was working on the Hill in the 1950s, recently recalled the day he went into the old Carroll Arms Hotel lounge for a late lunch and found the old chairman already soused to the eyeballs and still ordering drinks.

"He was in such bad condition," Don recalled, "that as he would pick up his drink and down it, some of it would dribble out of his mouth and down his suit. Some of us were worried about how it looked to outsiders, and I remember that one of South Dakota Senator Karl Mundt's staff got up and went over and talked to him, to see if he still made sense. He didn't, so a couple of us simply got him out of the chair, half carried him out and put him in a cab.

"I guess someone gave the driver his address. He may have been one of the worst demagogues I have ever known, but he certainly ended up a pathetic mess. The next thing I heard was, I believe, that he had died of cirrhosis of the liver in a naval military hospital."

Speaking of McCarthy, the wild man of the Senate, reminds me that until he married, late in life, he was not known to have his own apartment or house in Washington—he seemed to live at an aide's home, in a maid's room that had been converted to his use. Even at the height of his power, McCarthy was a lonely figure. Those who didn't hate him too much were very happy when he finally got married to a beautiful woman and had a more regular life.

But compared with another senator, McCarthy had a practically normal life. I'm thinking of another wild man of the Senate, Cotton Ed Smith, a South Carolina

Democrat. Cotton Ed put a cot in his office and wouldn't budge. He slept in there and lived in there. The maids refused to enter the place to clean because Cotton would spit all over the place when he chewed his tobacco—not even aiming at the spittoon.

Cotton Ed might have been the sloppiest man of the Hill, but he was the neatest at turning a phrase. Ken Black, the president of the Bull Elephants Club, was telling me one day how neatly old Cotton burst Olin Johnston's balloon when Johnston was trying to grab his Senate seat away from him in 1938. "Elect me," said Johnston in a speech, "and I'll go to Washington and I'll bring back the bacon."

Cotton Ed got up and said, "Governor Olin Johnston tells us that if he is elected to the Senate he is going to go to Washington and bring back the bacon. That sounds just fine, but what he didn't tell you is *whose* smokehouse he's going to *put* it in."

One man on the Hill had a wife who would make surprise raids to see if he was hiding whiskey—and he usually was. The poor wife enlisted the help of the office staff but the staff, not wanting to get fired, were very poor searchers for bottles.

Congressman Mendel Rivers had periods in which he seemed always to be under the influence—for days he didn't draw a sober breath. Behind his back, his friends called him "the bottle baby," and they covered for him as best they could.

Rivers was a brilliant man and some said he could be President if only he could conquer old John Barleycorn. If there wasn't a couch for Mendel Rivers to stretch out on when in his cups, he had been known to stretch out on a floor.

When his time came, it wasn't drink that got him, it was open-heart surgery. He didn't survive the operation. When I think of Mendel Rivers—and I often do, with affection—I think of all the people who had jobs because of him and the good that he did in various ways.

Rivers was always fighting to keep defense plants from being closed, as much for the jobs as for defense. As he would tell me, "It's all well and good for these weak sisters to yell, 'Close up the defense plants,' but if you do, you are throwing thousands out of work. The military is seventy percent of the budget. How are you going to give these young men jobs in this modern world?"

Rivers was also greatly concerned about the inadequate pay given the military. When Lyndon Johnson thought he was being very big by recommending a five-percent raise for the military and patting himself on the back, Mendel Rivers blasted him and put through a ten-percent raise.

Even the housewives had reason to bless Rivers. Years back, he thought it was unfair that women had to color their own margarine, which, because of the milk lobby, could only be bought looking like lard, and then colored with a little pellet of gold coloring that came with it. To buy oleo that was already colored meant the housewife had to pay a stiff tax. Rivers fought the milk lobby and the congressmen from the milk states to make life easier for her.

I remember when a plane, which was supposed to be transporting Brother Rivers, the chairman of the Armed Services Committee, arrived without him but with a couple cases of Scotch to show Rivers' intention of at least trying to get aboard.

Some of the worst bitching and bellyaching I have seen on the Hill concerned the natural enmity and sometimes pure hatred between the House and Senate members, which sometimes made it almost impossible to get a bill passed.

More than once, the House and Senate would have to get a time extension on appropriations bills because neither side would walk over to the other side of the Capitol to attend a meeting on the bill.

Clarence Cannon, Democrat of Missouri and chairman of the House Appropriations Committee, could not stand Senator Carl Hayden of Arizona, his Senate committee counterpart. The feeling was mutual. Like a couple of sixty-year-old brats, they would get so mad at each other that they wouldn't cross the center of the Capitol building to meet in conference. Usually, after keeping a bill hanging and having to get a time extension or two, Clarence Cannon would be prevailed on to bow to Carl Hayden's superior age and Cannon would cross over to the House side.

Finally, the matter was resolved when the front of the Capitol was extended outward 32½ feet. A special conference room was built straddling the House and Senate so that both sides could be in the same room and still within its own bailiwick or jurisdiction.

If anyone ever gets down here from Mars, we are going to have a hard time explaining our American form of democracy.

Old Bob Doughton, Democrat of North Carolina, would not go to the other side of the Capitol under any circumstances—for which he was called, and richly deserved to be called, "Muley" Doughton. Though the Other Body is supposed to outrank the House, Senator Harry Flood Byrd, chairman of the Senate Finance Committee, for years one of the most powerful men of the Senate, would have to come humbly to H208 in the House wing of the Capitol to deal with old Muley.

Even till this day, Russell Long, son of Huey, now chairman of the Senate Finance Committee, must go to H208 because Al Ullman, Democrat of Oregon, not only inherited the chairmanship of Muley's old Ways and Means Committee, but his attitudes.

When Congressman Albert Thomas of Texas slipped an appropriations bill through with amendments that Lyndon Johnson, Senate Majority Leader, didn't like, Lyndon proceeded to make life hell for him on any joint legislation.

What had happened is that Thomas, who was head

of the House Appropriations Committee, had sneaked in an amendment after the House and Senate had agreed to a *sine die* resolution that both Houses quit for the rest of the year. The Other Body didn't know until Congress had gone home that the amendment was there.

Another set of bitter enemies—in this case, both in the House—were Clarence Cannon, and "Muley" Doughton, who used to argue with mikes on cords around their necks and forget they had them on. They would get so angry that they would start to walk away from each other to show their contempt and the cords would suddenly jerk them off their feet.

Clarence Cannon was a great parliamentarian. But he would never smile, even at the Democratic Convention where he would be the final word on procedure.

But one day at the Democratic Convention in Chicago in 1952, the photographer caught him smiling in front of the Chicago stockyard where the convention was being held. The congressmen who knew him well said that he was not really smiling. He was just smelling the aroma of the stockyards and it reminded him of home.

Clarence Cannon was especially testy when the Democrats found themselves out of office in 1947, and John Taber of Auburn, New York, became Republican chairman of the committee, leaving Cannon simply the position of ranking minority member.

Cannon and Taber came off the floor after a heavy argument and headed for the men's room, right off the chamber. Cannon had been complaining that Taber was trying to shortchange the poor folks of the country in such matters as welfare and it had disintegrated into a squabble that reached its climax against a backdrop of urinals.

Cannon reached way down and brought his fist up from the floor and it crashed into the glass jaw of Taber. Taber, who was a giant six foot one and over two hundred pounds, went down with a single blow. His eye was closed for two days and remained black, blue and green for a week.

Sometimes, however, what everyone thinks is a feud is pure fake, staged for publicity and home consumption. I knew that was the truth about the famous "feud" that existed between Vito Marcantonio, the ultraliberal Democrat from the sidewalks of New York and my old mentor, Bill Colmer, the ultraconservative Democrat from my hometown of Pascagoula, Mississippi, who, as chairman of the House Rules Committee, controlled which bills came to the floor for vote.

When I would see this duo together behind the rail on the Democratic side, I knew they were cooking up another headline-making confrontation for the following day. Sure enough, Bill Colmer would rise on the floor and accuse Vito of being "soft on Reds" and "selling America down the river" and Colmer would proceed to lambast the New Yorker for a good ten or fifteen minutes.

Colmer would glance up to the press gallery to make sure that his followers had assembled. Before the confrontation, word had filtered through to the press gallery that the Colmer–Marcantonio feud was about to erupt again and reporters would come rushing into the gallery with notebooks.

Then the great liberal, who prided himself on having campaigned on street corners standing on an onion crate, would rise with all the dignity his small stature permitted—having no onion crate—and would tear into the chairman, accusing him of not knowing what the score was in the modern world and being against all progress, especially in fair employment practices. "FEPC, I'm afraid, is just a quaint arrangement of letters to the gentleman from Mississippi. How long must the poor wait for his enlightenment?"

The only thing that stopped these two men—watching how well their words were received in the press gallery—was the Speaker gavelling them down and saying their time had expired.

Even as their stories were being flashed on the wires across the country and set into type at the newspapers, the two men were back in the Democratic cloakroom slapping each other on the back and congratulating themselves and each other on a good performance.

But sometimes the feud is no joke. John Rankin, Democrat of Mississippi, a noted bigot, had been baiting and making life unbearable for a Jewish congressman, Morris Michael Edelstein, for some time, referring to Edelstein as the "friend of the *Daily Worker*," formerly the name of the communist party newspaper.

This particular day, Rankin put it on stronger than ever, questioning Mike's patriotism and casting him in the role of warmonger. It was June 1941, just six months before Pearl Harbor, and I still have the *Congressional Record* that gives Rankin's goading speech which caused such dramatic and terrible consequences.

Of course, that would be the expurgated version, corrected by Congressman Rankin before printing—but even so, the words leap up at me.

Mr. Rankin: "Mr. Speaker, Wall Street and a little group of our international Jewish brethren are still attempting to harass the President of the United States into plunging us into the European war unprepared; and at the same time the Communistic elements throughout the country are fomenting strikes by harassing industry and slowing down our defense program . . ."

He went on and on about Jews, and Edelstein rose to ask for a minute to answer. Choked with feeling, he gave a short retort that I feel is still important today:

"Mr. Speaker, Hitler started out by speaking about 'Jewish brethren.' It is becoming the ploy and the work of those people who want to demagogue to speak about 'Jewish brethren' and 'international bankers.'

"The last speaker, speaking about international bankers, coupled them with our Jewish brethren. The

222

fact of the matter is that the number of Jewish bankers in the United States is infinitesimal. It is also a fact that the meeting which took place yesterday on the steps of the Subtreasury was entirely controlled by persons other than Jewish bankers.

"I deplore the idea that any time anything happens, whether it be for a war policy or against a war policy, men in this House and outside this House attempt to use the Jews as their scapegoat.

"I say it is unfair and I say it is un-American. As a Member of this House I deplore such allegations, because we are living in a democracy. All men are created equal, regardless of race, creed, or color; and whether a man be Jew or Gentile he may think what he deems fit."

The House erupted into applause because someone had finally stood up to the bigoted old hellion of the House. And that applause was the last thing that Congressman Edelstein ever heard. He walked off the floor and fell dead, practically at Rankin's feet.

The strain of his final battle with Rankin had been too much for him, and almost immediately, other members of the House were on their feet eulogizing the dead man, who had been a noted New York lawyer before coming to Congress.

I wish I could say that this event changed Rankin and made him a sweet old man and a penitent one. Nothing could be further from the truth. As he got more senile, he continued to spout anti-Semitism and his next target was Sammy Weiss, a congressman from Pennsylvania, another good friend of mine—in fact, we used to go to football games together.

This time the year was 1944, and we were deep in war. Weiss had gone to Cleveland to make a speech. The next day, the newspaper headlines said, "Congressman Says Fascist Bloc in Congress Hinders War Effort."

One would think that Rankin, who could dish it out,

would not be sensitive. But he proved to be very thin-skinned and insisted that he had been insulted in the speech. He demanded Weiss be censured.

But this time Rankin was dealing with a tougher cookie than Edelstein had ever been. Weiss managed to defend himself ably on the floor.

The score was nothing to nothing.

When it came to bitching and name-calling in more recent times, Democrat Wayne Hays, the "Hairshirt" of the House, chairman of the House Administration Committee, deserved the prize. He had fiendish names for everyone. He called Congressman Don Fraser, who dared stand up to him in the matter of signing a voucher, a "mush head." And almost everyone suffered the name of "potato head" at one time or another, including me.

Hays was never happier than when he was ruining careers. I don't know whether Senator William Fulbright ever knew that Wayne Hays credited himself with having kept Fulbright from being chosen secretary of state by President Kennedy.

According to Hays, Jack Kennedy called him and asked what he thought of the idea of making Fulbright secretary of state. Everyone on the Hill, incidentally, fully expected Kennedy to give that cabinet post to him. According to Hays though, he told the President, "You've got to be kidding, Fulbright dealing with African nations when he's been against all civil rights legislation?"

He left the question dangling and Kennedy, he said, had been amazed he hadn't thought of it himself, and thanked Hays saying, "You're right, Wayne, absolutely right. I hadn't realized that." Since Hays was on the House Foreign Affairs Committee, though down the list a bit, his opinion would be of some interest to the President, but it's impossible to know who else Kennedy asked.

Hays used to laugh and say, "Fulbright wanted that

post so bad he could taste it, and it's been bugging him ever since. Ha, ha."

I sometimes wondered what would have happened if Fulbright had been secretary of state. I thought of it again after Fulbright left Congress and started representing the Arab interests. Could Hays have done the country a good turn in advising against him? Only history can say.

I always wondered when Hays' vitriolic tongue would bring about physical violence. Once a liberal New York congressman, Ben Rosenthal, started to throw a metal pitcher of water at Hays in a committee room during a meeting of the International Relations Committee after Hays made an anti-Semitic remark, but he was stopped by colleagues.

Ethnic slurs came easily from the Bully of the House. He referred to Ralph Nader and his followers as "a bunch of Jew-boys led by an A-rab."

But seldom is anyone punished by his colleagues. In its whole existence, up to the bicentennial year of 1976, the House had censured only eighteen members plus one delegate. For all his cavorting with stripper Fanne Foxe, Wilbur Mills was not censured. He merely lost his chairmanship for what one of his amused colleagues called "conduct unbecoming even to a congressman."

And to show how lenient the Congress has gotten in recent years, all but one of the cases of censure dated back to the nineteenth century.

The way they break down, seven cases involved the use of "unparliamentary language," meaning cussing; two involved "utterance of treasonable language"; two involved insults to the House through the introduction of "offensive resolutions"; and only five involved "corrupt acts." Only two involved actual assault or conspiracy to assault a fellow member—and those dated back to the last century.

Not all the best fights were in the far past. Senator

225

Strom Thurmond, Republican of South Carolina, who ran for the presidency on the States Rights ticket before he came to the Hill, has always kept in marvelous shape. He had a scuffle with Texas Democrat liberal Ralph Yarborough. In no time at all, Thurmond had Yarborough on the floor, and the Texan walked away muttering that it still merely proved that might doesn't always mean right.

THE HOT BREATH OF SCANDAL/WAYNE HAYS AND WILBUR MILLS ARE NOT ALONE

I cannot remember when we haven't had scandalous situations on Capitol Hill. Most get swept under the rug. Only a few know when there has been a near miss of ruining someone's career with those big ugly headlines.

Like all roads lead to Rome, in any discussion of recent Hill scandals the names of Wayne Hays and Wilbur Mills are invariably evoked. In my book, Wayne Hays and Wilbur Mills are pikers compared with the biggest swinger of them all—Adam Clayton Powell, Jr.

But before I tell you of the "King of Harlem" and how I happened to find myself a part of the tangled mess of his unprecedented scandal in the 1960s, let's look over the Hill territory—scandal-wise—to get the lay of the land, so to speak.

As a landmark or guidepost, let me say that because of Adam Clayton Powell, the House, to prevent scandals and to censure those who misbehaved, formed the Ethics Committee. It took ten years from the time the Powell furor began for the Ethics Committee to move again against a congressman—this time for the Sikes conflict of interest.

Robert L. F. Sikes, Democrat of Florida, a thirty-years man of the House, stubbed his toe on Capitol Hill when he was accused of doing too much that would improve his *own* welfare, such as acquiring stock in defense industries without making this fact known. The trouble was, he was chairman of the subcommittee on Appropriations for Military Construction.

227

The Ethics Committee Report asked that Sikes be merely reprimanded for three alleged offenses, the other two having to do with owning stock in a bank which he had used his official position to establish and which he had sold for a profit of $8,500.

The Hill was still playing games, as it had with Powell, by calling it a *reprimand*. If a member is censured, the embarrassment is more acute because he must walk to below the Speaker's desk at the front of the House and stand there listening as the Speaker reads aloud the censure verdict.

I remember a happier time, when Sikes was having a wedding anniversary party in a hearing room at the Rayburn House Office Building. Secretary of Agriculture Earl Butz was one of the honored guests and Sikes wanted to impress him.

Sikes said to me, "Fish, be sure when suppertime comes that the secretary gets some of this nice wild turkey. Would you do this for me?" So I watched the secretary proceed around the reception table and I went over and spoke to him as he stood before the platter of turkey.

Butz looked at the turkey, tasted it and said, "Fishbait, Bob Sikes said this is wild turkey, but it looks to me that's an old Tom that he got last Christmas, tied him up in the backyard and fed him rocks and other things to make the texture of its meat seem as though it were from a wild turkey."

He tasted it again and made a face. "What a way to treat the secretary of agriculture. Even I know you can't fool Mother Nature. And if you tell him, I'm gonna haunt you. But to make him happy, I'm going to have one of the waiters here fix me up a little package of this turkey meat. It really isn't too bad, but it ain't wild turkey."

The Library of Congress made a study and found that from 1904 to 1974 a total of twenty-five congressmen have been indicted for a criminal offense while in office. Of these, sixteen were convicted. Only two congressmen were indicted after they had left office.

Ethics means many things to many people on the Hill. Stephen J. Skubik, who collected *The Republican Humor Book,* likes to repeat the story on Ethics told to him by a member of the Republican National Committee.

A congressman who had been accused of unethical practices was asked by his teen-aged son just exactly what the committee meant by the word *ethics.*

The congressman allowed as how it was a hard word to define but that he thought he could make his son understand best by giving an example. "Let's assume," he said, "that my partner and I own a retail store. A customer comes in and buys something for $5 and gives me a $20 bill. I give him change for ten. Now ethics is, should I tell my partner?"

The brush of scandal is a wide brush and it touches all kinds of people as it makes a wide sweep around Capitol Hill.

Just before Speaker Carl Albert announced he was not running again in 1976, he was brushed by the charge that his hideaway room—the one we called "the Board of Education"—had been used for sex orgies. But he personally was not linked with such escapades.

Congressman John McCormack was deeply embarrassed when it developed that one of his top aides in the Speaker's Office had been influence-peddling and had even imitated his boss' voice on the phone.

The aide was quickly out of office and it was never charged that McCormack was aware of his activities. Even so, I think it helped the Speaker make up his mind not to run again. It was too much of a jungle up there, even for a Massachusetts politician.

Eyebrows were raised when it was reported that another Massachusetts politician, Tip O'Neill, the

229

House Democratic leader, was not only distributing campaign funds to needy Democratic candidates who had tough competition in 1974, but also generously gave money to candidates who had no opposition. It might not be illegal, but reformers wondered whether campaign contributions should be dispersed to help a powerful man become more powerful.

Even Jimmy Carter felt a slight touch of the brush before he had gotten well into his campaign, with a report that some of his $1,000 contributions were coming from names which belonged to children scarcely out of the cradle. The serious point there, which goes beyond Carter, is that kid contributions could become the sneaky way of getting around the $1,000 limit on donations from any one person. Also, since taxpayers were footing much of the bill in 1976, for the first time, by matching the first $250 of each private donation, this could amount to quite a bit of loot and be unfair to those of us who pay taxes.

Hubert Humphrey was touched by the brush in 1974, when certain campaign funds were being investigated. As a result, a top official of the milk lobby, David L. Parr, pleaded guilty to providing illegal corporate donations to Humphrey's campaigns, not once but in several elections in a row.

Parr was charged in 1974 with felony in allegedly conspiring to make corporate contributions not only to Humphrey's campaign but those of Jim Abourezk, senator from South Dakota, Wilbur Mills and Dick Clark—congressmen from Arkansas and Iowa. Eventually, Parr was sentenced to four months in prison and fined $10,000.

Let me tell you what kind of money Parr was alleged to have funneled to Humphrey, so you can see the kind of figures we're talking about—$63,500 in 1968 for a "Salute to the Vice President" dinner, plus another $38,000 for presidential campaign expenses in various states. Plus $23,950 in 1970 to help in the

230

Humphrey senatorial race. Adds up to $125,450.

Senator Henry Jackson and Congressman Wilbur Mills were touched when Gulf Oil Corporation pleaded guilty to making illegal corporation money contributions to their presidential campaigns.

Ed Gurney of Florida, the handsomest senator on the Watergate panel, found his own tail in the crack on charges of bribery and conspiracy in setting up a slush fund. But the case had a happy ending when he was found innocent.

It's hard to know where to start or end in talking about corruption or possible scandals on the Hill.

Remember when Nixon got into trouble during his first run as Vice President with Eisenhower in 1952? He almost got tossed off the ticket until he made a great TV appeal, in what was called his Checkers speech, defending his slush fund of $18,000 to pay for political travel and staff.

Well, that kind of fund is fairly routine these days. Now many, many congressmen have slush funds called "office funds donations." Some of these funds are treated as taxable income from which business expenses are deducted. Such a fund is that of Charles Rangel, Democrat of New York, who took in $5,200 in just one day for something called the "Rangel Educational Fund." The fund, his office said, would pay for a newsletter and would pay for young constituents coming to Washington.

He's *one* who is telling what he gets. Others won't tell.

It is estimated that about one hundred congressmen keep unreported office funds. But now that campaign laws have been changed, it may be that such funds will have to be made public. And also there is the question of whether such contributions can legally be made by unions or corporations.

Some say it is legal if the corporation gives money to a congressman for running his office but it is not

231

legal for campaigning. So the question is, can a congressman use his office money, supplied by Uncle Sam, for campaign purposes and his corporation contributions for running his office?

Finances on the Hill can be very tricky.

Maybe Congressman Jerome Waldie, a Democrat from California, was right when he retired from Congress mid-term at age forty-seven—after eight and a half years—saying, "I don't believe anyone should be in Congress more than nine years. The danger of being there too long is that it's very hard to leave and go elsewhere."

What he didn't say is that it also gets harder and harder to stay scrupulously honest and above the taking of any easy path.

After I was out of office, Jack Anderson sent his reporters to the Hill to see what dirt they could come up with about me and what came out was a very amusing column—the humor at my expense. It was all about how I was supposedly making money on ladies'-room sanitary napkin machines and also making money on empty soft drink bottles that I had been seen picking up.

Just to set the record straight, the House Committee on Accounts did not supply money for the very necessary supply for the machines in the ladies' rest rooms and I had no choice but to order the delicate product in large quantity for the female restroom attendants to keep the dispensers filled. I had my own small revolving fund for this purpose, but as for making money, it went the other way because the machines were broken into and robbed on a regular basis once a month.

As for the bottles, I certainly did pick them up wherever I found them—they were unsightly and a danger to congressmen not watching where they were walking. But what I did with them is take them to the nearest Capitol snack bar or restaurant for them to get the refunds, if any.

But I know how afraid the Congress in general is of Jack Anderson's column. I remember when we were returning from a trip to Austin, Texas, after the dedication of the Johnson library, a bunch of the congressmen wanted to play cards and were all set to deal when one of them said laughingly, "Do you suppose a spy for Jack Anderson is on this plane?"

They decided to put the cards away, muttering that they could not afford to tangle with Anderson.

I remember one of Anderson's reporters, Bob Owens, phoned me at home after my retirement to ask a lot of questions about the bottles and the sanitary napkins. I tried to explain, but the story came out anyway—without giving my side. I remember too that the reporter asked, "What's this about you making three phone calls in December and not paying the $3.05 when your successor James T. Malloy notified you about it?"

I explained that Mrs. Miller had written the check and mailed it to Malloy the day we got the letter from him telling us about the calls I still owed for. (When I had left office, the December bill hadn't arrived yet.)

Then Owens brought out a silly question about whether it wasn't true that girl pages refused to come to my office because I would follow the Biblical admonition of 1st Peter, chapter 5, verse 14, to "Greet ye one another with a kiss of charity." And I agreed with him that it was not true. I did follow the Biblical admonition, but not with little girl pages and I knew my limitations. Also, I assured him that, far from ignoring my office, the girl pages were popping in all the time for soft drinks, peanuts and other goodies I kept for staff and congressmen.

It's hard to say what is completely behind a story when a scandal breaks. Sometimes a man is almost an innocent victim of people trying to get at someone else. The story on the Hill was that forces must have been trying to tarnish the Kennedy image when Stewart Udall was put through so much agony after being picked up for shoplifting.

I had known Stewart when he was elected to Congress and took his oath of office on January 3, 1955. He was a model congressman, had a fine personality, did his homework well, served with distinction and President John F. Kennedy appointed him secretary of the interior. He resigned from Congress January 18, 1961, to take the cabinet post, and he served until January 1969 when Nixon came into office.

What happened on that unfortunate occasion of his arrest is that Stu had gone into a drugstore in McLean, Virginia, to buy some cigars. Then, as he told the story, and I believe him, he had remembered something his wife wanted and had gone to another section to get it. Without thinking, he stuck the cigars in his pocket and forgot they were there.

Instead of just reminding him of what he had done, the store had him arrested and a lot of unfortunate publicity took place.

He was fingerprinted and photographed like a common criminal, over the 95 cents worth of cigars. That was on January 17, 1971. Eleven days later, Stu appeared before Judge J. Mason Groves in Fairfax County and the case was dismissed because the store did not press charges. But it had been a devastating experience. As Stu said later, "I'm shocked at how dehumanized the store protection systems are. Everyone acts like an automaton. There is no room for normal human communication." He explained that even though he had readily admitted what he had absentmindedly done and assured the store that he had no intention of cheating them, no one would listen.

"Once the arrest was made," he said, "everyone

234

I turned to, including the arresting officer, the justice of the peace and the store manager, refused to listen to me and said, 'It's out of my hands.' " I consider this a sad page in the story of our democracy.

When is nepotism a scandal and when isn't it? Supposedly, the hiring of relatives is outlawed, and has been since 1967, but the question then arises, is it still nepotism if a member of a representative's or senator's family gets a job on a colleague's staff or committee? In the summer of the great Bicentennial year of 1976, I was surprised at how little progress had been made by the nation in keeping wage earners on the Hill confined to only one per family. All kinds of relatives showed up on other members' payrolls—just to mention a few, two children of William Clay, Democrat of Missouri, surfaced on the payrolls of Charles Wilson of California, and Louis Stokes of Ohio (both Democrats); the daughter of Republican Edward Derwinski turned up on the payroll of Robert Michel of Illinois (Republican, of course); and the daughter of Democratic Congressman John McFall showed up on the House Post Office and Civil Service Committee.

But to correct any impression that only female members of families were involved in the job game of musical chairs, the son of Gus Yatron, Democrat of Pennsylvania, surfaced on the payroll of the House Administration Committee and one of those children of Bill Clay, who was mentioned earlier—the one who went to work for Congressman Wilson—was a son.

People ask me, "How are you going to keep congressmen and senators from getting rich or corrupted in office?" I reply, as truthfully as I can, that I just don't know how to keep them completely above board, unless they already are.

Lobbyists can do a lot of favors. How can everything be covered? If they give stock to the wives, how can the watchdogs know? Many things that can be done to help a congressman get buried and he can act completely innocent. Money or stock, or whatever, can be given to his child. Senator Dirksen kept most things in his wife's name and everyone knew it.

The congressman can hint that he's worried about his family and wish that something be done to help one of his children. I heard that even FDR, right from the White House, was drumming up a little business for a son who was in the insurance game.

And many congressmen and senators belong to law firms. Though they may not be practicing law for the firm while they are in Congress, a constituent who chooses that law firm knows he isn't hurting himself. The congressmen do keep in touch with their old friends in the firm and may someday return to it. All these points add up. The congressmen know that someday they'll go back and they'll get some rewards if only in the increased value of the firm.

But for instant money, when lobbyists play poker games with congressmen they suddenly become lousy players and many a man on the Hill has found himself a card-game winner. On the Hill, if a man wanted to protect his reputation, he almost had to be careful who he gambled with. And incidentally, if a man couldn't play bridge, they would have played the child's game "Fish" if that would land money in the congressman's pocket.

Lobbyists around the Hill would always tell me what they were doing was perfectly proper, pointing out that even the Constitution says in the First Amendment that people have the right "to petition Government for a redress of grievances."

So what happens is companies hire the individual who is best at petitioning and they have some smoothies. But really, the smoothest ones are not even lobbyists at all but lawyers who simply stay behind the scenes and advise clients about which person is a friend of which congressman, what this and that congressman really wants in life or what the congressman's problems are.

My job was to keep out the cleverest of the lobbyists, the ex-congressmen. According to the House rule which was passed in the last century, former congressmen cannot come on the floor of the House during debate if they have a financial interest in a bill.

It had gotten so bad with past congressmen coming on the floor and making deals and standing like watchdogs to see that "the man" continued to vote "right," meaning "as bought," that a rule was necessary.

In the Roosevelt administration, a start was made in requiring some lobbyists to register so the congressmen and the public could know that a man was being paid to say what he was saying. It wasn't just from his heart. And the Truman administration encouraged Congress to expand the number of lobbyists who had to register. They usually don't call themselves lobbyists, however, they call themselves "industry representatives" or "trade group representatives" or just plain "Washington representatives."

Only one time did I have to throw out a lobbyist. He was a man of the cloth—a Catholic priest—so I hated to do it, but he was buttonholing all the members right in the doorway as they came into the House Democratic Cloakroom and telling them to vote for aid to Spain.

I was standing there debating what to do, but Congressman Wright Patman of Texas quickly took in the situation and said, "Fishbait, you know that's illegal. Remove that priest." So I did.

There's nothing wrong with lobbyists *per se*. As they say on the Hill, "If it weren't for the lobbyists, half the bills would never get passed through Congress," or even written for that matter.

Most of the good bills were pushed through by

237

lobbyists pressuring congressmen, explaining, helping to write the bill and all that.

The bad part comes in when a lobbyist bribes a congressman in one of a hundred ways so that the congressman isn't thinking of the bill and what it will do for the country, but only what it will do for him. He's offered things like trips on yachts with girls supplied for any purpose the congressman chooses—he's king for a day; things like plane rides, jobs for relatives, tips on the stock market, little attentions at Christmas, parties for fund-raising.

But heck, lobbying isn't an evil in itself. Also, not all lobbying is to get a bill passed. Sometimes it's to get a bill stopped. Or just to get a congressman in a good frame of mind for when the lobbyists do have a bill they'll want passed or stopped in the future.

Ken Gray of Illinois was one of many congressmen who turned lobbyist. One of the best dressers on Capitol Hill, he was one of the most successful of the lobbyists—with a big boat moored at the marina.

I remember when a secretary on the Hill told me that she was taking her husband to the Gray yacht. "My husband's been indifferent to me lately," she said, "and maybe what he sees there at a fun party will turn him on enough for me to take over when we get home."

That was long before another Hill secretary stepped forward to say that she had been on the Gray yacht with Elizabeth Ray when Senator Mike Gravel of Alaska had been another guest and that she had just happened to see, through a window, Elizabeth Ray and the senator together in a compromising position.

To put it as bluntly as Colleen Gardner did, she said she saw Liz and Gravel having "sexual relations." Senator Gravel indignantly denied it. He could not even remember being on the boat. Ken Gray could not remember either. Nothing came of it and many turned on Colleen, saying she was just trying to get in on some of the publicity that Liz Ray was enjoying.

What made it especially hard for Colleen to get her point across was that she was involved in another kiss and tell case. In fact, she had been trying for three years to get someone to believe her charges against Representative John Young.

The beautiful Colleen Gardner, a 28-year-old divorcée, claimed that Congressman John Young of Corpus Christi, Texas, had given her raises so that she finally earned a whopping $25,800 because she went along with his sexual advances.

The Hill gang, who had been feeling sorry for the 59-year-old Young because of his very poor eyesight and trouble with a cataract, were amazed. They didn't think he had it in him. Though the pretty Colleen insisted that she had been trying to interest the FBI authorities in her case, nothing came of it because Colleen actually was performing her duties as a secretary as well, so there was no effort to defraud the government. What she chose to do besides office work was her own business.

The difference with Liz Ray and the reason that Wayne Hays got his tail in a crack was that Liz insisted that the government had been defrauded. She had been paid $14,000 a year, she said, on Wayne's House Administration Committee, to do nothing but be available for servicing him sexually. "I can't even type and I can't file," she protested.

It was ironic that when the man most feared on the Hill was toppled, it was by a self-acknowledged dumdum.

But let's examine the situation from Liz's standpoint.

Why was Elizabeth Ray getting herself talked about unfavorably and thrown out of a job? It didn't make sense at first. She was making this wild accusation that made her look bad—and who on the Hill would hire a girl who kissed and told?

What had happened was jealousy. Hays, one of the

sexiest men on the Hill, had decided to get married. He really loved the girl who headed his Ohio office, Pat Peak, I believe.

He had been known to be involved with Liz Ray and had been very careful not to sit at the same table with her, even when both ate at such places on the Hill as the Monocle or the Rotunda. He would be at one table with staff or friends, and she would be at another with friends.

But off the Hill they had been seen together plenty at a particular hideaway restaurant in Virginia, near Liz's apartment. And the facts are that Hays had hired Liz and had given her a fine office where, she said, she fixed her nails and didn't even answer the phone because she didn't know how to answer the questions about committee work that she might be asked.

Everything seemed to be coasting along fine until Hays dropped the bombshell, telling Liz not to get excited or make waves but that he was going to marry Pat Peak, his secretary in his Ohio office.

Liz claimed to be grief stricken and asked to be invited to the wedding. The congressman, she said, refused. She said he promised that after he was married things might still be all right between them.

Why Liz decided on what to do next, I wonder. What she did was spill the beans about a book that she was writing as a novel based on her own life. And she spilled it to reporters she had called in. She may not have learned how to type, but she had learned how to leak a story effectively.

The book—a paperback entitled *The Washington Fringe Benefit,* with a heroine having Liz's own name —told of Liz's affair, not only with the main character, a powerful congressman, but with other congressmen and senators around the Hill, all with fictitious names. And it was assured its own fringe benefit in short order —financial backing for the making of a movie with nude scenes and Liz Ray in the starring role, playing herself. The Hill crowd had to admit, though ruefully, that it was a most historic first.

But even as Liz was flying to England to publicize her book, Wayne Hays lay near death. Hays, who had at first denied everything and then had admitted the affair in an unprecedented speech on the floor, was in a hospital back home in Ohio, suffering the effects of an overdose of sleeping pills.

The Hill crowd murmured that they had never seen anything like it—usually the girl who tells loses her job and slinks away in shame, and here was a girl who was striding away into the sunset in a storybook happy ending.

Now let's look at the situation from Wayne Hays' standpoint. To see why the Hill crowd chortled when the hot blaze of scandal hit him and there was not enough sympathy to put into a teardrop in the corner of an eye, you would have to have seen Hays in those final days leading to that sexploitation exposé.

Hays was in a vicious mood in the early months of 1976, and it was like an old morality play, the way he rose to the most feverish pitch of obstreperous behavior just before his own downfall. First, in January, he was very abusive of Thomas B. Curtis, chairman of the Federal Elections Commission, who was checking into an elections complaint about a member on Wayne Hays' House Administration Committee.

When poor Tom Curtis, a dear friend of mine and a former congressman, had the misfortune of appearing before Hays' Administration Committee, Hays subjected him to a vicious attack and threatened that if Curtis ever tried to audit his campaign expenses, "I'll take you to court so damned fast you won't be able to pronounce your name."

Hays was just as tough in talking to Max L. Friedersdorf of the White House several months later, threatening to close up the whole United States Information Agency by blocking its emergency funds if President

241

Ford vetoed a revision of the campaign reform laws.

Warning that the President better not veto the bill "until he sees what the hell he's going to veto," Hays made one of his typical bullying moves, guaranteed to injure a lot of innocent bystanders by taking the bread out of their mouths.

"Two people can play this veto game," Hays said, "and if I don't bring up the USIA authorization bill, that's a kind of veto because if they don't get $4 million or $5 million soon, they'll be out of business."

Almost anything set Wayne Hays off in those early months. Once it was the service he had received in an Eastern Airlines plane that triggered his temper, and he rose to his feet on the floor saying that he had just sent a letter off to Frank Borman, president of Eastern and former astronaut, after being informed that the airline was seeking a fare increase.

"I replied to Mr. Borman this morning," Hays said, "and I told him it had been my misfortune through an error on the part of one of my staff to be booked on Eastern Airlines to Miami last Tuesday. I had never been on a dirtier airplane with ruder personnel in my life.

"I was in the first-class section, which had been reconverted from tourist. It had not been very well reconverted. As far as the food I was served, I am sorry I did not have any hogs on my farm because I would have saved that food and taken it home to them. . . ."

Hays ended his assault by saying that if Borman could not clean up the plane, get better service and "be polite . . . I suggest he might want to return to the Moon and stay there."

Wayne Hays' temper did not improve as his remarriage approached. Just before he got married, he had his office send a document for translation to the Library of Congress. The next day, he asked his secretary what had been done about the translation.

242

Her reply was, "Mr. Chairman, I'm advised that it will take about three weeks to get that."

This was just the kind of answer that set him off. He said, "Well, I don't give a damn what they say, get that man on the phone."

When the secretary got someone from the translation section on the phone, the conversation was brutal. Evidently the man on the other end had said that he could get the translation done in three days if it was that important. Hays said, "I don't give a damn if it's going to take three days. I want it in six hours today or else heads will be rolling in the Library of Congress. Remember, I'm a member of the Joint Committee on the Library."

He hung up and he had his translation within three hours. I can imagine that every available man was immediately put on the job, as always happened when Hays cracked his whip.

The day the congressman was to be married to Patricia Peak, he was to have a reception at his committee office. He alerted the whole police force, telling them that the same strict parking regulations were to be followed as was usual for a Joint Session or Joint meeting.

Fortunately, Congress adjourned early that day and quite a few parking spaces opened immediately.

Hays was the kind of guy who was too nervous to let anything develop naturally. If he asked me for extra tickets, he would write it on a piece of paper and say, "I'm going to check up on you."

I would say, "I'll put your name down and I will send the tickets over to you." He would keep coming over so that I would not give his tickets to anyone else to deliver to him. "Damn it, I'll conduct my own business," he would say. For some reason, he didn't want to owe any favors.

Yet he was capable of doing some strangely generous things himself, which made others very grateful to *him;*

for example, he took the *maitre d'* of the House Restaurant, Ernest Petinaud, on one of his trips abroad and newspapers had seized on it.

Ernie came back saying it had been no lark. "I never worked so hard in my life. I don't care what Jack Anderson says." Petinaud, a black man, is a linguist speaking four foreign languages and he did quite a bit of translating for Hays.

When Hays was laid low by Liz's knockout punch, I thought of how truly ironic it was that once, years before, as you will soon see, Hays had been on the side of righteousness when, as a committee chairman, he questioned an employee of Adam Clayton Powell and illicited information similar to what Elizabeth Ray was spilling—in the Powell case, that she had taken trips for nonworking purposes.

And I also thought of the vast difference there was in the attitude of their colleagues when Wayne Hays and Wilbur Mills got their tails caught in the crack.

With Mills, there was great consternation and sympathy because he had been such a good guy. He just had gone temporarily adrift.

But with Hays, it was different. He had been so mean to so many people that, instead of clucking sympathetically, his colleagues were drinking toasts to Liz and practically dancing a jig.

It took a Republican, Pete McCloskey of California, to tell it like it was, saying Hays had chewed out so many people it was time he was getting some of his own medicine—to which many on the Hill said amen.

When Hays took himself out of the race by resigning, I doubt there was a wet eye in the House, except maybe that belonging to some staffer who might have trouble finding another job.

I have to tell you that I like Wilbur Mills a lot. I know for a time he seemed gone on a stripper-dancer and she almost ruined his marriage and that he fell from grace on Capitol Hill. But he is a dear man. A sweet man and a great man. Years from now, they will tell about how wise he was—until love blinded him in his sunset years—and how much he did for the country.

And he was one of the most hard-working men on the Hill. Maybe that was part of his problem. He worked too hard. When I first was in the House Post Office, he was trying to get ahead even then, and his wife, Polly, would come on Saturdays, bringing the children and keeping him company as he studied legislation and caught up on his office work.

To help him keep his office quiet, I would take the little kids with me. I would give each one a silver dollar for being good and they still have them and remind me when they see me that those dollars are now worth $5 apiece.

To show the caliber of the man, when Mills arrived in Washington from Kensett, Arkansas, another freshman congressman came at the same time from the same state, William F. Norrell. In respect for the other man's older age, Wilbur Mills stepped aside and let Bill be the dean of the Arkansas delegation, which Norrell was until his death in 1961.

Wilbur Mills has always been my friend and I consider him my friend today. Nothing can change that. He was one of the keenest minds on the Hill, but I think he cracked up for a period of time as a result of two things: one was his love of booze—he was one of the hearty drinkers of the Hill—and the other was his love of the presidency. He really did want to be President very badly, and when no one took him seriously it broke his heart.

He had been serious all his life and so, as a reaction, he suddenly flipped and became very frivolous. He just didn't seem to care about his Hill work any more the way he had all through the years. I felt very bad, seeing him go downhill, and I knew he was spending too much time nightclubbing at a strip joint, of all things.

But I do believe that for one mad moment Wilbur Mills did truly love the stripper Annabel Battistella, who danced under the name of Fanne Foxe, the Argentine firecracker. Maybe he would have gotten a divorce like so many other men on the Hill did to marry a younger, more sexy looking woman.

But Mills was one of the lucky ones. He *didn't* blow it all on a will-of-the-wisp dream. He *did* get help and he *did* come back to his senses. And what was wonderful to me is that his long-suffering wife, Polly, whom I've known all through the years, hung on that extra time it took for him to get straightened out and even went with him to keep him company at a sanitarium. Later I heard him say, "It's a miracle. I'm coming out all right and I feel better than I have in twenty-five years. I've got a good feeling inside, and I feel too damn good to give it up for a drink of whiskey."

I believe that physical pain might also have intensified his drinking problem in the early 1970s. Few people knew that he was suffering with a bad back. He finally had a disc operation which corrected his back problem in 1973.

Though Wilbur lost his chairmanship of the Ways and Means Committee, which once made him the most powerful man in the House next to the Speaker, and though he decided not to run for reelection in 1976, I still call this a story with a happy ending.

It's amusing that when congressmen get caught with their tail in the crack these days, their fortunes go down but the fortunes of the girls they were involved with zoom up. When Fanne Foxe went on to write a book about her life with Wilbur Mills, her value as a top stripper went sky high. The word on the Hill was that she was going to make a movie and that might have given Elizabeth Ray the idea that her own life was movie material, too.

The Silver Slipper, incidentally, where Mills had watched Foxe dance, became a mecca for tourists hoping to catch a glimpse of Fanne or some famous congressmen. But the publicity Mills had gotten had frightened away other Hill customers, and the word was that nearby Archibald's, with its topless dancing girls, was a lot safer for the Hill crowd in search of a little visual stimulation.

At Archibald's, the management watches like a hawk for reporters, photographers and other snoops and alerts its sensitive Hill guests of any such invasion. Usually, a congressman wanting to watch topless go-go girls caper and to be served by topless bar girls brings a gang of males with him for camouflage. Also, someone phones ahead to make sure that the coast is clear and there are no press people around.

In Washington, there is a unique situation—the press people memorize the faces of congressmen, but headwaiters and congressmen memorize the faces of reporters.

And this might amuse you: Jack Anderson once brought his own cameraman and wanted a picture with me—when he inherited the column from Drew Pearson—to show he was in the know around the Hill.

Not everything practiced on the Hill is what congressmen like to call "he-ing and she-ing." There are some men that the congressmen delicately describe by saying, "He wears lace panties."

Senator David Ignatious Walsh of Massachusetts had a big puffy face and sounded like he had a mouthful of buttermilk in his mouth when he talked.

The story was told and retold on Capitol Hill that a Boston department store magnate had said he would trust his daughter with Senator Walsh, even across the ocean in a yacht, but that he wouldn't trust his son to the Senator's benign care across the Charles River in a canoe.

Walsh made waves when he was picked up by police during World War II in a Boston joint which was patronized by sailors. Civilian men were known to come there to meet sailors.

The FBI was suspicious that espionage might be taking place, so they raided the joint and found no subversive activity—but they did find Senator Walsh.

Another congressman who got into a little trouble with the police concerning activities with members of the same sex was picked up by the police when he was parked in the Virginia countryside in an automobile with a young boy. As the amused congressman explained the situation on Capitol Hill, "He was not prosecuted because he had swallowed the evidence."

I was talking with an economist-historian, Jack Ben-Rubin, about the masculinity of the Hill men through history, and he brought a book to show me—*Woodrow Wilson: American Prophet* by Arthur Walworth. In it, President Wilson disgustedly said of a particular senator that he was "so feminine that it was immodest of him to wear trousers."

As I wrote this book, word had just come from South Carolina that a man who appeared unsuccessfully before the Senate Judiciary Committee after being nominated by President Nixon for the Supreme Court —G. Harrold Carswell—was arrested by a vice-squad policeman in a parked car in a wooded area.

The officer making the arrest in this case was already in the car. He had driven with Carswell after allegedly permitting himself to be picked up by the former Supreme Court nominee in the rest room of a Tallahassee, Florida, shopping center which had been staked out because of complaints of homosexual activity.

The officer said that Carswell had "touched" him in the car and that, under the Florida law, this constituted "battery." Since Carswell was not a congressman, and this was 1976, he did not fare so well. No longer were the newspapers delicately alluding to gay world activity as "an offense too loathsome to mention in the Senate or in any group of ladies or gentlemen." In fact, the *New York Times* said in the lead of its story on October 2, 1976, that Carswell "was accused of making homosexual advances to an undercover police officer" and that he had been convicted of "battery."

Carswell pleaded no contest, was found guilty and fined $100.

On the Hill, there would frequently be rumors about some congressman or senator who would be willing to pay $20 or so to be "serviced" by a young man, and there were several male staffers who allegedly padded their income with this pin money.

There also were some congressmen and senators who gave little gifts of $20 or $25 to Hill monkeys—those of whom it was said, "they hold their job by the tail."

We had one congressman on the Hill who was known as "the Gay Millionaire," and "the Gay Caballero." He was a bachelor and he made no effort to hide his sexual preference or to get married as a cover, but James Fulton did draw the line at one thing—he wouldn't tell his age.

Fulton, a Republican from Pittsburgh who died in Washington in 1971 while in office, was a fine legislator for twenty-six years and a progressive who wouldn't let anyone—including leadership—tell him what to do. He led a comfortable life, with a home in Pittsburgh and a nearby farm called "The Golden Pheasant Farm."

The way Brother Fulton tried to hide his age had the Capitol Hill crowd swearing his hair was "the blackest thing in the House." He would touch it up himself and it seemed always to be full of dye—pitch

249

black. Secretaries would say they hoped they would never have to touch it.

Jim Fulton's age was omitted even in his biography in the *Congressional Directory*. The closest he came to telling was to say he had been with a law firm in the early 1930s and had been a member of the Allegheny County Board of Law Examiners for eight years, beginning in 1934.

Naturally, when the good gentleman died in October 1971, the first thing his colleagues did was to find out when he was born and figure out that when he died he must've been about sixty-eight—considered a fairly young age around the Hill.

There was a particular congressman who prided himself on the gargantuan size of his male organs. That is, he prided himself until one of the female monkeys drew the line at him. In a moment of revelation, she confided to me that she would not have anything to do with this monster. "I told him no thanks, I didn't need any little presents. There was nothing I wanted to buy for myself. I wouldn't have anything to do with that one for a $40 present. He must be half-animal."

Until he found someone else more accommodating, the congressman went around with a furious temper directed at everyone on his staff or committee.

When I first came to the Hill in the 1930s, congressmen had a little trouble getting privacy when they found a pretty girl they were trying to seduce. They had to share their own office with their secretaries. When I worked in the House Post Office, I noticed that certain congressmen's secretaries were forever being sent over to us on some little errand. As I got acquainted with the congressmen, I learned why. They would send their secretaries out on any errand so that the coast would be clear.

Of course, the most powerful congressmen and senators have always had extra little hideaway offices. I remember once seeing a certain congressman peeping

250

out the door of his hideaway as if looking for someone. As I passed by that office again a half hour later, I saw the congressman upbraiding a certain Hill secretary for keeping him waiting. "You made me call you," he blustered, as if a congressman having to handle a telephone himself was the greatest indignity.

"I know I did," said the secretary soothingly. "And I'm sorry. I thought a *lady* always waited to be called."

Enormously amused at this thought, the congressman slapped his leg and roared, and then put his arm around her tenderly as he drew her into the unmarked room.

Staid senators can behave like hot-headed cowboys in a western when they find someone making time with their gals. A certain senator, known as a fine family man, became so jealous when he found his secretary with another man that he charged him like a mad bull. The man returned in kind and hit the senator over the head with a chair. This particular girl must have had something very special. She quit the senator and went to work for another government bigshot who also became enamored of her. So much so that he later died of a heart attack from exerting himself too much while with her in her motel room. As for the senator who had endured the chair over his head in her defense, he as it turned out was the lucky one—all he suffered was a black eye.

The fact that Congressman Allan Howe of Utah was a Mormon made it especially hard on him in June 1976 when he got his tail caught in a sex-for-hire trap. What can a young congressman do when he is arrested in Salt Lake City on charges of soliciting sex from two female police-decoy prostitutes and his religious leader, Spencer Kimball, president of the Church of Latter-Day Saints, calls for him to resign? As does the senator of his state, fellow Democrat Frank E. Moss.

He could do two things. He could resign or he

251

could get other important people to demand that he stand and fight and clear his name. That's just what Allan Howe did—the latter—he amassed an impressive group to help him stand and fight.

In a fund-raising party which followed on the heels of the "unfortunate incident," Marlene Dee Howe stood beside her husband to say she had utter faith in his innocence. One after another, the Democratic hierarchy of the House stopped in at the fund-raiser to stand before the microphone and put in a good word for "this fine man." Even Speaker Carl Albert and Majority Leader Tip O'Neill came to express their solidarity.

That is the more unusual way such charges are handled. Usually the case does not go to court, as Howe's did, and usually everybody on the Hill sort of closes their eyes and tries to pretend nothing has happened, unless the case gets the publicity that the Wilbur Mills' and Wayne Hays' got. In such cases, the rest of the congressmen usually try to avoid even being seen talking to the member who has been seared by the hot blaze of publicity—until it all dies down.

And what was the outcome of Howe's court case? Thirty days, suspended sentence.

About the last person you'd expect to find caught with his tail in the crack is young-looking 62-year-old Harry Flood Byrd, Jr., of Virginia. I remember his senator daddy who built up the apple orchard business in Virginia and became the "apple king" of America. Never was there a breath of scandal about him, except that LBJ, who used to visit Byrd, taking along the White House dogs, said that the way the Byrd dog treated his beagles was a scandal. Harry, Jr., seemed to be following in his father's footsteps, but in the Bicentennial year of 1976 a young woman claimed that she had gone to the senator for help and had been *helped* to a bed instead. The case was very strange and got weirder as it went on.

Had the story been permitted to run its normal course, it might have died an early death. Or it might not even have been taken too seriously since it was just an item in Jack Anderson's column under the subtitle of "Capitol Hill Bedroom Survey."

But the famed *Washington Post* suddenly got righteous and did not carry this particular column. That made editors all over the country ask their reporters to look into the case of Harry Byrd, Jr., to see what the *Post* wouldn't print.

Adding fuel to the fire, the executive editor of the *Post*, Benjamin Bradlee, felt called upon to write a five-column editorial on why he had killed the story. What his explanation amounted to was a contention that everything about the woman involved was so strange that it seemed to discredit her—and besides, she had filed no legal complaint about the senator seducing her.

Basically, the story is that a voluptuous young woman claimed her husband had disappeared and she suspected he had been done in by the Mafia and had gone to see her senator, Harry Byrd, Jr.

The senator had listened to her and invited her to come to his in-town apartment—he has a gorgeous home in Winchester, Virginia, too—in order to hear more about it. Instead of assisting her in finding her husband, however, the senator had, according to the bereft wife, tumbled her into bed. So desperate was she for help that she had gone along with it at first, she said, only stopping when she realized the senator would not or could not help her.

In his column, Bradlee said his reporter had found out that the lady in question had complained many times to the Fairfax, Virginia, chief of police about other matters, but never about the senator. For example, she had complained about "female neighbors [who] were having homosexual affairs *al fresco* on the back porch of a neighboring house." And that people

253

were digging holes in her backyard in the middle of the night.

But what the neighbors said about her was equally odd. According to Bradlee, his reporter Donnel Nunes had been told that the lady in question would tie her dog up with rope outside when it was in heat and stand watching with her daughter as all the male neighborhood dogs took turns mounting it.

But the question before the Senate was not whether the senator had or had not had an affair with the voluptuous dog *voyeur*. The question was and is whether he used his office to receive something of value—sex—under false pretenses. In the Ray–Hays case, the charge was that the congressman had made the *government* pay for sex that *he* had received. In the Byrd case, the woman's charge was that he made the lady give something of value for service which he should have *given* as part of his *duty* to his constituents for which the taxpayers paid him.

The congressmen, confused by the sudden topsy-turvy world of ethics and scandals, were hurriedly saying they weren't there to judge men's private lives but they were there to protect the public purse and would hound down anyone who used the taxpayers' money to finance their sex lives. "Play on public pay" was not to be tolerated.

Even the shielding of public officials when they got into trouble for being naughty with hookers was being discussed by local Washington police, who had thrown away many a traffic or sex-offense report when it concerned a high official.

The rule in Washington police circles in the past was that a congressman could only be arrested on a serious charge like murder or treason—while Congress was in session. The history of that went back many years to the early days of the Capitol, when legislation might be held up because of little misdemeanor charges against one of the early congressmen.

254

But that leniency was stopped abruptly in July 1976 after the chief of police, Maurice J. Cullinane, consulted with the mayor of Washington, D. C., Walter Washington, and the House and Senate District Committee. All decided that congressional types would just have to behave themselves like anyone else. Amen.

Now, finally, let me tell you about the "King of Harlem," Adam Clayton Powell, Jr., himself. I was personally involved because I started as Brother Adam's friend and ended up being sued by him as one of five who were keeping him from taking his congressional seat, to which he had been duly elected.

Powell was the first man to teach me street talk. He would say, "How you doing, baby?" and I would be shocked at first. I once challenged him on it, asking him why he didn't call me Fish or Fishbait like everyone else since I was certainly not a girl.

He said, "Well, Fishbait baby, I know that. I call everyone 'baby.' I call the President 'baby' to his face, so why should I treat you different?"

I got used to Powell's way, and I cooperated with his tall black secretary, Louise Maxine Dargens, who phoned me many times during the day to find out what was happening on the floor. She had a keen mind and was Powell's eyes and ears, keeping him informed of legislation pending on the floor whether he was in Washington or on his trips.

Part of the time I was so busy with Speaker John McCormack's needs that I couldn't handle her calls and McCormack's assignments at the same time. McCormack would write me little notes of instructions and some weeks I had as many as one hundred missives from him. Fortunately, most of them said, "Dear Bill, please remind me . . . ." But just being the Speaker's memory was job enough.

From the first moment Powell hit Capitol Hill after winning the election of 1944, he was nothing but a thorn in the side of his white colleagues. He had been cock-of-the-walk in Harlem, and he intended to be the same in the House of Representatives.

And he was. He was already having an extracurricular romance. He had married a divorced dancer, Isabel Washington, against the wishes of his father, a Baptist minister, but Powell was being seen everywhere with another star—Hazel Scott, pianist.

Adam had said he was going to Washington to get rid of Jim Crow and as soon as possible he called the demagogue, John Rankin of Mississippi, "the leader of American-style fascism."

Rankin said he would not sit next to Powell—though nobody had asked him to—and Powell replied that he, too, refused to sit next to Rankin because only Hitler and Mussolini were qualified to sit next to him and we had already taken care of them.

I got acquainted with Powell because he really wanted to learn the ropes in getting along on the Hill—or so he said, and I believed him. I taught him what I knew and he taught me what he knew—black problems. We would talk about his sermons as we stood behind the rail in the back of the chamber. He would not write his sermon until late in the week, then rush back to New York to his church—the Abyssinian Baptist, in Harlem—and to his girl friend, Hazel. When he came back on Monday, he would tell me some of his best moments in the sermon. He loved to preach.

His first goal, he told me, was to get rid of Jim Crow on the Hill and his second was to get rid of it around the rest of the country. At the time he came, the staff restaurant of the House did not seat blacks, but in his fury he ordered his black staff to go there and order something, even if they brought their lunch from home. He also sent them to use the barbershop which, at that time, did not accept blacks. And he was the first black man to jump into the congressional swimming pool.

256

The water did not change color, but some of the congressmen did. They demanded that I do something. There was nothing I could do. The Powell people were staff just as much as anyone else was staff, paid for by the taxpayers. I checked with the leadership and it was decided not to challenge Powell or his office help, even though the other black congressman, Bill Dawson of Chicago, had followed the unwritten rule.

I remember when Adam Powell took the oath of office and brought Hazel to the ceremony. For months thereafter, he complained to me about how he had tried to take her to a movie in which she had a big role—Gershwin's life—and they wouldn't let her in at the downtown Washington theatre. He had made a stink about it and the manager had come out to explain that, even if she was the only star in the movie, it was against the rules for her or the congressman—to go inside.

Looking back, it is amazing how much good Powell did. If only he had kept his tail out of the crack, they would probably be erecting statues to him just as they do to Martin Luther King.

Powell was a dynamo, fighting job discrimination and segregation. He didn't mind attacking even the White House. When Hazel Scott, who became his wife in his first year in the House, was not permitted to appear at Constitution Hall—the same hall where the Daughters of the American Revolution had barred black singer Marian Anderson—he blew his stack.

What really made him angry was that Bess Truman, Harry's wife, didn't resign from the DAR as did Eleanor Roosevelt, but instead went to a DAR tea. Powell made Truman furious by calling First Lady Bess, the "Last Lady of the Land."

Harry dropped Powell from the White House guest list, a bad slap in the face, but as Truman told me when we had a talk at the White House before he left, there was no way of knowing what Powell would do if he were invited there. "He had no discipline," said Truman.

I should have guessed that Powell was bound to get into trouble for liking money too much when he wouldn't let the press take pictures at his marriage to Hazel because he had *sold* the photo rights.

From the first, I really felt sorry for Hazel. She was a lovely woman and didn't know what she was getting into. She had been so proud when Powell threw a party for her on the Hill so that the congressmen would hear her play, even though they couldn't go to Constitution Hall to hear her. And both were proud when Hazel had a baby who was promptly named Adam Clayton Powell III.

But then everything started downhill. With his wife busy with the baby, Adam was busy with other beauties. And he started making trips to the Caribbean, taking along his pretty secretaries. Manny Celler of New York was one of the first congressmen to get annoyed after trying to help Powell, only to find Powell off having fun. "I am trying to help the man with a civil rights bill—exactly what he has been shouting about," Manny told me, "and where is he? Is he here helping on the debate? No, he's off somewhere with his cuties."

If I recall correctly, Brother Adam was off on a junket to the glamor spots of Europe that particular time, and being photographed with a beauty on each arm.

Not only was Powell in trouble with his political party liberals, but he was in trouble with Uncle Sam. In 1952, the Internal Revenue Service started an investigation on Powell and he had to pay over a thousand dollars on his back 1945 taxes.

From then on, it was one investigation after another. The Other Body got interested in Congressman Powell when it learned during a hearing that Powell had hired out two of his office secretaries to a Tenant's Protective Association, of which *he* was president, and the money had gotten lost in the shuffle. Powell said fire had destroyed the records of what had happened to $3,000.

Then came a kickback charge. Uncle Sam said that a woman who belonged to his Abyssinian Harlem church, and who had been Powell's secretary in Washington for a few years when he first came to Washington, had continued to be listed on the payroll from 1948 to 1952—Hattie Freeman Dodson.

Appearing for the government was a Harlem tax consultant who knew the records and who claimed the secretary had kicked back her salary but had been permitted to keep tax refunds that resulted from it. The secretary was sentenced to a seven-month prison term and a $1,000 fine.

For a while, it really looked like Powell finally had his tail firmly caught in the revolving door behind him. But he went to the White House to see Eisenhower, who was running for reelection, and he came out a different man. Instead of supporting Adlai Stevenson, in his second run against Ike, Adam announced he was supporting Eisenhower's bid for a second term.

Now none of the Democrats wanted to sit near him on Capitol Hill, but as he told me, "Screw them. They never helped me." The word around the Hill was that Adam Powell had struck a deal with Ike and that Ike would call off his Justice Department dogs concerning tax charges if Powell would bring in the black vote of Harlem.

Powell thumbed his nose at the Democrats and also endorsed Jacob Javits, a Republican, for the Senate, and Javits made it. So did Ike, of course, and a little while later the word on the Hill was that the Justice Department investigator in charge of Powell's tax case had been switched to work on another case.

But Powell's troubles were not over. For one thing,

Hazel Scott decided her career was more stable than marriage to a congressman and divorced him right after the 1960 election. And true to form, he married immediately thereafter the secretary he had met and hired in San Juan, Yvette Marjorie Flores, whose grandfather had been a mayor—"a Republican mayor," as Adam told me with high glee.

Again he had a son and again he named it Adam Clayton Powell now adding IV. I kidded him about the name and he said, "Can I help it if it's my favorite name? Can you think of a better one for a man that's going to grow up and save the world, right where I leave off?"

I had to agree that the Powell name could do it.

And again came the same old song, like a cracked record—money paid for questionable reasons. In fact, it was uncovered that a salary raise, from an original amount under $5,000 to something over $12,000, had been authorized by Adam for his new wife, even though she was living in San Juan and had never come back. When reporters finally got to her at the congressman's lovely new beach home, Yvette Powell protested that she did so work—she answered the letters Powell received from Puerto Rican people in his New York district, who wrote in Spanish. She got the letters because he personally *brought* them to her on weekends.

But this was only one-half of Brother Adam's troubles. The other half stemmed from a 1960 TV appearance in which Powell really got his tail trapped in the crack in the door by charging an elderly black New York woman with being "the bag woman" for corrupt New York police.

The woman, Esther James, was furious and at first asked for a public apology. Adam was too arrogant to comply, so Mrs. James hired a lawyer and sued Powell for $1 million for defamation of character. Adam was too arrogant to bother with court appearances and the case was tried without him present, and with Mrs. James winning $211,500 in April 1963.

But time went on, and three years later she still hadn't received a penny. Process servers were laying for Adam in New York, but he only sneaked into town on Sunday to give his sermon—when process servers on civil cases didn't work. Though Powell's lawyers had managed to get the original court's verdict cut down to less than a fourth of the original amount, the creeping court costs and penalties were bringing it back up to the original amount.

Brother Powell was really something. Instead of sitting around worrying, he again stuck his tail in the crack. He started travelling not only with a black secretary but a white one as well. In 1962, he took along Corrine Huff, his white receptionist, and Mrs. Tamara Wall, a black lawyer on his Labor Committee, to study employment of women overseas, and he authorized his own trip since he was chairman of the House Labor Committee.

This, in my opinion, was the straw that broke the camel's back and made Congress determined to get Powell. When he had relatives on the payroll and got kickbacks, that was something some congressmen shared, but when he mixed the races, they were livid with rage. "I could forgive him almost anything," congressmen muttered to each other in back of the rail, "but when he takes a white girl and a 'nigra' at the same time, that tears it." More and more, they were saying, "We've got to get that bastard out of here."

In view of later history, it was ironic that Wayne Hays, who would later meet his own Waterloo in the person of a female staffer, got the first crack at Powell. As chairman of the House Administration Committee's subcommittee on Accounts—which deals with money and its use and misuse—he questioned the staff of Adam Powell after studying the records.

Hays had found that Powell had not only taken the

261

beautiful Miss Huff on trips to Bimini, but he had hired a new girl on the Labor Committee and taken her along to cook and clean house for them.

In questioning another pretty office helper, Chairman Hays acted quite shocked to learn that Powell had listed her as taking several dozen trips to such places as New York and Miami, whereas she swore under oath that she had only made three trips.

It's interesting, in view of the fact Liz Ray was later to claim she had no office duties, that Hays elicited the same kind of response from the lovely Emma Swann. "Did you have to do any kind of work on these three trips that you took with Chairman Powell?" Mrs. Swann was asked. "Did you do anything like take dictation or any such thing as that?"

"No I didn't," Emma assured Hays. "I was just going. I had no business." And through repeated questioning, she held to her story about what amounted to vacation trips with Powell.

What kept saving Powell's hide was that he really was good at helping Kennedy and then LBJ in putting across their pet legislation. In fact, LBJ sent Powell a letter complimenting the chairman and his House Labor Committee for accomplishing the passage of many "bedrock pieces of legislation," including anti-poverty legislation, and anti-poll tax and anti-discrimination bills.

But by now, another committee of the House was interested in Powell's nonlegislative activities. The House Administration Committee found that Powell was violating a law which had been passed to correct his kind of payroll abuse. In 1964, Congress had outlawed any payment to staffers who did not work either in the congressman's Washington office or in his home state office.

Puerto Rico was *not* Clayton Powell's district. In 1966, however, it came out that Yvette Powell's absentee salary had been upped to over $20,000 a year. He had hidden her name under her maiden name, Y. Marjorie Flores. Only when it hit the papers and the public was writing letters to the editor did the House itself take Yvette off the payroll.

In January 1967, when the new Congress came in, Powell was asked to stand aside and not be sworn in. I was ordered not to let him take his seat. A committee was formed under Manny Celler to investigate him.

It hurt me to leave my fellow Baptist out in the cold when I was advised by leadership to stay on my toes and be sure that I followed the rules laid down to me—that Powell was not to be allowed on the floor.

That's when he started his lawsuit against me— Fishbait Miller—as Doorkeeper; Speaker John McCormack; the chairman of the Judiciary Committee, Emanuel Celler; Zeake Johnson, sergeant-at-arms; and W. Pat Jennings, clerk of the House. In fact, I thought this was just a lark until the case had progressed far enough that we had to be subpoenaed. Even then, I didn't think the marshall actually could serve papers in the hall of the House of Representatives.

The marshall said, "On the contrary, I have looked up the ruling and it states emphatically that you can be served in the confines of a government building, especially the U.S. Capitol."

The committee brought in Powell's wife, Yvette, who testified she had gotten only several of the checks after her husband quit sending her Spanish mail and quit coming to see her. And she was financially desperate. She said she had come to the States to see him, but he would not see her or pay her hotel bills if she stayed.

By now, Puerto Rico had lost its charm for Powell, and he was spending his time at Bimini. In fact, he made it famous. People who thought it must be a new kind of bikini suddenly learned it was a fun island in the Caribbean and planned to spend a vacation there.

I wasn't the only person who was amused when Powell first instituted his suit to take his seat. Most congressmen thought it was pretty hilarious that Powell could even think the courts would do anything about it. Hadn't he heard about the separation of powers? The judiciary couldn't tell the House how to run its own affairs and anyway there was a precedent or two.

For example, in 1870 a congressman named B. F. Whittemore of South Carolina had made a little side money by putting a price tag on his help in getting sons of wealthy men appointed to the military academies.

When Congress threatened to expel Whittemore, he fooled everyone by resigning. And then he did a clever thing—he ran again for the same seat. He won, but when he showed up, the House moved to exclude him.

And another congressman—a George Cannon of the territory of Utah—was excluded for practicing polygamy, which was in keeping with his Mormon religion.

The congressmen were only sorry that they could not *expel* the upstart Congressman Powell rather than merely *exclude* him. The reason they couldn't call it expulsion is that the deed for which one is expelled has to be committed after, instead of before, an election, and Powell had just been reelected.

Manny Celler had recommended that Powell's punishment be something different—that he be *censured,* stripped of seniority and fined $40,000. Celler, who had studied all the evidence of Powell's manipulation of travel funds, misuse of office salary allowances and nepotism, still felt Powell should be seated. But the House was in a *hanging* mood, as Celler termed it, and voted, against his advice, as an indignant member said, "to bar the bastard from the House

264

That's the side view of the Capitol behind me, where I have met all the greats of the world—including our own. This book is dedicated to all the congressmen and senators who have paced its floors—to the winners and the losers, to my friends and my enemies, bless them all! *(Dev O'Neill and Keith Jewell)*

A little tête-a-tête with President Jerry Ford in his Oval Office. I knew him all through his congressional and executive careers, and though he was on the opposite side of the political fence, we had a lot of little adventures together. Some said I should be voted out of my Doorkeeper's job because I dared to be buddy-buddy and call Gerald Ford "Jerry" after he was President, but Jerry Ford was too big a man to be concerned with that trivia. *(White House)*

In November 1969, President Richard Nixon was still a new President, and he had come up to the Hill on a little private visit with some of his old friends, especially Minority Leader Gerald Ford. I'm in the background talking with Bryce Harlow, Nixon's special assistant; Carl Albert is in the foreground—he was Majority Leader then, but destined to become Speaker of the House in 1971.

This is my favorite picture of Nixon addressing a Joint Session—in January 1972. It's one of the most dramatic pictures I've seen, giving an intimate feeling of what it's like when a President speaks to Congress. Notice all the men who wanted to grab his job at one time or another—at the right, Ted Kennedy who probably could have made it, and might yet; as well as George Romney; Ed Muskie, another still possible; Hubert Humphrey, an almost made it. And to the left are Elliot Richardson and Frank Church, both of whom would have had a better chance if they'd loosened up a little bit, Incidentally, that's me fixing my glasses for a better look. If you wonder how the photographer got that dramatic effect of the steep-looking aisle, it was taken from the House Press Gallery on the third floor, looking down on the House Chamber, which is on the second floor. *(United Press International)*

Republican Whip Les Arends puts his arm around Julie Eisenhower with warm affection as her husband, President Eisenhower's grandson David Eisenhower, argues some point with me. Julie and David were a dear couple and my heart went out to them when Julie's daddy got his tail caught in the crack over Watergate. *(Dev O'Neill and Keith Jewell)*

In the Family Gallery the night President Nixon gave his first State of the Union Address in January 1969. Julie Eisenhower was still practically a bride, and Tricia wasn't even married yet. How young they look. And how much happier Pat Nixon looks compared with later years. Here, Henry Kissinger, who was a White House advisor, uses his considerable wit to make the First Lady smile. Notice the row of cabinet wives behind them and Martha Mitchell wearing dark glasses even at night. I started the practice of bringing the First Lady into the Family Gallery to a standing ovation from the floor back in Mrs. Truman's time. Before that First Ladies sort of sneaked into their seats without fanfare.

I got a laugh from the congressional crowd on August 6, 1965, when I led the way for LBJ to speak at the Rotunda of the Capitol. "Ladies and gentlemen, the President of the United States, you all hear?" I bellowed. Lyndon was making news by signing the historic Voting Rights Bill at the Capitol instead of at the White House. *(Jack Brown)*

I am sitting at my usual seat while Lyndon Johnson gives his State of the Union Address. These special occasions were about the only time I got to sit down in the House Chamber. Presiding behind Lyndon is House Speaker McCormack, and beside him is Vice President Hubert Humphrey. Before any President spoke, it was my formal duty to precede him into the chamber and announce, "Mr. Speaker, the President of the United States." If you saw the movie *All the President's Men*, you saw me leading President Nixon in and doing my bit, because that's the way the movie opens. Lyndon had an ego that wouldn't quit and wanted his presidential seal in front of his lectern when he spoke. But McCormack said nothing doing, even the Speaker of the House does not have a seal there and after all, the President is just a guest when he goes to Congress. *(United Press International)*

Lady Bird was always sweet and ladylike around the Hill, and I always enjoyed looking out for her. Here I am holding her purse and book so she can have two hands free for meeting guests at a little gathering on Capitol Hill. With her and the President is bachelor Congressman Jim Fulton of Pennsylvania.

You can tell by this picture that there was still a little tension between me and President John Fitzgerald Kennedy. I guess he always remembered that I had been part of the clique that helped Speaker Sam Rayburn keep him from getting the vice-presidency in 1956 and had tried to keep him from getting the presidential nomination in 1960. But in spite of that, on and off we managed to have a bit of fun, kidding each other and telling jokes. Kennedy was probably the wittiest man I knew for snap comebacks.

Jack Kennedy had more persuasiveness than any President when he spoke. But when he got through, Congress slipped back into its own rut and still bucked him and refused to pass most of his proposals. It is ironic that Kennedy is going down in history as the man of vision, though it was Lyndon Johnson who finally got the Kennedy programs passed and scored high while Kennedy scored poorly on important legislation passed—I mean things like civil rights. *(United Press International)*

(Left) This is one of the happiest and saddest days for me—the laying of the cornerstone of the Rayburn House Office Building. Speaker Sam had not lived to see the fulfillment of his great dream: the completion of a heroic building that would show the Senate that the House was every bit as good as it was. But I could feel the presence of the man who had been like a twin brother to me (you can see part of my head and the stem of my glasses at the extreme left) as President Kennedy joked and helped Sam's successor, John W. McCormack, plaster the cornerstone in. I was not the only one to look a little misty-eyed; there were many there who had been helped up the slippery ladder to political success by Brother Sam. *(White House)*

Yes, Jacqueline Kennedy was beautiful, but never so beautiful and dignified as this day when she was walking down the steps of the Capitol. She was a great First Lady and I felt especially proud of her because I had watched her grow up and knew her even before she dated Jack. I used to help her when she was trying to be a photographer and would come around with her great big *Times Herald* camera. I would look out for her and phone her to hurry to the Hill because there was a big news event coming up. I would even hold her place for her if she was late. That's the kind of loyalty she inspired.

This is the broad view of the House Chamber when a President speaks at Joint Session. Here it's good old Ike—President Dwight D. Eisenhower—addressing the House and Senate. The cabinet is in front of him. Ike was sensitive about the baldness on top of his head and had makeup put there at the direction of Hollywood star Robert Montgomery, whom we all called Monty around the Hill.

I like this photo because it's a happy moment during the last State of the Union Address that Ike gave—the date is January 9, 1959. He was in a good mood; I guess he was glad to be retiring. That's Speaker Sam—Rayburn, of course—leaning over to share a joke, and that's Richard Nixon as Vice-President. How long ago that seems. I can't believe that's me in the front row clapping, because my hair seems to be parted in the middle. How fashion changes. What's left of my hair is parted a little more to the side now. *(United Press International)*

Ah, Memories! See Herbert Hoover to the right of Ike and Mamie at the oath of office ceremony at the Capitol? Well, when I arrived in Washington during the Roosevelt administration, he was the hated man, but in later years I got to know him well up at the Capitol and I developed a real affection for him. The date on this picture is January 21, 1957. The President had been sworn in at the White House on the proper date—January 20—and had reenacted the event the following day on the Hill. *(United Press International)*

I was closer to Truman than to any President, and before he left the White House he called me over for a visit and to review the events we had shared together through the years. He was still sensitive on the subject of his firing of Douglas MacArthur and still justifying it. I don't think there'll ever be another man like Give-'Em-Hell Harry, and it's a pity.

(Right) This was my great moment at the 1949 inauguration of Truman and Barkley. I held his hat and coat while Alben W. Barkley took his oath of office, and I was later kidded by the Hill crowd who swore they couldn't tell who was taking the oath of office—Barkley or me. As a footnote to history, this inaugural was the only time I saw the Bible kissed at such a ceremony. Both Truman and Barkley kissed the Bible. That is Justice Stanley Reed, a dear friend of Harry Truman's and Barkley's, who is administering the oath. Since Truman's victory was so unexpected—practically a miracle— this inauguration was called by newspapers "the most enthusiastic in the nation's history."

I think this is my favorite picture in the book because it shows my two favorite people and our good luck emblem which has a great history. That's our Victory Donkey, which had magical good luck powers. One of the smartest things I ever did was give someone a dollar for this old wooden beast at the 1952 convention. I lugged it home from Chicago, personally. I bribed a fellow with a bottle of Scotch to paint "Victory in '54" on it and damned if it didn't happen that we voted out the Republicans and had a Democratic Congress from then on. Every year, a bottle of Scotch took care of changing the date, and as long as the good-luck charm was in my office, we always had a Democratic Congress. The Victory Donkey was famous on the Hill. *(United Press International)*

All the best to Publ...
from his friend —
George McGovern

(Above) The most botched up presidential race I have ever seen was that of my good friend Senator George McGovern. It was as if the furies had been unleashed against him. As you will see in the book, there was even a Keystone Kops incident along the campaign trail that made everything seem a little ridiculous. But I must say the Ford-Carter race of 1976 wasn't much better. Here are Brother George and I at the 1972 Governor's Conference talking with Republican Governor Daniel Evans of Washington, at left, and Democratic Congressman Don Fuqua of Florida, at right.

(Top Left) This was Adlai Stevenson during the 1956 Democratic Convention, his second time around. Eleanor Roosevelt supported him and adored him, and this was a big bash given by Adlai in honor of the former First Lady. You see me between Delegate Richard Mirabelli of Elizabeth, New Jersey, and Stevenson, making the introduction. This circus-style event was something of a record; I called out the names of 11,000 people coming through the line during a fast-paced three hours. It was the big opening event of my favorite convention of all the many I attended, usually as Convention Doorkeeper. It was held in Chicago with the odor of the stockyards coming through loud and clear. But I didn't care, I was in my element doing the bidding of my hero, Convention Chairman Sam Rayburn.

(Lower Left) Hubert Humphrey hated the nickname "Gabby" and once I got into deep trouble over it. But look at this picture—now I ask you! I think HHH would have made a great President in spite of that mouth, and it is one of the tragedies of our nation that he didn't win over Nixon. You will read in the book the hilarious account of how I locked the whole damn House in one night slaving to get a bill passed that would have helped Brother Hubert win in 1968. You'll have to read it to believe it. And even then it's pretty unbelievable.

I always got a hug from Jack Dempsey, former heavyweight boxing champion of the world. Whenever Dempsey was invited to a Hill luncheon, he always wanted Gene Tunney there, too, and they would stage a little mock bout. *(U.S. Army)*

Senator Estes Kefauver does not look happy in this picture, and you can hardly blame him. It is the 1952 convention and the candidate with the famous coonskin hat has been told by Speaker Sam that he must wait and that he will not be nominated for Vice President this time. Sam Rayburn did keep his promise and Brother Estes did get his chance in 1956, but it was a bad year for Democratic presidential and vice-presidential candidates. Standing behind Estes to comfort him is Governor Mennen Williams of Michigan, who everyone called "Soapy" and who was known for his polka-dot bowties. *(Walter Bennett)*

Here is Princess Elizabeth on the day I flubbed the dub on protocol and, as a result, had to go to school at the State Department to learn how to cope with royalty. That's Prince Philip, over to the right, looking slightly amused. That was his usual look to cope with having to be "Mr. Princess." I felt sorry for the guy—he had to tag along and always remember *she* was the star. But if you have to have royalty, Elizabeth is very nice.

A politician and a Doorkeeper find themselves doing a little of almost anything. Senator Ed Muskie, who lost a presidential nomination by a teardrop in 1972, gets a little help from me in cutting the ribbon for a new seafood restaurant in Washington, D.C. I don't know which of us got to keep the lobster—probably the senator.

General Douglas MacArthur came to the Hill many times after his famous "Old Soldiers never die" speech. Here he is getting "the treatment" from Robert McNamara, secretary of defense and later president of the International Bank for Reconstruction and Development, at the annual "Bird Luncheon" that Mendel Rivers would give featuring quail from his state of South Carolina. I got to know MacArthur pretty well, and I want to say for the record that I was there to announce him when he made his historic speech.

Here I am with good old Henry Kissinger on Inauguration Day 1973, just before President Nixon's world started to crumble. Once, a few years earlier, Kissinger told me, "I've only been here a little while but I know who runs the House." Great sense of humor, that guy.

Who says Congress has to be stuffy? All the brethren on the Hill counted on me to liven up their little luncheons and meetings with show-business greats—and I did. Here I'm measuring the "schnozz" on ole Jimmy Durante himself. And Congressmen Oren Harris, Democrat from Arkansas (left), and Clifford Davis, Democrat from Tennessee, get a chuckle, because I prove it takes a ruler with an extension to do it. Incidentally, it was Brother Cliff who got a bullet in the leg when the Puerto Ricans shot up the floor of Congress.

For John Wayne, who's got a grip like a giant, I even put on my special dignified look. But I didn't have to. He was a regular guy and we soon were calling each other "pardner." We agreed that we didn't want each other's jobs—I couldn't handle his horses, and he couldn't ride herd on Congress and keep the mavericks off the floor. *(Dev O'Neill and Keith Jewell)*

Pearl Bailey is another gal who has a heart as big as the world. She had the word "Love" embroidered on her evening coat the night that we got together at the White House News Photographers Dinner, and on her head was a crown of diamond hearts. The picture was taken in 1971 and since then she has been assigned to spread a little love around the United Nations. She's the gal who can do it. Even when she's insulting you, it's a pleasure. I had just finished telling her all my job responsibilities, and she is saying, "You ain't foolin' me for a minute, Fishbait baby. You don't know what tired is. You got the easiest job on the Hill. Now me, baby, *I'm* tired." Joining us is Arnold Sachs, a photographer who is a dear friend of mine.

Edie Adams is just about the sexiest woman of all the hundreds of beauties who came to call on us at the Capitol. I mean even with her clothes on and pitted against such sexy gals as Jayne Mansfield, who came to visit us in the Capitol and purposely shifted one shoulder to let one nipple escape from her dress while the photographer was shooting the scene. That picture of Jayne became a favorite pin-up in the back rooms of Congress and I have it, too, but I prefer this one where I'm pinning a corsage on that living doll, Edie. As I told her, "I'm a nonsmoking man, but for you I might even pick up a Muriel." *(United Press International)*

(Lower Left) When Bob Hope and Justice William O. Douglas got together during a 1967 reception, it was a battle of wits on who could travel fastest. The Justice, who was famous for his hiking and mountain climbing, claimed he could hike faster than old ski nose could talk. When they got to who had been to the coldest places, Bob Hope said he'd taken his troupe to some mighty cold outposts, but again the witty Justice topped him, claiming that in the Himalayas it was once so cold that the candle froze and they couldn't blow it out. Thoroughly enjoying this byplay is Jane Morgan.

My favorite VIP was Winston Churchill. He was a spellbinder when he talked, and he also held me spellbound when I watched how much he could eat. The date on this photo is January 17, 1952. By now, we were old friends. That's me, incidentally, standing beside him, and it's Speaker Sam and Vice President Alben Barkley standing and leaning forward.

A bear hug from Billy Graham who was a frequent guest on the Hill as well as at the White House. This time, in 1971, it was his greeting at a Prayer Breakfast.

Here's how the old homestead looks before the daily session begins. The symbol of authority is the Mace. On the wall behind the Speaker's stand are two plaques of the cruel Mace with hatchets which was used in ancient Rome. Our Mace has an American eagle instead of a blade, but it is still used to quell a fist fight on the floor.

Majority Leader of the House Tip O'Neill and I, taken in 1973. Tip, whose full name is Thomas P., Jr., was a very close friend of President Jack Kennedy, came from the same state of Massachusetts, and also shared the same kind of Irish wit. One of the funniest speeches Tip ever made on the floor of the House was after Jerry Ford finally announced that he was going to run for the presidency in 1976. Tip can devastate any opponent with humor, and as they said about Tip on the Hill, "He's all heart—but his heart's all Democrat." *(Dev O'Neill and Keith Jewell)*

Paper work, paper work! Words, words, words! If you want to know how many words are spoken in the House and Senate, take a look at this picture dated October 22, 1966. Speaker of the House John McCormack, seated, House Minority Whip Les Arends and I, standing, are going over the congressional records and journals of just two months.

I call this picture "The Power Brokers." And I also call it "The Bugged Room." The date is May 11, 1971, and these are the big guns of the Hill gathered on the occasion of Congressman William M. Colmer's annual luncheon for the President. Bill Colmer, Democrat of my state of Mississippi and the man so important in my life because he sent me to college and brought me to Washington, gave this posh luncheon in his capacity as chairman of the powerful Rules Committee, which controlled which bills came on the floor. As you will learn in the book, I was aware that each year before Nixon arrived, his men came by and placed bugging equipment around the room and maybe I should have made a fuss about it. Maybe if I had, the nation would have learned a lot sooner about Nixon having the White House Oval Office and other places bugged, and the Watergate revelations might have started sooner. But somehow I thought they ought to know what they were doing and to have a good reason for doing it. Who knows what congressional secrets came out on the tapings in the off-the-record luncheons—especially secrets spoken by congressmen away from Nixon's side of the table. Anyway, this is the Speaker's Dining Room which Nixon had bugged when he attended special luncheons there. Getting ready to sit down are Speaker of the House John W. McCormack, President Richard M. Nixon, Majority Leader Hale Boggs of Louisiana (mysteriously lost with his plane in Alaska), and Chairman Colmer. *(White House)*

(Lower Left) Lyndon Johnson as Senate Majority Leader and Sam Rayburn as Speaker of the House in the fateful year of 1960, when they thought Lyndon could capture the Democratic nomination from that young upstart Jack Kennedy. I don't mind saying Speaker Sam was my idol and I helped him toward many of his goals. Very few people knew the tragedy of his life—his unsuccessful marriage, which I tell about in this book. Because he had no children of his own, he took a great interest in LBJ's daughters Luci and Lynda Bird and my daughter, Sarah Patsy. Few knew that every year on his own birthday he had a party for children. He was a very secretive man, even the way he helped FDR bring about the recovery of the nation is scarcely known.

When the big guns get together, everyone acts a little cagey at first until they relax and start to let their hair down. Here is a little high-pressure group getting together at a pre-Christmas reception on the Hill in 1970: Lawrence F. O'Brien, chairman of the Democratic National Committee, whose office would be burglarized as the start of the Watergate scandal, and Mrs. O'Brien greet Democratic stalwarts Ted Kennedy, John McCormack and Carl Albert.

I sure miss good old Mendel Rivers, as you will see in the book, one of the most colorful congressmen the Hill has ever produced. Actually L. Mendel—he never would tell that the "L" stood for Lucius—came from South Carolina, and the big joke on the Hill was that if he, as chairman of the Armed Services Committee, got even one more military installation for his state, he would sink the shoreline and put Charleston completely under water. In this picture dated June 19, 1952, which shows me table-hopping, the fellow seated next to Brother Mendel is Jerry Beven, Billy Graham's public relations man. Mendel died right after Christmas 1970.

Here I am with Shirley Chisholm, Democrat of New York, on January 20, 1972. I give her a lot of credit for effectiveness. I'm on her side, even though, when she's home, her husband does the cooking. *(Dev O'Neill and Keith Jewell)*

The famous fun-loving Congresswoman Coya Knutson of Minnesota could always be counted on to bring her accordion and liven up a party. Here in happy days at a Women's Democratic Club, is Coya and her accordion and me, with Katie Louchheim, deputy assistant secretary of the State Department. Katie had a long and colorful career. A great gal, she was one of the LBJ crowd who would spend long summer afternoons in Lyndon's backyard arguing politics and eating the good Texas food that Lady Bird cooked with her own hands.

Daniel Inouye as he first arrived in Washington back in 1959, after being elected to the House of Representatives in a special election. I'm orienting the congressman in this picture, introducing him to the newspaper *Roll Call* which is aimed exclusively at the Hill crowd. Inouye, who later became a senator, spent the first few years getting people to quit feeling sorry for him or treating him differently because he had lost an arm in World War II. He proved he could do with one hand what some people are too clumsy to do with two. A great guy.

Congressman Frank Boykin, Democrat of Alabama, went around the Hill shouting, "Everything is made for love!" Here, in 1959, he and I pose on the Capitol steps with the pom-pom girls with the Alabama football team. The girls were visiting the Capitol that spring to see Congress in action. As one congressman commented, perhaps what Congress needs is some pom-pom girls to cheer them on.

Congress took its baseball seriously in the old days. Here I am practice catching wtih Congressman Jimmy Roosevelt, Democrat of California, for the Odd Sox, the softball team of the Hill. Jimmy, the member of the family who helped FDR and made it look as if President Roosevelt could walk, tried to follow in his father's footsteps, but it was too tough.

It's that historic game of 1953 and I'm giving the Democrats' team star, Congressman Hugh Addonizio of New Jersey, a kiss for scoring the run that beat the Republicans 3 to 2. The Democrats baseball team would go to Florida every year and practice at the Red Sox training quarters. We would always repay the hospitality by playing a game for charity.

I had two offices. This is the official or ceremonial office in which I met with State Department officials concerning visits of foreign dignitaries to the Capitol or planned logistics of the President's arrival for the State of the Union message. *(Don Gangloff)*

(Lower Right) That's Speaker Sam Rayburn escorting the Mardi Gras Queen to a Louisiana State Society ball. And attending with Sam, who was like a brother to me, was my wife, Mable, and me. I'm sneaking this picture into the book because Mable, in contrast to me, is so shy that I'm sure she would demand that I cut her out of it or tear it up. But I'm proud of her—no matter how I kid about her—and want the world to meet her in at least one picture.

But the office I really used and had fun in was the work office, in which I kept the Victory Donkey, the good-luck charm of the Democratic congressmen. As long as I had it and kept its date repainted every two years, we never lost a congressional election. The "Gefilte Fishbait" can on my desk has an interesting history. Congressman James C. Corman of California had it specially made up as a gag gift, and it cost him all of $2.85 to have it sent to me airmail special delivery. I treasured it. Incidentally, Brother Corman was the man who took over some of Wayne Hays' duties when Wayne got his tail caught in the crack. Corman moved up to sign checks for the Democratic Campaign Committee—an important position of trust.

This is introducing Sarah Patsy, back when I had hair to burn and all of us were a little younger. Today she's an English teacher in Atlanta, Georgia, and she has a little shaver of her own, John William Knight. I want to go on record as saying that Sarah Patsy has never seen my manuscript and is not responsible for it in any way—including my personal use of the English language.

This is my pride and joy, my 1947 Dodge sedan. Though it is not an antique yet, I call it a senior citizen. Only one man has ever worked on it, and it's a journey of several days each time I take it back for its check-up. What mother treats a baby any better? Old '47 has many memories, and those famous names of Capitol Hill would come back to haunt me if I ever got rid of the car they used to love to ride around in—such men as Speaker Sam, Manny Celler and Mendel Rivers.

That's me in retirement visiting with the Honorable Maynard Jackson, the mayor of Atlanta, where I now live, and Dr. James P. Wesberry, Sr., the pastor of Morningside Baptist Church where you'll find me on a Sunday morning. The mayor says this is the quickest takeover he has ever seen, and he warns me that though I may have been a living legend on Capitol Hill and Washington, D.C., he intends to run his own city.

It's an occupational disease! Here I am still politicking in retirement, visiting the Honorable George Busbee (center), Governor of Georgia, with his friend Dr. James P. Wesberry, a former Acting Chaplain, U.S. House of Representatives. But I swear that when I chose Atlanta for my retirement home, I did not know that Mr. Peanut would be our new President. *(William Birdsong)*

That's me winking at you and saying that's all I'm gonna tell you. I'm going to let you read the book. Then drop me a line through the publisher to let me know if you didn't have a few surprises and learn a few things you didn't already know. This is Fishbait signing off for now. Bless you all. *(Ken Heinen, The Washington Star)*

altogether." They didn't want "to look at him" they said. The only question in the minds of most of the top men of the House, including my old mentor, Bill Colmer, was whether to tell the courts themselves to mind their own business or to hire a lawyer to tell them off for Congress—and, of course, we five who were singled out.

Jerry Ford was one of those who suggested that Congress itself should not dabble in court business but get a lawyer to "go down there and tell them it is certainly none of their business." Lawyers were hired, and before the case was over almost a quarter million dollars were billed to the House for legal fees. I was happy that I did not have to pay my one-fifth.

The case went up as high as the Supreme Court and we lost. What the Court ruled was that it is the *people,* the *electorate,* who exercise the safeguard of punishing a bad congressman by not reelecting him. Other than that, Congress had the right in extreme cases of misconduct to expel a member with a two-thirds vote. Then the Court quoted Alexander Hamilton, one of the authors of the Constitution, who said, "The people should choose whom they please to govern them."

I'll never forget Bill Colmer's disgust with that decision. He said he could quote another famous man to reply to that, Andrew Jackson, who hadn't liked a Supreme Court decision back in 1832, and had said, "John Marshall has made his decision. Now let him enforce it."

Powell was seated. The decision was handed down on June 16, 1969. Not only that, but he ran for reelection while relaxing in Bimini and was reelected by his ardent Harlem followers. But we hardly ever saw him on the Hill anymore. He had been cut down to a freshman congressman and been given a small office in the Longworth House Office Building which looked pretty dismal after his fancy Rayburn diggings. Also, he had lost his chairmanship of the Labor Com-

265

mittee. I really think he lost his will to live, even though some said he was as arrogant as ever down in Bimini.

At any rate, early in 1972 he died of cancer in Miami, where he had been flown for treatment. But he didn't want even his body to be a part of the United States. He had ordered his ashes scattered over the island he had made famous.

ALL YOU'VE EVER WANTED TO KNOW ABOUT THE HISTORY OF THE CAPITOL BUT WERE AFRAID TO ASK

I envy the tourists for the joy of being awed as they set foot in the Capitol. When I came to the Hill in 1933 to be a humble worker in the House Post Office, I too knew the thrill of being awed by the majesty of the names I heard every day.

John Nance Garner, our illustrious Vice President under the new man in the White House, Franklin Delano Roosevelt, had been a congressman and his name was on almost everyone's lips because he had just left his post as Speaker of the House in the Seventy-second Congress to accept the nomination as FDR's running mate.

And just the session before—in fact, from the Sixty-ninth to the Seventy-first Congress—the famous Nicholas Longworth had been Speaker of the House. I was overwhelmed to be walking in the same corridors once trod by the wealthy Longworth of Ohio, who had married the daughter of a President—Alice Roosevelt—and who had continued through the administration of Hoover to walk in and out of the doors of the White House at will.

And Charles Curtis, who was Vice President under Hoover, was still another bright memory on the Hill. He too had been a graduate of the halls of Congress. Curtis was dismissed as "Indian Charlie" for his claim —which nobody doubted—that he was half-Indian.

Very quickly, I started to learn that congressmen—

even Speakers—were human. It was a great relief to hear the great Longworth blasted like any other mortal. The Democrats were saying he had never sponsored a single bit of legislation of any consequence, that he had used the House as "a rich man's hobby" and that he had certainly known how to make the most of "good connections and a flapping tongue."

John Nance Garner was put down as an old reprobate whose "best judgment dealt with picking the right Bourbon." The only reason FDR had picked Garner, it was said on the Hill, was that he had made a splash with labor by earlier exposing how the secretary of the treasury, Andrew W. Mellon, had quietly given billions of dollars of tax refunds to big corporations.

And besides, with the country in deep depression, they said, FDR needed to take attention away from the fact that he was a rich man. He needed a scuffy, unpressed-looking wardog of a running mate who was really a man of the people. And that was Garner.

When I arrived at the Capitol, the Hill gang was still talking about the big flap at the White House in which no one could decide who outranked whom— the sister of the Vice President, Dolly Gann, or the wife of the Speaker of the House, Alice Roosevelt Longworth.

The White House had a big party at which bachelor Vice President Charlie Curtis and Speaker Nicholas Longworth were both invited.

It's hard to remember how that was resolved—I think Dolly Gann as the sister-hostess of the Vice President sat higher than acid-tongued Alice.

Dolly Gann had worn a lot of green around Washington and the Hill. The color was called "Gann-green."

When I arrived, the Hill was certainly different looking than now. There was only one House office building. Every congressman had one room for an office and he shared it with his secretary or assistants.

He wasn't overwhelmed with helpers because he had just a $5,000 yearly allowance for office employees. If he'd been in the House for a long time, it got harder for him every year because he had to share his cramped quarters with an ever-expanding row of file cabinets.

In those days, it really paid to become a committee chairman because then you got some extra space. Space was the status symbol.

When I arrived, they were building the second office building, so relief was on its way. And I would be on the Hill long enough to see a third office building built as well. One day, I was in a congressman's office as he and a group of other congressmen were watching the driving of the pilings for that third office building, which had been the brainchild and special project of Sam Rayburn and which he promised would be the most elegant building on Capitol Hill. The congressmen crowded around the window, looking to where the loud noise was coming from, and suddenly one of them laughed ruefully and said, "Well, there goes Speaker's Sam last erection."

And the Speaker's "last erection" was named for him, the Rayburn House Office Building. It became known as the most wasteful office building, costing more than twice what it had been intended to cost and having the vast interior space of a Roman forum. It has two-story hearing rooms and marble stairs rising elegantly but which are unneeded and unused. There are vast unused areas—including one where stands a dwarfed statue of Speaker Sam, trying to look a little bigger.

It's interesting how the House office buildings were named. The building the men stood in, looking out at the pile driving, was the Longworth building, named for the Speaker who had accomplished nothing but good will. And the first and original House office building was named after the worst-tempered Speaker of the House, Joe Cannon, who was known as the tyrant,

269

the dictator, the Napoleon of the House—take your pick.

History is full of reasoning like that.

So suddenly the three buildings that had been known simply as the Old House Office Building, the New House Office Building, and the "New, New House Office Building," were named in one big emotional binge on the House floor, which became known to history as "House Joint Resolution 711, Eighty-seventh Congress, May 21, 1962." With enactment into law and the signature of the President, it became Public Law 87-453.

It took the Senate ten years, until October 11, 1972, to follow the House lead and name its Old and New Senate Office Buildings for Senate leaders. Senate Resolution 296, Ninety-second Congress, names the Old SOB "the Richard Russell Building" (Russell had died just the year before), and the new SOB became the "Everett McKinley Dirksen Building."

Dirksen, who had served in the House before improving his life by going to the Senate, is remembered most for his gravel-voiced elegance and his campaigning for the marigold as the national flower—a campaign in which he died still unsuccessful. I don't remember what Richard Russell was famous for besides bachelorhood. But neither one was anything like the kind of tyrant that good old Joe Cannon was on my side of the Hill—the House side.

To show you what I mean, the effect of Joe Cannon's tyranny is still felt on the Hill but now it is felt with affection. I am referring to the damn bean soup that some say is the best in the world and some say is the worst, and the recipe of which is in this book.

Bean soup had been featured even before Joe Cannon came to Congress. One hot, hot day, when Joe was in his heyday, he went into the House Restaurant and couldn't find it on the menu. "Where is the bean soup?" he demanded irritably. "I'm looking for the bean soup."

The waiter explained that it was a muggy day and the chef had decided it was too hot for bean soup. "Hell and thunderation," roared Speaker Joe. "I had my mouth set for bean soup. Get me the chef."

The poor man came out and was read the riot act by Joe in front of the waiters and congressmen who might not have been properly aware of Joe's powers. "From now on," Speaker Cannon said sternly, "hot or cold, rain, snow or shine, I want bean soup on the menu every day." Bean soup has been on the menu every single day since.

Tourists always ask me about firsts—who was the first black, the first Jew, the first Catholic, the first member elected who had served time in jail, the first anything.

The first convicted felon elected to Congress was Matthew Lyon, an anti-Federalist congressman from Vermont who had violated the Sedition Act of 1798 by publishing a letter critical of the government. If the Sedition Act were in force these days, we'd all be in jail, but back in October 1798, Congressman Lyon was sentenced to four months in the pokey and a $1,000 fine. That was a very big fine—about the cost of a little house in those days.

To show how the voters felt, they reelected him while he was still in prison. Years later, a special bill was enacted refunding his fine to his heirs.

The first black also got to Congress as the result of legal problems, but not his own. He was Joseph Rainey of South Carolina who was elected to finish out the term of Benjamin Franklin Whittemore. Rainey was sworn in on December 12, 1870.

Whittemore hadn't died. He had gotten into trouble and been charged by the House with "corruption." The House had tried to expel him but failed. Instead, they just declared his seat vacant.

271

Catholics in the House came with the first Congress—Thomas Fitzsimons of Pennsylvania served in the first three Congresses, 1789–1795, and a second Catholic, Charles Carroll of Maryland, who served 1789–91, was also present at the first session.

In the Ninety-second Congress, Robert F. Drinan became the first congressman who was also a Roman Catholic priest, elected in 1970 and reelected to the following two Congresses.

I was very much surprised to see him when he came, but I took to him immediately—he was a very brainy man, interested in everything that would help Massachusetts and the country.

After the Catholics came the Jews. The first Jewish congressman was David Levy Yulee, elected in 1840 and serving until 1845—but he couldn't vote in the House. That's because Florida was still a territory and he had only delegate status.

The first Jewish member who could vote in the House was Lewis Charles Levin, elected from Philadelphia in 1844 and serving until March 3, 1851.

So far, there have been no rabbis elected to Congress but in 1860, Morris Jacob Raphall of B'nai Jeshurun, New York City, became the first rabbi to open the House with prayer. That was in February, during the first session of the Thirty-sixth Congress.

Then came the Japanese. Daniel Ken Inouye of Hawaii became the first congressman of Japanese descent to serve in the House, representing Hawaii, and was sworn in by Speaker Sam Rayburn on August 24, 1959. He served in the House until 1962, when he ran successfully for the Senate. He was a World War II veteran who had suffered the loss of an arm in the war. I used to want to help him, but Inouye spurned all help and prided himself on even being able to light his own cigarettes with a package of safety matches.

The first congressman of Japanese ancestry to represent a state on the continental United States, however, didn't take office until January 14, 1975—Norman Yoshio Mineta of California, who was sworn in by Speaker Carl Albert.

The congressman with the most exotic background so far was Dalip Singh Saund of California, born in Amritsar, India, elected to the Eigthy-fifth Congress in 1956 to represent California. He must have done something right—he was reelected in 1958 and in 1960.

For a while, the other congressmen couldn't get used to his dark good looks, his straight jet-black hair and his Indian features, but very soon he was one of the crowd, deluging them with little gifts, dried seedless dates and California oranges sent fresh from his home state. He amused them too with his story of how he had been elected to the court in Imperial County to serve as judge too soon to be sworn in, because he wasn't even a citizen yet. He had to run again the next term.

But in the House of Representatives, evidently, rules are made to be broken. I cannot understand it, but the record for the youngest member to be sworn into the House is that of a 22-year-old—William Charles Cole Claiborne of Tennessee—who was sworn in on November 23, 1797.

Maybe they figured the constitutional requirement of twenty-five years of age didn't apply because he was elected to fill an unexpired term—that of the future President, Andrew Jackson, who at that point was leaving the House because he had won an election to the Senate.

At any rate, Claiborne went on to serve in many other political posts—governor of the territory of Mississippi, governor of the territory of Orleans, governor of Louisiana and finally U.S. senator.

The oldest congressman to serve died in office at the age of eighty-nine years, seven months and twenty-five days. He was Charles Manly Stedman of North Carolina, who died just three years before I came to the Hill.

But a senator whom I did get to know beat him by a few years—Theodore F. Green of Rhode Island, who in 1960 decided to retire and enjoy himself. He was ninety-three at the time and still a bachelor.

Many said Green's long life was due to the fact he had never married "or worn himself out in the hopeless and hapless pursuit of heartless women." The senator's idea of fun was to walk from his hotel to the Capitol and back. I used to try to give him a ride but he refused to be spoiled by me.

Longevity in office is a different matter. The man who was on the Hill the longest, serving in both the House and Senate, was Carl Hayden of Arizona, who toted up fifty-six years, ten months and fifteen days—starting his career on February 19, 1912, and ending it on January 3, 1969.

But the man who served longest in the House was Carl Vinson of Georgia who spent an unbelievable fifty years, two months and thirteen days on the Hill. That was from 1914 to 1965.

Second place goes to Emanuel Celler of New York —forty-nine years, ten months, from 1923 to 1973. Third place belongs to Sam Rayburn—forty-eight years, eight months, from 1913 to 1961.

Joe Cannon, who had such a stranglehold on Congress as Speaker, comes in fourth with forty-six years of service.

Is there a congressional cemetery? Yes, there is, but it hasn't been used for a long time. It really was the first national cemetery, being older than Arlington National Cemetery.

Even in 1793, before the days of the "federal city" of Washington, the Maryland legislature acted to solve the problem of possible deaths among legislators who might pass away while attending Congress. Transportation of the body back to the home state was not feasible, so a plot of ground was purchased to be administered by the Christ Church Washington Parish.

There was room for one hundred gravesites, but in 1820 the honor of being buried in the Congressional Cemetery was extended to cabinet officers and their families and the families of members of Congress. Since 1960, there have been no members of Congress buried there and many who were have been—with modern transportation—reburied in their home states. But the place still contains the grave of a representative who gave the political world an important word— Elbridge Gerry of Massachusetts, whose political activities included helping recut a district to make sure his political party won its vote.

As the story goes, someone said, "My God, that district looks like a salamander." "No," said another, "it looks more like a Gerrymander." And thus a new word was born. Gerry may be gone, but gerrymandering is still very much alive. And he's very much remembered by me because he set up the Office of the Doorkeeper, bless his heart.

I should explain the history of the seating arrangement in the House. Back in the earliest days it was first come, first served, but some congressmen who had to come from faraway states got angry at the special luck of the Virginia and Maryland men. So in the Twenty-ninth Congress, which began in 1845, members drew for their seats with the exception of the ex-Speakers and members of long service. Such honored men were allowed to keep their previous seats, or select new seats.

There is a touching historic scene that members still draw upon when talking of the seating problem. That was when John Quincy Adams returned to the House after having suffered a paralytic stroke. As the story is told, the former President-turned-congressman

275

entered the House on February 13, 1847, while the whole House was in committee on the State of the Union. As soon as they saw Adams, the members rose to welcome him and Andrew Johnson congratulated him "on being spared to return to this House." Then Johnson led him to the seat he had saved for him.

That scene took place before the House moved to its new quarters, ten years later in 1857. At that time, there were individual, carved oak desks and chairs. But the members couldn't make up their minds which they wanted. First, in 1859, they replaced chairs with benches, with the political parties opposite each other. But the members didn't like that, so it was back to the desks in 1860. Since there was no room to move around, smaller desks were designed and installed in 1873. In 1888, still fussing about the chairs and desks, James Bryce is reported to have said, ". . . the desks are a mistake, as encouraging inattention by enabling men to write their letters . . ." In 1902, smaller desks were brought in. Then, in 1914, it was rip out the desks again and bring back the benches as in 1859—with the difference that the benches were really a row of chairs arranged as long benches.

And there it rested even until today. Though there are still no desks, there are padded armrests.

As for what seat to sit in, the members are really back to the First Congress. Again, it's every man for himself. The arrangement changes day by day, with congressmen grabbing any chairs they like just as long as the Republicans stay on their side, on the left of the Speaker, and the Democrats stay on their side, on the right of the Speaker.

I should explain about that pesky rule on hats. Back in the early Congresses, members wore their hats during sessions for two reasons. First, it was a sign of independence in the House of Commons of England—and the members of Congress liked that. Second, there was just no safe place to put them.

Plus, there had been some problem of water dripping down from the ceiling above on the heads of the legislators.

Some members had started agitating as early as 1822 to have members remove their hats. It was more polite. But it took until September 14, 1837, for the gentlemen to adopt the rule that "no member shall wear his hat during the sessions of the House."

Of course, they had no idea that over 120 years later some woman named Bella Abzug, who was famous for her hats, would be a member of the House.

The ban against smoking came after the ban against hats—in 1871. Since the members quibbled and said that meant one could smoke on the floor until the Chair gavelled the House into order each day, the rule was changed again on January 10, 1896, at which time it was made clear that smoking was prohibited at any time in the House Chamber.

Needless to say, this made a lot of tobacco chewers out of smokers and spittoons became more than necessary around the floor. For years, there was one spittoon for every member. The floor was a mess, and even those who prided themselves on aim did not always hit the mark.

Snuff was always available. It was supplied under the stationery fund. Snuff was good because it required no spitting—just a lot of handkerchiefs.

Only one woman has added any historic first in the line of smoking and that is Congresswoman Millicent Fenwick of New Jersey, who took office in January 1975: the first lady on the Hill to smoke a pipe.

Going back to the early days of the Capitol Building itself, what is now Statuary Hall was once the scene of a general marketplace, with men and women setting up little stands to sell things—liquor, candies, flowers, fruits, watches and sundries—to congressmen.

Years and years ago, there used to be houses of ill repute, which the Congressmen called "monkey houses," on a little street half-way down between Independence Avenue and C Street. It was called Carroll Street.

Some of the ladies took to coming over to the Hill and sitting right on the floor with the congressmen, and it was giving the House a bad name. So the leadership, in all its wisdom, decided to make a rule that it was not proper for lady folks to be on the floor.

That was the way it had been all through the years and how it was when I arrived. Not even a female secretary may come on the floor to consult her boss.

On the Senate side, a female secretary may come on the floor if she has special permission from her senator. But in the House, never. Only one exception exists and that is that at the time the House is considering a bill, a committee staff member, even if she is a female, may come on the floor to help the congressman. But she cannot be a secretary from his own office. That is a no-no.

Only one male from each senator's office is permitted to go on the floor at any time on the Senate side. On the House side, no members from a congressman's staff can go on the floor. If it's a Democratic congressman, the staff member goes to the East Door and a doorman will call the member off the floor. If it's a Republican congressman, the staffer goes to the Main Door and a doorman calls the member off the floor. In either event, they still enter the Rayburn Conference Room—H207. Republicans and Democrats mix and mingle once they are in the conference room, but they must come through the right door. And the congressmen all go through the same door to get to the Rayburn Conference Room.

Through the years, some people have dared to suggest that the rules are a little crazy. One of them has been Sarah McClendon, the newswoman famous for making Presidents like LBJ and Kennedy squirm with her questions. She pressured Speaker Sam Rayburn

278

through the years, but he was too shy to tell her about those ladies of ill repute who used to be on the floor and what havoc they caused when they enticed men out in the middle of floor business.

Then came Speaker John McCormack, and lo and behold Sarah got wind of the fact that I had permitted male White House Fellows onto the floor but had not permitted female Fellows. I caught hell in all directions—from Sarah, from McCormack and from the Fellows.

Sarah led a delegation of female reporters to the Speaker's office and I was called in to explain the situation to Sarah. I said, "Mr. Speaker, it was just one of those things that happened when we are applying the rules of the House, which we have had all these years—that no women are allowed on the floor of the House if they are not members of Congress."

I did not bother to go into the one exception for committee staff under certain circumstances. Nor did I remind the Speaker that after Rayburn died, I had said, "Boss, are we going to have any changes in our operations—are we going to let women on the floor?" He snapped, "Hell, no, the rules were good enough for Speaker Rayburn and they're good enough for me."

After Sarah had gone, Speaker McCormack said gruffly, "That woman makes me so mad. She could at least be gentle. From here on, you handle her, Mister Doorkeeper. Keep her out of here." But of course I couldn't.

Thomas Jefferson, when a young man, entered the competitions not only for the design of the "President's House" but also for the Capitol Building, and he lost out both times. The man who won out was a young doctor from the West Indies named William Thornton.

George Washington was entranced with Thornton's design even though the doctor had no previous ex-

279

perience as an architect and Thornton was awarded the $500 prize.

Washington laid the cornerstone of the Capitol in 1793, little dreaming that the inexperience of the original architect would cause there to be many strange nooks, crannies and stairways leading nowhere and that, in fact, even with corrections by various future architects, there would be some seventy little cubby-holes and hideaways that would be used for good and ill by congressmen of seniority and power who needed a place away from their own office to snooze, study or engage in dalliance.

After the British soldiers did their thing in gutting with fire the incompleted Capitol in 1814, the House Chamber was rebuilt and used until 1858. Then, each state was invited to send statues of two of its most famous citizens—not necessarily political—and Statuary Hall was born.

The statues admittedly are not among the greatest works of art, and Mark Twain, seeing them for the first time, could not resist saying that if you went to the Capitol, you could walk through Statuary Hall where all the sculptures were, "but what have you done that you should suffer so."

There are all kinds of interesting tidbits I have learned about the Congress through the years. The first congressional act, for example, was signed by George Washington on June 1, 1789, setting rules for when and how oaths of office would be administered.

In the early days, the Congress didn't spend in a whole year what is now spent in one hour. The first billion-dollar Congress was the Fifty-second—March 1891 to 1893—which appropriated a little over a half billion dollars for the first year of the term and a bit more than that for the second. The nation was shocked, according to records, "and viewed with alarm."

The year after I left the Hill—fiscal year 1976, ending June 30—the budget for the year was $231.9

280

billion, which was $5.5 billion less than the appropriation President Ford had asked for.

Now even the date of the fiscal year has changed. And in the future, the fiscal year will end September 30 to give congressmen more time to do their homework and get their fighting done.

The longest session of the House was before my time—246 days actually in session between December 1917 and November 1918.

The easiest years on the Hill were 1939 and 1961, each with only 147 days of actual session. And I was there.

When women came to the Hill in 1917—the first woman was Jeannette Rankin—all kinds of firsts were added to history. Alice Mary Robertson of Oklahoma became the first woman to preside over the House. That was during a special session on June 20, 1921, deciding on a $15,000 appropriation to send a commission to represent the United States at the Peruvian Centennial. The vote was 209 yeas and 42 nays.

Mary Teresa Norton of New Jersey became the first congresswoman to head a congressional committee—the District of Columbia Affairs Committee—serving from 1931 to 1937.

When I left at the end of 1974, Margaret Chase Smith of Maine was still the only woman to have served in both the House and Senate.

There is one black woman who should go down in history as one of the most beautiful congresswomen. She arrived on the Hill to take her seat in January 1973, and more than one commented that she was beautiful enough to follow Lena Horne into movies, but she was not interested. She was the serious-minded Yvonne Brathwaite Burke of Los Angeles, a Democrat.

The daughter of a janitor at MGM studios, she is another one whose life would make a movie or musical. Even her love life is storybook, marrying as she did during her campaign to a successful businessman—William Burke, a few years her junior.

Many remember that she was vice-chairman of the Democratic National Convention in 1972. She will be forever in the book of records of the Hill not for her physical beauty, but because she was the first to ask for and receive maternity leave from the U.S. Congress, giving birth to a baby girl with the beautiful name of Autumn.

There have been a lot of hot-headed men in the House. And even some known for calmness have gotten unruly in the midst of a floor debate. At such times, the custom, strange as it seems in this day and age, is to run between them with the Mace.

In olden days, the Mace was a cruel weapon, a long pole with spikes or sharp axes at the end, capable of smashing through a man's armor, or at least bashing his head in.

The Mace in the House of Representatives is a much more civilized-looking object. It's almost four feet tall, and consists of thirteen ebony rods—representing the thirteen original colonies—which are tied together with silver strands crisscrossing up and down the pole. At the top is a globe of the world with a solid silver eagle standing on it, wings outspread.

We've had the Mace since December 1, 1842, when it was made by William Adams for a price of $400. Today it is priceless. Every day when the House is called to order, the sergeant-at-arms or his assistant—who at one time was me—places that symbol of authority into a cylindrical pedestal of beautiful green marble, standing at the right of the Speaker's chair. As long as the House is in session, the Mace remains in place, but when the House resolves itself into the committee of the whole House, the Mace is removed to a lower level to a pedestal beside the sergeant-at-arms' desk.

By looking at the Mace, members coming into the

chamber can tell at a glance if the House is in session or in committee. The current Mace is not the first we have had in the House. The first Mace used by the House, starting with the First Congress in 1789, was destroyed by the British Army's burning of the Capitol on August 24, 1814. A quick replacement was made of wood, and it served for more than a quarter century until our current splendid one was ready.

Our Mace is patterned after that of the British, and to show what the British thought of their symbol of authority even in modern times, one of the members of the House of Commons was suspended in 1930 for showing disrespect to it.

What had happened was that John Beckett, a member of the Labor party, was protesting the suspension of a member of the House of Commons. He grabbed the Mace, saying, "it is a damned disgrace," and attempted to leave the chamber with it. But the sergeant-at-arms wrestled the Mace away from Beckett and returned it to the Speaker's table.

No such thing has happened yet in this country.

Usually, since members themselves are able to correct the *Congressional Record* and delete things they have said which put them in poor light, there is no sign in the *Congressional Record* of the use of the Mace.

Let me give you a modern example. The black Representative Ronald V. Dellums was on the floor complaining, as he frequently did, that America was "a third-rate power" when it came to solving the problems and human misery of the ghettoes. Congressman Robert D. Bauman, a Republican and former page, could stand it no longer and jumped up to say that Americans had done "more to bring freedom to minorities than any nation on earth."

There followed a general rumpus with a few catcalls, and Richard L. Ottinger, a very liberal Democrat from New York, charged that Bauman had made a "racist" remark.

Now it was Bauman's turn to flip his lid. The very conservative Bauman from the eastern shore of Maryland jumped up and shouted out, "I'm not going to stand here and let this pip-squeak lecture me about racism."

Yet, the next day not a word of this could be found in the *Congressional Record*.

Back in 1847, when the country was heating up toward the Civil War, two men were having a fight about slavery just before there was to be a vote on electing Representative Robert C. Winthrop of Massachusetts to the speakership of the Thirtieth Congress.

William Duer of New York and R. K. Meade of Virginia were arguing because Duer accused Meade of being a disunionist. The argument grew into a heated floor dispute about slavery, during the course of which they called each other names. Duer finally accused Meade of lying.

The word lie is a very dangerous word on the floor and pandemonium broke loose until the sergeant-at-arms ran between the two irate congressmen with the Mace.

The vote on Winthrop continued and he was elected to the speakership. And in tribute to the Mace, which had done its work so well, Winthrop had it elevated to a place of honor beside him at that time. It has held that place of honor ever since.

In the 1890s, John A. Heard of Missouri and W. C. P. Breckenridge of Kentucky got into a scuffle on the floor and the sergeant-at-arms ran between them with the Mace and brought them to the Speaker's desk. Each then apologized to the House and to each other and that was the end of it.

But a few years later, in the case of Charles L. Bartlett of Georgia of the Fifty-fifth Congress, it wasn't so easy. Bartlett was a real hothead—there have been a few of those in the House—and he actually threw a book at a colleague, James M. Brumm of Pennsylvania. The book, a volume of the United States Statutes, fell on the floor and the sergeant-at-arms ran between Bartlett and Brumm with the Mace. Both sat down and Bartlett didn't get into trouble again until the new century had begun and we were into the Sixtieth Congress.

This time, Bartlett was the ranking minority member of the Committee of Accounts, and New York Congressman George Southwick made some caustic remarks on the floor because the committee had failed to provide an increase in salary to a House employee.

Bartlett, though he was only a member of the minority of the committee, chose to take the matter personally and rushed at Southwick "brandishing a knife," as the story is recorded. Fortunately, before he could get to Southwick, a fellow congressman held Bartlett back until the man with the Mace could get there. For some reason, Bartlett was not expelled or even censured.

Even the 1838 incident of Kentuckian William J. Graves killing a fellow representative in duel did not result in expulsion.

On the other hand, Thomas L. Blanton of Texas was moved against for expulsion from Congress in 1921 for the mildest of offenses—a little bad language that he let slip into the *Congressional Record*. True, Blanton was known for having the filthiest mouth in Washington, but that alone was not enough to get him in deep trouble. The plain truth was his colleagues didn't like him in other ways. And sooner or later, if they don't like you on the Hill, they will catch you some day with your tail in the crack. When they caught Blanton, his high crime was to have permitted the use of vulgar language in material that was printed in the *Congressional Record* under his name. It wasn't even what he personally had said.

As I have indicated, every congressman gets to correct his statements in the *Record* before printing, so usually any slip of the tongue is caught in time. However, the congressman, in recording a conversation of other people, did not check it over carefully himself afterwards and it was printed with a few cuss words, which would be considered fairly mild by today's standards. The House was much more straitlaced in 1921. Eventually, he was merely censured.

Now, though members are still a little careful of what goes in the *Record* that is read by friends and political pundits of the nation, their language off the floor is alive with colorful curses and casual vulgarities, lightly used and with no offense intended.

From the beginning of Congress until 1975, there have been twenty attempts to expel members and only three times has it been done—all three cases involving Southern congressmen who took up arms against the government of the United States and fought for the Confederacy—John B. Clark and John W. Reid of Missouri and Henry C. Burnett of Kentucky.

The case of Adam Clayton Powell, Jr., is different. He was denied his seat in Congress but the Supreme Court held that the House had done it illegally.

In the time leading up to World War I, Congressman Tom Heflin of Alabama, who was known for advocating war with Germany, made some remarks that questioned the patriotism of members who were opposed to passage of the resolution that put the United States into war. Congressman John L. Burnett of Heflin's own state sweetly inquired then as to why his colleague didn't go to war himself. Heflin rushed at Burnett and only the arrival of the Mace stopped the exchange.

Yes, the Mace has not sat around idle during the years. In fact, in one Congress, the Fifty-first—1889 to 1891—known for its roughness, the sergeant-at-arms would frequently pace up and down the aisles, just carrying the Mace.

I once checked the Library of Congress and found that the first brawl in the House took place in 1798, during the administration of John Adams, when Congress was using rented quarters in Philadelphia even before the move to the newly built Capitol in Washington, D.C., or Federal City or Washington City, as it was variously called.

Congressman Matthew Lyon of Vermont spit into the face of Roger Griswold of Connecticut in the course of an angry exchange, and the House immediately entertained a resolution to expel Lyon. The debate lasted about ten days, with Lyon acting as his own lawyer. In spite of Lyon's defense of his behavior, the expulsion resolution carried 52 to 44. Still, Lyon was not expelled because that was not the two-thirds majority necessary for expulsion.

The nation was impressed with the brother act of the Kennedys, in which John Fitzgerald Kennedy was followed into the Senate in later service by his brothers Robert, of New York, and Edward, of Massachusetts.

But there is a still more amazing brother act in the history of the Hill—four brothers, three of them serving simultaneously from different states. And none with a White House connection. First came Israel Washburn, Jr., a Maine Whig who was sworn in on March 4, 1851. Then came his brother Elihu, also a Whig, from Illinois, sworn in in 1853. Elihu was followed two years later by Republican brother Cadwallader Colden Washburn of Wisconsin. All three served simultaneously from 1855 to 1861. The fourth brother, William Drew Washburn, Republican of Minnesota, arrived in Washington eighteen years later, after his victory in 1878. He served three terms.

For those who like statistics, here's a rather interesting one: Of the 9,510 congressmen who have served in the House through June 1974, all of 339 have been brothers.

Of course, no record of the House is complete without the record on the fattest man to serve. White House buffs point with pride to President Taft, who was so fat he had to have a special bathtub installed—a truth the White House denied until the bathtub was torn out years later.

Well, the House is proud to have had a man who would have made Taft and his 320 pounds look like a baby. He was Dixon H. Lewis of Alabama, who was in office from 1829 to 1844. He resigned in the latter year because he had been appointed as a senator to fill an unexpired term in the Other Body.

Old Dixon Lewis was a rare man, a lawyer who fed his mind as well as his body, and he had ballooned up to over five hundred pounds. So it took two chairs for him to sit in the chamber, until a special chair was built just for him.

Lewis proved that his courage matched his size when a coastal steamer he was on was wrecked and people were pouring into lifeboats. Lewis bravely refused to get in, saying his weight would "jeopardize the safety of others." Virtue was rewarded in this case and the rotund congressman was eventually rescued.

Bathing used to be a luxury to congressmen and senators who came a long way from home and stayed in Washington rooming houses. For their convenience, lovely hand-carved marble bathtubs were ordered from Italy and installed in the Capitol. These tubs became as popular on the Hill as karate is these days.

Members used to call the sport "tubbing," and some spent a great amount of time in the luxurious marble *objets d'art* once they got their turn. Unfortunately, his turn led to the death of Henry Wilson, the Vice President, who enjoyed sitting in the tub more than he did

288

presiding over the Senate. He caught his death of cold on a chill November of 1875.

If you want another oddity of history, you don't have to go further than the fact that we once reelected a dead man to Congress. I don't mean it was a case like Hale Boggs, who disappeared in an airplane over Alaska when we waited for months not knowing if he was alive or dead—in fact, we still are without proof either way as I write.

In this case, it was a man reelected posthumously to the Eighty-eighth Congress. He was Clement Woodnut Miller, Democrat of California, who was killed in an airplane accident near Eureka, California, on October 7, 1962. He had been in Congress since 1959, and I liked him well and called him Clem, as did all his friends.

But they didn't like him well enough to elect him as a dead man. The problem is that under the election laws, certain states, including California, require a sixty-day notice before a special election can be held.

So in November 1962, the month after his death, Clem was reelected and his staff was paid until his successor, Donald H. Clausen, was elected and took office the same day, January 22, 1963, just eleven days after Clem had been "sworn in."

When you say party leaders or leadership in the House you mean the Speaker of the House, the Majority Leader of the House and the Whip in the House. If you're speaking of the party not in control of the House, the party leaders are the Minority Leader of the House and the Minority Whip.

The Officers of the House are the Clerk, the Sergeant-at-Arms, the Parliamentarian, the Chaplain, the Postmaster and the Doorkeeper. I can only say that the office of Doorkeeper has been a noble one. There has been a Doorkeeper keeping the rowdies out and announcing honored guests, starting in 1789 with Gifford Dalley, whose native state is unknown. But

289

surely Dalley must have seen George Washington arriving by carriage, as well as such men as Thomas Jefferson, John Adams and James Madison. He served through three Congresses. The Doorkeeper who served longest was Thomas Claxton, manning the door through thirteen consecutive Congresses—from 1795 to 1821.

I'm proud to say my record of service over a hundred years later is next—I served through twelve Congresses, the Eighty-fourth through the Ninety-third, and earlier than that in the Eighty-first and Eighty-second Congresses. In other words, I served in that post from 1949 through 1952 and then from 1955 through 1973.

Though thirty-three men had been Doorkeeper at the time I was retired, only three, of whom I am one, were called back to serve again once they had left office. Only one Doorkeeper ever won election to the House, and that was Walter Preston Brownlow of Tennessee, who was elected to seven terms from 1897 until his death in 1910. And only one congressman reversed the order, becoming Doorkeeper after leaving office—Charles Henry Turner of New York, who had the job of Doorkeeper from 1891 to 1893.

The House of Representatives has been a good training ground for all types of advancement. Of the four hundred men and women who served on the cabinets of various Presidents through 1971, almost one-fourth —ninety-seven—had prior service in the House. And the cabinet officer who served the longest in a presidential cabinet post—in the Department of Agriculture, sixteen years and one day—had served first as a congressman from Iowa. James Wilson served under McKinley, Teddy Roosevelt, William Howard Taft and at the beginning of Woodrow Wilson's term.

As for Vice Presidents, the record is simply amazing. Twenty-one Vice Presidents were former members of the House. And of these Vice Presidents, a lucky six became Presidents—John Tyler, Andrew Johnson, Millard Fillmore, Richard Nixon, Lyndon Johnson and Gerald Ford.

You don't work on the Hill long before you realize that each congressman and senator feels he is somehow different. The vote of the electorate has turned him into some kind of god. I've seen them start humble and lose their humility fast.

It's as if each elected man is trying to emulate the man in the White House and have the same luxury situation for himself.

The public learned there was a swimming pool in the White House in which Kennedy liked to swim in the nude. Well, the Hill has two swimming pools in which the men can swim nude and for several hours a day they used to graciously get out so the ladies of the Congress could have their turn.

The swimming pools are in the Rayburn House Office Building, said to be the biggest monument to one man's ego. Let me explain about the Rayburn building. I was there when the building was conceived and Rayburn was my closest friend and idol on the Hill, so it hurts to hear what they say, but it's true. I think somehow the plans got out of control. But if you can figure out how to keep another Rayburn building from happening, you will also know how to keep congressional heads from swelling.

And let me confess, I was part of the system. I was one of those who helped congressional heads swell. I gave men such good service that they fought over me. I was supposed to take care of Democrats, but the Republicans liked what they saw as well. They got a little jealous and were going out of their way and coming on the Democratic side to give me their work to do. They liked the Fishbait treatment.

Now about that Rayburn building. I remember when Sam Rayburn got his inspiration for a monument to himself. It was true the congressman needed a little more room. He chortled happily as he worked out his clever idea of how to turn the simple need into a super building "for all time and for all ages."

As he told me, "Fish, the senators need to be shown that congressmen are every bit as good as those damn senators are."

One of the biggest selling points that Rayburn came up with was that Congressman Dante Fascell, Democrat of Florida, was so crowded in his office that he had to put one of his secretaries in the hall leading to his own executive bathroom. Rayburn had crocodile tears in his eyes as he explained to the House members how dreadful and embarrassing *that* was.

And what he suggested was simply for the House Appropriations Committee to put $25,000 into the budget for a study on the problem of congressional space shortage.

But when the supplemental appropriation bill got to the floor, Rayburn, flush with power, pulled a switch and said in effect, forget the $25,000 and let me have $2 million to acquire land and start construction right away and I'll come back for more when needed.

In this way, Rayburn got around the rule of having the matter properly studied and an authorization passed. But once Rayburn sneaked the original legislation into law, like topsy the thing just grew.

Things got added as Rayburn tried to put the Senate in its place—a fantastic gym with a sixty-foot swimming pool, not one but five dining rooms, a huge cafeteria for the lesser lights. Not to mention inside parking for 1,500 cars—enough space for any number of guests who might show up at a cocktail party held in one of the committee rooms.

The committee rooms, incidentally, were grand enough, with huge two-level ceilings, to inspire terror in timid witnesses. The halls of the building were marble and wide enough to drive a Cadillac through. The outside, too, has marble—Georgia marble—but then, in a sudden attack of humility, Speaker Sam decided to have the lower part of the exterior made of modest stone—granite from New Hampshire. But so ugly does it look against the marble on the building that ivy is being encouraged to rise up and cover it as fast as possible. The building took from 1955 to 1965 to finish, and the ivy is following suit in not moving very fast either.

In Rayburn's last years—he didn't know until the last few months of his life that he had cancer, a secret that I helped him keep in 1961—the thing that gave the Speaker the greatest joy was his pet building project.

"It will be the first thing you see as you come up the Hill," he would gloat. "I'm going to have marble rest rooms for the ladies, the best ever designed. This building is going to have far better rest rooms than the members of the Other Body ever dreamed of."

It certainly does. It has so many rest rooms that office help in the neighborhood drop in just to use the facilities. There are some ninety public rest rooms. Plus, there is a private rest room in each three-room suite for the congressman or woman occupant, and a rest room for the staff. However, in most offices, the staff rest room has been gutted to make it into an additional work space.

Instead of everyone wanting to work in the Rayburn building, most still prefer the Cannon, or the Longworth building which gives a better appearance when one enters an office suite.

The trouble is that the Rayburn building is all show on the outside and waste space on the inside on great hallways you could hold concerts in. But the rooms for the help are pitifully small.

When the building first opened, there was such fighting over who was to go in that it was decided to let the lucky people be those with the most seniority. Even being chairman of a committee did not bump a person on the list with greater seniority.

One congressman made his reputation as great humorist by his comments on the Rayburn building. He was Bill Ayres, Republican of Ohio. He had been one of the lucky ones to get space in the new building.

Well, good ole Bill moved in and was delighted with his refrigerator and, in fact, complete kitchen. But then he made the mistake of turning on the water in his kitchen sink. Zounds! There was no drainage. This was particularly funny because Ayres, before he came to Congress, was a plumber. It became a circus as the reporters and photographers rushed in to photograph Ayres mugging with his sink. The ranking minority member of the Education and Labor Committee became more famous over his sink that didn't work than over his legislation that did.

What had the Rayburn building cost? It cost $81 million—but the land and a few other things, such as an underground Toonerville trolley to ride the congressmen to the House floor in style, added a few million more.

When Rayburn died in 1961, there wasn't a doubt in anyone's mind about what the palace would be called. I remember, before he knew he had cancer, how I used to kid Speaker Sam, saying, "They'll have to name that building for *you,* Boss." And he had said, "Why do you want to say that Fish? They can't until I die. Wouldn't be proper. They'll just have to call it by number like they do the other two."

Then he laughed. "Heh, heh, heh. Or maybe you've gotten to be such a character around here, they'll name it for you—'The Fishery!'"

He would be gone before the building was finished and there would be no problem as far as its name went. All three office buildings would cease to be nonentities with names of "the Old and the New" and would now be named for three fallen leaders.

If you wait long enough, history comes full circle. Now I have been informed that Congress is thinking of expanding its facilities to take care of all those extra employees. And what will the cost be? Would you believe $84 million? Only this time, the House members say, they will get much more for their money than Rayburn did.

The $84 million is a bargain rate if the new building is combined with the old Cannon building, which was finished in 1914. If Congress starts fresh and has to buy existing homes to demolish to make room for the new building, the cost goes up to $180 million.

I'll bet Rayburn's ghost did a few dance steps on that note.

At least this saved the second Library of Congress annex. The House was hellbent, for a while, on appropriating the new building in the final stages of construction, though it had been designed particularly to handle books, magazines and papers and to solve the problem of congestion in the Library of Congress and its annex. Just to convert a library to an office building would have wasted millions, and of course another library building would still have to be built.

A final question I am always eventually asked is, "Are there ghosts in the Capitol? Are there ghosts in any of the buildings up on Capitol Hill?"

I don't know. I wish I did.

Through the years, some of the night guards have sworn they saw something weird. One lost his job for what he thought he saw. What is true is that the ghost stories are certainly a part of Capitol Hill history.

I myself have heard strange noises that I could not identify—something like the clucking of a chicken.

There is not just one ghost story about the Capitol, but several. Some say the curse on the Capitol goes back to the building's very beginning and that the

295

reason it keeps sinking and swaying and needs supports even today is because of that very curse.

The story begins with the design of the building by William Thornton and the attempt of the follow-up architect, Benjamin Henry Latrobe, to make the plan workable. George Washington had laid the cornerstone in 1793, but in 1808 they were still building, and that year, Latrobe had an argument with his construction foreman, John Lenthall, about a certain arch that Latrobe designed to serve as a support. Lenthall, who was extremely concerned with the appearance of his workmanship, said the arch was not needed and that he would prove it. He started to pull out a support and some stones fell down, crushing and killing him. It is said that his dying words were a curse on the Capitol.

Another man died or disappeared in the building of the Capitol. He was a stonemason and some believe he was killed in an argument with a carpenter and was sealed into a wall with his own tools. Now and then through the years, someone has reported having seen a ghostlike figure with a trowel in his hand pass through a solid wall on the Senate side of the building.

One particularly tenacious ghost story involves a demon cat who is supposed to roam around Statuary Hall before national tragedies and changes of administration. It is said to seem perfectly natural at first and to be purring. But then, as a guard or other person approaches, the cat becomes frighteningly large and the purr turns into a snarl. One guard of bygone years screamed in sudden fear at the sight of the snarling, swelling cat as it leaped at him. It did not land on him, however. Just as it reached him, it disappeared.

I have not seen the demon cat, but I must say that Statuary Hall can seem eerie at night. Yet there are others who say there are definitely ghosts who return there. One guard said that as a clock struck twelve

296

one night, he saw some figures float down from their pedestals. As he approached, he saw the ghostly figure of General Grant shaking hands with General Lee. And then, he added, the other figures came to life and all started dancing around in utter silence. He had tried to scream but couldn't, and he had run right out of the building. He told the Capitol police, who relieved him of duty. They didn't believe him, but others did.

My own favorite Hill ghost story concerns another Statuary Hall visitation. This one involves John Quincy Adams, the only President to become a congressman after serving in the White House. When Adams served his terms in Congress, from 1831 to 1848, what is now Statuary Hall was the House Chamber.

Adams had risen to speak out against the Mexican War, which had just been won. The date was February 23, 1848, and he was furious that Congress was going to honor those who had won an "unrighteous war against Mexico." His speech was never finished. Adams suffered a stroke and was carried to the Speaker's Room, where he died within days.

Workers around the Capitol, who were still finishing the rebuilding work necessitated by its being burned by the British in 1814, swore they had seen Adams' ghost returned to that room, still finishing his speech. And they pointed out the spot—the same spot where Adams had been stricken.

But the saddest ghost I've ever heard about is that of Pierre L'Enfant, the great French engineer who never was paid for laying out the city of Washington and had to be buried in a pauper's grave.

A few have seen L'Enfant's ghost with a roll of plans under his arm walking in the hall of the Capitol and shaking his head sadly, still waiting for Congress to appropriate the money.

As most people know, President James Garfield lay in state at the Capitol Rotunda, after being assassinated by a disgruntled office seeker. While his body lay in the Rotunda, his own ghost was said to have been seen walking around the halls nearby. Sometime later, a guard swore that he had seen Garfield's assassin, Guiteau, starting down a stair at the Capitol. He said he chased the man, thinking he had escaped from prison. Then, as the figure evaporated into air, the guard remembered that Guiteau had already been executed for his crime.

Yes, it really is eerie in the Capitol at night.

PROFILES IN POWER

Top star in my life was Sam Rayburn, the Speaker of the House. Some said we were as close as a pair of twins, but I never took advantage of my closeness.

I didn't want to call him by his first name, out of a feeling of respect, though I could have. So I called him "Boss," and he liked it. It was the right title, any way you looked at it. Rayburn called all the shots and I carried out his orders.

I was one of the few men to know the truth about Rayburn's private life, and people would ask questions. Was the guy a celibate? What about his half-hidden marriage? What was he really like? I didn't tell. But I will in this book since he has been dead for over a dozen years.

Joe Martin, another bachelor, was important in the power-structure of the House. It was strange indeed that at one point in history, the top job of the House vacillated between these two bachelors—Martin, the Republican and Rayburn, the Democrat. Joe Martin, incidentally, was one of the few men on the Hill who refused to reveal his religion.

Then there was John W. McCormack, the only man who insisted on calling me Bill. The reason was that McCormack's wife disapproved of nicknames. "Harriet won't let me," he would say. And hearing this, Sam Rayburn would shake his head in disbelief at one woman's hold over a man. McCormack was the most compulsive and sentimental man on Capitol Hill. He never missed a meal with his beloved Harriet, often causing havoc on Capitol Hill when he walked out for his "date."

Harriet had given up a career as a singer to marry John. Speaker Sam and I would sit on a bench at the

299

end of a day's session of Congress, gossiping about what had happened that day, and we would see John rushing out. Time and again, Sam would turn to me and say, "Damn it, isn't it lucky we don't have such closely held ropes around us." But of course, Sam Rayburn *did* have a closely held rope around himself which was his all-consuming love—Congress.

Speaker Carl Albert was very short in stature, just a little over five feet, and boyish in looks. One time when he first became Speaker and was passing the desk of a brand-new freshman congressman, on his way to the Speaker's stand, Carl was mistaken for a page. A freshman snapped his fingers importantly and said, "Boy," as I had told him to do if he needed anything.

Carl Albert looked around and saw that the congressman meant him. He was sure that he had not misunderstood when an instant later the freshman thrust some publications at him and told him to take them over to a colleague. Albert, much amused, did as he was told and delivered the papers to the startled colleague.

As the Speaker took his place at his desk on the top level of the three-tiered Speaker's stand, he paused before rapping his mallet and cast an impish glance at the freshman congressman. The frosh, who by now was aware of whom he had turned into an errand boy, was rather hard to see. He was slumped down in his seat, shrinking to the smallest size possible.

Powerhouse Wayne Hays, Democrat of Ohio, was nicknamed "Chairman Skinflint" and he relished the name. It isn't always death or elections that terminate a man's position of power. It's saddest when the downfall comes as a result of indiscretion, as it came to Wilbur Mills and Wayne Hays. It is hard to remember that some of these men were superstars—worshipped and feared by the run-of-the-mill congressmen.

Hale Boggs of Louisiana was another of my bosses who rose in power, first becoming the Democratic Whip, then Majority Leader. I remember that Hale and his wife, Lindy, who managed his campaigns and knew just about as much about politics as he did, would always have a spring party at their home in Bethesda, Maryland. They would have about 1,800 guests. I had to stand in line beside Hale and tell him the names as the people came by. It was one of my annual chores—and I loved it.

The annual party certainly helped Hale's rise in power. When he disappeared, Lindy Boggs inherited his job and his power. The fact that she was the first woman in history to be permanent chairman of the Democratic National Convention in 1976 was just one sign of it. I feel that Lindy, who is a dear friend, is the woman to watch on the Hill.

If there ever is a woman Speaker, she may be it. Sister Lindy—whose given name is Corinne—is not just a woman legislator, she's a powerhouse. She has also been involved in very important legislation dealing in the use of atomic power for energy.

Men of power are very competitive in strange ways. The urinal in the men's room off the floor was frequently the place at which members tried to show off by how far they could stand from the receptacle. The older a member got, the farther back he would stand and the more he would brag about the distance he could achieve.

The younger men said the old bastards were acting like they were some kind of long-distance runners or athletes getting in training for the Olympics. The behavior of the congressmen was of more than a little interest to me because, being in charge of the restroom attendants, I was involved in trying to keep the place presentable. It couldn't be done.

A story about Senator Theodore Bilbo of my home

state was circulated on the Hill. It seems that "The Man," as Bilbo called himself, was in a hotel room while on a trip and was seen and recognized by another guest across the court—a man with frequent business on the Hill.

The man caught Bilbo standing at a window in the act of looking down and examining his equipment. Hiding behind the drapery at his own window, the man called out, "Senator, are you pointing with pride or viewing with alarm?"

The blind crashed down in a hurry. Bilbo may have suspected that it was no accident that his colleagues on the Hill were frequently mentioning "pointing with pride" at something or other in his hearing.

Sam Rayburn was very sensitive about the call to nature. One thing I had to do for Speaker Sam, whenever we were going to a strange place for him to make a speech, was to locate the men's room and find a short-cut to it. I would take him through kitchens, after making a dry run and tipping all the cooks and waiters along the route. That way he could disappear and no one would realize what he was doing. But once, a couple of the Congressional Club leaders—wives of Congressmen—wanted to talk to him and they tracked us right through the kichens and all of a sudden burst right into the men's room, not realizing what it was.

After I had escorted them out, Speaker Sam said with a shy smile and a blush, "People do follow the public leaders blindly, don't they?"

Most people don't know that Republicans do not use the same urinals as Democrats. The men's room off the House floor is strictly segregated by political party. There is an aisle down the middle with three Republican potties and four urinals on one side and three Democratic potties and four urinals on the other side. It frequently happens that a mischievous Democrat will slip over and use the wrong urinal and go out gloating "I 'blanked' all over the damn Republicans."

In the no-man's land, belonging to both parties, is a very expensive scale of the kind used in some doctors' offices, so that members do not have to peer down over their paunches to see if they are holding their weight.

Only twice did we Democrats lose our standing on the Hill—in 1947 and in 1953. You would think Rayburn and McCormack would say, "Well, we've had our turn long enough, let the Republicans have a turn." But no indeed, they were a little bitter, especially John McCormack.

He had been Majority Leader in the Seventy-ninth Congress, second in power only to Speaker Sam, but when the Republicans took over in the Eightieth Congress in January 1947, Brother McCormack was back to being only the Democratic Whip.

He told Rayburn, me and a group of other Democrats that he felt like the pig that had lost his standing in the community—a neighbor had cut off its testicles for spite, and the farmer was suing the man who had done this terrible deed.

It was a real lawsuit and McCormack had paid close attention to the outcome about the time of his own reelection in 1946 to a Congress that had gone GOP. When the Eightieth Congress met in January 1947, he was still talking about it and making a comparison between himself and the pig.

"I'm like that pig in Boston, but I have no lawyer to defend me," he said. "I have been castrated and there's nothing I can do about it. I've lost my standing in the community."

In 1953, when McCormack again lost his standing in the Hill community, he decided he was going to be the best Minority Whip ever. He set me up in a little basement room—now known as Hernando's hideaway—gave me a typewriter and a phone and a lock for the door.

My job was to contact the regional whips and work up a fact sheet quickly on how the House was going to vote on certain important matters. And after a vote, he wanted to know immediately how everyone had voted. He could have waited until the next day and gotten it all in the *Congressional Record,* but he wanted it immediately in order to discuss strategy with now Minority Leader Sam Rayburn.

That's how men got power and stayed in power—they never let up. And once in power, almost anything goes—or has at least been tried.

More than one man found that it doesn't pay to buck the Hill powers, or to insult the Congress. Claude Pepper was a senator when he tried to be funny about Congress, and it didn't go over. In fact, he got demoted to congressman. Truman could get away with insulting Congress, but that was because he was President. Back in 1947, Pepper had said, "One man has described the present Congress as the worst in twenty-five years. I wouldn't go that far. It's only the worst in fifteen years."

Pepper's constituents, like his colleagues, had resented his poormouthing Congress and gave his job in 1950 to a young man with enthusiasm and appreciation—George Smathers. Claude became just plain citizen-lawyer Claude Pepper of Miami Beach, Coral Gables and Tallahassee.

Eventually, Claude Pepper got back into the Congress but it was to the House, not to the Senate. However, when I saw him, Pepper was mighty happy to be back on the Hill at all—it had taken him twelve years to return.

At first, it was rather hard for Pepper to get used to being a House member after all the privileges he enjoyed as a senator. One morning Claude appeared in my office and said, "Mr. Doorkeeper, it's been a hard morning. Do you have any snake-bite medicine here? It might help calm my nerves."

I told him that I ran a dry office, but I directed him to the office of the sergeant-at-arms where they knew how to handle these things.

Congressman Sam Steiger of Arizona learned in his second year in the House that one just doesn't insult the big guns of the Hill. Something of a loner and a Republican to boot, he went on a radio talk show and rambled on about how incompetent Congress was and how most members weren't even fit to push a wheelbarrow.

So when it came time for legislation to bring new projects and government contracts flowing to his district, his colleagues would line up and object. In fact, one day three members waited all afternoon on the floor, just to kill his bill.

It only takes three objections to knock a bill off the Consent Calendar for the rest of the session, and after he had been bumped three times, Steiger was almost on his knees saying he was sorry and pleading to get a bill through to a vote.

Eventually Morris Udall of his state, though of the opposite party, took pity on Steiger and helped him to get a bill passed—especially because his constituents asked him to. But Steiger never did feel completely at home in the House, and in 1976 he decided to start fresh by running for the Senate.

Speaking of Udall reminds me that I have had my feuds and power struggles too, in holding on to my particular job of Doorkeeper. At the end of the Ninety-third Congress, when I was deposed, it was the combination of Udall and James V. Stanton, a Democrat of Ohio, that did me in.

For some reason, as soon as Stanton arrived on the Hill with the Ninety-second Congress, which took office in January 1971, the man had it in for me. The word was that he was determined to get me out and put someone more to his liking, James Malloy, chief of the Finance Division of the House, in my place.

From the beginning of his term, Stanton started throwing out sledgehammer hints in my direction. One of the first times he approached me, even while I was trying to be friendly and helpful, he said, "Fishbait, I've been hearing about you too long, what a great fellow you are and how long you've been here, that you know how to help everybody and know all the ins and outs of the workings of Congress. And I don't see why old as you are you don't think about retiring."

And with that he walked on. No smile, no slight show of friendliness.

The second man to whom I owed my defeat was Mo Udall. I had come to him, asking him to second my bid for the continuation of my job as Doorkeeper, when it would come up at the end of December 1974. Instead of saying he would, Udall said, "I don't know, Fish. I'm running for President, and I don't think I can have that albatross around my neck. I can't have my name associated with yours."

Both Stanton and Udall won, and I lost my bid for another term as Doorkeeper by a vote of 100 to 150 in Democratic caucus.

I thought of each of them as they too met their waterloos. I saw James V. Stanton after his defeat when he had tried to become the head of the committee investigating the CIA. The committee had wanted Nedzi and not Stanton, and now he knew how it felt. He was walking along, his head low, slouching dejectedly on his way down the House steps. I knew it was wrong, but I was gloating a bit. I couldn't resist giving him a little finger wave. He got the message.

As for Udall, he did not get the presidency which he had wanted so bad he could taste it. Though he was a liberal and a fine man, that wasn't enough. He didn't have enough friends. One must be faithful to

306

one's own friends. And though I was only a very small potato in the potato bin, and he could afford to throw me away, the man who throws away one friend is apt to throw away others.

I want to tell you that the fall from power is a mighty bump. Especially when you've been flying high. I remember, and have the *Congressional Record* to prove it, when on January 20, 1971, right after the invocation by the chaplain on the opening day's session, the day was proclaimed "Fishbait Day" in honor of my birthday.

And this was a bipartisan event, no less. The men who stood to proclaim it were Republicans Gerald Ford, Minority Leader, and Elford Cederburg, ranking minority member of the Appropriations Committee; and Democrats Hale Boggs, Majority Whip, and Robert F. Sikes, chairman of a subcommittee of the Appropriations Committee.

One great truth I have learned on the Hill is that doing someone a favor can cost you your life or hurt your career. Hale Boggs was doing Nick Begich of Alaska a favor when the terrible thing happened of the plane's disappearance. Because Begich had voted against Boggs when Boggs was trying to become Majority Leader, Boggs was trying to win Begich over by helping him in his bid for reelection. It cost Boggs his life. It almost cost me mine, since I had been scheduled to go, too.

Jack Kennedy was trying to do Lyndon Johnson and the Texas delegation a favor by going to Texas to help them heal their wounds and bring about "solidarity." It cost Kennedy his life.

And speaking of Hale Boggs reminds me that he was almost the victim of friendship in his bid for the majority leadership after the 1970 election. He asked Wayne Hays to campaign for him and help drum up the votes needed to get a majority of votes against several contenders.

307

Hays promised he would. Instead, Wayne pulled a fast one and tried to grab it for himself. Fortunately, Boggs was still popular enough to get a majority on the second ballot.

One way you can measure power on the Hill is by the number of honors one receives.

When you are on the Hill, all kinds of honors come your way. Some are worked for, some fall into your lap. You can imagine how many honorary degrees a congressman or senator gets in the course of his term in office if I tell you that this is just a partial list of mine:

I'm a Kentucky Colonel, an Alabama Colonel, a Mississippi Colonel, a Texas Honorary Citizen, a Nebraska Admiral in the State Navy, a Louisiana Colonel, a Georgia Lt. Colonel, an Oklahoma Okie Colonel, and I have an honorary Doctor of Laws from Atlanta (Ga.) Law School.

I'm an honorary Sergeant of the U.S. Marine Corps, based at Quantico, Virginia; and a Flying Colonel of Delta Airlines.

Showing that honors rise above party affiliations, Rogers B. Morton, secretary of the interior and President Ford's campaign manager in his bid for reelection, made me an honorary deputy game warden of the U.S. Fish and Wildlife Service.

But, as long as I'm being immodest, the thing that means the most to me is my standing in the Masonic world. For fellow Masons and Shriners around the country, the list goes like this: Shriner-Kena Temple, Alexandria, Virginia; Aide to the Imperial Potentate, Member, U.S. Capitol Hill Shrine Club, Washington, D.C. I am an honorary member of the following Shriner Temples: Hamasa 61, Meridian, Mississippi; Aloha, Honolulu, Hawaii; Wahabi 127, Jackson, Mississippi; Yaarib 52, Atlanta, Georgia; and Islam 15, San Francisco, California.

Now we get to the Masons and I am looking at my ring which I proudly wear as a Scottish Rite Mason, 32nd degree, Alexandria Consistory in the Valley of Alexandria, Orient of Virginia.

Working my way up through the years, I have achieved the honor of becoming a 33rd degree Mason. I am Inspector General Honorary Member of the Supreme Council 33rd degree, Ancient and Accepted Scottish Rite of Freemasonry of the Southern Jurisdiction, U.S.A.; and an honorary Inspector 33rd degree, Grand Tyler of the Supreme Council.

Further than that, I am a member of the Royal Order of Jesters, Alexandria, Virginia, Court No. 162; a Master Mason of the Cherrydale Lodge Number 42 A. F. and A. M. of Arlington, Virginia, and also knight Commander of the Court of Alexandria Consistory.

So much for formal honors. For a different kind of honor that gave me a big kick, I remember when a Republican friend, Congressman Jim Johnson of Colorado, asked his family what they wanted to call their new dog. All members immediately piped up with, "Let's call him Fishbait." It's nice to have a namesake, if only a dog. Jim's wife came to see her husband one day and told me not to get worried if I'm visiting their house and hear the children ordering "Fishbait" around.

I'm happy to say, however, that I have acquired another namesake in recent months, John *William* Knight, a grandson born to Sarah Patsy, who, though an English teacher at Georgia State University, has no responsibility for this manuscript, which she has never seen.

I'm not ashamed to say I almost worshipped Sam Rayburn. He would laugh as I used to say, there is nothing I wouldn't do for him short of murder and that only at my own discretion.

All kinds of famous names hitched their wagons to a star on the Hill and grew in stature as a result. Lyndon Johnson hitched his wagon to the same star as I did, Samuel Taliaferro Rayburn—that was his full name and he hated it.

And Walter "Fritz" Mondale hitched his wagon to a star named Hubert Humphrey, starting when, as a student, he helped Professor HHH with his first campaign. Mondale stuck to Humphrey like glue on the Hill, getting his best advice from him.

So I was not surprised that when Mondale was picked to be Carter's running mate at the 1976 Democratic National Convention, HHH was there to nominate him.

I didn't aspire to public office, but my rise in the administrative side of the Capitol came directly from Speaker Sam's guidance and that of another of his protégés, John W. McCormack.

Rayburn always expanded my mind with the great truths he would suddenly come out with. For example, I would be tired or I would wonder why he was not tired and he would say, "If you say you're tired, you will be tired." He would never admit to tiredness, so neither did I, and it made a big difference in how much I could get done.

Rayburn had a peculiar rule about his mail. If a man or woman wrote to him in pencil, he answered in pencil. If it was in ink, he answered in ink. He never upstaged anyone, even in a letter, and he always told me, "Fish, I have greater trust in people who send me postcards or letters on tablet paper, using a lead pencil, than those who use the telegraph office to deliver their message." He put his greatest faith in what he and Lyndon called, "the little people."

Even when he was getting old, he was all for progress, saying, "There's only one thing I hate more than an old fogie and that's a young fogie." He had

310

no patience with congressmen who weren't open to new ideas. Unless it concerned women.

Of course, he was the boss of the Democratic party on the Hill and he always preached to the newcomers something that Lyndon picked up from him, "To get along, go along." But Rayburn always added, "But I will never ask a man to do something that will ruin him back home with his constituency."

Even though Speaker Sam had enough power to choke a mule, he had a little bit of shyness and humbleness about him. That's because he saw the House as much bigger than himself. "It's a wise man who knows that the church is bigger than its pastor," he would say, and "the damn fool who becomes conceited or arrogant in a job wasn't big enough for the job in the first place."

Rayburn would turn aside praise and act embarrassed by it. "I'm only doing my job," he would say, and he would give me a dirty look if I didn't act equally humble, when I had done something I was proud of. "Damn the man who wants praise and credit," he exploded once, as a rather conceited congressman left his office after patting himself on his own back. "If he does what he's supposed to do long enough, he'll end up getting more credit than he's entitled to."

It is true that someone can be powerful and you can feel very sorry for him. I felt sorry for Rayburn because he had lost the woman he loved. He hated to talk about it, but sometimes he would be dreaming of the past and he would give me little hints of how it had been. And the rest, I learned from others.

His wife was the sister of Marvin Jones, a Texas congressman who had been Sam's roommate at the time of World War I. Rayburn had known him before that in college and they had been friends, and they met again when Marvin Jones came to the Hill. The two men shared an apartment in the Washington

311

Hotel, which was popular with Hill people for years.

Sam Rayburn took a fancy to Marvin's kid sister, Metze, who was only eighteen years old, and he started writing letters to her. This was in 1918, when Sam was thirty-six and should have known better. He just sort of had an obsession about that girl—she was tall and slim, a dark-haired beauty from all reports.

To show the kind of dedicated man Sam was, he kept writing to her for about ten years. And when his mother died in February 1927 at the age of eighty, he quickly proposed to Metze.

Rayburn had had a relationship of closeness to his mother that few men had. When he used to go home to visit her, she would pack box lunches for him to eat on the train and would send him letters of encouragement when he was a big shot in Washington. He was still carrying around his mother's letters when I first knew him.

Anyway, he must have been terribly lonely and he pressed Metze to marry him as quickly as possible. They were married in the fall of that year—he was forty-five and she was twenty-seven or twenty-eight. Their honeymoon was the trip back to Washington in a car Sam had bought for the purpose.

But Metze was unhappy from the first. She didn't like the trip to Washington and didn't like having to wait for their apartment to be ready for them at 1616—16th Street, then called "the street of embassies and churches."

Metze also didn't like the political friends Sam had and the fact that they drank. The couple had arguments over his drinking and Sam would mention now and then "the driest Christmas I ever had—the Christmas of 1927." She even scolded him in public when he took a drink. And worst of all, she was jealous of his sister Lou's position in his affections. Lou had taken care of his mother and I would have to be very careful with her when she came now and then to act as Sam's official hostess.

Speaker Sam would tell me, "I've got Miss Lou here again. She keeps me up half the night going to those parties, then she sleeps all day while I work my tail off." But he expected me to roll out the red carpet anytime she was coming and I would have to make sure a certain easy chair was ready for her.

"Now, Fish, you know this has to be done right because you have a dear sister at home too," he would say.

When I knew Speaker Sam, his marriage was over. In fact it lasted something short of two and a half months. Early in January 1928, Metze went back to Texas for a visit and never came back. She went to work at Neiman-Marcus in Dallas and soon divorced him. She remarried but he never did. He just grieved for her the rest of his life and tried to keep the memory of her from surfacing too many times. But he always kept watch over her from a distance, and when her child by her second marriage got polio, Sam immediately got the girl into the Georgia polio center that FDR made famous, the Franklin Roosevelt Warm Springs Foundation.

When I knew Sam Rayburn he had found consolation. There was someone he went to see once or twice a week and he was very secretive about it. But as was his way, he was very loyal to that one woman, whoever she might have been. I never found out who she was and he didn't volunteer to tell me. His chauffeur would be ready and waiting to take him to her, and afterwards the chauffeur would say with a little smile, "Well, he saw his gal again." He was glad that his boss had found a bit of happiness and so was I.

Speaker Sam had a proverb even for that—"The old only start to complain about the conduct of the young when they've gotten too old themselves to set a bad example."

I believe Rayburn's unfortunate marriage changed the history of the country to some extent in that he held back progress. I really think his own wife had been so excessively straitlaced and had given him such a hard time in those scant two and a half months of marriage that he decided women were not good for the Congress and didn't belong in the House Chamber because they cramped a man's style. I think that sometimes just seeing an attractive woman gave him bitter memories.

When people would ask him how he felt about congresswomen, he would say in the privacy of his office, "It's not their time yet. Let them stay home and raise their children."

He hated anything that resembled women's liberation, though the phrase hadn't even been invented yet. But this did not stop him from advancing women in another way. The first advice he would give every new congressman who came to see him privately was this, "When you set up your office, don't put a boy in there to run it, get you a lady." His reasoning, as he confided to me, was that a male administrative assistant would get all his secrets and then run against him on his own.

Rayburn practiced what he preached and his top assistant for forty-two years was Alla Clary, who had been a schoolteacher before he hired her.

Rayburn liked the bottle but didn't smoke. John McCormack didn't drink but loved a good cigar. The two struck a deal. McCormack gave Rayburn all the booze he got for Christmas and Rayburn gave McCormack all the cigars he received. "I'll do your drinking for you if you do my smoking for me" is the way Speaker Sam put it. But Sam had to hide the best of the cigars for McCormack because the Majority Leader's wife used to like to give them away to the Catholic priests as little presents. It was McCormack's

314

one little deceit. He let her get her hands only on the second-rate cigars.

Both men cussed as naturally as they breathed. John McCormack was so used to cussing that he couldn't stop himself if a priest was around. He would just cross himself and say, "Forgive me, Father." He was always saying, "Goddamn it."

Sam Rayburn would usually say, "Damn it," and try to leave God out of it. When he would say "She-e-e-et," drawing the word out, I knew he was still good-natured. But if he said it fast, like, "I don't want to hear a lot of shit from you," I knew I was in trouble.

Some of my happiest memories concern going fishing with Speaker Sam. We would get together a little group of congressional friends and rent a fishing boat. We would take along our own skillet and salt and pepper and cornmeal. The cornmeal was to make corn bread and also to roll the fish in before frying.

I remember how the Speaker would work up to the mood of closing shop to go fishing. Those were the good old days. He would say, "Fish, I don't feel too good. I think I'm getting a temperature. I think I need a doctor."

I would agree that he didn't look good and say, "Well, Boss, maybe it's something that you could cure with a day in the sun, smelling sea air."

He would agree, and suddenly he would declare a two-day recess of Congress, and we'd drive over to the Chesapeake Bay and spend the whole day on a rented fishing boat around Solomon's Island.

Sam would be the overseer of the cooking. He would be the one who had to determine if the fat was hot enough to drop the fish in. And he would always comment, "Now there are two proper ways to do this. You can piss in it or you can spit in it to see if it sizzles." But then he would sigh and guess he'd better test it with a drop of branch water.

315

Though this was in the days before "the pill," birth control was still one of the subjects aboard the fishing boat. I remember one story about a doctor who had invented a birth-control medicine.

The doctor was a little startled when an old, old woman came hobbling in and wanted some of the medicine.

"What are you going to do with it, mother?" asked the doctor. "You know you can't have any more babies. Why do you want my birth-control medicine?"

"So I can pour a little in my ears," the granny said. "It's all in my mind."

Congressman Howard Smith of Virginia, a gentleman farmer, chairman of the Rules Committee, had a trick for getting a holiday. As soon as the sun was shining in the spring and he had crops to put in, he simply took off. Rayburn would curse and practically wring his hands, but there was nothing he could do. You can't drag a man back who says he is "sick." All kinds of legislation would be hanging in the balance, waiting for Smith to make up his mind to "get well" and come back.

During the forty-nine years that the Honorable Sam Rayburn was a congressman from Bonham, Texas, he did many things of great importance to the nation, but he never forgot to solve the little problems of his constituents. At the Sam Rayburn Library, in Bonham, I saw row on row of file cabinets covering just one subject—thank-you letters for good deeds done.

Historians, though, will probably remember Rayburn best for some of his early legislation, and these were the things he liked to talk about most—for instance, how he had fought John Foster Dulles on one of his first bills. It was the Truth in Securities Bill that he had introduced because people were being ripped off through the sale of worthless stock.

Dulles, an important international lawyer, had come

316

to Washington to fight the bill on behalf of his clients and had acted pretty arrogant, Rayburn felt.

"I cut him to ribbons," Speaker Sam would gloat, remembering back to that time of 1933. "I showed him up as not knowing beans about the bill and we got it through."

Another bill he was proud of, dating from the early New Deal days, saved the railroads. On this bill, Jimmy Byrnes, who was then in the Senate, credited Rayburn with the great victory, as did Franklin D. Roosevelt himself. The situation was that railroads were going broke during the Depression and 50,000 miles of tracks were in the hands of receiverships. The railroads were $250 million in debt.

Rayburn came up with the idea for the Railroad Rehabilitation Act, which banned holding companies from railroad ownership.

I am convinced that Sam Rayburn was so much the mentor of Lyndon Johnson that Lyndon would not have taken up Jack Kennedy's offer of the vice-presidency at the 1960 convention if Rayburn had said no.

When that job was offered to Johnson, Kennedy's selling job had to be done through Rayburn and not to Johnson. I know, because I was there when Jack Kennedy came to Rayburn's room with hat in hand, so to speak, and true humility, to ask him to let Lyndon be his running mate.

And I can give you another instance to show which one was the boss. It was down in Bonham, Texas, in 1957 when they were getting ready to dedicate the Sam Rayburn Library. This was four years before Rayburn's death and he was still in the pink of health.

Speaker Sam was sitting on his porch with a bunch of Texans, and Lyndon Johnson, who was Senate Majority Leader, had wandered off to the yard in the back of the house. Suddenly Rayburn sent me to get Lyndon, saying he needed him for a minute. Johnson was talking to others too, and though I relayed the

317

message to him, he waved me aside once or twice.

The third time I told him that Rayburn wanted him, he exploded, "Damn it, you tell him I can't come. And another thing, I don't like you bossing me around in my home state. I don't mind so much in Washington, but when you come around to my home state in Texas and tell me what to do, I think that's the end of the line."

He stood glaring at me. I said, "Well, Lyndon, shall I go tell the Speaker you're not coming?"

"No, damn it," he said quickly. "Tell him I'll be there real soon," and he almost beat me back. Lyndon never sent for Rayburn, he always came to him, even though Rayburn was the boss of the lower house.

Every spring, most people get spring fever. But Rayburn would not be affected until a little later in the season when the first sweet corn was ready, and then he went slightly berserk. I had to personally go out in the countryside and get several dozen ears.

Rayburn would go on a sweet-corn eating binge for about a week, downing at least six ears at a sitting. And when this madness came upon him, he would not eat meat or any other things normally associated with a balanced meal. All he wanted was sweet corn and a huge whole white onion sliced with some tomatoes and covered with oil and vinegar.

That would be the week that no one would come closer than arm's length from him because he would reek of what he had eaten.

Dr. George W. Calver, attending physician of the U.S. Capitol, had suggested to Speaker Rayburn that he walk around the outer fringe of the Capitol grounds four times each day for his exercise. But not with me, or he would talk more than walk.

Then, seeing me with the Speaker so often, the doctor suddenly took a good look at me and said, "Fishbait, you're in worse shape than the Speaker. You're fat. I want you to take the same exercise but not at the same time as the Speaker does. Go at a different time, walking, not talking."

So after I had been walking the border of the Capitol grounds for three weeks and was about ready to drop, Dr. Calver finally noticed how much walking I did and he said, "Fishbait, stop. With the walking you're doing in the line of duty and the walking I have you doing, you're going to collapse on me. So cut it out and we're going to try something else."

What he did was much worse—he restricted my calorie intake. I was in agony until he brought me down 76 pounds, from 255 to 176. I'm back to 189, but just thinking of Dr. Calver almost frightens me into going back on his diet.

People would say, "What do you and Rayburn talk about all the time?" We were both very busy, but when we'd relax at the end of the day we found a lot to talk about. I filled him in on my home life. He was interested in hearing about Sarah Patsy since he didn't have a child of his own, and he was also intensely interested in Lyndon Johnson's children.

I loved to listen to Rayburn's candid impressions and predictions—even when they were wrong. For example, he said he didn't like Khrushchev, thought he had a mean face and wouldn't be surprised if he started World War III.

He really liked Kennedy when he got used to him as President. Kennedy catered to him, as an elder statesman, which helped. Every Tuesday morning, Rayburn would go to have breakfast with Kennedy along with a few other congressmen and what he admired most about Kennedy was that he had the brain to hire the best brains in the country to advise him. Rayburn had no patience with men who were too bullheaded to get someone else's opinion.

I was really startled to learn one day that Speaker Sam credited Calvin Coolidge, of all people, with saying the smartest thing he'd ever heard outside of the Bible. Rayburn himself liked to speak in a biblical fashion now and then and one of his favorite lines was, "There is a time to fish and a time to mend the nets."

What impressed Rayburn so much was that Coolidge had told him once at a White House breakfast, "I found out early in life that you don't have to explain something you haven't said." Rayburn believed and taught me not to volunteer too much information and was always telling about the men who had gotten their tail caught in the crack as a result of doing so.

He added to my lore on Coolidge by telling about the time everyone was hovering around Coolidge, who was seated at the breakfast table, and how they wouldn't go sit down because they didn't want to leave their places near the throne. The seats on either side of the President had already been grabbed by the early birds.

Coolidge looked around at them with that sour little look he had, Rayburn recalled, and then Coolidge said, "Sit down any place, gentlemen. Eating is just as good one place as another."

Rayburn chose Truman as his favorite President, even while everyone else was blasting him. He said, "Just you wait, Fish, history is going to be very kind to Harry Truman. History forgets all the little things it doesn't like about a President, like the foul language he uses or the few extra drinks he might take. It's going to forget that silly-ass stuff about Truman and realize that when he approved the Marshall Plan, he saved Europe from communism."

Rayburn always gave a President benefit of the doubt. He even defended Harding, saying he could not have known about the Teapot Dome scandal, but must have been the victim of his friends. Speaker Sam always said the office ennobled the man. I wonder what he would have said about Nixon.

The day Kennedy died, Speaker McCormack was in the House Restaurant having his favorite lunch—a bowl of Joe Cannon's bean soup and a double order of soft chocolate ice cream—when the news arrived. Someone came running in, out of breath, wanting to know if anyone at the Speaker's table had heard the bad news.

Everyone gave a negative reply, and as the Speaker heard the news that the President had been shot in Dallas and was on his way to the hospital, he tried to stand up and had a dizzy spell.

He sat back down and regained his composure and said, "Boys, I've got to go down to my residence before Harriet hears this." So with that, George Donovan, his driver, had the car ready and proud license Number 18 raced down Pennsylvania Avenue, turned right at the Treasury and parked in front of the Washington Hotel.

The Speaker dashed out of the limousine, took the elevator to the eighth floor and had just finished telling Mrs. McCormack when there was a loud knocking at the door. He got up quickly and some of the dizziness returned.

As he told us later on the Hill, as soon as he opened the door and started to step outside to talk to the men who identified themselves as being with the Secret Service, they shoved him back abruptly into the room, saying, "Mr. Speaker, you've heard the news and you are next in line to succeed if something happens to Johnson."

At this time, it was not known whether it was an international plot and whether Kennedy would be the only one assassinated.

McCormack told them, "Goddamn it, get the hell out of here. I don't want any protection." They started to argue with him, but he stopped them saying, "It's an infringement on my private life."

The Secret Servicemen, baffled this way for the first

321

time in their lives, returned to the White House and told their chief that McCormack would not cooperate. Thereafter, I was a party to the Speaker's "invisible" protection. The new President, Lyndon Johnson, had ordered the Secret Service to protect McCormack whether he liked it or not, but to do it inconspicuously. Since I was the Doorkeeper, I had to know in order to help.

We lost another man who was in line for the presidency through resignation—Spiro Agnew—and a similar case developed. It was Speaker Carl Albert who was immediately surrounded by Secret Service.

But Speaker Albert was an entirely different type. He cooperated fully. Suddenly, no one could go in or out of the Speaker's office unless cleared through Mike Reed, Carl Albert's legislative assistant, who had been cleared by the Secret Service and knew everybody on the Hill.

Every time Albert moved, whether to go to the little boy's room or to his front offices—H203 to 206—word would be passed by walkie-talkie that he was on his way. The agent stationed at the door of H205, the main entrance to the Speaker's suite of offices, had already had the place cleaned out so there would be no one but staff.

Two Secret Servicemen always walked with the Speaker. One of the plainclothes detectives of the Capitol police force would lead the way. Other plainclothesmen would be lurking inconspicuously in the background.

I felt so sorry for the men who had to stand on the hard marble floors that I ordered strips of rug to be cut for them to stand on. The men kept the pieces of rug in their lockers overnight so they would not be taken as souvenirs.

After Nelson Rockefeller was sworn in as Vice President in the Senate Chamber on December 19, 1974, the happiest person was not Rocky, but Carl

Albert. When it was over, Albert's wife, Mary, said, "Thank God, we can go where we want now, and nobody's tailing us." From what she said, I judged that Albert was one rare man on the Hill who did not want to be President.

Joe Martin, the Minority Leader back in Rayburn's time, was different. He wanted to be President. He was third in line on the two occasions that the Republicans won the leadership and he became Speaker. He would proudly explain how close he was to the presidency. But there was always a Vice President around— Alben Barkley, under Truman, and a man named Richard Milhous Nixon, under Eisenhower.

Joe Martin was a strange little man. He was like Speaker Sam in that he had no wife, but he had never married—not even Rayburn-style. He didn't date, to my knowledge, except occasionally to take a newspaper gal to dinner. He belonged to the job. Martin, too, lived at a hotel—the Hay-Adams, from which you can see the White House across Lafayette Park.

Joe Martin was so virtuous that he never even smoked or drank. But what intrigued me was that he would never tell his religion. He had the feeling that religious differences alienated people and he wanted none of his colleagues or constituents to feel a barrier. He said that Jefferson had felt the same way.

Speaker John McCormack had retired but was still living at the Washington Hotel, right across the street from the Treasury Building, when his beloved Harriet became ill and went to Providence Hospital, a Catholic institution. John was so concerned that he took the room next to hers and never left her side until she died months later.

She was too ill to have company, but I would go three or four times a week to see the former Speaker and give him a feeling of normalcy. We would visit in his room and I would fill him in on all the gossip

323

of the day. He loved it and would laugh and take several puffs on his cigar before egging me on to tell him more.

One day I took my chief page, Turner Robertson, along and this time, to show the Speaker that everything was normal, I hit him up for a contribution to the missionary program of my church—Memorial Baptist Church in Arlington.

I could see that Turner was horrified at my poor taste in asking for money under these circumstances. But McCormack said mildly, "Well, Bill, I guess it's that time of year again. Did you bring a pen?"

I pulled out my pen.

"Do you remember what I gave last year?" he asked, puffing on his cigar as he tried to remember.

I said, "Boss, don't you remember you gave $50 in memory of Lottie Moon for World Missions?"

McCormack said, "Oh yes, who'd you say Lottie Moon was again? Oh, I remember. The missionary who was in China for fifty years. I'm glad to see you keeping up with that because some day we're going to get you in our Catholic church and you'll know what to do about charities and missions."

As he handed me the check, Turner said, "Mr. Speaker, I don't see how you put up with him."

McCormack replied, with the same mildness, "Now, now Turner, you don't know that this is one of God's special children. He goes out with his Bible under his arm and knocks on the doors of those who haven't come to church to find out what's wrong with them. And also, Turner, I do believe that if he'd asked me for $100, I'd have given him $100. But he's a dear fellow and he only asks for $50."

As we left, he said, "I'll tell Mrs. McCormack that you did wish her well."

In all the time I was up there, my forty-two years, only two times did the Republicans win the House and Senate—the Eightieth and the Eighty-third Congresses. I can give the reason for these defeats, as I always explain elections. People do not vote *for* someone. They vote *against* someone. They also vote *against* situations they don't like. Even in a presidential election, people don't vote because they love one candidate, unless they are married to him. They vote against the candidate they can't stand. In 1972, people didn't vote for Nixon because they loved him—they voted against his opponent.

We lost the 1946 election because we were still rationing things. We were using the point system to buy red meat and we had to have tickets to buy gasoline. People were angry. There was all the meat in the world, but you couldn't get it. We flucked the duck, flubbed the dub.

The other time, in 1952, everyone was sick to death of Democrats, who had been in for twenty years—and besides, they were afraid of Adlai Stevenson. He was too much of a gentleman to straighten out the country. And so the people said, "Let's give that tough soldier Ike a chance, and let's give him a Congress that will work with him and save the country and make America a better place to live." History will have to record whether he and his Republican Congress made the country a better place, not Fishbait Miller. He's liable to be biased.

I was happy to be with the party in power—the Democrats. As they say, "I've been rich and I've been poor and rich is better," so they can also say about power. We've been in power and out of power—*in* power is better.

Wayne Hays is my favorite study in power. He was the same kind of wild man in the abuse of power as Adam Clayton Powell, except that Hays had a mean streak. Powell was just a fun-loving guy who used rules and people for his own advantage. I mean Powell took advantage of funds to travel and womanize

325

and have a good time, but at least he prided himself on helping blacks gain greater civil rights.

With Wayne, it was a little different. He seemed to love to terrorize people. He did things that were downright mean. Just as soon as he had become chairman of the House Administration Committee, which oversees the housekeeping activities of the House, he cut the pay and the work hours of the House Restaurant workers.

The workers were upset because they needed the money. But Hays made no bones about his motive—he was determined to show what a good manager he was by cutting the food deficit. But then he spent what money he'd saved staffing a new committee called the House Restaurant Committee. He also eventually invaded my province, the barbershops.

Before Hays took over the position of the House Administration chairman, the job was pretty routine—sign payroll vouchers for committee aides and House Restaurant employees, sign committee-approved travel expenses of House members. But by the time he was through, he put a stranglehold on all vouchers and acted as if it was only through his goodwill that the people were paid. And he could hold up a payment indefinitely. Some people came to me in alarm and had to borrow money till they got their pay.

As he threw his weight around and seemed to enjoy doing it, he got the nickname of "Hitler Hays" and "Chairman Skinflint." He loved it. Even Speaker Carl Albert was afraid of him, and I hated to see this because it only made Hays more arrogant. I would overhear Carl Albert say, "Something must be done to stop him. Hays is getting to be an impossible bully." But Carl would never really confront him.

One time, to goad Albert, Hays invaded his area and refused to honor Albert's appointment of a man to replace a retiring aide in the House press and TV galleries. Hays notified the man that his vouchers would not be processed. In other words, he wasn't going to be paid if he chose to stick to the job.

Speaker Albert finally summoned up the courage to ask Hays what he was doing. Hays said he was cutting nonessential staff. But, if Albert insisted, he would sign the vouchers. So the man's job was safe, but Albert's pride wasn't. Hays sneered behind Carl's back, but making sure enough people heard so it would get back to him, "I thought McCormack was the damned weakest Speaker in history, but this guy Albert is making him look like Superman."

Carl Albert wasn't the only congressman to suffer. Once Hays didn't like the fact that an aide to Don Fraser, Democrat of Minnesota, had used his own discretion to summon several witnesses to testify before his subcommittee, of which Hays was chairman.

Hays became furious, accusing the aide of going over his head, and point-blank refused to sign the aide's pay voucher. Poor Congressman Fraser had to use desperate means to get Hays to sign his aide's voucher, calling for quorum counts and holding up all other House business until he signed. Had Fraser not stood beside his aide in this way, Hay's action would have had the effect of firing the aide of a fellow congressman, considered most unethical.

I know from personal experience that Hays loved it when people came begging to him for favors. He would sort of wet his lips and savor it. Once I was the one after him to get a voucher signed. He put it off and put it off, telling me I had too much power. But I kept going to his office with it.

"You goddamn son of a bitch," he exploded. "I'm not going to sign that fuckin' paper."

I said, "Mr. Chairman, I'm sorry about the second part but, on the first part, I didn't know you were interested in my ancestry."

"You son of a bitch," he said, "aren't you afraid of me?"

"No," I said, trying to look merely amused.

"Well, damn it, man, you'd better at least act like you're afraid of me."

Having helped him get the meanness out of his system, I said again, "Mr. Chairman, are you going to sign this voucher for me?"

Hays smiled a dry little smile and said, "Oh, well, I guess I have to. It's the law."

Only Ron Dellums, a black congressman from California and a psychiatric social worker by profession, knew how to handle Hays when Hays tried to kill one of his social welfare bills after Dellums had made an unflattering comment about "uncaring congressmen" the day before.

Dellums confronted Hays, bluntly accusing him of trying to destroy the bill without a bit of feeling about the "human misery" the bill dealt with. "I've heard that you are out to get me," Ron said, "and I just want to know if that's true."

Hays was taken aback and sputtered, "If I were out to get you, you would have known about it before this."

I really had very mixed emotions about Wayne Hays even when he was an SOB, giving me and everyone else a hard time. The reason I felt sorry for him is that he had a miserable childhood. I was a sucker for a poor childhood story.

In one of his nicer moments, he had told me that he used to be so bashful that he would cross the street so he wouldn't have to talk to someone. And he had been so poor as a kid that he had worked as a caddy to make a little money, and had dug ditches when he was a little older.

I wanted to like Wayne Hays, but it was impossible to stay his friend. He would be too mean, insulting anyone in front of an audience, sometimes when the person was there and sometimes behind his back. He was what was called an "unreliable." On the Hill, it was considered better to have a known enemy than to have a friend who was an unreliable.

THE JOKERS ARE WILD

The public would be amazed at the antics of their elected heroes. Some of their play is in the nature of dirty tricks that the "Watergate" crowd might have envied.

One congressman, Bill Green, Jr., the late Democratic political boss from Philadelphia, would cover the cloakroom phone with a handkerchief and call his hated competitor, Vito Marcantonio, a member of the ultraliberal American Labor party, off the floor, pretending to be an important constituent from New York City.

Brother Bill would berate Brother Vito for his voting record, his lack of attention to work or whatever fitted the occasion on that particular day. He would have poor Vito sweating and protesting.

Brother Vito could never understand how the phantom constituent knew so much about his every move. "Fishbait," he would say, shaking his head, "I've got spies down here and they report my every move. I've really got a tough gang back there, giving me hell every day. Did you ever see anything like it?"

I had to look innocent and say I never had—which was true as far as it went. If I had squealed and told what I knew, the word would have gotten around and I'd never have been trusted again by my secret sources, who shall be known only as "Deep Mouth" and "Flap Tongue."

And if I didn't have "Deep Mouth," how would I know that a certain member, who shall remain nameless, had gone so far as to place an X-rated bill in the hopper. It concerns taxing the only thing which has not yet been taxed:

330

93d CONGRESS
2d SESSION   H.R.

IN THE HOUSE OF REPRESENTATIVES

Mr. (Peterson) introduced the following bill; which was referred to the Committee on AFFAIRS.

A BILL

Be it enacted by the Senate and House of Representatives of the United States of America in Congress assembled. That this Act may be cited as the Peter Taxation Act of 1974.

SECTION 1. The only thing these great United States have not taxed is our peters.

SECTION 2. This is mostly because 98% of the time it is not in use, and the other 2% of the time, it is in the hole.

SECTION 3. Beginning January 1, 1976, the peter of the American male shall be taxed according to size in the following manner, to wit: 10–12 inches, luxury tax; 8–10 inches, polo tax; 6–8 inches, privilege tax; 4–6 inches, nuisance tax; and under 4 inches shall be eligible for a refund.

On the Hill, we knew it was spring when it was time for the annual paddleball party for a bunch of congressmen who patronized the House gymnasium.

Each person supplied a food specialty from back home. For example, John Fogarty of Rhode Island furnished the lobsters; Congressman LaVern Dilweg, the all-American football player who played professionally with the Green Bay Packers, brought tremendous Wisconsin cheeses; Congressman Emmet O'Neal represented the most important state of all because he furnished the Kentucky dew—Old Grandad, Old Crow, old anything as long as it was Bourbon; and a couple of New York State boys handled the Scotch.

Minority Leader Joe Martin and Majority Leader Sam Rayburn would usually come empty-handed. Leadership is never expected to contribute.

What did I bring? The best shrimp in the world, shipped up from Mississippi. It would cost me $70 or $80, but this night was worth it.

After each spring annual, we would be told by the hotel management that we were barred from returning. The drinks would flow and somewhere along the line practical jokes would begin. People would leave the room at the end of the night with their pockets leaking ice cubes and dripping salt. Several congressmen would engage a victim in conversation—arms around him and each other and with much backslapping—while another would fill his pockets with salt, pepper and plenty of ice.

Sometimes physical fights would break out, and once Speaker Rayburn, small as he was, found himself holding two husky giants apart, each at arm's length, and threatening that if they didn't behave, "I'm going to send you two adolescent boys home. I'm going to have Fish drag you right out of here." What I could have done to drag those two brutes out, I don't exactly know, but fortunately they listened to their leader and the fight subsided.

But there was nothing Rayburn could do about the throwing of rolls, wet napkins and ice cubes, and I knew, as I looked around the private banquet room of whatever Washington hotel we were in, that we were also not going to be returning here.

The highlight of these annuals was the giving of an award which the member then held for a year— the "Shit-ass of the Year Award." Surprisingly enough, a man would be honored to be known by his colleagues as "Shit-ass of the Year" and he would go around the Hill bragging about it the next day.

One year, it was Clair Engle, a feisty fighter from

332

Red Bluff, California, who was so honored. And he went on to become the senator from his state. Another year, it was Congressman Thomas B. Curtis from Webster Groves, Missouri, who went on to become chairman of the Federal Elections Commission.

The Paddleball Club group stuck together to such a degree that if Speaker Sam saw several of them missing, he would send a page to go get them at the gym or at a certain member's office where a gin-rummy game was almost always in progress.

Poker was the chief sport of the Hill leaders in the old days. John McCormack would trim them all. He was so tricky and astute at memorizing the cards that he would walk away with a bundle of money. I would be in the background now and then as the men played —frequently in the Mayflower Hotel apartment of Congressman Adolph Sabath—and I would keep an eye on McCormack. No matter what was in his hand, he never changed expressions in the slightest. It was a very grim game, with the stakes sometimes as high as $3,000.

I would frequently drive Congressman Sabath to his hotel just to keep him from having to find a cab, and he would always be lecturing me against gambling. He was obsessed with the game, and was always trying to break the gambling habit but not making it. He was especially disgusted when McCormack's poker face had caused him to give up a pretty good hand because the stakes had gotten too high and McCormack won with nothing.

"Poker is a cruel and useless pastime, and I love it," Sabath said. "But that's why I'm warning you now, Fishbait. Don't ever get started and you won't ever have to give it up." Others who would be in the games on a more or less regular basis would be Leo Allen of Illinois; Senator George Bender of Ohio, Majority Leader of the Senate; Scott Lucas of Illinois; and Bill Colmer of my hometown.

Since Sabath claimed he couldn't stand some of these men politically, I asked him why he played with them if they were that bad. "I'll tell you why," he said. "Because Democrats and Republicans and even Democrats who act like Republicans all play with money that's green."

My friend Gordon Smith, vice-president of Gottlieb and Associates, a top public relations firm around Washington, was reminiscing with me the other day about how a certain kind of phony dignity has gone from the Capitol. Men on the Hill are much less concerned now about keeping a stuffy image.

As an example of how prim and proper some congressmen were in the old days, Gordon recalled how he had needed to get some publicity to help one of his clients who represented the Dutch flower-bulb growers.

Senator Ken Keating of New York had promised to cooperate in having a picture taken with a pretty Dutch girl. The fact that she had been born during the battle in which her town of Eindhoven, Holland, had been liberated by the 101th Airborne Division of the U.S. Army was a plus.

To commemorate the liberation, thousands of tulip bulbs had been planted at 101st Airborne Headquarters at Fort Campbell, Kentucky, and the Dutch girl, after her stint with Senator Keating in Washington, would end up at Fort Campbell for a big ceremony.

The moment came in Washington when Senator Keating was supposed to have his picture taken with the costumed Dutch girl and the tulips in the background, and a wooden shoe for further authenticity.

To make the picture memorable enough to be used by the wire services, the photographer and Gordon had come up with the idea of the senator kneeling and, like Prince Charming, placing the wooden shoe on the girl's foot. But here they hit a snag. Keating maintained that it was absolutely beneath the dignity of a senator to kneel in front of a girl.

The situation was tense and it seemed that there would be no picture coming out of the session good enough for newspapers to use. But then the senator came up with his own solution. He asked, "Why not have the young lady kneel and place the shoe on *my* foot?"

It was a reverse of the Cinderella story, but she did, he did and the picture appeared all over the country.

The Hill always makes fun of its members—like Lawton Mainor Chiles, Jr., the Florida senator—who march on foot across the state or take every backroad where they can drum up three votes. But most have been guilty of the same thing in their early years.

Both sides of the aisle tell the same story to illustrate this, but since I'm a Democrat and it's my book, I'll tell it as our side does. "Chiles, one of our Democratic brethren, was starting his campaign early, going around the countryside and stopping wherever he saw a crowd gathered, from one end of Florida to the other.

"Well, one day he saw a crowd in a farmer's barnyard, where the neighboring men were helping with the threshing. There was no place he could stand so they could all get a look at him and be heard by him, so he just climbed aboard a manure spreader that happened to be sitting there and he said, 'Gentlemen, I must apologize, I feel a little uncomfortable talking to you from up here because it's the first time I've ever spoken from a Republican platform.'"

Republican Senator Paul Laxalt, who became famous in 1976 for managing the Reagan campaign, would kid the Democratic members about their political party. He said he heard a candidate giving a campaign speech and the candidate said, "And in conclusion, let me tell you that I was born a Democrat, I have always been a Democrat, and I expect to die a Democrat."

And from the back of the hall came the comment, "Not very ambitious, are you?"

Members were always trying to beat each other out on proving how poor they had been in childhood. But the Hill crowd gave the crown to Alben Barkley, who had the ultimate illustration of poverty: "We were so poor that we had to use hoot owls for watchdogs."

Congressmen loved to summon up the stories of other political greats, and Lincoln is still quoted a lot on the Hill. The favorite is Lincoln's answer to Peter Cartwright, his opponent for Congress in 1846.

During a debate, Lincoln was being harassed by Cartwright, who kept demanding to know where Lincoln was going—to heaven or to hell. Lincoln rose and said, "Brother Cartwright asked me directly where I am going. I desire to reply with equal directness. I am going to Congress."

When the book *Dog Days at the White House,* by the dogkeeper, Traphes Bryant, came out, telling of eyewitness accounts by the dogkeeper that he saw President Jack Kennedy skinny-dipping in the White House pool with young lovelies other than his wife, the Hill had its answer. Congressmen went around trapping each other with this one.

"Have you heard about the government official who got arrested for skinny-dipping in his pool?" they asked.

The first time I heard it, I bit, saying, "Oh, isn't that too bad. Where did it happen?"

"I told you," the congressman said, "he got arrested for skinny-dipping in his own pool. Unfortunately, it was his typing pool."

There is a vast array of humorists on the Hill. Some spend their time dreaming up practical jokes and gag gifts.

Congressman Bill Ayres, Republican of Ohio, at one point went around a Hill restaurant collecting $5

336

bills. The victims waited and waited to see what the money was for. Ayres left them waiting. He simply pocketed the money and walked out.

My co-author knows from personal experience that Bill Ayres would go around the dining room in a place like the Monocle or the Rotunda (posh Hill restaurants) collecting $5 bills, because she was there having lunch with him. She said once, "Are you going to give this money back?" He said, "Of course not." And he had a great laugh. Then he said, "Don't worry, I'll probably be taking them to lunch or something." He was very generous and some of the time he would, just as suddenly, start passing out presents. He did outrageous things and was known for it. And anybody who didn't feel like parting with a $5 bill just wouldn't; some would dip into their pockets and give him other things instead—a penny, a quarter, a handkerchief or a stick of gum.

And when Bill Ayres was on his collecting binges, he would sometimes confuse the issue further by taking one man's $5 bill and giving it to someone else. It would become a hilarious hodge podge of money changing hands and if Bill gave the money to a third person, she noticed the rightful owner would sometimes reach over for it, or the beneficiary would sheepishly walk over to another table and say, "Hey Jim, did Wild Bill take this from you?" And he'd give it back. But so well liked was Ayres by his colleagues that when he pocketed the money, they never complained. It was sort of an honor to be chosen by Ayres for one of his practical jokes.

When President Kennedy moved into the White House with wife, family, and new baby, John-John, Bill Ayres went shopping and arrived unannounced at the front gate with his gift—a baby buggy. The guards phoned inside, expecting to be ordered to get rid of this nut but instead, the President, who had been a friend of Ayres from congressional days—

though on opposite sides of the political ball park—invited him in and made a big fuss over Bill and his gift.

Once at the Statler Hotel, Ayres was leaving a party when he ran into Liz Carpenter, Lady Bird's press secretary. She was leaving in her White House limousine in evening clothes with her husband, columnist Les Carpenter. Pressing them into service, Bill ordered them to drive him to his destination. Only when he had gotten into the car would he tell where he was going—directly across the street to the Gaslight Club.

Congressmen would sit around over a drink and make up definitions, which would then be passed around the Hill. Once Ayres came in with a list of things at which Republicans would draw the line:

> Republican boys date Democratic girls. They plan to marry Republican girls, of course, but they feel they're entitled to a little fun first.
>
> Democrats buy books that are banned. Republicans draw the line at buying them. They form censorship committees and read them aloud as a group.

I remember once when Republican Bill Ayres and some of his Democratic friends were coming up with all the amazing court decisions and laws that were still on the books in various states.

The list was endless but I saved a few. As Ayres pointed out, cream puffs had been banned in Marion, Ohio; and in Columbus, Ohio, cornflakes could not be sold on Sunday.

Texas Congressman Olin Teague topped him with the information that in Houston, Texas, it's against the law to buy Limburger cheese on Sunday, but if you do buy it, you cannot take it out of the store.

Then someone from Indiana piped up. If you live in Gary, Indiana, and eat garlic on any day of the

338

week, it's illegal to go into a theater or ride a streetcar for four hours thereafter. Which led Glenn Cunningham, Republican of Nebraska, to inform the boys that in his fair state, in the town of Waterloo, barbers are forbidden by ordinance to eat onions during working hours.

That stopped everyone for a while until someone remembered that in Corvallis, Oregon, in an effort to keep its young ladies from getting sexually agitated, an ordinance was passed forbidding girls from drinking coffee after six o'clock—since it was once considered an aphrodisiac.

"It still is," said Congressman Ayres, consulting his notes again and reporting that in a certain town of New York it is illegal to eat peanuts and walk backwards outside a concert hall while a performance is in progress. And also that in Detroit, for the protection of horses, it is illegal to throw banana peels on the street.

Kansas was heard from next—it's illegal there to eat rattlesnake meat on Sunday and it's illegal any time for a restaurant to serve an alcoholic beverage in a teacup.

Manny Celler of New York recalled that a court ruling during the war held that it was legal to serve pickles as a substitute for butter. "That's how seriously we took the war effort," Manny said sanctimoniously.

"That's nothing," said Torbert MacDonald, a Democrat from Malden, Massachusetts. "You don't know the word serious until you tangle with the formula for Massachusetts clam chowder."

To show how seriously Massachusetts people take their clam chowder, Torbert swore that in that state it is against the law to use tomatoes in the chowder.

The one that stopped everyone cold, though, was a Lexington, Kentucky, ordinance making it illegal to carry ice cream cones in your pockets. "The ways of law are inscrutable," said Bill, "just like some of my constituents think who write to ask what you Democrats are up to." Bill Ayres was a most unusual congressman. Though a Republican, he never campaigned as a Republican but just as "your Congressman." The Democrats of his district were his greatest supporters.

As I recall, there were two laws the gentlemen decided they really ought to get passed into national law. One was a New Jersey ordinance that made it a misdemeanor punishable by fine to slurp soup in public. The other was a Connecticut court ruling on fresh pickles. According to the court, if you dropped a pickle from a height of one foot and it collapsed, and did not bounce, it was not a fresh pickle and the seller could be arrested.

The "boys" of Congress come up with rougher humor as the situation inspires. When they were annoyed by a female member who was being rough and tough in fighting for a bill—having learned all the dirty tricks from the male members—they passed the word in the back of the chamber, "She can't wear short skirts. Her balls would hang down."

Which reminds me of some of the stories brought back by junketeers returning from far-flung corners of the world. One congressman, who refused to reveal who the incident happened to, told of attending an elegant dinner at the American embassy in an Eastern country at which many diplomats were present.

According to him, there was a strikingly beautiful blonde at the table and someone of the American party—surely not he—had the good luck to sit beside her. Encouraged by her smiles, the junketeer began to pat her knee. Things went on from there, and as the delighted explorer began investigating a little further under the table, the girl suddenly put her face to his ear and whispered, "Don't change the expression on your face when you feel my balls. I'm a foreign agent."

The Hill crowd had a great interest in the food quirks

340

of some of their most illustrious colleagues, especially Speaker Sam, who was always worried about his bowels.

Speaker Sam swore by his tablespoon of honey. He said a thousand times that if everybody would just take a full tablespoon of honey before breakfast, everybody would keep regular and be in good spirits and the world would be a much more peaceful place.

He got the honey from Congressman Charles Hoeven of Alton, Iowa, and it was of such good quality that Speaker Sam even forgave Hoeven for being a Republican.

Sam's honey finally had a little more effect than keeping him regular. It influenced another man—Congressman Eugene Siler of Kentucky, who was not very talkative. In fact, Siler was the most silent man on the Hill and no one could open him up, though the Capitol jesters frequently took turns trying.

The Hill routine for Rayburn and Siler and several others started with a very early breakfast in the House Restaurant. This particular morning, when Speaker Sam entered the room, Siler and John Kyle of Iowa were already at the special breakfast table ahead of him.

Speaker Sam said good morning and Gene Siler didn't even open his mouth but merely grunted. Then Sam said good morning to Kyle and Kyle gave a hearty "Good morning, Mr. Speaker," and proceeded to give a few pleasant comments on the day.

Then, ceremoniously, Speaker Sam asked me for his fresh supply of honey and proceeded to extract the spoonful with his usual speech. All through the breakfast, everyone talked except Silent Siler but when Speaker Sam left, Siler suddenly turned to Kyle and said, "That was most remarkable. He did say to take a tablespoonful every day didn't he?"

It was Kyle's turn to be amazed. He was so surprised to hear that Siler had a voice that Kyle could

341

only nod. "Yes, that's most remarkable," repeated Siler. "I must get a bottle and take it home."

When I told Speaker Sam what had happened, he refused to believe me. "If I didn't know you were a total abstainer, I'd say you were drunk," he said.

Speaker Sam's honey addiction was matched by old "Muley" Doughton of North Carolina who could not kick the sweet-potato habit. He lived to be ninety-one and he attributed his sexual powers to it. At the age of ninety, he was still tearing off, or at least ripping, girls' clothes, when the mood struck. He would buy them a new dress and they would be much amused at the incident.

However, there was a little sigh of relief when the doughty Doughton decided to retire in 1952 and not run again after forty-two years in Congress. He went back home to Laurel Springs and was dead within the year. On the Hill, the girls who knew him said that was because he hadn't had anyone to keep him supplied with his raw sweet potatoes. The girls had taken turns bringing them in each day, peeled and sliced. All day long, Doughton would go around munching away on them.

During World War II, the patriotic thing to do in America was to have meatless days or find substitutes for grain-fed beef cattle.

About that time, Congressman James Domengeaux of Louisiana, whose home was in the Bayou country, said his people wanted him to get a little publicity for this patriotic idea they had which was to have a day in the Speaker's Dining Room and serve nothing except stewed muskrat, sweet potatoes and okra, all from the South.

The day arrived. The chef, Ernest Zahm, had done his best considering the rank odor of the meat. The Louisiana congressman had talked Speaker Sam into having still photographers and newsreel cameras going

342

for this important event, as the Speaker personally set the good example for the nation.

Everything was ready and headwaiter Carl E. Sommers had the food placed on the table when Rayburn came in and sniffed and turned a little green. In answer to his dirty look in my direction, I whispered in the Speaker's ear, telling him not to worry because the muskrat family washed everything that went into his mouth just like the raccoon did.

This didn't help Speaker Sam too much, but as the cameras rolled he managed to keep a fixed smile as he popped a piece of muskrat into his mouth. Somehow he swallowed, still grimacing as if he enjoyed it.

Then he turned the tables on me, ordering me to do my patriotic duty and finish it, while he surreptitiously ordered a steak to be flung on the fire for himself.

One time, I had to eat rattlesnake. We had a congressman from south Texas named West, and another congressman from west Texas and his name was South.

Nothing would do but that Milton West was going to make everybody eat rattlesnake, whether they liked it or not. In fact, he was not going to tell them what it was until they had eaten and digested it so they couldn't say it had made them sick.

His plan, to which he made me privy, was that he would serve it at the regular Texas "eating–meeting" affair. Every Wednesday was Texas luncheon day, and different members of the Texas delegation would bring the goodies of their district for fellow Texans and a few lucky outsiders to enjoy.

South had already had his big day when he had feted the gang with shrimp and fish which he had not even gotten from his own district but had *imported* from a friend on the coast. South had said, "All I could serve from my district is billygoat, and I'm not about to disgrace my district."

But he as much as anybody else looked forward to

343

the mystery dish that West had announced under an exotic French name. On the day of the luncheon, everyone had high praise for the dish of fancy-cut small pieces of white meat that seemed to be some kind of frenchified chicken.

The host, Milton West, ate as much as the guests, which was plenty, and nodded pleasantly as they praised him for his treat, but he would not tell exactly what it was. When they said, "This is great chicken," he merely smiled and nodded some more.

Days later, when big, hearty six-foot-four West dropped his little bombshell in the form of his revelation that everyone had been eating rattlesnake, the Texas delegation was about to ride him out of town on a rail. But then they had a better idea. They skipped him two times in his turn for supplying the main course and for playing host.

At first, South was the most annoyed of all, but he grudgingly admitted that if you didn't know what it was, it might even beat the billygoat of his district.

On the Hill, they say there are only three sure things, death, taxes and Joe Cannon's bean soup.

Tourists take this bean soup very seriously—though I must say at my house, Mable makes much better bean soup—and many ask for the Joe Cannon recipe. I don't know how many women have come to me to get them that prize. As I say, tourists take the bean soup seriously, but it has been the subject of continual hilarity on the Hill. When someone charged that the wrong kind of beans were being used—Great Northern beans instead of Michigan beans—a member quipped, "Yeah, they're using the wrong kind of beans—the nonrepeating kind."

Soon bumper stickers appeared on several cars around the Hill. One read, Eat More Joe Cannon Beans—Solve the Gas Shortage. But things took an ominous note when Congressmen Bob Traxler, a Democrat from Michigan, demanded that only Michigan beans be used from this time forth. The fact that ninety percent of the Michigan beans are grown in his 8th district was strictly coincidental.

Traxler brought the great bean controversy to the same kind of conclusion that had once made Joe Cannon so famous. In front of everyone, he called forth the dining-room manager. He called forth the chef. He called forth the headwaiter. And in tones loud and clear, he declared that henceforth Great Northern beans, which are grown out West, were not to enter the House kitchen but only Michigan beans.

I had a quiet conversation with some of the restaurant staff after this traumatic experience and they assured me that the public and Congressman Traxler can rest easy in the knowledge that there will be only Michigan beans from now on, even though the Michigan beans are in short supply and harder to get.

Undoubtedly this is the congressman's answer to the energy shortage, said one of them grimly. He's picked the bean with enough go-power to make everybody self-propelled. In production of gas, the Great Northern bean just isn't in it.

So with that introduction, here finally is the recipe you've been panting for:

> RECIPE FOR BEAN SOUP SERVED IN U.S. HOUSE OF REPRESENTATIVES RESTAURANT
> 2 lb. No. 1 white Michigan beans
> Cover with cold water and soak overnight
> Drain and re-cover with water
> Add a smoked ham hock and simmer slowly for about 4 hours until beans are cooked tender. Then add salt and pepper to suit taste.
> Just before serving, bruise beans with large spoon or ladle, enough to cloud. (Serves about six persons.)

And would you believe that the Other Body, being jealous of the more famous Joe Cannon bean soup of the House also has its own bean soup recipe and claims that the original bean soup on the Hill started with a twinkle in the eye of some senator?

The only difference that I can see between the two recipes is that the Senate adds some chopped and browned onion to the mixture while it's cooking, definitely a good idea.

Some of the Hill crowd have pet economies. Senator Frank Moss of Utah refused to get rid of his shoes until they had been resoled beyond repair. He was a depression boy and would brag about how he would patch his own shoes in those dark days. In fact, he said he still had a pair of shoes that were twenty-five years old.

Minority Leader Jerry Ford had two habits that drove his staff up the wall but were probably a good example to all of us—he went around turning out lights, including those in congressional halls, and he wore his pencils down to little stubs.

Senator William Proxmire wasn't just jogging for his health when he ran from home to office and back again at the end of the day. A careful man with a buck—whether it was the government's or his own—he once said he had figured out that he saved $1,200 a year by using his feet instead of a taxi.

What really challenged the Capitol Hillers most was any colleague's excessive pride. They did not rest easy until such a member had suffered his comeuppance.

Congressman F. Edward Hébert, Democrat of Louisiana, was proud when his rise in power and seniority finally gave him a lovely office with a small entryway in which he grandly installed a little fountain. The others on the Hill were green-eyed with jealousy until the story came around of how old F.

Hébert had been taken down a peg or two by a constituent.

The constituent had come up from New Orleans and had been shown around the office by the congressman himself. Afterwards, someone asked the man what he thought of the office and he said, "Well, it was all right, but the man ain't got no class. He keeps a urinal right in his outer office."

At last, everyone was happy.

When the Duchess of Windsor came to Washington, D.C., to be the guest of honor at the Women's National Press Club, which after it started taking in male members became the Washington Press Club, I introduced a female reporter to her as the "Duchess." For a while, the real Duchess believed me, and actually it was half-right because among the delightful nicknames in the Capitol city is that name appended to Esther van Waggoner Tufty.

Senator John Tower liked to tell tales that had to do with American history, and his favorite was one which explained why George Washington, who had been born in Tower's state of Texas, ended up in Virginia. The way Tower told the story, little George had gone out and chopped a mesquite tree and his father had been alarmed and asked what happened.

"I did it, father," said little George. "I cannot tell a lie!"

George Washington's father shook his head sadly and said, "Pack your things, son. You'll never make it in Texas. We're moving to Virginia."

Back in the 1950s, the name G. Mennen "Soapy" Williams, governor of Michigan, was something to reckon with and it looked for a while as if he might get a chance at the presidency or vice-presidency. So everything that happened to Soapy, who always wore a polka-dot bowtie as I recall, was bandied about on the Hill.

347

One incident we heard was that Soapy Williams had arrived at Boysville school in his home state to attend a Christmas party for the youngsters. To make him welcome, the boys had made placards, each one with a different letter, that were supposed to spell out "H-E-L-L-O G-O-V-E-R-N-O-R." But in their excitement at greeting a governor who might become President, the boys got confused. When Soapy stepped out of the car, they were standing in a line behind their placards that spelled out "O H-E-L-L G-O-V-E-R-N-O-R."

When I ran the first time for Minority Doorkeeper, George P. Miller went up to Sam Rayburn and said, "I am in need of some guidance. I don't know how to put down the name of that Fishbait character."

Speaker Rayburn said, "I'm going to just write 'Fishbait' and put it in the ballot box." Miller sneered a bit and said, "I believe I can do a little better than that. I have something else in mind."

He drew a fishhook and placed a worm on it and just put it in the box and it was counted. I won that election for Minority Doorkeeper.

The Hill was delighted when one of its own was honored on the cover of a book. The book was put out at the height of the streaking craze and showed Minority Leader Gerald Ford, phone in hand, learning about streaking for the first time. He is repeating, "Oh, you take off your clothes and what?"

LBJ started all the jokes about Gerald Ford's mental capacity. Lyndon always did cut down his enemies with his acid tongue and Gerald Ford, as the head of the opposition of the House, had chopped up many of Lyndon's pet bills and foiled many of Lyndon's best-laid plans.

So Lyndon, remembering the facts that Ford liked to chew gum and spoke a little slowly, though a

348

Northerner, had passed the word that the trouble with Jerry was that he couldn't chew gum and walk at the same time.

But when Ford got into the White House, the Democratic Hill gang never let up. Every chance they got, they made up a new Ford joke. When the photographers were barred from taking a picture in Ford's helicopter, they said they were banned because the President didn't want them to see where he forgot to duck and banged his head on his chopper doorway so many times that the paint was chipped.

When Jimmy Carter got rolling on his campaign, his toothy smile was what the Republicans zeroed in on. "How much does he really smile?" asked one. The other answered, "Well, when he came back from his vacation on the beach, he suffered sunburned gums."

The National Press Club can always be counted on to engage in fun nights with the Capitol Hill crowd. I remember when Felix Cotton, an I.N.S. correspondent who was president of the club in 1943, got together with the Hill pranksters to set up a spelling bee.

Five congressmen and five congresswomen were going to compete and Speaker Sam was going to be the schoolmaster. Even with Rayburn present, the superstar of the show was Representative Clare Boothe Luce, who outsparkled everyone and started out both gracious and glamorous but ended up being a spoilsport.

Speaker Sam got it off to a laughing start when he announced he would begin with "four-letter words." From the beginning the contestants treated the spelling bee with irreverence. Given the word "frog," George Dixon, writer of a Washington column, immediately spelled "Rayburn." Speaker Sam stifled a chuckle and gave the next word.

Bending the rules further, one of the contestants,

Atlanta newspaperman Gladstone Williams, leaned over and whispered to the chairman of the entertainment committee, Howard Acton, telling him to order Sam to give him the word "feline." Gladstone, given the word, jumped up and spelled it "Luce."

The hundred or more guests laughed hilariously— Luce was known to have written a play, *The Women,* on the very subject of cattiness, hadn't she—but Clare was furious. Her face turned white and she faced the laughter without a smile. She deliberately misspelled the next three words so that she would be out of the game, and she rushed off the stage and left.

For the next couple of weeks, members of the club took turns seeking out La Luce to apologize and butter her up. After about three weeks, one of the other women members of the House told Felix Cotton that she thought Clare was "getting over it." Just recently, I was talking to Felix at the club and he commented on the fact that the woman with the most acid tongue of any congresswomen also had the thinnest skin.

Then there was the time the National Press Club held a National Chili Cookoff Contest among senators, each of whom came armed with buckets of his own state's brand of chili. On this auspicious occasion, Senator John Tower's Texas Chili won against such tough competitors as Howard Cannon's Nevada Chili and Barry Goldwater's Arizona Chili.

Before the final judging, I sampled them all and thought Goldwater might have the edge over the others. I said to Goldwater, "Isn't it great to be a winner?"

Goldwater snorted, "I don't know. I never was one."

It's only fair to give you the recipe that made Senator John Tower of Texas the crowned chili king. The recipe comes from John himself.

CHILI RECIPE OF
SENATOR JOHN TOWER OF TEXAS
Used at Chili Cookoff, April 4, 1974,
Washington, D.C.

At the National Press Club

3 lbs. chili meat (sear until browned)
Add 15-oz. can tomato sauce and 1 cup water
Add:

1 tsp. tabasco
3 heaping tbsp. chili powder or
    ground chili peppers
1 heaping tbsp. oregano
3 heaping tsp. cumin powder
2 chopped onions
garlic to taste
1 tsp. salt
1 tsp. cayenne powder
1 level tsp. paprika
1 dozen red peppers, chopped
4 or 5 chili pods
Simmer for 1 hour, 15 minutes.
Add thickening (2 heaping tbsp. flour mixed
    with water).
Simmer additional 30 minutes.

Needless to say, this makes a *very* potent chili.

One member of the Other Body whom congressmen loved to quote was Senator Sam Ervin of North Carolina, who was a legend on the Hill even before he presided over the Watergate hearings. His background in law and as associate justice of the North Carolina Supreme Court was very impressive. Members would quote him on what he had said concerning landmark cases such as the banning of the teaching of evolution in public schools that was being contemplated in his state.

"I can think of only one good thing that can come of this," Ervin was quoted as saying. "The monkeys in the jungle will be pleased to know that the North Carolina legislature has absolved them from any responsibility for humanity in general and for the North Carolina legislature in particular."

But my favorite Sam Ervin story is a down-home tale about two friends who are discussing their possessions and trying to brag a little. The first friend says, "Whatever became of your old hound dog?"

The other one replied, "Didn't you hear? I sold him for $5,000."

The first man said, "Come on now, you know you never got $5,000 for an old hound dog."

"Well I didn't get it in cash," the friend admitted, "but I got it in trade—I got two alley cats in exchange, each of which are estimated to be worth $2,500 apiece."

I think though that what the Hill crowd liked best of all Sam's sayings was his comment when there were reports that Martha Mitchell wanted to appear before his committee in spring 1973. "I'd have to meditate a long time on a voluntary witness," the senator said on that occasion. "The only other voluntary witness I've had is a man who calls me several times a week to tell me that the Lord has communicated with him on Watergate. I advised this caller I would be awful glad to have the Lord come as a witness, but I could not permit the caller to testify because it would amount to presenting hearsay evidence."

I remember a great poem that was circulated around the Hill in xerox form in August 1973 during the depth of the Watergate days, and it gave the members quite a lift. It was written by my good friend Ken Hoyt. "I wrote it in atonement," he said, "for having been executive officer of aviation for Nixon in the 1972 presidential campaign." By twisting Brother

352

Ken's arm, I got his permission to share this goody with you:

THE WATERGATE FOLLIES

We've buggers and sluggers and under-the-ruggers
Who work for King Dickie the Tricky.
We've capers with tapers and shredding of papers
As if in an X-rated flickie.

All hail to the kiddie named G. Gordon Liddy
Reluctant to tell us why did he.
The Watergate mess is who will confess
To taking the lid off of Liddy.

Magruder denied it and Mitchell defied it
Protesting that somebody blew it.
A squealer named Dean was spitefully mean
Suggesting that Tricky Dick knew it.

There's Ziegler, the wiggler and would-be "finigler."
Reporters say he's always nagging.
From Dickie's bad press, we hazard a guess
He zigged when he should have been zagging.

They say of dear Julie, her tongue was unruly
In hinting that daddy might exit,
While Martha unrulier, far beyond Julia
Says that she hopes and expects it.

Now Haldeman's through and Erlichman, too.
The tapes have been all disconnected.
And still unrepenty at old San Clemente
King Dickie has hidden, dejected.

He pours out his woes, oh, to Bebe Rebozo
And Billy can pray for those sinning.
But Mr. Sam knocks. And Archibald Cox!
The fireworks are only beginning.

Another man whose comments would be bandied about the Hill was Bob Orben of the White House, who frequently supplied President Ford with tidbits. The one I especially liked was Bob's definition of smart: "Smart is when you believe only half of what you hear. Brilliant is when you know which half."

Congress in general is very sports-minded and the first baseball game of the season was very important, with the President throwing out the first ball for the Washington Senators. Most people don't know that it was President Taft, way back in the century, who started the whole thing.

Harry Truman used to have fun showing he could throw the baseball with either hand. He was very proud of being ambidextrous.

To Nixon, it was a bore. We heard he much preferred to watch the game on TV.

Jack Kennedy made a splash each year bringing his whole family with him. It looked like a big clambake.

We once had some mighty good players on the Hill and we made good use of them—Eugene McCarthy and Scoop Jackson could have become pros in their youth. Jimmy Roosevelt, FDR's son, was not bad, either.

We had two Hill teams. We had the softball team called the Odd Sox. Then we had two baseball teams—the Republicans and the Democrats. When they played each other at Griffith Stadium—in the days before the RFK stadium was built—to raise funds to send underprivileged children to camp, the crowd once totalled 17,000 people.

Of course, it helped that we were being sponsored by the *Washington Evening Star,* which gave us plenty of advance publicity. In those days, the congressional players were given unusual inducements for playing in the form of prizes for home runs. I remember the game when Mendel Rivers played center field and was damn good. That was before he had switched to elbow-bending as his favorite sport. Dillard Rogers

354

helped catch and the honorable Harold Cooley of North Carolina, chairman of the House Agriculture Committee, was out in left field.

The Republicans were up at bat and the ball was coming at Cooley. He heard the crack of the bat and he tried to get the arc of the ball in his sight. He zeroed in on it but he, ran too far. The ball went over his head. The Republican got a home run and won the prize, which was a washing machine—appliances were hard to come by during World War II.

One time, Eugene McCarthy, the same man who was later to try for the presidency, had a most unfortunate encounter at home plate. He had belted one out toward left center. It was a hellacious good lick. It looked like he might make a home run until it suddenly looked like he might be *out* at home base as Tom Curtis came at him to catch the ball that was being thrown. The ball, Tom Curtis and McCarthy all arrived at home plate together. The score was one home run, one banged head and one dislocated shoulder. McCarthy's mind was addled for a few minutes, but Tom Curtis was out of commission for several days, exiting by stretcher, which gives you an idea of how seriously we took sports on Capitol Hill—we played for blood. We always had two doctors, two trainers and two ambulances standing by, and we used them all.

We had another congressman, this one from San Diego, who broke an ankle playing second base. That was Clinton McKinnon, who felt the cleat of a Republican who came sliding in.

These brutal affairs finally drew the attention of the leadership of the House, and the day after one of our bloodier games we were called to the Speaker's stand and ordered not to have these games anymore for fear that someone would be maimed for life.

The games were discontinued for about ten years, and then they started to play again on an easier system, where no one was hurt and no one was playing for blood. Looking back, I can only say they don't make congressmen the way they used to.

President Nixon once participated in a gag birthday party for me. I was invited to the White House on my birthday, which seemed like a nice little coincidence, and I told myself on the way over that I must remember to tell the President that it was my birthday.

But when I got there, the surprise was on me. They had fixed up a make-believe door for me that had a handle thirty inches high to open it. The top calligrapher of the White House, Sandy Fox, who did all the formal handwritten invitations to royalty, had taken the time to do the lettering on my door.

Congressman Brooks Hayes of Arkansas—not to be confused with Wayne Hays—was one of the storytellers of the Hill. He was, incidentally, one of the few people up there who did not call me Fishbait. He called me "Kingfish. You're too important up here to be called Fishbait."

When the Congress was contemplating some legislation that Hayes felt did too much for people that they could do for themselves, he told a story to demonstrate what he meant. "When I was practicing law down there in Little Rock," he said, "I had a fellow who committed a terrible crime. He had stolen firearms and money at the same time. I did the best I could but the jury said he was guilty, so they sent him to the pen.

"Spring came and he wrote to his wife. He said, 'Dear Momma, I know you're having a terrible time. But when you get ready to plant this year, don't dig up that ten acres I usually use because I've already planted some things there.' The warden assumed he had the guns and money buried there, so he put ten deputies to work and they ploughed up the whole ten acres.

356

"In the next letter, he wrote his wife, 'Well, I heard by the grapevine they didn't find anything, so you might as well get those potatoes in.'"

Maury Maverick, Democrat of Texas, was a bouncy roly-poly and was the inventor of the word gobbledygook, although some people credit Clare Boothe Luce with inventing it. At any rate, Maverick, like his name, was a little different from the herd. My friend Ken Hoyt, the aviation specialist, reminisced with me about him and recalled the time when Ken went to Maverick's office one day and heard strange jingling noises before he opened the door.

Ken caught the congressman in the act of playing horsie with a set of old sleigh bells draped around him. His secretary was so used to him, she just kept typing and paid no attention. Maury ended his dance, explaining he had just bought the bells at an old antique shop and was trying them on for size.

I remember when Congressman Marion Zioncheck was passing out pen and pencil sets with this advertisement: "Maisie's Emporium, Where the Customer Always Comes First."

And I hear Gerald Ford received a toilet seat with the seal of his old university on it—University of Michigan Class of '35—and he liked it so well he had it installed in the White House.

One gift killed a Hill friendship. It concerned Speaker Sam, who had been, from old pictures of him I had seen, well-endowed with hair in his youth, and quite handsome. But when I knew him, he was about as bald as a billiard ball and very sensitive about it.

A congressman, Luther Patrick of Birmingham, Alabama, didn't know how sensitive Rayburn was, and in a little ceremony, gave him a gag gift during the Christmas season—a comb and brush set. Speaker Sam looked very strange and tried to smile a little. He hurried to his office as soon as he could and after that the friendship just kind of collapsed. Rayburn

357

didn't try to retaliate in any way, he just kind of avoided Patrick.

Bill Hungate, a Democrat from Truman's state of Missouri, had been on the Hill since 1964, when he was elected to serve out the term of Clarence Cannon, who had died in office.

Hungate wasn't a punster or a giver of gag gifts. He was a spinner of stories on the order of Mark Twain, whose hometown of Hannibal was in Hungate's district.

Bill really came into his own on the Hill with the Watergate scandal. Even when the Watergate scandal seemed so far away and remote that it was merely a "caper" he had written a song which brought it close to home. He sang it himself as he played the piano—*Down at the Old Watergate.*

As a member of the House Judiciary Committee, Bill got annoyed with the way Republican apologists for Nixon were pooh-poohing the evidence against Nixon by calling it "inference and therefore not solid." He said, "We sit through these hearings day after day. I tell you, if a guy brought an elephant through that door and one of us said 'That is an elephant,' some of the doubters would say, 'You know, that is an inference. That could be a mouse with a glandular condition.' "

On another occasion, he got tired of all the technical legal language some members of his committee were using to obscure their meaning.

"All these technicalities," Bill said, "just remind me of a story of the old Missouri lawyer. The fellow was kind of a country lawyer and finally got a case in the Supreme Court, and he was nervous. He got up there and was arguing along and one of those learned judges looked down at him and said, 'Well, young man, where you come from do they ever talk about the doctrine of *que facit per alium, facit per se?*'

"The country lawyer wasn't going to plead ignorance, and he shot right back, after only a moment's thought, 'Judge, they hardly speak of anything else.' "

Another time, Hungate found excessive technicalities of language had bogged down a conference. He recalled the story of a young couple who wanted to get married and who gave their license to the judge, only to have it handed back with the criticism that they had recorded the date on the wrong line.

"Go back to the clerk and have it corrected," the judge demanded.

When they returned, the judge found yet another cause to send them back to the clerk for correction. When they returned after the fourth correction, the judge asked who was the small boy with the couple. The groom replied that it was his son.

"You realize," the judge said, "that makes your boy a technical bastard?"

The man replied, "What's the matter with that? That's what the clerk said *you* were."

I was really sorry when Bill Hungate decided not to run again in 1976. I once asked him why some men never gave up and kept running until they were old men. Bill said it was the competitive situation. "It's like Hale Boggs once told me," he said. "It's that SOB who thinks he can take the job away from you that won't let you quit."

Some thought that Senator Robert Taft of Ohio, called "Mr. Republican" in his day, had no sense of humor. However, I remember one story he would tell to show that Congress is truly representative of all kinds of people:

"When Senator Smoot of Utah was elected to the Senate, there was a little consternation about having a Mormon in the Senate since Mormons still believed in polygamy. As soon as Utah achieved statehood and held its first election, a delegation of the righteous rushed to see an old political boss to voice their alarm.

359

"The political boss looked over the members of the delegation and spied one of them who was a notorious womanizer. Looking sternly at the culprit, he observed, 'I would much prefer a polygamist who doesn't polyg to a monagamist who doesn't monag.' "

It was traditional for the members to play a little prank on the freshmen who were finally honored, for the first time, by being asked to preside while the Speaker left his post for a few minutes. A note would be sent by page to the freshman member sitting so proudly in the Speaker's chair: "If you had any last night, smile."

Some would blush. But all would smile.

The two-hundredth anniversary of the nation found Capitol Hill prepared. As one there told me, "They're going to have new rates on the 14th Street hookers' strip—the $20 girls are setting up a special bargain price of $17.76 for the Bicentennial year. But that's only for Minute Men."

Even my losing the election to continue as Doorkeeper was seized on by the wits of the House, who sent me many light notes that I cherished even more than the sentimental good-byes.

Bob Casey of Texas, the Democratic chairman of the subcommittee on Legislative Affairs of the Appropriations Committee, sent one of my favorites:

Dear Fishbait,

Since your departure I have honestly tried to adjust, but it has been extremely difficult. Without the familiar ring of your voice, my feet don't know to stand me upright to recognize the distinguished gentlemen coming down the aisle . . .

Sincerely,

(Signed) Bob

Bob Casey

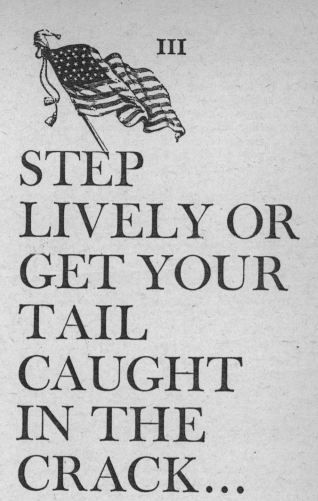

III

STEP LIVELY OR GET YOUR TAIL CAUGHT IN THE CRACK...

CONVENTION FEVER

When I went to a convention, I was married to the convention. I hardly slept. I did all the little errands that the permanent chairman couldn't do for himself. It was viewed as highly significant if he was even seen going to talk to someone, so I would run ask the question he wanted an answer to or I would pass the word.

I loved knowing the secrets. I loved the crowds, the bands, the smells, the tension in the air. But most of all, I loved the smoke-filled rooms. I loved being in the background and listening in on how the bosses wheeled and dealed—how Rayburn would get a promise of something for his support on something else—not for himself, he was not a greedy man, but for what he thought the country needed.

Usually the permanent chairman of the convention was someone I already knew from the Hill. In 1940, my first convention, it was Senator Alben Barkley. In 1964, it was Speaker John McCormack. In 1968, it was Carl Albert, who had such a bad cold that it was the worst Democratic convention ever for hearing what the chairman wanted or what was going on.

In 1972, they tried having co-chairmen to bow toward the emerging women's libbers. There was Yvonne Brathwaite Burke, black congresswoman from California, and the chairman of the Democratic National Committee, Lawrence F. O'Brien, who was soon to make another kind of news when his personal office was the subject of the original Watergate break-in by Nixon's "plumbers."

But my favorite chairman was Speaker Sam Rayburn, who chaired the conventions an historic four times, from 1944 to 1956.

363

Ah, 1956. That was my favorite convention. Humor was high, the dealing was low and that was the year they stole Jack Kennedy's chance to run for Vice President. The year 1956 would have been a red-letter convention if only for the fact that no woman's voice shrilled the "Star-Spangled Banner." Instead, it was a joy to the ear to hear a man's voice sing the national anthem—Leonard Warren of the Metropolitan Opera.

In 1976, the convention's idea of fun was seeing a film clip of Jimmy Carter's life. How dull! I remember when, in the 1956 convention, there was some improvised humor that blasted the other side, which is what a convention is all about.

The little skit was based on the popularity of money-making television quiz shows like the *$64,000 Question* and the temporary chairman of the convention, Governor Frank Clement of Tennessee, had a conversation with several of the quiz-kid winners, the youngest of whom was Lenny Ross, eleven. But at eleven, Lenny was more than a match for the governor.

Governor Clement: "Aren't you the young man who won the $100,000 on *The Big Surprise*?"

Lenny Ross: "I am that individual."

Governor Clement: "Well, how in the world did you keep from turning Republican with that much money?"

Lenny Ross: "I was going to ask *you* that."

Governor Clement: "All right, question number two: The Eisenhower administration has proposed a huge tax-relief measure to help us all, they say. Now Lenny, if you were a steel worker under this bonanza, earning your living by the sweat of your brow and making $5,000 a year and you had a family of two children, how much taxes would you have to pay under this proposal?"

Lenny Ross: "$420 a year."

Governor Clement: "And if you were the owner

364

of U.S. Steel stock, getting $5,000 a year in dividends, how much taxes would you have to pay?"

Lenny Ross: "Only $200."

Governor Clement: "Under the Eisenhower plan, it would seem to be better not to work, wouldn't it, Lenny?"

(Cheers and applause.)

Just thinking about it now, I can hear the voice of Florida Governor LeRoy Collins announcing the permanent chairman of the convention and trying to build a little suspense: "We recommend for permanent chairman of this convention the man we feel unquestionably is the unanimous choice of all Democrats assembled here and of all Democrats everywhere. A great American, a great leader, he has served our party and nation in conspicuous distinction and ability as Speaker of the House of Representatives longer than any man in all history. Mr. Chairman, your committee proudly presents as permanent chairman, the Honorable Sam Rayburn from the state of Texas."

By that time, there is wild applause and the band strikes up "I've Been Working on the Railroad," known in Texas as "The Eyes of Texas Are Upon You." Same song, different words.

This then was that glorious 1956 convention. The next convention—in 1960—the "heartless bastards," as Sam's friends labeled them, would cut out good old Rayburn completely. And who would replace him? Why LeRoy Collins, of course, the man who said all those nice words.

Words, words, words. Any convention would make a full book in itself, and if you knew what was going on backstage—the sex and seduction in some rooms and the political seduction and screams of anguish or demand in other rooms—you would have a book. The plot would be a masterpiece of intrigue. The pomp and ceremony would be as great as for kings.

Now comes the appointment of the Committee of

Escort—all chosen for being famous or useful names from every corner of the nation, including a token woman or two. Among the committee are Warren Magnuson of Washington, Hale Boggs of Louisiana and the Honorable Beatrice Schurman, national committeewoman from Vermont, on hand to escort a glowing Sam Rayburn to the rostrum.

Anything that happened to Speaker Sam was as exciting as if it was happening to me. I was his shadow and would soon be up there in the shadows behind him, looking after his every need.

Now Speaker Sam is acknowledging the great outpouring of love. Almost everything he says gets a round of applause or laughter, or both. "There need be no parade, because I am not a candidate for anything." (Laughter.)

The applause comes as he credits Democrats for the prosperity that incumbent President Eisenhower is bragging about in his bid for a second term: "Now the Republicans boast about this great prosperity. Who laid the foundation for this prosperity? It was the Democratic administration of Franklin Roosevelt and Harry Truman and the Democratic Congress who supported them."

Now he proceeds to lay Ike, the incumbent, low. Rayburn was one of the trickiest, cleverest speakers of the whole Democratic party. "Now we are *not* going to make the health of the President of the United States an issue in this campaign. The Republicans are doing that because every day of their lives they are trying to prove that the President is a *well* man. And *we* pray God for his speedy and his complete recovery because we are people with a *heart*."

I could just imagine good ole President Ike cringing in the White House as he heard our Sam on TV:

"Personally, I like President Eisenhower. He was born in the district which I represent and everybody down there who remembers him says he was a good

366

baby. Then he moved off to Kansas, and after he was sixty years of age he decided he would be a Republican. And I feel sure that, with his trouble with these Republicans in Congress, he regrets every day that fatal decision was made."

This was the window dressing. All the real work was done back in the hotel rooms. Now all kinds of people would nominate favorite sons and national leaders, but only Speaker Sam and a few others would know who was going to get it. They had it all planned, down to when they would start a stampede in the right man's direction. As Sam would say, "Now we've got to be patient and let each one get it out of their system and then I'll give you the signal." The signal would be for certain delegates to start throwing support to one man and it would all look spontaneous.

So, though Henry "Scoop" Jackson of Washington nominated Warren Magnuson of the same state for President, and John Connally of Texas nominated Lyndon Johnson of the same state for President, and Raymond Gary, governor of Oklahoma, nominated W. Averell Harriman of New York for President and a lot of other people got nominated for President, Rayburn already had decided that Adlai Stevenson deserved another chance. That was the word. Sure, Adlai had lost the time before—but this time, who knows. That was Rayburn's way of playing the game of politics.

Why didn't LBJ get the nod in 1956? "No," said Speaker Sam, "his time hasn't come. This will be a step up the ladder for him—get his name circulating. Give him a chance to be talked around and get delegates to thinking about him for 1960. That's his year. That's when we move for Lyndon."

Well, as it turned out, Paul Butler scotched that by taking the next convention away from Sam Rayburn, which gave John Fitzgerald Kennedy his chance.

Had Rayburn been in charge of the convention it would have been the other way around—Lyndon for President and perhaps, but he wasn't 100 percent sure yet, that young man Kennedy for Vice President.

But this was 1956. Rayburn was, in a way, protecting LBJ's career. "It's gonna be murder to try to take it away from that Texas turncoat in the White House," he said. "It's a freak of history when it happens—like with Hoover—that you sweep out a man before he's had his full eight years. No, the country is too damn prosperous to shove Eisenhower out now. Might as well let Adlai butt his head against Ike one more time and everyone will be happy. Everybody deserves a second chance."

And Sam smiled virtuously. Because the truth of the matter was that he didn't love Adlai the way he loved Lyndon, and he didn't mind throwing Adlai to the wolves. In fact, it was a nice touch that he was being noble in helping Adlai get it, knowing his chances were so slim.

Now it came to the nomination of the Vice President, and again came the favorite sons as choices—Senator Albert Gore of Tennessee was nominated for Vice President by Jared Maddux, lieutenant governor of the same state, and LeRoy Collins was nominated for Vice President by Congressman Robert L. F. Sikes of the state of Florida, and on and on. But there were only two names that I knew were important—Senator Estes Kefauver of Tennessee, nominated for Vice President by Mike DiSalle of Ohio, and Senator John F. Kennedy of Massachusetts, nominated by Governor Abraham Ribicoff of Connecticut.

The crowd wanted Kennedy. He was the handsome young senator whose marriage had been treated like some royal event. He was almost a prince among the old political crowd, or at least a knight in shining armor. But Rayburn didn't want him. He had a promise to keep elsewhere. And John McCormack didn't want him particularly. Kennedy belonged to the competing political family of Massachusetts. And friends stick together.

Still, there were the amenities. Kefauver had been seconded by Senator Richard L. Neuberger of Oregon and by a former President's son, James Roosevelt, a congressman from California. So Rayburn had twisted McCormack's arm and got him to at least be the second seconder of the man from his own state.

The first of the seconding speeches for Kennedy's vice-presidency was given by Senator George A. Smathers of Florida, and he gave a warm, wildly enthusiastic speech saying over and over how "there is nobody" who can do the job of vote-getting like Kennedy can—"Jack Kennedy's name is magic in Ohio—Cincinnati, Akron—California and other areas. It will be great for us to have him on the ticket.

"There is not another man who can do as much in the highly industrialized areas such as Michigan." He went on and on, ending with the comment that "I am happy and highly honored to second the nomination of a young man with wide experience and great wisdom, a young man with a big heart who will be a great campaigner and who will make us a great Vice President—Jack Kennedy."

By contrast, John McCormack's speech was dry bones and almost grudging in its sound. Nowhere was there a glowing word about Kennedy the man or the candidate. Instead he talked of everything else, how the man chosen should be one who was agreeable to the presidential nominee, Adlai Stevenson, and how all the men who had been placed in nomination for Vice President were "fine Democrats" and how he would be willing to vote for *any* of them.

Then, almost grudgingly, he told how he had weighed the situation. "Now there are certain considerations," McCormack said. "Frankly, as I view the situation confronting our party in the coming election, the second place from a basic angle should either go East or to the agricultural area. I am frank in saying that. Those are the basic considerations." Then he said that as a secondary consideration they needed "a man we can go to the country and sell and, at the time, a man who will bring strength to the ticket." And finally he came to his faint-hearted approval of Kennedy.

"I am here to second the nomination of an experienced man, one to whom public office is a public trust. I am proud and happy to second the nomination of Senator John F. Kennedy. I hope he is nominated."

And it was good he added the last line, because those listening to him hadn't been too sure. But at least he had done his duty. And in case by some fluke Jack upset the plan and got the vice-presidential nomination and Adlai and Jack by some miracle went on to win, McCormack would have a good working relationship with the White House. That's what it was all about. And you always look eight years ahead to the White House.

So what happened to Kennedy's chances? The closer you get, the worse it smells. First of all, Kennedy and Stevenson were supposed to be friends—Kennedy had even given the nominating address for Stevenson in 1956. That's supposed to be a sign of friendship. But in this case, friendship took a backseat to politics.

Let me explain about that. If Stevenson had wanted to have Kennedy as his running mate, he could have passed the word. But instead, in 1956, he went to great lengths to avoid naming a vice-presidential candidate of his liking and, in an unprecedented move, threw the selection of the Vice President open to the floor of the convention.

Why did he do this? Well, part of the reason was Rayburn. Speaker Sam had made a half-commitment elsewhere and Adlai, if nothing else, was a team player.

To understand the full story, we have to go back to 1952, the first time Adlai was nominated for President. My job at the convention hall in Chicago was to guard the privacy of Speaker Sam, the chairman of the convention, as usual, and do whatever he wanted me to.

After Stevenson was safely nominated and it was time to think of Vice Presidents, all kinds of people were letting their availability be known. I was one of the few who knew that John Sparkman was the man. I had been up all night in the smoke-filled hotel room with Sam Rayburn, keeping out the riff raff—which meant, in those days, whomever Rayburn wanted kept out.

Rayburn's word was law on the convention floor. He was like an orchestra leader giving a signal here and a finger wiggle there to someone he wanted to have play the right tune. Standing at the platform protecting Rayburn, I saw coming together from the rear of the hall two men who spelled trouble—Senators Estes Kefauver and Paul Douglas. They had been trying to get recognition, but Rayburn didn't want to recognize them and now they were taking the long walk up to confront him.

I told Speaker Sam what was happening, and he said, "Fish, tell you what let's do. Let them in and don't lay a hand on them. Put them back there behind the rope. In the meantime, put an extra chair there for me and don't let anyone get in with them. Not newspapers, radio or TV. No notes accepted.

"I don't even want anybody passing near them."

Then Mr. Rayburn went ahead and recognized the people who were to nominate Sparkman. So while one man was talking for ten minutes about the glories of Sparkman, Speaker Sam turned over the gavel to Majority Leader John McCormack and went to talk with Estes and Paul. In effect, he made a deal that if Kefauver did not make waves in 1952, he would get his chance later.

"Now Estes," said Rayburn soothingly, "you served in the House with me. And Paul, your dear wife, Emily, has served in the House with me. And I want you both to know this is not Estes' time. Be available later. Estes, you go home and get yourself reelected, and your time will come."

So now it was 1956, payoff time. But leadership wasn't really that crazy about Kefauver. When Adlai threw the vice-presidential nomination open, something even worse was happening from leadership's standpoint—that upstart young senator from Massachusetts, John Fitzgerald Kennedy, was just about to waltz away with the vice-presidential nomination. He looked like a virtual winner.

In fact, at about this time I looked up and saw Jack Kennedy's brother, Bobby, coming toward me with an air of great excitement. "Fishbait," he said, "I have to ask you a question. My brother says you have all the answers, so will you tell me this. If my brother gets the nomination, what is he supposed to do?"

I squatted down to talk to him and said, "Well, Bobby, all I can tell you, my dear friend, is this: Wherever he is or whatever he's doing, our friends here at the convention know. And if lightning does strike him in the form of the vice-presidential nomination, he will be picked up and brought immediately to the Stockyards Inn next door and guarded while awaiting the results of the balloting."

But even as I said it, I knew Kennedy was too late. It was going to be Kefauver. Bobby thanked me and walked away and I was not surprised when the Honorable Albert Gore, who had been trying to be recognized for a while to make it look good, was finally called by master musician Rayburn.

Gore, the aristocratic senator from Tennessee, spoke and graciously gave up his own aspirations by throwing his votes to Kefauver, his fellow Tennessean, though a raggle-taggle one in his coonskin hat and tail.

Kennedy was swamped and, as the convention loves to do to show solidarity, it was decided to make the nomination unanimous for Estes. I later learned from Speaker Sam that many had wanted Richard Russell of Georgia for the number two spot. But once the leadership had made up its mind in those days, it was all over but the applause.

In 1956, it wasn't particularly that Rayburn was anxious to keep his word to Kefauver, but Sam *was* a man of his word and besides, Kefauver was a handy tool to stop Kennedy. In my mind, it was clear beyond a shadow of a doubt that Jack Kennedy was cheated out of the vice-presidential spot on the Democratic ticket.

So the ticket was Stevenson and Kefauver—Adlai and Estes. But as Speaker Sam commented later, disgustedly, "Adlai with Jesus couldn't have won." But just maybe Adlai and *JFK* could have.

And by 1960, Paul Butler, according to Sam, had shafted him and paved the way for Kennedy. As Rayburn said later, after the 1960 convention, "It didn't just happen, Fish. And it didn't hurt that Paul Butler was on the same side of the religious fence as Kennedy, who had the Pop he did. That's real Pop power."

And it didn't hurt that Paul Butler had been the chairman of the arrangements committee for the 1960 convention and had helped pick a permanent chairman of the convention from Florida, which just happened to be where the Kennedy clan spent its winters.

The inside story was that Joseph Kennedy, Sr., himself, an early backer of Franklin Roosevelt, really saw himself as President and had every reason to believe it would be his turn after FDR. But the big upset was that FDR had gotten greedy and wanted a third term himself in 1940, the year that was supposed to be Joe Kennedy's. The senior Kennedy had vowed that he'd fix FDR's wagon and hated him from then on. And he vowed that the White House would have a Joe Kennedy one day, damn it, his son Joe. But the son was killed in World War II and Kennedy, Sr., then started grooming his next son, Jack. He had a good product, Rayburn grudgingly admitted, even though in Jack Kennedy's early career in the House and Senate, Rayburn said he wouldn't have picked him as a future President against almost anyone else.

Rayburn felt that Butler had done a slick job of easing the amazingly young candidate through to victory, with the help of John McCormack, who had defected from Rayburn to become Kennedy's floor manager at the 1960 convention.

For a while, it put a little strain on the Rayburn-McCormack friendship. But when it was all sorted out and the ticket read Kennedy for President and Lyndon Johnson for Vice President, the two men were solidly friends again.

But I'll never forget how sad it seemed at the 1960 convention when, after four times as the star, Rayburn was alone and lonely—as he watched someone else in *his chair*—eating his heart out and trying to get Johnson nominated for the presidency. McCormack was now the man next to the throne. As a sop to Sam's ego, the arrangements committee offered to him an honorary chairmanship. Speaker Sam didn't come cheap and he said, "I may accept the honor if it also entitles me to a car and chauffeur, a hotel accommodation and meals, of course, and a few hundred extra tickets."

As I recall, they did pick up some of the tab for him. And a group who loved him very much picked up the tab for me because Rayburn had always relied on me at the conventions.

In 1960, in Los Angeles, I recall that LBJ was furious that Kennedy was playing around with girls off somewhere at the hotels—"probably got himself a half dozen starlets"—while he and Rayburn were working their tails off to gain delegates. It sounded to me like Johnson was not just envious of JFK's delegate popularity but of his girl popularity too.

And Rayburn put his finger right on it when he said, "Now, now, don't be jealous, Lyndon. You don't have to be jealous."

Johnson said, "Jealous? Chickenshit. I'm not jealous. I'm just pissed off that I'm working my ass off and he's playing tiddlewinks."

Of course, Johnson had a lot going for him, too— queen-bee hostess Perle Mesta to entertain for him and cowboy singers with gee-tars. But he didn't have girls.

It's natural to ask why a smart politician like Lyndon didn't get the nomination, especially since he had the help and support of the greatest student of practical politics of his time, the Speaker of the House.

The thing that happened in the 1960 convention is that LBJ and Rayburn outsmarted themselves. The mistake had happened, really, a little earlier in the year when Jack Kennedy had gone dashing around the country winning friends and primaries, and Lyndon hadn't made the primary scene at all.

Lyndon had reasoned that he could do it as Majority Leader and that his combination of age, experience and hard work would really show up "Jumping Jack." LBJ wanted to be able to say, "Look, delegates, I stayed on the job and took care of your business while Jack ran around having fun and getting votes." It was a reasoning that Speaker Sam believed would work too, and he was bitterly disappointed when it didn't. He was at the convention buttonholing delegates and state leaders. He seemed out of step with the times. He was passé.

The greatest triumph for Rayburn at the 1960 convention came when he suddenly found himself in the position of strength with the Kennedy forces wanting

Johnson for the number two spot on the ticket. Because, though Rayburn might not control the convention, he still controlled Johnson.

For a while, I thought he was going to physically bar the door and keep Lyndon from accepting Kennedy's offer of the vice-presidency.

Eventually, it turned into a love fest "for the good of the party." Rayburn loved Kennedy the way McCormack loved Kennedy. But eventually the honeymoon was over and there was competition again between the White House and the Hill, and especially between the warring political families of Massachusetts—the McCormacks and the Kennedys. And when Speaker John McCormack's nephew ran and lost against Jack's brother, Ted, Speaker John was bitter.

I thought of all this not long ago when I received a letter from the retired John McCormack and saw that on the envelope he had pasted a 13 cent Kennedy stamp. I laughed and thought that this was the closest McCormack had ever come to a Kennedy since the Democratic Convention of 1960.

After he was nominated, Jack Kennedy sought out Everett Dirksen for advice concerning his throat. Jack asked how Dirksen managed to keep going for hours without a throat problem. He said that he could hardly speak anymore because his throat hurt so much from talking and he wondered whether he should try to get rid of his Boston accent because people were finding it funny and laughing about it.

The Republican Senator told the Democratic presidential candidate, "No, Jack, don't try to change your accent. All that laughter is friendly laughter and it will get you votes. But if you can't talk at all, that will lose you votes." Dirksen advised Kennedy to find a voice teacher and learn to speak from his diaphragm so that his throat would not be strained. And the fluffy gray-haired Republican leader proceeded to give the candidate his first voice lesson. They were very good friends.

I remember I got in bad with Jack Kennedy at the time of the 1960 nomination. I was always getting in bad with him because he didn't care much for my Southern ways. And I'm afraid he never forgot what happened in 1956 and the sneaky way I handled his brother, Bobby, while the vice-presidency was slipping away to Kefauver.

And, of course, Kennedy knew that I had been at Rayburn's side trying to keep him from getting the nomination.

But *I* liked *him* anyway. And besides, this was right after Kennedy had won the nomination for the presidency and now all was forgiven and forgotten and we were having a big meeting of fund-raisers. It was called the "750 Club," and they were the top contributors as far as personal generosity goes.

They were meeting in a conference room, and I was stationed outside to usher Kennedy in and announce him at the strategic time. Adlai Stevenson was speaking, and suddenly Jack Kennedy arrived and stood waiting. I thought I had seen Rayburn nod to me to bring in the nominee.

At any rate, I advanced into the room in the middle of Stevenson's plea for funds and bellowed, "Mr. Speakah, the next President of the United States."

Kennedy was furious. "That was stupid," he hissed, hitting his head with his hand. "He hasn't even finished his pitch." He was blazing mad, probably thinking he'd miss out on some money.

But the deed was done. I had announced him, so he had to go forward, especially since the crowd was on its feet and simply roaring its approval of Kennedy. When the cheering died down, Stevenson's humor popped up and he said, "When I heard that appreciation, I thought it must at least be Miss America."

In the political game, all that counts is winning, and

since Kennedy won, he must have gotten enough contributions in spite of my little mistake.

Stevenson had a real gift for the sudden quip, the perfect comment. Other than that, it was hard to know why he was considered such a good speaker. He had to read his speeches, and he couldn't even keep track of where he was. His voice sounded almost as bad as Eleanor Roosevelt's. And he wasn't gutsy. The leadership complained that he couldn't make up his mind whether to be a liberal or not, and of course they called him "egghead."

Nor was he so original. When Eleanor Roosevelt died and he said that great thing about her at the first Eleanor Roosevelt Memorial Candlestick award dinner, "She would rather light a candle than curse the darkness," everyone gave him credit for being a great phrasemaker. Then it turned out the Chinese had said it first. It's an old Chinese proverb: "It is better to light one candle than to curse the darkness."

I knew, as did men like Rayburn, that though Adlai was getting credit for his great speeches, the truth was he had great speech writers. I'm not faulting him. Almost everybody on the Hill has great speech writers. If congressmen had to go back to writing their own speeches, I'll bet there would be a lot of fresh faces on the Hill.

I'll never forget Lyndon Johnson telling me how he had told one of his speech writers to get the hell out. "I told him that to be able to write for me and know how I feel, a feller has to know what it's like to walk barefoot in a barnyard full of chickenshit," he said, "and feel some between his toes."

So I'm not faulting Stevenson for the great thing he said about Eleanor Roosevelt, I just wish he would have admitted where it had come from—unless he thought his speech writer made it up. What he had said swept the country, and he was praised for it over and over. I would not have known where he had gotten it if a reporter hadn't found it in an old book of Chinese sayings.

Adlai tried to beat Ike in 1952 and again in 1956 and failed both times. Then Eleanor Roosevelt, who really believed in him, tried and failed, in a last-ditch stand in 1960, to get the convention to give Adlai just one more chance now that Ike was safely out of the way.

I guess the reason Kennedy was so mad at me for cutting short Adlai's speech in 1960 was that Kennedy wanted to be a gracious winner. He could afford to be—Adlai was down for the long count and wasn't apt to try for the presidency again.

Recently I was reminiscing about conventions with Edgar A. Poe, a collateral descendant of the poet, who is more famous in Washington, however, as former president of the Gridiron Club, president of the White House Correspondents Association and correspondent for the *New Orleans Times-Picayune*.

We were talking of how a convention is a big love-in, and how, with TV cameramen egging me on, I had kissed Mayor Daley of Chicago two times on the head at the Democratic Convention in Chicago in 1968 to counteract the hate that was being demonstrated outside the convention hall. But Ed maintained that I had slowed down a lot because he had kept count at the 1960 Los Angeles convention that nominated John F. Kennedy and claimed that I had kissed ninety-nine feminine conventioneers.

This led us to recall a story that was being told at the 1960 convention about another man whose name was placed in nomination for President, at the same time as Kennedy's—Ross Barnett, governor of my state of Mississippi. Ross, we decided, illustrated perfectly how a politician can get his tail in a crack and come up looking like a man who should be President.

The way the story goes, Governor Barnett, when he was running for governor of Mississippi, got trapped in a crowd at the Neshoba County Fair and someone dared ask a political question on this great social occasion. "How do you stand on this here forty-hour work week?"

Ross Barnett bellowed, "I'm agin it!"

A thunder of boos swept over the listeners and some overall-clad men suggested loudly that he be run out of town.

After the pandemonium died down, the tall candidate's voice boomed over the loudspeaker: "As I was saying, forty hours are *too dang long* for any man to work." Whereupon applause and shouts of "Hurrah for Ross," broke over the fairgrounds.

Every candidate running for President at a convention is a humorist—more or less—usually at the expense of a competitor. I was shocked to hear Senator Muskie at the 1976 convention still taking potshots at Hubert Humphrey as a presidential candidate and saying, "Hubert couldn't stop running even if he fell into a vat of Kaopectate."

And for his part, Humphrey at the same convention was still taking out after poor Richard Nixon and his Republican party's promise, when he became President, to take crime off the streets. "They've taken crime off the streets all right," Hubert said. "They've taken crime off the streets and put it into the White House."

I remember when Lyndon Johnson was going to run for President in 1964, after having served out Kennedy's term, the Hill was much amused that he would have to pick a running mate *at all,* let alone one as powerful as Hubert Humphrey. "Lyndon doesn't need a running mate," a member of his own party said. "Lyndon's running mate is his inner self."

What's in a name? A lot, if it belongs to a candidate for President.

Senator Barry Goldwater almost got a new name

380

during his 1964 presidential campaign when the chairman of some ladies' club got over-excited and over-awed and introduced him this way: "Ladies and gentlemen, the next President of the United States, Goldy Bearwater."

The "Tricky Dick" label didn't stop Richard Nixon from squeaking through to victory in 1968 and then winning by a landslide in 1972.

Maybe that's because his fellow candidates had worse things done to their names. To show that Humphrey was still under the thumb of retiring President Johnson, and was as much a part of the Johnson family as Lady Bird and Lynda Bird, the opposition came up with a devastating name for Humphrey—Hu-Bird.

And as if that wasn't bad enough, a cartoon was passed around the Hill that showed Johnson sitting on an egg and the egg has opened and poor Humphrey is trying to get out of it. The caption says, "I'm hatched, chief, would you please get off my back?"

Hubert Humphrey could play the name game too. He reworded the commercial which talked of Excedrin headaches and admitted to audiences, "I have a 'Present Administration' headache." There was more than a little truth in that.

When Lyndon Johnson chose Hubert Humphrey for his running mate in 1964, I was aghast because each was a powerhouse on the Hill and usually a man is happier with a more subdued candidate.

I was right that LBJ would feel that old competitive urge and would cut HHH down to size in whatever way possible. He made Humphrey get on a horse and look ridiculous down on the ranch in Texas, and according to Humphrey's own account in his memoir, he suffered more than a little abuse at the hands of LBJ. In 1968, as a final putdown, Johnson waited until it was too late to help before he gave his Vice President his real support.

Poor Humphrey. He would have been one of the brainiest Presidents we have ever had. But everything conspired against him, even the times, which had not been of his making. I'll never forget Chicago in 1968. Streets blockaded. Barbed wire fence around the hall. It was like a concentration camp.

My biggest problem was trying to see that Senator McGovern's wife and a doctor always got through to their box seats at the convention. We never did find out why a doctor was always with Mrs. McGovern, but we were told that the presidential hopeful was "sick" and needed a doctor near. Anyone would be sick with that hostile atmosphere. McGovern was not a candidate this time, but was there as an important delegate.

Four years later, the same doctor was there with the McGoverns when the victory and the cheers were for George. And I still did not find out exactly what the doctor was needed for. But it was ironic that very soon in the campaign that followed it was the health problems of *his running mate,* Thomas Eagleton, that caused McGovern's downfall in the race.

In 1968, my part in the convention started in the Statler Hilton Hotel in Washington, even before I got to Chicago. I was the sergeant-at-arms for Hale Boggs and his committee on the platform for the Democratic party. To get to the convention on time, we suddenly had to pack up kit-and-caboodle and catch a plane at Dulles Airport, bringing everything along to finish before the convention opened.

We worked in strictest secrecy almost around the clock in Chicago at the Blackstone Hotel, except when we rushed for two hours to a meeting each day at the convention hall, passing through the barbed wire in our two big buses with police escort.

But somewhere along the line, there was dirty work afoot. One day when we returned, one of our plain-clothes detectives suddenly held up his hand for silence,

382

put his finger to his lips and then pointed at a little wire. He had discovered that we were being bugged with two microphones in the room and the other ends of the wires terminated in the basement of the hotel.

Hale Boggs was sure it was a TV network job and, though we had some evidence of just who the bugging sneak thieves were, we kept the secret for the duration of the convention, which already had enough trouble.

But I'll never forget Hale Boggs bawling me out as if it had been my fault that it happened. Though I protested that I was only gone for two hours of sleep and two hours of meetings, he said, "Damn it, if you can't do better than that, you'd better sleep right here."

And I did, from then on. And we had no more news leaks.

The best thing I can say about the 1972 campaign is that at least they had a little fun. When McGovern dumped Eagleton as a running mate, he decided to get someone from the Kennedy crowd to give the campaign a touch of class—Sargent Shriver, husband of Eunice Kennedy. In fact, McGovern learned about Kennedy-style fun, when some of the gang would toot Shriver aboard the McGovern plane playing "Hail to the Chief" on a couple of kazoos.

Shriver did have the old Kennedy sense of fun. On the Hill, they said McGovern had himself "a Kennedy once removed" as a running mate.

But once removed wasn't good enough, and the only state they won in the election was the Kennedy stronghold of Massachusetts—plus the District of Columbia.

I attended and helped in every Democratic National Convention, starting in 1940 with Roosevelt's bid for a third term through the 1972 convention, which was the opening gun of the most botched-up campaign of my experience.

Altogether, I've seen eleven conventions. I was assistant sergeant-at-arms until 1948, when I was made assistant doorkeeper of the convention. I was assigned to go up and down the aisles to keep them clear and then to stay around the platform in case Rayburn needed me.

Then in 1952, I was made doorkeeper of the convention. And from then on I sent the assistant doorkeeper to clear the aisles.

Republican conventions are no more virtuous than those of the Democrats. Though I didn't go to the Republican conventions, of course, being a henchman of the Democratic leadership, I got the word on what skullduggery went on straight from my buddies who did attend.

The inside story is that Herbert Hoover, who was elected President in the 1928 election and voted out in the election of 1932, did not give up his fond dream of regaining the presidency as vindication for the humiliation of not being permitted a second term—a great rarity in American politics. But there were many top Republicans who were determined that he wouldn't be President again.

In 1936, a beautiful blonde led a snake dance for Hoover on the floor of the convention hall. There was supposed to be a great stampede for Hoover and there almost was, but when he got up to speak, as the former President of the United States, by some unfortunate coincidence the mike broke down and he couldn't be heard.

In 1940, at the Philadelphia convention, Hoover was again discouraged, but with more finesse. My good friend Ken Hoyt, who was with the Republican National Committee in 1936 and in 1940 was the director of publicity for the "Taft for President" campaign told me that when he arrived in Philadelphia, a rough

384

and ready local politician told him, "The mike broke down for Hoover in 1936 and it was no accident. This can happen again if necessary."

But that wasn't really necessary, because they had come up with something much better. In the offices under the galleries, the radiators had been fully turned on. There was no air conditioning, of course, in those days. Every chair was a hot seat. The hundreds of press people covering the convention were oblivious to what was going on, as usual. They only knew it was terribly, miserably hot and you could hardly hear Hoover, who looked about the size of a tiny doll from the galleries. And that for some strange reason, the back doors of the hall behind the platform were opened facing the Pennsylvania railroad track and every few minutes the rumble of trains drowned out what little you could hear of the poor man.

When Hoover had risen to speak on that warm June night of 1940, the audience was really in agony—those who were still awake, that is. Because, to play it perfectly safe, the Willkie faction had taken the precaution of turning down the microphone volume just enough to blur Hoover's voice.

Sam Pryor was the arrangements chairman for the 1940 Republican National Convention The "arrangements" included many psychological tricks, including dirge music for unwanted candidates and the packing of the galleries with local gas and electric company employees to shout, "We want Willkie," dinning the ears of the bewildered delegates. Willkieites had gotten in with phony general-admission tickets, grabbed the seats of legitimate holders, and were overflowing the steps—against all fire regulations.

For Taft, they had used "Love's Old Sweet Song," which begins, "Once in the dear dead days beyond recall . . ."

Taft had been the leading candidate at the convention, but his forces were eroded by this fierce assault

385

upon the delegates. A week before the convention, all the best political reporters had been predicting a Taft win.

Ken said, "I knew the Willkie tricks going on and the total situation and told only one newsman, the 'Periscope' editor of *Newsweek,* who was unable to use it until the convention was all over." The story got in the *Congressional Record* and was the subject of House speeches.

Even Congressman John Rankin of Mississippi, our worst rabble-rousing Democrat, said it showed that the Republicans ran a boss-ridden convention. But the Democrats did not make much of an issue since our own convention a few weeks later featured propaganda over a hidden mike, planted by an employee of the local sewer and sanitation department. So it was called, "A voice from the sewer."

The sewer voice gave a running line of patter on how great FDR was. It had been plugged into the loudspeakers. How well I knew. I had been in Chicago helping along in any way I could to make Democratic history by getting Roosevelt a third term.

As I told Ken, "They just don't make conventions like that anymore." To which he added a dry, "Fortunately, I guess."

I asked Ken what he now thought, looking back at the 1940 convention at which his man Senator Robert Taft didn't make it, and he said, "I have to say it was a blessing that Taft wasn't nominated. He would have lost World War II for England. He would have used obstructionist tactics to keep America from helping England with destroyers." Then he added, "All of Europe might have fallen to Hitler. Who knows?"

It is staggering to think of how much the progress and state and condition of the whole world rides on who is elected to the American presidency.

FDR set out immediately to help Britain, as soon

as he was reelected. But as Ken and I recalled, Taft had said in speeches in the midwest before the convention, "We can deal with Hitler. It will be unpleasant, but we can do it."

As for Willkie, the best part of his story is what happened after the convention and after his loss of the election to Franklin Roosevelt. To keep his name alive and gain knowledge in international affairs, which had been his weakness in the campaign, he took a trip around the world.

In Egypt, he learned a little more about international affairs than he was looking for and almost caused an international incident when he popped into his hotel room from his bath, stark naked, into the midst of a group of Egyptian dignitaries who were there to honor him and talk with him. The dignitaries rushed out in consternation because it was a great offense to their Moslem laws to be in the presence of a nude Christian.

That was Willkie's first mistake. His second, which he bragged about when he returned to the U.S., happened in Russia, after Stalin welcomed him and warmly received his views about all nations living in peace and tranquility in "one world." Willkie was sure he had really made a friend when the Russian leader asked if he had ever flown over Russia and then gave him a plane, a pilot, a copilot and a beautiful interpreter to make a leisurely survey.

With the door safely locked between the cockpit and the luxurious interior, Willkie and his beautiful companion relaxed and did what came naturally. But these were the days before pressurized cabins, and the high altitude, Willkie felt, strained his heart. Maybe it did, maybe it didn't. His book did sweep the country under its catchy title of *One World*, but he never was able to prove whether he could have made it into the White House.

Within a short time, Willkie was dead of a heart

attack, and on the Hill the word was that Stalin, in his inscrutable way, had done him in.

I've saved the best for the last. It concerns how Eleanor Roosevelt changed the course of history.

Few people realize that Harry Truman really owed his presidency to Eleanor Roosevelt. The story starts in Washington in 1944 before the Democratic Convention, when FDR had been advised to pick Jimmy Byrnes, the secretary of state, for his running mate on his fourth term go-round.

Jimmy was greatly respected on the Hill and had had a long historically significant career and all the background experience needed to make a well-rounded President. And FDR had passed the word that he wanted Jimmy, and Jimmy had been informed and had even told his wife that he was going to be the next Vice President.

But FDR had played it real cute, cards close to the chest. In order not to anger Henry Wallace or his liberal following, Roosevelt had given the convention a half-hearted sort-of endorsement, saying that he had no objections to having Wallace as his running mate.

Well, as everyone now knows, Franklin Roosevelt was in terrible health in those days—and even approaching death. He did not attend the convention. He acknowledged and accepted the nomination by long-distance hook-up. And when it came time for the vice-presidential nomination, Henry Wallace was indeed nominated. But what the public doesn't know is that it was Eleanor Roosevelt who changed the course of history, and really was, in a way, like Edith Galt Wilson, who was running the show when President Woodrow Wilson suffered his stroke.

Hearing that Jimmy Byrnes was to be *the man,* several top liberals of the country talked to Eleanor Roosevelt and told her how unhappy they were. They said *that* Southerner would never get the Negro vote.

Taking matters into her own hands, Eleanor asked who they would like. And they suggested this nice fellow Harry Truman who was doing such a good job with his War Investigating Committee and was from an acceptable state—Missouri.

Without waking up the President, the First Lady gave the word to the powers that be at the convention that FDR had changed his mind and wanted Harry Truman.

When FDR found out what his wife had done, he almost had a stroke then and there. As for Harry Truman, when he found out that *he* was scheduled to be *the one,* he could hardly believe his good luck and gasped something like, "Why, I've hardly been to the White House."

As a matter of fact, Harry Truman had come to the convention fully prepared to nominate Jimmy Byrnes. Byrnes was never nominated. Instead Truman *was,* by a respected fellow senator of his own state—Bennett Champ Clark.

As for Jimmy Byrnes, he resigned from the cabinet soon thereafter, still smarting under the humiliation.

I never did tell Harry Truman the full inside story of how he had become President. Once a man becomes President, even though you are pretty close to him and reminisce about things, there is a certain barrier and you do not tell him things that put him down in any way. Maybe he would have thought it amusing, but the last thing I would have wanted to do would be to hurt old Harry's feelings. But I always thought of Eleanor when Truman would comment about how surprised he had been to find himself Vice President.

It seemed that it was Truman's destiny not to receive the love shown other political stars, no matter what he did. At the 1948 convention, which should have been a triumph for him because he did get the nomination, Harry Truman suffered every humiliation.

First of all, after he was nominated, the convention

officials kept him cooling his heels outside the convention hall for simply hours. And by the time he got to make his entrance and give his acceptance speech, the prime time of radio was long over and hardly anyone was listening—either in the hall or across the nation.

And just to make sure he got the message that he wasn't too welcome, some of the delegates had turned the "W" around on their signs and greeted poor Harry with placards that read: "I'm Just Mild About Harry."

But the final humiliation at the 1948 convention concerned some birds that were supposed to represent the doves of peace—healing the wounds of the Democratic party and the wounds of the war-torn world. Only they, too, had been waiting too long, cooped up. When they were finally released, instead of soaring up and away like good little doves of peace should, they angrily dive-bombed around and "pooped on I-oway," as the old toast goes, as well as on Truman's loyal state of Missouri.

PRESIDENTS I HAVE KNOWN BEFORE THEY WERE PRESIDENTS— FROM TRUMAN TO FORD

When I see the great outpouring of love to Harry Truman now that he is dead, I shake my head and remember how he was once Truman-the-hated on Capitol Hill and how during the dark days there was even danger of starting impeachment proceedings against the "pig-headed bastard from Missouri." His firing of Douglas MacArthur was viewed by many as "the second great day of infamy."

But no matter what others said of Truman, Sam Rayburn was always his defender.

One of the greatest assemblies of members of Congress ever held outside the Capitol was one which was brought together by the Civil Air Patrol after World War II and held at a Washington hotel.

The Civil Air Patrol was the volunteer corps of flyers who patrolled our coasts against submarines and maintained air services nationwide throughout the four years of conflict. The purpose of the love fest was to thank Congress for the privilege of having served their country. This was a switch because most people ignored their congressmen unless they wanted something, so most of Congress was there and happy that night. But as a matter of fact, as it turned out, they *did* want something very big—an independent Air Force. They wanted to separate it from the stranglehold control of the Army. So on the night of the banquet, every state was represented and a majority of both the House and Senate was there. Their hosts

391

had forty-eight tables for the wing commanders of each state plus an Army Air Force general.

My friend Ken Hoyt attended as the public relations man for the Civil Air Patrol. The master of ceremonies was to be Speaker Sam and the guest of honor was President Truman. Colonel Earle Johnson, the CAP national commander, was on pins and needles to be sure everything went right and he knew that Rayburn needed to be briefed on the story of the patrol.

Ken Hoyt was nonchalantly smoking a cigarette in the VIP room where the most distinguished guests were assembling and having cocktails before being led to the head table. "Quick," said Colonel Johnson. "Write Rayburn a speech. He's drunk as a billy goat." Actually, Johnson had underestimated the capacity of the Speaker, who, of course, performed with his usual smoothness in spite of his condition. But Hoyt hurriedly scribbled some notes which he explained and gave to Rayburn.

After using a bit of Hoyt's notes to commend the Civil Air Patrol, Rayburn launched into a most flowery introduction of the President imaginable, calling him "the *loved* man, the *wanted* man."

It was too much for Truman. He was so overcome that he choked and said, "I had a nice little speech, but you've knocked it out of me." He threw away his speech and proceeded to reminisce about how he had been the first to use an airplane in a political campaign. For a clever stunt before an election in Missouri, he hired a pilot with an old open-cockpit, two-seater plane so he could drop leaflets. "But," he said, "as I became airsick, on one side of the plane I dropped my leaflets and on the other side, ooh . . ." He lowered his head and leaned far over with his mouth open—and the crowd roared.

People ask whether I got to know the Presidents because when they came to the Hill to speak before

Joint Sessions and entered the hallowed chambers, I shouted out, "Mr. Speakah, the President of the United States." No indeedy. By the time they get to the Hill to speak on those austere occasions, there is no time to make friends.

No, I became friendly with Presidents before they were Presidents. I knew one from his Senate days, and four Presidents in a row were former members of Congress. Jack Kennedy was one I had known this way. He came to the Hill in the Eightieth Congress and stayed through the Eighty-second—1947 to 1953 —before making it into the Senate. Of course, I had known Truman on the Hill, because he was a senator before FDR—or I should say Eleanor—tapped him to be Vice President. And while he was Vice President, I got to know him even better because he presided over the Senate and I was always involved in some matter or other that had to do with the cooperation of the House and Senate.

But getting back to Presidents who had served in the House, Lyndon Johnson did, too, from 1937 to 1949, as did Richard Nixon—1947 to 1950—and Jerry Ford—1949 to 1974.

Of the thirty-nine men who have been President of the United States, seventeen served previously in the House. That's a proud number. And some of the names back there in history, a bit before my time, made me even prouder to have served in any capacity in the House. Taking them from the top: James Madison, Andrew Jackson, William Henry Harrison, John Tyler, James K. Polk, Millard Fillmore, Franklin Pierce, James Buchanan, Abraham Lincoln, Andrew Johnson, Rutherford B. Hayes, James A. Garfield and William McKinley.

It's kind of strange that between McKinley and Kennedy, exactly fifty years apart in their presidential administrations, there were no Presidents coming out of the House.

I sometimes wonder what would have happened if I had made the country aware that President Nixon was having places bugged outside of the White House, even on Capitol Hill, before the Watergate case broke. Maybe if I had sounded an alarm, the leadership might have gotten so incensed that the resulting publicity would have stopped him from ordering the bugging of the Democratic headquarters. But then, we would not have had the Watergate case which showed up all the rest of the bugging that was going on. So it's just as well that I let nature take its course.

What happened is that President Nixon was invited to be guest of honor at a luncheon hosted by the man who gave me my first job, Bill Colmer, chairman of the House Rules Committee. It was a tradition that Mr. Colmer annually invited whoever was the President. Other guests were the leadership—the Speaker, Majority Leader, Minority Leader, Democratic and Republican Whips. I noticed that the signal corps was bugging the Speaker's Dining Room, where the luncheon was to take place. In fact, one of the waiters alerted me to it and said, "Be careful of what you are saying in this room and even how you answer phones. This room is full of bug juice." That was what some of the people around the Hill called bugging—bug juice.

Actually, I believe that for possibly three years in a row the room was bugged and Nixon must have had a record of what the congressmen were saying about him even before his arrival, or what is worse, what they might have been saying about him on the other side of the table, where they thought he couldn't hear. The time was the early 1970s—1971, 1972, 1973. One time when I was aware of this bugging, I did mention it first to a few of the men who entered the room but since the congressmen didn't get excited, I just forgot about it. Anyway, for all I knew, someone had gotten permission for this bugging. Only after the Watergate story broke did I realize how serious the bugging might have been.

Actually, Congressman Wright Patman, chairman of the Banking and Currency Committee, had recognized the seriousness of Watergate long before Senator Sam Ervin's committee and wanted to have a House investigation. Wright Patman explained to me how even in 1971 Nixon was trying to gain control over Congress in a very sinister way by refusing to spend money that Congress had appropriated.

Patman said, "That man in the White House is using the Congress as a distraction to hide what is happening. He is trying to camouflage a grab for power such as we have never seen before." Congressman Patman was very worried about Nixon and what he might do with this power he was after. A little later, there were stories on the Hill about how Nixon was setting up shadow governments around the country, duplicate agencies to the Washington one, and he was training his own henchmen in the White House and then putting each one in control of an agency. I'm glad we didn't get to find out what this could have led to.

Each administration had its own flavor, its own feeling. Even having lived through the Nixon years and hearings that could have ended with his impeachment, I still say I have never witnessed so much hate as that directed toward FDR and then Harry Truman, the first two Presidents I served under.

At worst, Nixon inspired a cold contempt, but with FDR and Truman, even congressmen showed such great hate that they would practically froth at the mouth. Some men on the Hill, like Rayburn, loved them dearly, but others hated them so that you even had to be careful who you talked to about them or else you were in trouble.

One congressman, Joe Byrns, Jr., of Tennessee, son of the former Speaker of the House, was famous for his gross and devastating imitation of Eleanor Roosevelt in the back rooms of Congress.

It was perfect in voice and even in the way he curled his lip—after inserting a wad of paper—in imitation of buck teeth. He was for a time during the Roosevelt administration the most popular man in the cloakroom. I'm afraid I laughed as much as anyone else, while feeling guilty at his cruel jest.

In those early days, the talk on my side of the aisle was of how lucky we were to have gotten rid of that "cold fish," Hoover. A congressman told how one of Hoover's friends had said to him at a dinner party, after Hoover was elected, that he was sorry to confess he had voted for Al Smith, but now that it was over and Hoover was in, he was happy for him and wished him luck. Hoover gave him the iciest look he had ever experienced. The friend waited nervously but Hoover did not answer and never talked to him again.

Those who were around the White House in Hoover's day laughed that Hoover had issued an order that no staffer was to pet his dog, King Tut, because too much of a fuss had been made over the dog and one day the dog didn't bother to come to the President when he called. Nixon also had trouble making his dog come to him and was distressed by it.

That's the kind of thing that Jerry Ford would have found funny and would have retold many times. He loved jokes on himself. But Nixon and Hoover were both uptight men and possessive even about their damn dogs.

Ford had a well-developed sense of humor in the old days on the Hill, so I was not surprised to learn that at the White House he had trained his dog, Liberty, to help him get rid of visitors. On a signal, Liberty would march into the Oval Office, giving Ford an excuse for getting up and changing the subject, terminating the conference.

President Ford did have a natural wit. Before the recent Republican convention, a baseball star gave him four baseball caps "because we don't know your head size," and Ford quipped, "That depends on the way the polls go."

He loved to make fun of his own game. About his golf swing, he said, "I have a very wild swing. I'll tell you how wild it is. Back on my home course in Michigan, they don't yell 'Fore!' they yell, 'Ford!' "

About his golf game, he said, "You know all those Secret Servicemen who follow me? Well, whenever I'm playing golf, they go on combat pay."

As a matter of fact, he considered himself a jinx to other players, as he explained at the opening of the World Golf Hall of Fame, which happened to be held on the night before the World Open tournament.

"Tonight I have good news and bad. The good news is that four of our honorees—Jack Nicklaus, Arnold Palmer, Gary Player and Sam Snead—will be competing in the World Open beginning tomorrow. The bad news is, today they shared the course with me— I'll tell you what I mean.

"In 1972, I played with Sam Snead in the Pro-Am before the Kemper Open. He *didn't* go on to win the tournament. In 1973, I played with Miller Barber before the Kemper Open. And he *didn't* go on to win the tournament.

"This year, I played with Tom Weiskopf before the Kemper Open. And I played with Dave Stockton before the Pleasant Valley Open. *Neither* of them went on to win the tournament. In Washington, I'm known as the President of the United States, but in golf, I'm known as the 'jinx of the links.' "

Then he added that he had figured out that Snead, Barber, Weiskopf and Stockton had blown $165,000 in prize money. "If you think they're unhappy," he said, "you should hear the Internal Revenue Service."

397

Good sportsmanship is frequently the subject of humor on the Hill, and Jerry Ford has enriched the repertoire with his much-quoted comment on the subject. "I'd like to share two memorable football quotations with you," he said. "The first comes from Grantland Rice: 'When the one Great Scorer comes to write against your name, he marks not that you won or lost, but how you played the game.'

"And the second," he said, "comes from Ohio State's Woody Hay: 'Hah, Humbug!' "

Religion once brought Jimmy Carter and me together when he was governor and I was the Capitol Doorkeeper on a visit to Georgia. I had the honor of giving the prayer at a luncheon that Carter attended.

I didn't dream he would become another of the surprises of history. If I've learned anything in Washington, it is that only on looking back do you know what really happened. And looking back and remembering how he sounded, I now realize that Jimmy was fixing to run for President some day.

A painted room meant something a little different to President Ford than to you and me. When he was a kid, he earned his allowance by putting the labels on paint cans for his stepfather, who had a small, struggling paint manufacturing company.

Jerry was naturally Jerry to me all though the years on the Hill—since he arrived in 1949, it would be natural that I still called him by his first name after he was Vice President. And he was still the same man when he became President, so it was still natural to call him by his first name. It seems to me that congressmen and friends who have been close to a man for many years need not suddenly be calling him Mr. President. That's silly to have to change. It's like wanting your children and parents to call you Mr. President.

Anyway, that's how I felt and it got me in trouble. The newly confirmed President came to the Hill—

same man I had been calling Jerry for twenty-five years—and I said, "Hi, Jerry," and he was not at all appalled. But I could see the people around him—especially Wayne Hays of Ohio and my nemesis from the same state, James V. Stanton—were agitated at what they thought was my brash nerve. They later circulated the story that this was the reason I had been voted out of office at the start of the Ninety-fourth Congress.

But I want to say right now that Jerry Ford was certainly not the reason the members did not vote for me for my fifteenth term as Doorkeeper. He was not the kind of man to be offended at not being called "Mr. President." But that gave my enemies a handle for telling the incoming "young turks" that I had offended the President.

They also claimed that I had "manhandled" the President. What I had done was grab the President to keep him from falling over Speaker Carl Albert when the President hadn't noticed him because Albert is so small. Jerry Ford had a way of barging ahead without looking, which was later to give him bad headlines for supposedly being clumsy.

I lost the election for a fifteenth term by 150 to 100 votes, which was not a shameful defeat. When I left, Brother Jerry Ford, who had no knowledge of this "manhandling" accusation, or I'm sure he would have risen to my defense, sent me a warm letter from the White House about what I had meant to him through the years.

When I think of Ford, I think of a guy who is a complete sports nut and who maybe missed his calling when he didn't become a professional athlete. He's great on long drives, but needs to work on his putts. He loves skiing. But what most people don't know is that he was boxing coach at Yale.

When Queen Elizabeth was visiting during the Bicentennial, and Bob Hope was at the White House as a guest and to entertain her, Ford said Bob Hope was trying to ruin his golf game. They'd been out on the course, said the President, and "just as I was getting ready to drive a long one, Bob said, 'You know, Mr. President, I'm going to the convention as an uncommitted delegate.' "

Yes, you weren't around Ford long before you knew his mind thought sports and gave everything else he talked about a sports twist.

I told him that my wife, Mable, had said I loved baseball more than I loved her.

"What did you tell her?" he asked with a slightly worried look.

"I said, 'Yes, but not football.' "

Ford had played outfielder—and a damn good one—on the House Republican baseball team against my Democratic team. Though we were not teammates there, we did share another experience on the same side of the fence. Each of us had been deserted by our father early in life. But Ford tried to do something about it legislatively.

The first day of every new Congress he would introduce his bill known as the "Runaway Pappy Bill." What it amounted to was a demand that the federal government help wives find the men who had deserted their children in order to get support money.

Since it is so hard and expensive to try to locate a husband in another state and then to institute child support proceedings, Ford felt the wives should have the help of the federal government, which has all social-security records.

I was one of the last people Truman called to the White House to say good-bye. "Right after the election," Truman told me, "I just couldn't help it. I had to do it. I wanted to call Ike's bluff because he'd been such a blow-hard and talked so big. I sent him a telegram and I said, after I'd congratulated him like a gentleman is supposed to do, I said, 'By the way, if you still plan to fly to Korea, I will put my plane at your disposal.' "

He said he'd heard from his spies and pals around the White House that "Ike was so shook, he couldn't hit his golf ball straight for a month."

Truman knew I had been in on the secret preparations to invite General MacArthur to speak at the Joint Meeting after Truman had fired him.

Truman said that if he hadn't fired MacArthur for insubordination the old General could have tricked the U.S. into a third world war, this one to fight Chiang Kai-shek's battle by invading China. I confessed that I had been impressed by MacArthur and thrilled to be a part of it when MacArthur came to the Hill, but now I wasn't so sure.

Truman resented the fact that many people thought he was just an accidental President and wasn't very smart because of his Missouri twang and his plain talk.

"Hell, Fish, I know all the words," said Truman. "I just don't drag them out every day. I wasn't a dummy. I read the Bible clear through before I was old enough to go to school. And I had a wonderful mother."

Truman said that if he thought about it, perhaps the reason he was in the White House was that she had started it all. She had gotten him a present of a blackboard with biographies of the Presidents on it and he had learned to think presidency.

Then he added, "But by the time it happened to me, Fishbait, I was certainly not thinking of that blackboard anymore."

What Truman liked most, I think, was reminiscing about how we both got our start in drugstores. I told him about how the men of the town would come in on a Sunday morning before church for their "medicine" and I, as a little shaver, had to sell them their shots of whiskey, hardly knowing what I was doing,

401

except that the money was not to go into the cash register but in another place.

Truman had been a little older than I was when he got his drugstore job—all of eleven. And he knew exactly what was going on. He'd simply put the bottle of whiskey on the counter and the men would pour their own. And they'd leave a dime for each drink.

Truman recalled how he had hated prohibitionists because he remembered what hypocrites some of the men were who made the most speeches for prohibition.

But he couldn't leave the subject of MacArthur alone. "Fishbait, it was as if *you* started to give Speaker Rayburn the orders instead of the other way around. You can only have one Speaker of the House and you can only have one Commander in Chief."

Truman explained in a tired voice that he had no choice but to fire MacArthur. "Hell, he was going to undo everything, just when we had the 38th parallel again, where we could begin negotiations of the cease-fire. He was going to expand the war and unleash Chiang Kai-shek's army and bomb China's industries and a whole list of things."

He paused and waved his hand as if to wave off the list. "And can you imagine, that bastard issued his own statement that he was going to meet with the enemy and that if North Korea didn't surrender to him personally, he would invade China."

Truman shook his head in disbelief and muttered, "I should have busted him long ago just for the insubordination of meeting me in that get-up without a tie and wearing an open shirt and those damned sunglasses."

I'd say that MacArthur was Truman's obsession.

History is never what you think it is. The bad are not that bad. The good are not that good.

Around the Hill, Eisenhower, who rode into office as the hard-working general, was known as a "snolly-

402

gaster"—a politician who is all words and very little action. Ike did not like to overwork or even give the impression of overworking, and this started way before he got into the White House.

I remember when he was campaigning and the story circulated around the Hill about how one of his supporters in some little town had written its whole history and political situation for him to background himself before he spoke there. And the great day came, and the man who had spent all his time getting this compendium together waited anxiously for the arrival of the great general.

So the great general arrived and the man handed him the manuscript. Ike took one look at it and said, "Young man, the whole battle plan for the Normandy invasion wasn't this big."

It took the fellow down to ground zero, but it proves a very important point about campaigning—don't overkill.

I didn't get to know President Eisenhower too well because he had not been on the Hill as a congressman or senator as so many other Presidents had. But I do recall that when he came to the Hill to deliver his State of the Union and other addresses, he liked to throw in a little military story to relieve the tension beforehand.

Once he was telling about a military game in which the rules were that a certain bridge that was there was not really there because it had been destroyed and so it was not to be used.

As the mock fighting progressed, General Eisenhower was shocked to see the enemy approach and march straight across the bridge instead of fording the river.

Afterwards, General Eisenhower had called the commanding officer down for it and said, "Didn't you see the sign that the bridge was totally destroyed and unusable?"

403

The enemy commander, according to Ike, thought a moment and replied, "Of course we saw that it was destroyed and out of commission. Couldn't you see that we were all swimming?"

The best kept secret of the Roosevelt administration was that FDR was really a wheelchair patient and couldn't walk worth beans. I knew this because I was there at the Capitol when the elaborate preparations were made to hide the fact that he wasn't really walking. We, who helped the Secret Service, understood that we were not to discuss it, and I never did until now.

I was just a lowly worker in those days, and I would help as the workmen set up an elaborate screen of shrubbery and a specially built wooden ramp for President Roosevelt to take a few steps to the microphone at the Joint Sessions of Congress for the State of the Union message.

I counted once and found that FDR made nine steps to the microphone, if you could call them steps. What would happen is that his son James, who was in uniform as his father's military aide, would help the elder Roosevelt out of the wheelchair and to a standing position, hidden by the shrubbery, of course. Then the President would slap the braces under his trousers to lock his legs into position. For nine steps, FDR would flip his feet forward and wide apart, like a robot. The legs were stiffly locked, and Jimmy was providing the balance.

FDR's children did not follow their father's path, but they tried. Jimmy Roosevelt and Franklin Roosevelt, Jr., were both in Congress in the 1950s. Jimmy was very well-liked and could have stayed in Congress as long as he wanted but FDR, Jr., who had succeeded a great man—Sol Bloom of New York—was a bit lazy.

He was a pleasant enough guy, but the other congressmen grumbled that young Franklin had not done his homework and they were not sorry when he didn't run for reelection in 1954.

Poor Daddy Roosevelt had his troubles, too. We knew on the Hill that his home life wasn't a bed of roses. Why would a woman get away from her home as much as she could?

One military man who was connected with flying Eleanor on her many trips—an air corps officer who served as her pilot or co-pilot on occasion—told how when they were travelling "RON"—which means "remain overnight" in military vernacular—the First Lady would come into his bedroom and give him a goodnight kiss as he lay in bed.

Because Kennedy was a Catholic—and the first Catholic President in the White House—everybody was always wondering exactly how Catholic he was. Did he go to church, or did Jackie make him go?

Well, I dealt a lot with Secret Servicemen because of the many visits Presidents make to Capitol Hill, and though they seldom let anything slip that they shouldn't, one day I couldn't help overhearing two of them talk about what had happened the Sunday before, when the Kennedys had gone to the Catholic church on Pennsylvania Avenue, only about eight blocks from the White House.

As one Secret Serviceman was telling the other, the First Lady had said to the President, quite angrily, "Come on now, you son of a bitch. You got yourself into this and you know your public demands it. So get your damn tie and coat on and let's go."

I remember Jackie Kennedy when she was Jackie Bouvier and a scared little newspaper girl trying to act very dignified and grown up. She would come to me to help her get some pictures for her column, which simply involved asking a question a day.

I would help her. I remember when she started going with Jack, she had come in to ask him a question. And he had appeared in her column. I think

405

she'd also used a picture of Dick Nixon in the same column.

I used to kid her about catching our bachelor and tell her to keep her hands off him. She said, "Oh, Fishbait, you people up here protect your own." Then I'd switch and say, "But if you really want him, Jackie, I'll help you get him."

She'd say, "Oh, Fishbait, you nut. If I need help, I'll advertise."

One of the nicer perks of the job is that I got to go to the White House social functions, now and then taking my wife. Once, in the Kennedy administration, Mable couldn't go so I got permission to bring our daughter instead.

Knowing the routine when the trumpets blare and the presidential party descends the stairs, I positioned Sarah Patsy and me where the President and Mrs. Kennedy would have to pass nearby and Sarah Patsy could get a good look. She worshipped Jacqueline. President Kennedy had dispensed with the formal line and just walked among the guests, shaking a hand here and there and stopping to talk to people he chose.

President Kennedy spotted me and I introduced Sarah Patsy and thanked him for letting her fill in for her mother who had been there the preceding year.

"I'm glad you let your daughter come instead of Mrs. Miller," he said, taking her hand. "I want to tell you what a great daddy you have. This is Thursday and in the Tuesday paper on the front page there was an article stating the the Doorkeeper has sent over $90,000 to the miscellaneous fund of the U.S. Treasury for the sale of waste paper from the House wing of the Capitol."

Jack beamed at her with that youthful grin and Sarah Patsy almost swooned. But she did recover enough to thank him for telling her. Then Jacqueline stopped to shake hands and I thanked her for letting Sarah Patsy come and she amazed my daughter even more. "Oh, Sarah Patsy," she said, very softly, the tones almost like music, coming from her throat, "I'll bet your father didn't tell you that I knew him when I was a photographer.

I saw my daughter's eyes open wide. Jackie chuckled and continued, "Oh, yes, and he would always telephone me at the *Times-Herald* and advise me that something important was going to happen. And when I arrived he had placed someone in the spot to hold it so I could take over and get my picture."

The First Lady laughed and I realized she had changed quite a bit from the days I knew her and seemed to be measuring out everything she did, even her laughter. But Sarah Patsy, who hadn't known the old Jacqueline Bouvier, was making little noises of appreciation. "Thank you, Mrs. Kennedy," she said excitedly. "I'll tell my mother that because she still doesn't believe he really knows you."

Seeing President Kennedy that day, it was hard to remember he was the same man who could cuss me out for bringing him into a room too soon.

For a while, little Sarah Patsy had new respect for her daddy.

When President Kennedy was assassinated, I was in my office, talking with Congressman Sparky Matsunaga, Democrat of Hawaii, and his guest, the sister of my old friend Governor John Burns of Hawaii, whom I'd known as a delegate.

I got a phone call from upstairs. "Have you heard the news?"

I said, "No, what's up?"

One of my boys shouted, "They claim they've assassinated the President."

I said, "That can't be—they've gone to Texas." With that, I reached over and turned the knob of my radio and heard it being talked about.

As if we had read each other's minds, we three fell to our knees and prayed for the survival of John

Kennedy and then I rushed to find Speaker McCormack to see what he needed.

It's sad to go as Kennedy did, but at least all the memories of him are of a young champion. Nothing is sadder than seeing a President grow very old, all power gone.

I knew my favorite, Harry Truman, had really gotten old when he entertained President Nixon, his old enemy, in his home—even though Nixon came with a peace offering, the piano that Harry had played at the White House. Nixon was giving the piano to the Truman library. I remember an earlier time when Harry Truman had said he would poke Nixon in the nose on sight if he ever saw the SOB face to face and I remember that the last time I had seen Nixon he had told me he still couldn't stand Truman.

I was at every presidential inauguration—from Roosevelt's second in January 1937, onward to the present. I was there and I participated, and I even had to wear white gloves in the old days as an usher, helping seat the congressional wives.

In 1949, it was my idea to help Harry Truman and Alben W. Barkley look better outside the Capitol building, as they took their oath of office on the specially built platform that cold January day, by holding their coats. Afterwards, everyone kidded me by saying they didn't know whether I or Alben Barkley had taken the oath of office for Vice President.

The most glamorous inauguration by far was Kennedy's. Never had a nation cared so much what a First Lady wore or whether a President had a hat on his head, in his hand or over his kazoo. I'd say Jack and Jackie Kennedy were the closest we ever got to having royalty—with the possible exception of George Washington.

Never had there been such an inaugural extravaganza as the gala put on by Frank Sinatra.

Capitol Hill was used to hi-jinks and wildness, but even the playboys of the Hill were a little shocked to hear that President Kennedy had left his own inaugural festivities, with its thousands of people, his family and all of officialdom, to have sex with a cutie. His excuse to his male friends was, of course, that he simply had to have sex every so often. He told various people on the Hill that he got a headache if he didn't have sex regularly—like you have to eat several times a day, he had to have sex several times a day.

He might have been exaggerating, he might have meant it when he said, as was reliably reported to me, "If I don't have sex every four hours, I get a headache." Exaggerated or not, I did not introduce him to any girls on the Hill when he pressed me to do so on several occasions. I figured, let him get his own.

Every President had a favorite actress or actor. Nixon had Pearl Bailey. Lyndon Johnson had Carol Channing, who gave his ego a big charge by singing "Hello, *Lyndon*" in a take-off on "Hello, Dolly."

Truman had his daughter, Margaret, the star singer in his book. He liked Bob Hope, too. Truman was much embarrassed when Lauren Bacall hopped up and sat on the piano while he played. He hadn't meant it to be that way at all. As he said, "I can do without that kind of publicity, Fish." At the time, Hollywood was being investigated for communist leanings, and Lauren and her husband, Humphrey Bogart, were testifying before Congress.

Ike had Robert Montgomery.

Ford shared Pearl Bailey with his predecessor and was so impressed with her ability to charm that he made her a UN official, to see if she could do a little of the same at UN headquarters.

Coolidge had Will Rogers, who said about him, "He didn't do nothing, but that's what we wanted done."

409

I've noticed that a President will take any amount of abuse if it comes from a fancy stand-up comic.

I never knew a President who relished the little tidbits about history the way Lyndon Johnson did. Before he appointed a new cabinet officer, he would have the history of the office researched so that he could come up with something both educational and amusing at their swearing-in ceremony.

When Nicholas Katzenbach became attorney general, Lyndon in his introductory remarks had a double-header because, as the guy who was known for going around the White House turning off lights, he was interested in economy. And, of course, he was always interested in history.

I remember the President said, "The office of attorney general is an old office in our American system. It was one of the first four that were created, but it is a much more honored and a much more important office today then when it was first established.

"The first Attorney General, Edmund Randolph, made the complaint that he was, and I quote, 'a mongrel between the State and the United States.' He had the title and the honor of being Attorney General of the United States, but he was left to support himself in the courts of his home state.

"President Monroe some years later reminded Congress that the Attorney General had no office space and no clerk and no messenger, and he had to pay his own fuel bill and buy his own stationery.

"I hesitate to observe to the Budget Director, but this might present some fine opportunities for economics that we should probably explore."

We always heard the best stories of what was doing with the Presidents, especially about those who had formerly served on the Hill. There was a great pipeline from the White House to the Capitol. The Hill people knew the best and the worst of these Presidents, and the Presidents weren't fooling anybody. In the memory of the Hill people, Kennedy was still a spoiled brat who never quit talking about girls or looking for a new one, even though he had graduated to the White House. Lyndon Johnson was still the "terrible-tempered Mr. Bang," though the most dedicated hardworker the Hill had ever seen.

The word on the Hill was that Lyndon had so much power and flashed it so much, that they didn't know whether to vote for him or plug him in. But he did a lot of good with his power. I think future generations will give him much more credit for the important things he did than we do today, just like Truman is a newborn hero. One date that will be remembered is July 2, 1964, when Johnson signed the civil rights bill into law. It is known now as Public Law 352 of the Eighty-eighth Congress.

I read in some woman's column in the *New York Post* that I, the Doorkeeper, was supposed to be a fanny pincher in the Capitol Hill elevators. That is false. They must have gotten me mixed up with Kennedy. He was the fanny man. But not a pincher either. He would sort of cup his hand and pat. And to my knowledge, no woman objected.

As for me, it is true that I was "the busser." I would give a girl or woman a little peck on the cheek, the kiss of charity that is mentioned in the Bible. And I did not bestow it just on cute little things who were young enough to be my daughter. I bestowed it on the left cheek of sweet little ladies of eighty and ninety as well.

Johnson was a great kisser, too. That was his Texas style. He kissed them all—some a little more ardently than others. Sure there was a lot going on in his office. He wasn't responsible for all of it. Whenever you get

411

a big staff working together like the Majority Leader has, things are bound to happen.

Lyndon and I shared one thing as fathers—we both had daughters attending Washington Cathedral School for Girls—Sarah Patsy was about Lynda Bird's age.

Each year that Sarah Patsy attended the cathedral school, her classmates would come to the Capitol for me to take them on the grand tour. Many told me afterward they had hated history class until they had heard me bring the past to life. "Oh, Mr. Miller, I can't wait to read more about all that death and destruction. It's so exciting. All we ever get are dates of battles."

Most congressmen try to be excessively polite to any President, out of respect for the office. Only Wayne Hays of Ohio, of all the congressmen I knew, was so cantankerous that he even enjoyed baiting Presidents. Once the Ohio Democrat got angry because there was a mixup at the White House gate and his name was not on the list. He was asked to wait a minute until it was checked and cleared up. Arrogantly, Hays said, "To hell with that, Nixon's the one who wants me here. Tell him I didn't want to come here to begin with. I've got plenty to do at my office."

By the time he got back to his office, the White House was on the phone apologizing and pleading with him to return. He said he couldn't. As Hays told the story, with relish, they then said they hoped he would be back for the evening reception for the same foreign dignitary that he was supposed to be meeting now. As Hays told it, "I told them to stuff it."

Eisenhower had handled armies, but he couldn't handle Hays. One of Hays' favorite stories was his put-down of the President when Ike invited him to a fancy luncheon for descendants of Presidents.

For his own reasons, which were that he wanted to needle Ike, Hays chose not to decline but went to the luncheon and then announced to Ike that he was not related to any President and that his name wasn't even spelled like Rutherford Hayes, who had an *e* in it.

He then proceeded to ask Ike what was new on his farm in Gettysburg and Ike had said sadly that he had been advised by the attorney general to get rid of his cattle.

Since Hays had cows too, the President had struck a responsive cord and Hays asked sympathetically what the matter was, thinking it must be something like hoof and mouth disease. But instead, the President said that the attorney general had said it might seem like a conflict of interest to keep the cows.

As Hays told his story, he had said, "If I were you, Mr. President, I certainly wouldn't sell my cows under those circumstances."

"No?" asked Ike eagerly. "What would you do?"

"I'd fire the attorney general," said Hays.

It's interesting how many Presidents have had near brushes with death in their early years, or who became very aware of death. Everyone knows about Kennedy and his P.T. boat incident during World War II— how he carved a message for help on a coconut and sent it with a native on a Pacific isle, after he had injured his back saving a man by swimming to shore with him after the loss of the P.T. boat.

Well, it's a pity nobody played up the brush Jerry Ford had with death during the same war. He was also at sea, on an aircraft carrier in the Pacific. Once there was a typhoon near the Philippines and three destroyers were sunk in high waves during the night. They hadn't been heavy with fuel, or it might have saved them. Anyway, there were very few survivors from the ships. And then Ford's carrier caught fire and Ford, who was running to help, almost got tossed off the side of the ship as it rolled. He just managed to catch hold of something in time. He was the lucky one. Five other men did get tossed overboard to their death.

I always thought that's why he didn't mind jokes about his clumsiness, if any—about falling up and down steps and walking into walls and being unable to walk and chew gum at the same time. All those jokes. He knew he would always fail-safe.

Why did Nixon pick Ford? He trusted him and all of that, of course. But more than that, they were fellow founders of the Chowder and Marching Club. Nixon had been in Congress two years and Ford was just arriving when they got together and formed this fun and work club to improve their minds politically and figure out how to get publicity so they could climb the political ladder to better things.

They got themselves tall chef's hats and big striped aprons and had their own emblem—a monster lobster-chef figure in the center and "Chowder and Marching Club" printed in a circle around the outer rim of the chef figure, as I recall—sewn on the bibs of the aprons. And they made sure the emblem was big enough so it would photograph well.

Well, they got together to study and talk issues and strategy and how they could help each other, and their members went on to all kinds of high offices—presidency, governorships, cabinet offices. And some became senators—though not all House members would agree that this is a step up.

When Nixon became President, I remember how he had gotten into the House in the 1946 election by red-baiting Jerry Voorhis of California. It was a great lesson in politics. Nixon had called him a communist, and Jerry wouldn't answer. This silence on Jerry's part had a tendency to snowball in Brother Nixon's favor.

Nixon, of course, as many know, had answered the advertisement of a civic group wanting a candidate and that is how he stumbled into the race to begin with. As Jerry reconstructed it for me later, at first he thought it would be "ungentlemanly to even dignify the young upstart's silly accusations." Only when it was too late did Jerry realize a great truth of politics: No charge is too silly to be ignored. And for a second point: Silence means consent.

I loved Jerry Voorhis—he was a wonderful congressman and a crackerjack idea man. But whenever I reminisce about his bout with Nixon, I have to tell a funny story about Jerry's unfortunate accident that was right in keeping with all his bungling in that 1946 campaign.

What happened was that he was on a plane coming back home after a campaign trip and was hand-carrying a briefcase with such secret information that he even carried it with him when he went to the little boy's room. And it's a good thing he took that briefcase, because when he got to the boy's room he couldn't get his zipper back up and had to sit in his seat with his briefcase in his lap all the way to California. He came back down the aisle of the plane gingerly carrying the briefcase in front of him, and like a girl in imminent danger of attack, he kept his legs close together.

At first, I disliked Nixon for what he had done to my friend Voorhis, but eventually I had to admit the man was exceedingly hard-working and serious. Even when Nixon was trying to make a joke, he was serious about it.

I had seen Nixon from the beginning of his career from close range, and when he was leaving I suddenly had to say, "Stop the music"—I had been getting the tickets printed up for his impeachment. It was something like getting the admission tickets ready for a public hanging.

THE OTHER BODY

The Senate is called "the Other Body" by the haughty congressmen, for the same ego reason a presidential candidate avoids mentioning his opponent by name. It also has its interesting people and their crusades—crusades which I relished as much as those on my own side of the Capitol.

For one that immediately comes to mind, I recall Senator William Proxmire up in arms over an $84,000 U.S. grant to study *why* people fall in love. "Right at the top of things, I don't want to know is why a man falls in love with a woman and vice versa," said Proxmire. But it might have helped Proxmire to know, since the senator's marital problems got so complicated for a time that he and his wife occupied his and hers homes up the street from each other.

I would say Senator Proxmire is the most doggedly independent and unusual man in the Senate. As a loner, his chances of becoming a powerhouse were very slim when he first came to the Hill—only team players get the help of their buddies for a quick goose up the ladder. But the seniority system has finally given him a great platform for his many battles and reform efforts. He has become the chairman of the Banking, Housing and Urban Affairs Committee.

Pick up almost any newspaper and you will find a story on something Proxmire is blasting that day. But it's the man himself who fascinates me—the health addict, the man who does two hundred pushups first thing in the morning and sits at his Senate office desk doing isometric exercises to strengthen his neck muscles.

Proxmire has an ego that won't quit. Others might have a little plastic surgery done to take out the bags under their eyes, but Proxmire practically put out releases about it. And he made no bones about feeling a senator should look as young as he is able to. He also had very conspicuous hair transplants—which look much better now—and he didn't try to hide them either. It was just part of being a self-improvement nut.

What everyone knows about Proxmire is his daily jogging to and from work. But what they don't know is that he continued doing it even after he was mugged one day in mid-street. The Hill gang laughed and said Proxmire probably welcomed the experience so he could put out another press release on it.

He used to have his wife involved in helping him. They had a TV show together that went back home to constituents and was aimed at the milk farmers, and they would end each show by drinking a glass of milk.

Then Ellen Proxmire rebelled and started doing her own thing. She formed a money-making company that put on weddings around town. And William Proxmire moved out. But not far. For some years, he lived in another house on the same street and kept in close touch with his children. The story had a happy ending when the couple got back together again.

Ellen is a lovely woman and I was genuinely happy when she shrugged her shoulders and said let's try again. She admitted that the Senate still takes "ninety-five percent of Bill's energy, strength and time, but there's a difference now. At least he phones me to let me know in advance when he's going to be away so I can make other plans."

As for the senator's cosmetic surgery, Ellen Proxmire claims she knew nothing about it and that it took place while she was on vacation in Jamaica. She had to learn of it through a phone call from a friend who frightened her by saying her husband was in the hospital. Ellen now thinks that she had grown resentful of her previous role in the marriage, which was total absorption in Bill Proxmire's career. But now that they

417

both acknowledge that he's a person and she's a person, each with a separate career, she thinks they'll make it.

Another health enthusiast is the amazing Strom Thurmond, former candidate for President on the State's Rights ticket, who at age seventy-four exercises daily, can outdo Proxmire on pushups and has started a second, young family with his South Carolina beauty-queen wife who is still in her twenties.

Usually a congressman or senator is happy about his nickname, but Senator Hubert Humphrey was surprisingly sensitive to one of his—Gabby. I know, because I really got my tail caught in a trap when I used it at an inopportune time.

It was back around 1960 and I was picked to help at a gigantic party for Speaker Sam. There were so many people expected—six thousand or more—that it had to be held in the armory in Washington. My job was to bellow out the names of the most distinguished guests.

About one-third through, I guess I got carried away, country boy that I am, and bellowed out, "And now ladies and gentlemen, it gives me great pleasure to introduce to you the senior senator from the great state of Minnesota, the Honorable Hubert 'Gabby' Humphrey."

The crowd roared and applauded. But less than twenty-four hours later, there was a committee of four Minnesota congressmen who cornered me and said, "Fishbait, are you tired of working up here on the Hill?"

I said, "Gentlemen, I don't think so, but seeing who you are, I presume you are concerned with my little *faux pas* on Saturday night."

That was dead right. The senator, it seems, was interested in getting rid of that image of the constant talker, an image that might impede his career. But worst of all, as Joe Karth put it, "Muriel is mad at you and she is going to give the senator the devil unless

418

you go over to see him and straighten it out. Maybe you didn't realize it, Fishbait, but we are trying to get away from that nickname of Gabby."

I promised I would go to the Other Body immediately and take care of it. The four left, acting as if they really didn't believe I would do it.

But I had been trained by Sam Rayburn never to let anything distasteful sit overnight but to get rid of it right away. He had also preached that the little slights or insults were the ones longest remembered.

At the Senate, I found that Humphrey was at lunch with a reporter. And I waited an hour and a half outside the door cooling my heels. He could see me and I knew he would eventually get to me. When he came out he took me to the Vice President's Lobby—the House Doorkeeper is also afforded the privileges of the Senate floor. The Vice President's Lobby is the equivalent of the Speaker's Lobby in the House.

By now, I was feeling a little distressed and debating how to begin, but before I could open my mouth, the Senator said, "I know what you're here for. Fishbait, as long as we are by ourselves, I am Gabby and you are Fishbait. But when we have ears other than ours that are listening, I am to be addressed as the Senator and I am to call you the Doorkeeper."

We shook hands, patted each other on the shoulder and I told the senator to give his bride my love and tell her I was sorry. When that was over, I walked back to the House floor and made my report to the four Minnesota congressmen. Several days later, after checking out my story, they all came as one and said, "Fishbait, you're a great fellow. We love you. You really kept your word. We checked on you."

HHH has done a lot of good—backed much liberal legislation, helped farmers, helped school children with their lunches, sponsored the Food for Peace Program, the Peace Corps, the Limited Nuclear Test

Ban Treaty, and on and on—but the truth is, he is long-winded.

Even President Ford has taken a potshot at Hubert's long-windedness: "Hubert is a dear friend of mine. I can still remember when I came to Congress and attended something. It was the first time I ever heard him talk. He was in the second hour of a five-minute speech. I didn't have a program, so I asked the fellow next to me what followed Senator Humphrey.

"The fellow looked at his watch and said, 'Christmas.'"

The Senate had two great talkers, Hubert Humphrey, of course, and Everett Dirksen, Republican Minority Leader of Illinois. Dirksen felt he had an edge over any other senator because, in his youth, he had written amateur plays and dreamed of a stage career. In his time, he was noted as perhaps the greatest political storyteller on Capitol Hill. His favorite, which showed a bit of modesty, concerned the politician who was asked by his worst enemy, "Why weren't you at my last meeting?"

"Well, if I had known it was your *last,*" said the politician, "I wouldn't have missed it."

Whenever Hubert Humphrey and Everett Dirksen got to competing with each other on the floor, staff people hurried to the galleries to listen.

I remember when it was the beautification of the Capitol grounds that had Hubert Humphrey on his feet in the chamber of the Other Body, treading on sensitive ground, as far as Dirksen was concerned. Dirksen considered himself the ultimate expert on flowers, and in fact had been campaigning to get the marigold the official flower of the whole United States. But here was Senator Humphrey rising to his feet at the end of April 1962, calling for something to be done about planting flowers around the Capitol. In later years, as a matter of fact, when Lady Bird Johnson came up with the idea of beautifying Washington, the capital city, I wondered if she had been inspired by the man who became her husband's Vice President.

Anyway, here was HHH telling in his usual long-winded but fascinating way how *he* had gotten the inspiration for Capitol Hill beautification. "I met my elder son for dinner last night," he said, "and in the early evening we walked across the Capitol grounds, particularly the grounds surrounding the Capitol Building itself. It was a beautiful evening. For me, it was a rare moment of relaxation, and I had a chance to look around the Capitol grounds again and to take a tourist's look at the great Capitol Building.

"I noted with surprise that in this city, where spring comes early, almost no flowers were blooming anywhere in the immediate vicinity of the Capitol Building.

"The calendar tells us that spring has come. If we step outside right now, we can feel that it is spring. The flowers which are blooming in the private yards and gardens throughout the Washington area tell us it is spring. The gardens surrounding the center of the executive branch of our government—the White House —tell us it is spring. Even the leaves and the trees surrounding the Capitol tell us rather plaintively that it is spring."

Everett Dirksen was chomping at the bit to get up and refute him, but Hubert charged on. "But there are no flowers in the eastern area of the Capitol grounds to tell us that it is spring. The beautiful fountain in front of the Capitol is dry; there is no water.

"I should like to see improved gardens and far more blossoms surrounding the Capitol. I think the thousands of American citizens who visit the nation's capital would like to see more flowers around the Capitol."

After many words were spoken by Humphrey, Dirksen finally got his inning:

"Mr. President, I am always transported by the profound observation made by my distinguished friend, the senior Senator from Minnesota [Mr. Humphrey]; but never am I quite so transported as when he ventures into the domain of flowers.

"Today he has made an eloquent entreaty to have the Capitol grounds fairly bedecked with nature's choicest flowers, to delight the eyes and hearts of the thousands of Americans who come here."

Dirksen then went on and on to the effect that the distinguished senator from Minnesota didn't know what he was talking about and that there would eventually be cannas blooming in profusion around the Capitol Building, as had been the custom for many years, and if he would just be patient, he'd have his flowers. But they hadn't been planted yet. And with good reason. And as he launched into his subject, it was further proof of what the Hill said—that Dirksen was the only man in Congress who could out-Humphrey Humphrey.

"I share the great interest of the Senator from Minnesota in this matter, but it does involve somewhat of a problem," Dirksen said. "You see, Mr. President— [it is protocol to address remarks to the Chair, when they are meant for a third person, or the Body as a whole]—insofar as I recall, the average date of the last frost in the Washington area is April 20; but the gardeners usually figure that there may be a frost as late as the first of May.

"Of course, there are frost-resistant flowers. For instance, let us consider the gentle, multicolored pansies. They can be planted in the winter; and when spring comes, after the winter has ended, we find them with their beautiful, dainty heads, helping to beautify the world.

"Then there is the daffodil, a hardy flower. I remember the little ode by Wordsworth:

'Ten thousand saw I at a glance,
Tossing their heads in sprightly dance.'

422

"But we cannot cover the entire Capitol grounds with daffodils."

By this time, everyone could tell that poor Hubert Humphrey was sorry he had ever mentioned the subject of flowers on the floor. But on the other hand, he was learning something about how his own captive audiences felt on occasion, as Dirksen wouldn't let go, "The gardeners have always graced the Capitol grounds with cannas, but of course they are not very frost-resistant, so the gardeners do the proper thing, and the cannas are planted later in the season," the loquacious senator from Illinois said, fixing his eye on the squirming Humphrey.

"The dahlias always entrance the eye; but one must be careful lest the tiny shoots of the dahlias come up before the frosts end, in which case it is necessary to do the work all over again.

"Then there is the gentle petunia, one of my favorite flowers. But one must be careful about when he plants them.

"Certainly I wish to see the Capitol grounds bedecked and beautiful, Mr. President; but I am afraid that my distinguished friend, the Senator from Minnesota, has failed to read the old almanac, which tells us that in April frost may occur at any time; and, of course, if frost comes, it is necessary to do the planting of flowers all over again.

"Thus it is, Mr. President, that the Senator from Minnesota and I and the tourists must wait for nature, and must permit nature to take its own sweet time. We must take into account the seasons and the time when the frosts end.

"Of course, I am an amateur; and I planted my cannas this weekend, in the hope that there will be no more frost this season. [Those who were there tell me the entire Body let out a groan heard round the world.]

423

"Certainly in due time there will be cannas and dahlias and prince's-feathers and, in due time, all the other beautiful flowers, that somehow engender a kind of introspection, assuage all the turbulance of the soul, and bring peace to the hearts of all those who labor here and of all the thousands who come here to visit. So, Mr. President, all in its own good time will be brought to pass."

Now finally Hubert Humphrey popped up.

Mr. Humphrey: "Mr. President, will the Senator from Illinois yield?"

Mr. Dirksen: "I yield."

Mr. Humphrey: "I am happy that the distinguished Minority Leader, the Senator from Illinois, has given us this note of reassurance, because my heart was troubled and my spirit was dampened by the knowledge that many of these flowers are not planted on the Capitol grounds. However; the reassurance we have received from the Minority Leader gives me a ray of hope; and I think I can hang on for a few days more.

"But I should like to say that although undoubtedly the Senator from Illinois is an expert on horticulture, he is much less expert when he deals with matters of temperature. I would be delighted to have the Senator stop by the neighborhood where I live in Maryland. It is far enough away from the Capitol so that the air out there is not quite as warm as it is here. I would like to have him see the beautiful flowers of some of my neighbors. It is a little more frosty in the country than it is in this urban area.

"There are also beautiful flowers at the White House. I did not know the power of the New Frontier was so great that it could draw the frost line where it wanted to, even though it might be helpful—" Dirksen was on his feet.

Mr. Dirksen: "Now, Mr. President—" HHH did not give him a chance to continue.

Mr. Humphrey: "I merely want to say to the Senator that he has been very reassuring. It was my hope that this colloquy would permit some further improvement on the grounds. I know now that I have strong, staunch support in this famous soldier of agronomy from Illinois."

Mr. Dirksen: "In my observations I should have mentioned the stately tulip but I am afraid my friend is making reference to shrubs—"

Mr. Humphrey: "No. The Senator from Minnesota knows the difference between a shrub and a flower."

Mr. Dirksen: "Shrubs such as forsythia and dogwood and other plants presently coming into bloom. But I remind my friend that 'Weeping may endure for a night, but joy cometh in the morning.' Be reassured."

Mr. Humphrey: "I join with the distinguished Senator and offer him my hand in the interest of horticulture and better shrubs and flowers."

Realizing all the hassle he would get from Dirksen if he pursued the subject of getting flowers for all seasons planted on the Capitol grounds, Humphrey ceased and desisted. But the story has a happy ending. Eventually, Humphrey realized his goal in his own way and it didn't cost the taxpayers a penny. He simply invited the florists and flower-growers around the country to contribute flowers and plants for the Capitol, which they were more than happy to do. And today the flowers are a beautiful sight for tourists and the Hill gang alike, in every season.

Senators have always assumed a little more lordly air than congressmen. As the perfect illustration, let me tell you what delighted the Hill crowd after Olin Johnston won the senatorial race in South Carolina in 1944 and arrived in January 1945 to take his seat.

Senator Johnston was driving grandly around town to look the place over from the vantage point of his big Oldsmobile, when he entered the wrong end of a one-lane tunnel near the Hill which was for streetcars only.

The senator heard the clang, clang coming toward him and screeched to a stop just in time to avoid a head-on collision. Olin leaned his head out the window and screamed at the startled trolley driver, "I want to tell you that I'm the junior senator of South Carolina and I want you to get that trolley car out of my way. Now back up."

With that, the trolley driver leaned his head out a little farther from *his* window and said, "And I'll tell *you* one damn thing. I'm the Senior Trolley Driver on this trolley and if you don't get that heap out of my way, I'm going to run over you."

The senator backed humbly out.

The Senate had its own mystique and its own set of stories about the noble past.

For example, they love to tell about Daniel Webster —how, when a senator, he rose in the chamber one day with one hand in his trouser pocket and the other brandishing a sheaf of papers. "Mr. President," he said, "I hold in my hand a memorial of the late war [Mexican]." A colleague quipped so that a small circle of members could hear, "Will the gentleman tell the Senate in which hand he holds the memorial?"

I don't think there's too much difference in the playing around of senators and congressmen, except that senators seemed to feel the girl is more honored because of his higher rank.

I must say the worst womanizer of the Senate, if not the whole Hill, was Estes Kefauver of Tennessee, who died at a hospital with a heart attack, far before his time. Small wonder. He must have worn himself out chasing pretty legs.

Many believed on the Hill that if Kefauver had tried half as hard to be President as he tried to make time with every passing doll, he would have been President.

Kefauver was colorful, with that ever-present coonskin cap from which swung the tail of the raccoon, and tall as befits a presidential candidate or a congressman

426

aspiring for something higher. But as soon as he opened his mouth and had to use his own words in a small speech, he was dull as lead.

Once a good-looking newsgirl was taken to interview Kefauver when he was still a congressman but was being groomed to be a senator and maybe President, if all went well. The man who had arranged the interview left the room a few minutes and Estes quickly started tearing the girl's clothes off, flinging her backwards across the table.

He was most unreliable in controlling himself, even when people were around. During campaigns, a battery of watchdogs took turns sticking with him to keep him out of trouble and on schedule. Even so, every time someone needed him, he had disappeared after the first lovely who gave him a come-hither look and a slow smile.

The senator had a good heart, but a lousy memory.

Estes Kefauver would try to be generous every Christmas. He would walk from one end of the Capitol to the other passing out silver dollars to any Hill employee he happened to see. I kept mine as souvenirs and still have them.

Estes would walk along and say, "Hi there. Mrs. Kefauver and I want you to have a Merry Christmas." And he'd hand over that silver dollar.

One Christmas a fellow called Hoppy, who looked after Speaker Sam, happened to be on the Senate wing on the first floor when Estes came by, recognized him and said, "Hi there, Hoppy. Mrs. Kefauver and I want you to have a Merry Christmas. And here's a silver dollar to help you along."

Hoppy was in a hurry because he had run an errand for the Speaker and had to get back to the House side. He got there just in time to again bump into Estes Kefauver performing his dollar miracles with the House employees. Spotting Hoppy, Kefauver again said the very same thing, "Hi there, Hoppy, Mrs. Kefauver and

427

I want you to have a Merry Christmas. And here's a silver dollar to help you along."

After he had gone, Hoppy said to me, "No wonder that man needs a speechwriter. With his memory, maybe I can do a repeat performance next year. Of course, with that jock, if I had been a pretty girl he'd have remembered me."

Senator Kefauver makes a certain current womanizer in the Senate look like an angel. This senator had only *three* mistresses. All from his own office. He could afford to play around—though not as wealthy as a Kennedy—and for a while he luxuriated in his unique situation.

This senator was and is greatly oversexed and so the girls didn't mind sharing him. They were quite amused, as a matter of fact, that the swinging senator thought he had them all fooled and that they did not know about each other. But they knew all right, and they would get together and be very tolerant and friendly with each other. They even compared how they were making out with him.

The senator prided himself on how cleverly he thought up excuses to keep his choice for the night staying after work, even with the others right there listening. "The stores are open tonight. Do you mind doing a little shopping for me?" "I have to get a package mailed, honey, will you stay behind and help me?" "Do you mind going with me to this cocktail party, so you can get me out of there in time. The hostess is a barracuda and never lets me go."

But all good things come to an end and what happened finally was jealousy. The girls themselves got tired of the situation and started fighting among themselves and telling the senator nasty stories about each other. Later, only one trimphant girl worked at his office and the other two moved on to other jobs.

A particular senator, whose wife rarely showed up in Washington, liked pretty women very much, and he would make a fresh selection almost every day of whom he would take out that night. He actually would pass off many of these girls as his wife. Since few knew her, he would have a lot of fun doing it and making the girl feel important.

However, the game backfired in one small way when he wanted to advance in an organization that was fairly straitlaced. When they investigated his character and learned of his reputation as a womanizer and his habit of introducing strange women as his wife, he did not make the grade. He never learned why.

Some members like "to charge up their batteries," as they call it, before they go out for the night, and they head for the House barbershop. "I don't need a shave so much," they have told me, "as I need to study up on the latest literature." Then they'd wink. The *literature* used to be the *Police Gazette* and *Esquire*. But now the magazines kept for them in the House barbershop are the ones with the nude girlie covers, such as *Penthouse* and *Playboy*.

I know many aides who left the House side to go to work for a more prestigious senator, only to find they would give anything to "come home to the House where folks are folks." On the Senate side, they found they seldom had any contact with the senator and were lumped together with fifty or sixty others working for the same man.

On the House side, only eight to ten persons work for a congressman or, at most, eighteen is the greatest number permitted to work for any representative.

Senators, too, who have served in the House have told me that they miss the greater friendliness of the House and the more intimate services rendered by House employees. Since senators tend to act more aloof than congressmen, the staff follows suit.

Many men want to get into the Senate because they feel it is a better springboard into the White House. I'm biased, but there is a bit of truth in that, even though Jerry Ford was never a senator. But then, he didn't get to the presidency through the ballot box. And the word on the Hill was that he got his chance through a deal that hardly needed mentioning but was just understood.

Senator Henry "Scoop" Jackson of Washington, could never get his presidential campaign off dead center even though at the outset, in 1976, he had more money than any other Democratic candidate.

Having seen a lot of candidates come and go, I knew what was wrong. Though Scoop had the presidential mind and the presidential money and even the presidential friends, he just didn't have the presidential *look*. If he had let his hair become more bushy, like Carter's, and loosened his collar once in a while, he just might have caught fire. He should have borne down on his nickname, which helps a lot, and quit acting so conservative. I'm convinced that Jimmy Carter would not have made it either at the primaries in 1976 if he had insisted on being called James E. Carter, Jr.

When he was in the House, Scoop Jackson was the ideal candidate and was one of Jack Kennedy's dearest friends. They left the House at the same time to go to the Senate in 1953. Had Scoop continued to change with the times, it might have been a different story, I'm sorry to have to tell my dear friend and fellow Odd Sox baseball teammate.

Senator Ted Kennedy is another man whose presidential chances went down the drain in one horrible night in July 1969. I remember it was like a morgue on the Hill when Ted Kennedy suffered the tragic incident of Chappaquiddick. He didn't have a mean bone in his body. He just had suffered an attack of "the dumbs." That's what bad judgment is called on the Hill.

Even his enemies felt sorry for Ted—it was all too terrible for words. A girl lay dead in his car and he had not gone around the neighborhood screaming for help. There was almost the same sadness and hushed shock as when his two brothers had been assassinated. Congressmen and senators went around saying "Why? But why?" And they still don't know, but every speculation has been made.

Birch Bayh, the junior senator from Terre Haute, Indiana, was another close friend of the Kennedy brothers. In fact, he had the dubious honor of being in an airplane crash in New England with Ted Kennedy when both were almost killed. But in my own thinking, God must have had something else for each of them to do and saved them for future use.

Kennedy became so popular that he became known as the man who refused to become President. Bayh became the author of an amendment to the Constitution that changed the course of history. It is the Twenty-fifth Amendment, which allows an incumbent President to fill a Vice-Presidential vacancy by appointing anyone he sees fit to become Vice President, after approval by the Judiciary Committee of the House and Senate and the approval of both bodies.

Before this, the nation would be without a Vice President until either the next election or the death of the President, also, in which case the Speaker would become the head of state.

Birch Bayh—I love that name—is a part of important history forever because of this milestone legislation which he struggled valiantly to push through for five years.

I was frequently around when the senators were at play. It's amazing how the public image of a senator can be so different from the way we knew him. On that score, Goldwater was the most maligned man on the Hill. Barry was anything but the fuddy-duddy he was pictured to be during the presidential campaign of 1964.

For example, he was given to comparing sex to politics —you don't have to be good at it to enjoy it.

Though a Republican, Goldwater acted like a relaxed Democrat; I placed at the other extreme Democratic Senator Robert Byrd of West Virginia, who acted like a super-straight Republican.

The people in Senator Robert Byrd's office would gripe about their boss's strict rule that no one could take more than forty-five minutes for lunch. It was all he allowed himself, too. He would brown-bag it. So they couldn't even complain that he was unfair.

He was just that hard-working and busy, as a Whip with ambition to climb up the next step of the ladder into the majority leadership. Byrd made a specialty of helping other congressmen get away from the Hill for trips. He would cover for them and see to it that their legislation got introduced or pushed toward a vote.

The office staff stayed put and worked like crazy, but they had a fringe benefit—when he came back from the floor in the middle of the afternoon, he always brought candy bars for the whole staff. It wasn't just that he was being generous, however. "Eat this, it's for quick energy," he said.

But to get back to Goldwater, the senator from Arizona could cuss with the best of them and was not at all the glum man the voters thought he was.

He got even funnier and more relaxed after he had gotten the madness of running for the highest office out of his system in 1964.

Years later, in 1971, the Alfalfa Club picked him for their "Potential Candidate for President" dinner and he gave one of the funniest speeches ever. It proved that he had no sensitivity about anything—about the fact that he was a conservative or that he had goofed in picking a running mate who had no chance of becoming a household word. I'd like to share a bit of his speech with you:

"You are to be congratulated. You have made the perfect selection. I am the ideal candidate. I have had experience. I have had an audience with the Pope. I have talked with Golda Meir. I have visited the Wailing Wall. I have been to Vietnam. The *New York Times Encyclopedia* has me listed as a Democrat. The Senate clerk calls me a Republican. Bill Buckley's *National Review* calls me a Conservative. And the *Washington Post* calls me a Neanderthal.

"I start off with twenty-seven million votes. I want to prove I can lose some of those.

"But I am really just an Episcopalian who is restricted to playing nine holes on Gentile golf courses because I am half Jewish . . .

"I hope you realize my first big task will be to find a household word to run with me as a candidate for Vice President. The last time out, Congressman Bill Miller was my running mate. I made an *elder* statesman of him in a hurry. I don't remember what he looked like, but I know he was wild. Candidates are easy to forget. But this will never happen to Spiro. If the public ever forgets him, every comedy show on television will fold up and a whole army of gag writers will have to go back to work. . . ."

Power is a heady thing and the senators usually enjoy their additional power. It's a lot more impressive to be one of two superstars of a state than to be one of a delegation of thirty congressmen.

The role of superstar in the Senate is very impressive. Alben Barkley was a superstar, long before they used that word. A humanitarian, a senator from Kentucky and Truman's Vice President, Barkley was a great man and an honest man. It's a pity he was too old by the time he got to the vice-presidency to try for the presidency. His training was perfect—he was in the House from 1913 to 1927 and the Senate from

1937 to 1947. He served as Majority Leader and Minority Leader. He had it all.

It's amusing how brother Alben—whom I saw often because he was a dear friend of Speaker Sam—got to be Vice President. He'd gone to give the keynote address at the 1948 Democratic Convention and did such a sensational and warm-hearted job, speaking without a note or printed word, that the crowd ended up demanding him for Vice President. It is interesting that Truman, the man who had been an accidental Vice President and accidental President, ended up with an accidental Vice President.

The whole Hill rejoiced with Barkley when he found love late in life in the form of a 37-year-old beauty named Jane Hadley, who was a house guest of Clark Clifford, the famous lawyer and friend of many Presidents.

Barkley used to sit and write love letters to her while presiding over the Senate, and he wasn't worth beans until they got married and got it over with. Alben behaved like a schoolboy, he loved her so. In fact, in the Vice President's former office, right off the Senate floor, his desk is still there and shows deep markings from some of his letter writing. Some sexy words had to be carefully rubbed out.

I think Brother Rayburn got a little wistful as it came time for his old buddy Alben to get married. Speaker Sam had missed out on some things, like a happy home life and watching children grow. Rayburn and Truman both attended Barkley's wedding. I remember when everyone on the Hill was crowding around Barkley and congratulating him on his forthcoming marriage and as usual he had a story to tell. He said that Lafayette had figured out the difference between a married man and a bachelor. A married man was a happy man and a bachelor was just a lucky dog.

I think Barkley was trying to make Rayburn feel better. The feeling was that if Barkley could find his

434

true love, there was hope for anyone, even Speaker Sam. Barkley had been born in 1877 and was over seventy when he married a woman in her thirties. A luscious woman in full bloom of life. Rayburn was born in 1882—he was five years younger than Barkley.

Alben Barkley well knew that the secret of great humor was that it poked fun at oneself instead of the other person, and he was always telling that kind of story. One was about a recent event at which he had given what he considered an important speech and an old friend came over and asked if he'd mind a minor point of criticism.

Alben assured the friend he wouldn't mind at all and would be grateful for it. The friend replied, "Well I have to tell you, Mr. Vice President, that your speech was much too long."

Alben said he had thanked the man and agreed that it probably was too long.

"And Mr. Vice President," the friend continued, "if you don't mind another tiny suggestion, you read your speech and you really shouldn't read a speech. It should be worth remembering."

Alben said he thanked the man again and said he was right, he probably shouldn't have read the speech. He should have taken the time to memorize it.

But then the friend administered the *coup de grace:* "But on the other hand, if you don't mind my saying so, you shouldn't have memorized *that* speech because I didn't hear anything that was worth remembering."

Truman was one of Barkley's best buddies. The two men would get together and drink and talk, and Harry would listen to Alben's stories. Truman and Barkley were one of the few presidential–vice-presidential teams I've ever known that were not competitive and who genuinely were friends.

When Truman moved back to the White House after the renovations were completed, the members of the Congress which had appropriated the money were, I believe, the first guests to come take a look. Though President Truman was around, the actual host at the opening was Senator Kenneth McKellar, the chairman of the Committe on Restoration of the White House.

Truman just enjoyed himself and didn't even stand in the receiving line. Poor McKellar had to do that and he was old and in bad shape, leaning on a cane.

I would have been happier if he had kept leaning on it, but since it took three and a half hours for all the Congress and Senate to pass through the line and meet Truman before wandering around the White House, McKellar, unfortunately, leaned mostly on me. "I prefer to lean on you, Fishbait," he said slowly. "You're like one of these strong pillars here."

I thanked him and said that was about the nicest compliment I'd ever had and I meant it.

Sam Ervin from North Carolina, who emerged from the Watergate trials as the lovable "Senator Sam," had special significance to me. I knew his brother, Joe, who was a congressman from the same state, and who died suddenly in office. Sam never got over it.

In December 1945, it was my sad duty to accompany the body of Senator Sam Ervin's brother to his final resting place at Morganton. Joseph Ervin, who had been a friend, had been afraid that he was going blind. It had gotten so bad that he could hardly see, and it troubled him deeply. So deeply that he took his own life.

That was the tragedy in the life of the star of the Watergate investigation, who delighted everyone with his marvelous sense of humor. I always felt that Sam, whom I loved and admired so much, turned to humor to ease his own pain. And I know that his brother was never too far from his mind.

Every time that I could, I journeyed over to the Other Body to listen to Senator Sam. He intrigued me. Almost every time he spoke, pearls of wisdom dripped from his lips. Like what he said about shallow people who sound so bright: "They are like lightning bugs—they carry their illumination behind them."

Sam Ervin once flashed a tiny piece of microfilm—no more than 1½ inches or so—and said this was the whole Bible. He said that someone who had seen it said that considering the difference in size between the Bible and the Constitution, it must mean that the constitution can be reduced to the size of a pin head. Sam Ervin told how he had answered the man, "I said I thought that is what they had already done with the executive branch [Nixon's White House], because some of those officials cannot see it with their naked eyes."

About his mental powers, however, he was very modest and said he was one of the few people in public life he knew who didn't complain how the press was treating him. "Oh, the press takes me to task every once in a while," he said, "but they have been very kind about not attributing my hypocrisy to bad motives. They always blamed it on a lack of mental capacity."

I was sorry when Senator Sam decided to retire. I knew the Capitol would be a much duller place without him.

It's good that the members of Congress generally have a sense of humor because it helps them when they have to take their lumps. When Senator Frank Church was not the one, on the list of six, to be chosen as the vice-presidential candidate by nominee Jimmy Carter, he did not wail or beat his breast at the convention in New York. Instead, he quipped, "I should have known two days ago that I wasn't going to get the vice-presidency. That's when I got the news that my house in Bethesda had been struck by lightning—I should have known that lightning never strikes twice."

I've had so many people tell me that if Frank Church had learned to cuss a little or tell a dirty story he might have been President by now. But they said, "He takes his name too seriously. Church. Christ, he's more like a cathedral." And some did call him Frank

437

Cathedral behind his back and say, "He's too nice to be President. He'd call in his wife to bawl someone out."

To my knowledge, no one has ever seen him let his hair down. But I must say he struck me as bright enough to be President and dedicated as all get out. He preached against "socialism for the rich and free enterprise for the poor," by which he meant that big business wants help from government and says "that's all right, but let the little guy help himself, sink or swim."

Frank Church, barely thirty-two when elected, was the youngest senator when he came to the Hill in 1956. It helped him get that "too nice boy" image.

Maybe he can do something to correct it.

When presidential nominee drop-out and loser Vice President Rockefeller arrived in the Hill to preside over the Senate, he was still in mourning over his many lost chances to be President. But being a good political soldier, he did not cry. Instead, he told a banquet of the Washington Press Club, "It's a real thrill for me to be here tonight, representing the Republican party. This has never happened to me before." Then he paused and muttered, "Not that I didn't try."

Senator Edmund Muskie had also suffered, not one but three—or possibly four—defeats, depending on how you count. The first time was in 1968, when *he* didn't make it as Vice President because *Humphrey* didn't make it as President. The second time was in 1972, when his angry tears in the New Hampshire confrontation with publisher William Loeb, who had accused his wife of drinking, cost him the presidential bid.

And finally came 1976, when he lost twice—first at the primaries and second when his name had been placed on Jimmy Carter's list of acceptable Vice Presidents, only to be passed over for Mondale.

Ed Muskie now has decided that silence is golden. He tells a story about a man who came to a town in his home state of Maine—a little coast town—and tried to start a conversation. Nobody seemed to want to talk to him. After trying unsuccessfully to get a few words out of various townsmen, he finally asked if there was some kind of law against talking in the town.

There was a long pause. "Not exactly a law," one man spoke up, finally. "But we have an understanding not to speak unless it improves on silence."

The best candidates know how to turn any disaster into a laugh against their opponents or the opposition party.

When Scoop Jackson, a Democrat, was campaigning and fell through a rotten floor, he looked pretty ridiculous until he looked up and said, "I'm standing on one of the planks from the Republican platform."

Once, when Robert Kennedy was making his ill-fated attempt to run for President, he happened to come into a room at the wrong time. It was some farm group, and it was very embarrassing as he walked in just as one of them was grumping about what a drain it would be on the national budget if all those nine or ten Kennedy children got into the White House.

Bobby turned the embarrassing moment into a great joke, when he quipped, "Yes, I've got ten kids that drink milk. Tell me anyone else who's doing that much for the farmer."

One of the highbrows of the Other Body was Republican Senator Hugh Scott, who collected pipes to smoke and Chinese art to study. He even wrote a book on the subject of Oriental art. He was quite a linguist. He studied Chinese and Japanese to understand Oriental art better, but he also could speak French, Spanish and German.

Scott had been in Congress since 1941, starting with the House of Representatives and graduating to the

439

Senate in 1958. But he won his spurs in 1969 when he bucked up against Senator Everett Dirksen who was backing Senator Roman Hruska, Republican of Nebraska, to be Assistant Minority Leader.

Scott won, Dirksen died soon after and Scott next won the election to succeed him as Minority Leader, this time beating out Dirksen's son-in-law, Howard Baker of Tennessee.

Scott loved to confound the Hill crowd by using words that sounded like cuss words but weren't. A favorite word with him was "pismire," which wasn't what it sounded like but only a red ant.

Finally, I want to talk a bit about Senator Mike Mansfield.

I first knew Mike Mansfield of Montana when he was a congressman. I was especially interested in him because he had beaten a famous woman, Jeannette Rankin, who had made such a splash voting against the U.S. entry into war. I wondered what kind of a guy had managed that. Mike Mansfield had one of the strangest and most touching stories in the power line-up on the Hill. He had suffered a kind of desertion much worse than mine, so I really felt close to him. But if he hadn't had tragedy, he'd never have gotten to Montana.

Mike had been born in the slums of New York and was not even in school yet when his mother died. His parents had come over from Ireland because they were practically starving there. When Mike's mother died, his father didn't know what to do with him, so he sent him to Montana to other relatives and that changed his life. I wonder if he would have become a senator from New York if he'd stayed in Hell's Kitchen.

When I met Mike and got to know him, as I tried to be helpful to any freshman, even before I was Doorkeeper, I was delighted to meet his wife for a special reason. He didn't mind telling that Maureen had been

440

the girl who had helped him with his English high-school-equivalency courses.

There are a lot of cases on the Hill where the wife helped make a polished gentleman out of a rough diamond.

What made Mansfield famous on the Hill was that Joseph McCarthy, the red-baiter, started calling Mansfield a communist dupe, because he was challenging one of McCarthy's pets for his Senate seat—Zales Ecton, a Republican.

McCarthy went into Montana to smear Mansfield, but the voters paid him no mind. So after the election, McCarthy thought he could shine up to Mansfield and bygones would be bygones. It was the talk of the Hill when the two men met for the first time after the victory and McCarthy grabbed Mike's hand and said heartily, "Mike. How good to see you. How is everything in Montana these days?"

The story goes that Mike removed his hand and said coldly, "Much better since you left, sir." And he just walked away, leaving McCarthy to pretend he didn't hear the snickers around him.

Lyndon Johnson liked the way nobody could scare or push Mansfield around and he made him the Majority Whip. Once a Whip, it's the big time, the leadership, and anything is possible, even the position of Majority Leader. Lyndon was picked by Kennedy to be Vice President and Mike slid into home base.

Mike told me and others time and again that he didn't enjoy throwing his weight around and being the top man. He was so anxious to be sure he was making the right decision, he would drive people wild waiting for him to make up his mind.

Eventually, he would. But he'd have it all written out on paper, exactly the way he had thought it through. I always thought the reason he wrote himself position papers was the continuing influence of his early English teacher, his dear wife, Maureen.

441

Maureen's influence shows in the great writing of the eulogy which Mansfield delivered in the Rotunda of the United States Capitol over the body of John Fitzgerald Kennedy, lying in state on November 24, 1963. There is an irony in the fact that Mike, one of the poorest men ever to enter the Senate, was chosen to eulogize one of the richest.

But a greater irony is that Mansfield, who had run away from school at twelve, had written words so beautiful that they became a part of history, quoted whenever great speeches are given. He wrote it himself and with passion.

I can't resist sharing those lines with you, and if you can read them with dry eyes, you're tougher than I am. I can see him now, that tall, gaunt man:

There was a sound of laughter; in a moment, it was no more. And so she took a ring from her finger and placed it in his hands.

There was a wit in a man neither young nor old, but a wit full of an old man's wisdom and of a child's wisdom, and then, in a moment it was no more. And so she took a ring from her finger and placed it in his hands.

There was a man marked with the scars of his love of country, a body active with the surge of a life far, far from spent and, in a moment, it was no more. And she took a ring from her finger and placed it in his hands.

There was a father with a little boy, a little girl and a joy of each in the other. In a moment it was no more, and so she took a ring from her finger and placed it in his hands.

There was a husband who asked much and gave much, and out of the giving and the asking wove with a woman what could not be broken in life, and in a moment it was no more. And so she took a ring from her finger and placed it in his hands, and kissed him and closed the lid of a coffin.

442

A piece of each of us died at that moment. Yet, in death he gave of himself to us. He gave us of a good heart, from which the laughter came. He gave us of a profound wit, from which a great leadership emerged. He gave us of a kindness and a strength fused into a human courage to seek peace without fear.

He gave us of his love that we, too, in turn, might give. He gave that we might give of ourselves, that we might give to one another until there would be no room, no room at all, for the bigotry, the hatred, prejudice, and the arrogance which converged in that moment of horror to strike him down.

In leaving us—these gifts, John Fitzgerald Kennedy, President of the United States, leaves with us. Will we take them, Mr. President? Will we have, now, the sense and the responsibility and the courage to take them?

I pray to God that we shall and under God we will.

DEATH AND DANGER ON CAPITOL HILL

I remember well what it was like on the Hill when various Presidents died violent or quiet deaths and lay in state in the Rotunda of the Capitol. FDR's body, however, was not brought to the Rotunda. It was kept secret, but I was told that FDR was cremated and that was why the casket was not brought up there.

I have seen more of death, working on the Hill, than I care to recall. I remember my first deathwatch assignment—accompanying the remains of President Franklin Roosevelt to Hyde Park for burial. I remember Eleanor Roosevelt in her heavy black veil.

Some congressmen fully believed the story that there were only ashes inside the casket, so I too, still believe it, based on their sources.

In the case of poor JFK, his head was so shot up that there wasn't an easy way or time to make him look good enough for an open casket at the White House or at the Hill—though I believe caskets have been routinely closed and flag-draped in the Capitol. Only those who had to, saw him to identify him.

I was the House liaison to the White House in that dark period, and I made six trips to the White House to make all arrangements that involved the House of Representatives.

There have been many terrible moments when death came to a congressman. I have saved the lives of several congressmen—cardiac cases. I had an intensive course in first aid for this purpose.

I also had training in security methods and techniques. We go to school on Capitol Hill for this—about fifteen classes are held right in the Capitol. We learned

444

a few tricks—how to query someone when you want to get him next time, how to recognize voices, danger signals, strange behavioral mannerisms.

Spread through the galleries are plainclothes officers of the Capitol police force that no tourist would recognize. And I took my training with them, though I was not required to wear a gun, blackjack, handcuffs or the "twister" worn on the back of the belt, under the coat.

The twister is a very effective devil. It stops violence before it happens. The plainclothesman sticks this little gadget on any finger of the disturbed person he can get hold of and simply twists the finger until the person is subdued—which only takes a minute.

I was there the day that the Puerto Ricans shot five persons in the House Chamber—two Republicans and three Democrats. One Republican, Speaker Joseph W. Martin, Jr., probably saved his life when he wrapped himself in a flag and hid behind a pillar. The year was 1954, only one of the two times in my whole career on the Hill that the House had turned Republican, or it would have been Speaker Sam in the most vulnerable spot—and who knows what he would have done. Surely, not wrap himself in the flag. His mind didn't work that way.

That day had grim results, although none of the men died. At first, it seemed that Alfred Bentley, millionaire congressman from Michigan, was the most injured. A bullet went through his chest and into his liver, and he was out of commission for six weeks. But it later turned out that Kenneth Roberts, Democrat of Alabama, who only was shot in the leg, was in much worse condition. The bullet had severed a nerve and an artery and Percy Priest, a Democrat from Tennessee who was affectionately described by colleagues as "ugly as homemade sin but sweet as honey," snatched off his own tie and made a tourniquet.

We thought everything would be all right, but Roberts had endless trouble with the leg and ended up

445

in a wheelchair for two years and had to have daily therapy.

Congressman Ben Jensen, Republican of Iowa, was shot in his shoulder so forcefully that it spun him around and he staggered into the Speaker's Lobby. Even so, a tough cookie, he hardly missed a day.

Clifford Davis, who has been called one of "Master Crump's puppets," of Tennessee, limped around for a week with a cane after they took out a bullet from the calf of his leg. But it was George Fallon, the old fun-loving Democrat from Maryland, who had to take all the teasing and abuse from his colleagues because of the indignity of being grazed in the right buttock. From then on, behind the rail, he was always referred to as "our half-assed" congressman.

All the culprits were apprehended—four men and one woman—and sentenced to prison terms of fifteen to twenty-five years. I'll never forget that terrible day, with blood on the floor and moaning, realizing it was my own voice that was shouting, "Get those litters moving!"

But it was not always as grim as the Puerto Rican incident. Once a woman shouted menacingly from the gallery, directing her remarks to the Speaker. "Mr. Speaker, damn you," she said, "I want you to put some teeth in this bill."

When we got to her, we found *she* didn't have a tooth in her head. Anyway, we escorted her out.

Since the Hill gets a cross section of Americans as tourists every day, it also gets a cross section of nuts and disturbed or potentially dangerous persons.

One woman came looking for President Kennedy. A Capitol policeman, realizing he might have trouble on his hands, told her gently that President Kennedy was dead. "Don't you remember when he died?" he asked.

She got so excited and distressed at this news that she started wailing and throwing off her clothes, with many curious tourists watching. The police stopped her, but not before she had become topless. After that, it was decided to send anyone who asks for a dead President directly to the northwest gate of the White House because there they were geared for such incidents all the time.

We've had all kinds of things happen on the House side of the Hill. Some nut, who was fortunately caught before he had caused too much damage, slashed three historic paintings outside the House galleries on the third floor—the most damage being done to the huge painting by Howard Chandler Christie of the signing of the Constitution. Even so, it cost $3,000 before all the repairs were made.

I remember one time when Rayburn was opening a brand-new Congress. It was the second day of the session and a woman had managed to get on the floor. The doormen and pages had not learned the faces of the new congresswomen yet, and they assumed this woman striding right down the aisle from out of the Democratic cloakroom must know what she was doing.

She walked right up to the Speaker's stand and said, "Mr. Speaker, I want to address the House." At about this time, I was starting to come to life and a moment later I heard Speaker Sam hiss, "Fish, you and Zeake get this damn woman out of here."

Zeake Johnson, the sergeant-at-arms, and some of his coworkers escorted the lady downstairs. We found out later that she was an escapee from a mental institution in Pennsylvania.

After the Puerto Rican incident and every now and again, the House debated over having bulletproof glass to protect them and much palavering went on. But the members finally decided they didn't want to have "legislature under glass" in this country and be like something in a museum case. They really like looking up and seeing the galleries, just as if they were actors on a stage looking up at an audience.

447

So instead of glass, there are many more security people than there ever have been. Anyone visiting the Capitol now shows the inside of his or her briefcase or purse, states his business if it is off-hours or at certain doors, and is pretty well looked over and sized up by guards and plainclothesmen. On the Hill, only the insiders know who is security.

Some congressmen have compared my job of Doorkeeper to that of St. Peter at the Heavenly Gate. The difference, they said, was, "He deals with angels and saintly souls, but Fish handles flesh and blood people—and live devils."

To thwart any "live devils," everything humanly possible is done to protect the President on his one-mile trip to the Capitol—including security on and in just about every building along the way. In fact, security has gotten so strict in the Capitol these days that any visitor even walking near the doors of the House Chamber must walk through an X-ray gate, just like at airports.

People who wonder what in the devil the Capitol needs a full-time Doorkeeper for should have been around when notification came from the White House to my office that the President of the United States was coming to the Capitol to deliver his State of the Union Address—or any other of his addresses.

Forty-eight hours before the President's appearance —at the *invitation* of both Houses, since under the division of powers no President is permitted to just barge in and address Congress without specific permission—I am notified to start putting it all together.

The first thing I would do was go see the Speaker of the House to get any special instructions he might have had and then I would confer with Lewis Deschler, who was the parliamentarian of the House until he retired in 1974, to see if there were any changes in regular procedure.

Specifically, I would need to find out whether the

President was bringing anyone more than his usual entourage of three who would need seats on the floor near him—his three being his doctor, his press secretary and his military aide. Usually Lou would tell me, "No changes, no changes. Whatever you have done in the past is how the President is doing it this time."

I would have a lot of calls to make to the personal secretaries of each cabinet member, but first I would call the Supreme Court, because those crotchety gentlemen are the hardest to deal with—worse than senators. Though there were only nine men, they could never make up their minds on whether they were going to attend.

In the case of the Supreme Court, it wasn't a secretary I would call but Marshall of the Court Frank M. Hepler, and I would say "Frank, the Old Man's coming up to make a speech. State of the Union. You find out for us now whether you can get them all together and get them over here. This is important, Frank. I've been asked to do this by the Speaker."

I would sort of wheedle and tell how "the Old Man" —the President is always called "the Old Man" by those who deal in protecting him whether he is as old as Eisenhower or as young as Kennedy—"would be hurt if the men in their judicial robes would not be there."

He'd say, "I'll do my best. I'll let you hear from me." If the occasion was for the President, they would eventually pull themselves together and let me know at the last minute that they'd be there. But if it was a foreign chief of state who was going to address the House and Senate, I would dread the calls when Frank would regretfully tell me, "I couldn't get a quorum, and we will not be present."

Then I would call the State Department, Office of the Chief of Protocol, and they were a dream to deal with in comparison with the Supreme Court. All I'd have to say is, "This is Fishbait. Here's what we've got

449

this time. Reach over and get your papers from the time before. We've invited you to come to the President's speech, prime time.

"We'd like you to be here not later than 7:55 and you people will supply your own security guards [they brought six] at the east steps at the document room door, at the first floor and second floor by the elevators. Our Mr. White [the architect of the Capitol] will have someone running the elevator. The elevator operator will stay there as long as needed and all your 118 diplomatic corps are safely out of there."

Then I'd tell Mr. King or Mr. Codus—assistant chiefs of protocol, with whom I always worked—all the rest of the little instructions that were so important when working with diplomats. "We'll have four or five secretaries to help your people hang their hats and coats, so you bring them to the usual place—H207.

"We'll also have to ask you to call Mr. Kermit Cowan at extension 2734, manager of the House Restaurant, to order your cookies, coffee and tea for the diplomats to have while standing around and waiting."

That is the way the diplomatic cookie crumbles around the Capitol. We make the State Department pick up that little tab, small as it is.

Then I would get hold of my contact colonel at the Defense Department and remind him to tell the five chiefs of staff to wear their dress uniforms with all the ribbons. "And since it's an 8:30 speech, I want them in the Speakers' room—H209—at 8:05 so we won't have a traffic jam." And I would tell my contact to tell the chiefs of staff to bring their own aids to look after them.

Then I would call the Office of the Commandant of the Coast Guard. John W. McCormack was the first Speaker to extend the courtesy of an invitation to the Coast Guard boss man, feeling as he did that the Coast Guard had been slighted in past history.

The commandant would sit at the end chair next to the fifth chief of staff.

Then I would sit down and call the private secretary of each cabinet officer. All the others so far did not need tickets because they were known to us. And they were invited as solos. The cabinet officers were invited to bring their wives, but they had to have tickets for them to sit in the Executive Gallery. I asked each of the secretaries to write me a letter and have their car come with the authorizing letter and pick up a ticket between the hours of 2:30 and 5 P.M. of the day of the Joint Meeting.

The diplomats, who are not as high in seniority as those allowed a seat on the floor, were seated in the Diplomatic Gallery, which is right next to the Executive Gallery. We even furnished two female security guards who verified the authenticity of the persons coming to that gallery.

All tickets, incidentally, are prepared for a two-year session at the beginning of each new Congress. However, I would have to rush-order a batch of tickets to the Government Printing Office to have the date overprinted in two places on each ticket. I always made sure that they promised to have them ready by nine o'clock the next morning, the day before the event.

Right about this time, I would put in a call to the Majority Leader of the Senate, the Honorable Mike Mansfield, and jog his memory. "I would like to put a bug in your ear that you prepare to leave your chamber in the Other Body no later than 8:14," I would tell him. "And please, sir, keep it in mind that we want you to be on time."

Mansfield would always grumble, "Now, Fish, what do you mean be on time? You know we'd never be late and upstage the President. And since you've told me something. I want to remind *you,* don't forget my damn tickets."

451

The Majority Leader and I always had a friendly feud over tickets. Each member of the Senate was entitled to one ticket other than for himself—for his wife, his child, his girl friend or whoever—and each House member was entitled to the same. One extra ticket was provided to the Majority and Minority Leaders and the Democratic and Republican Whips of both Houses. Mansfield, however, would invariably come up with company from home or another emergency to help in wangling a few extra tickets and he was never disappointed. I was very fond of Mike and, besides, I had learned early what side my bread was buttered on.

Now came the big security conference in my office to get ready for the safe handling of the President. The public would be amazed at how complicated a simple spin up Pennsylvania Avenue and an hour's talk in the House of Representatives could be, how many agencies and departments of government were involved and the conferences that took place.

The day before the President's visit, three Secret Servicemen from the White House would come to see me at my office. They would stay for an hour and a half, going over every minute detail of how the visit would be handled. They would tell me from which gate of the White House he would depart, the route he would take and every detail of the way he would be handled on entering and leaving the Capitol grounds. They would try to vary the procedure so no one would know which gate he was leaving from or exactly how he would approach the Capitol Building. At the same time, we were talking about routes, we would make arrangements for hot-line phones to the White House from various points in and out of the Capitol—to be installed by the Signal Corps.

Meanwhile, the architect of the Capitol set up a security meeting at his office which I also had to attend. That was a meeting of the U.S. Park Police, House and

Senate Capitol Police Force, both the uniformed and plainclothes detective branches of the Washington Metropolitan Police Force, the traffic bureau, two officers of the Canine Corps, the chief of the fire department, the chief of the bomb squad, and the Signal Corps of the Army. And finally, the attending physician of the Capitol.

Since I had been around the Capitol for a great while, and the architect and others at the meeting were practically brand-new, I would have to speak up and ask the *earthshaking* questions put to me by the Secret Service. "Are you going to put men on the top of the buildings—Rayburn, Longworth, Cannon, Library of Congress, Russell, and the entire roof of the Capitol?" "Are you going to have the usual number of ambulances ready, one at the front steps and five at the Senate garage, ready to travel at a moment's notice?"

Then I would say, "We have the attending physician here with us." The doctor would tell how many men and first-aid people he would have stationed throughout the galleries and House floor.

Usually there would be four doctors, five nurses and five corpsmen stationed in various places, with two doctors in easy reach of the President besides his own physician, who had come with him from the White House. I would usually say, "And will you station the usual doctor in attendance in the gallery where the presidential family is and another in Gallery 4 where the members' wives are?"

Before we were through with arrangements on the Hill, we would frequently decide to borrow fifty detectives and one hundred uniformed policemen from Baltimore so our own city police force would not be depleted.

The Washington Metropolitan Police would supply the big V of motorcycle police that precede the President's car and the Secret Service cars. Trailing along in the rear are two cars with press people and a truckload of photographers. There are no TV cameras on this truck—they have already been put in place early in the morning or the day before.

One of my questions would be addressed to our own architect and the chief of the Capitol police force: "Are we going to have the stanchions set up that are threaded with steel wire to keep the crowd back?"

My last set of questions would be necessary, as Doorkeeper. Namely: "Is the First Lady traveling with the President, or is she coming in a separate car? And will she have the rest of her party with her, and how many will there be?"

The White House had no idea how much more complicated they made it when the First Lady came in a separate car. That would involve additional personnel to greet her and get her up to the Executive Gallery. It would also mean losing her place in the order of precedence and seating her after, instead of before, the Diplomatic Corps—though she would still get her applause from the floor and galleries, members rising.

All that is prelude. Now comes the great moment and you are there. The sirens are screeching as the flying-V arrives at the south door of the Capitol. The presidential limousine is met, not by me—though I meet the cars of other dignitaries—but by the architect of the Capitol, George M. White, and the House sergeant-at-arms, Kenneth R. Harding.

The first person to pop out of the President's car is the presidential press secretary. He is the one who usually helps the President out of the car to be greeted by the two Capitol officials. A moment later, the First Lady is helped out by a Secret Serviceman and joins her husband in chatting with Harding and White.

That's the last that the First Lady will be with her husband for a while. She and her entourage are taken by my assistant chiefs, Hicks and Anderson—accompanied by two Secret Servicemen and two lieutenants of the Capitol police force—to the gallery level.

The President, his doctor, his press secretary, his military aide, and his Secret Servicemen go with the architect and the sergeant-at-arms to the second floor Speaker's rooms—and an elevator has been held to speed the President to his destination. Waiting for him are his cabinet and the Committee of Escort made up of members of both houses of Congress.

The House of Representatives, being in recess, would be called back into session as soon as the Senate appeared. I would have to see the whites of their eyes before I would give the signal to Luke Hicks, my chief assistant, who would be standing in the front of the chamber close to the George Washington painting. He would pass the word to the parliamentarian that the Senate had arrived. Parliamentarian Deschler has been waiting at the door to the Speaker's Lobby to signal the House Speaker to come in. Together they mount the steps to the Speaker's stand, where the Speaker raps his gavel and states, "The House will be in order."

At that moment, I would walk into the chamber, nod to the Speaker, walk to the third row from the back where one microphone has been placed for the whole radio and TV media on a pool basis. I would pull in my tummy, stick out my chest, take a deep breath and say, "Mr. Speaker, the Vice President of the United States and members of the United States Senate."

As they walked down the aisle, they were escorted by the secretary of the senate, Francis R. Valeo, and the sergeant-at-arms of the Senate, William H. Wannall.

I would escort the Vice President to the right of the Speaker, but if the Vice President could not make it and the President pro tempore was in his place, I would take him to the left of the Speaker. Only the Vice President may sit to the right of the Speaker.

The next order of business is that the Vice President picks up his list of names comprising his Committee of Escort and reads them aloud. This committee usually consists of four or six senior members of the Senate. Right after the Vice President is finished, the Speaker reads his list of escort. As soon as members hear their names, they start rising to hurry to room H210 to be there when the President arrives and greet him.

As soon as I hear the Speaker name his last name, I look up at the Executive Gallery to see if the page is going to signal me that the First Lady is ready to enter the door of the gallery about twenty-five feet above us. If he signals yes, I turn around and start applauding and those I have tipped off to start the applause look up at her, rise and applaud too.

Invariably, in the last two administrations which were Republican years, I would have to admonish some of my Democrats, who would not stand up to applaud Nixon or Ford without a little hard encouragement from me that someday we might have another turn at a First Lady who was Democratic and we might need a little Republican help.

I started this practice of special applause for the First Lady back in 1949, when Bess Truman entered the Executive Gallery for the first State of the Union Address by her husband, Brother Harry. And once something like that is done, it quickly becomes a precedent.

Now back to the ceremony. With the First Lady seated, I go outside the double door called the Main Door, the same door through which all honored guests are escorted. The Diplomatic Corps is now waiting. I make a little bow to the dean of the corps, Dr. Guillermo Sevilla-Sacasa, ambassador from Nicaragua, then shake hands with him and ask him if he's ready to travel. He says, "I'm ready to go."

I knock four times on the double doors and the two pages inside are waiting for my knock. There are no handles on the other side of the doors, so I push the

456

doors open slightly and the pages grab hold and swing the doors wide. I go back to my place at the mike, and bellow, "Mr. Speakah, the Ambassadors, Ministers and Charges d'Affaires of Foreign Governments."

I lead them down the center aisle to the well of the House. I have learned through the years that the dean of the diplomatic corps enjoys his rituals as much as I do. So, to give him full stage, I step to the left and watch as he makes a full sweeping bow toward the Speaker and the Vice President. Then I seat them in a large block of seats set aside on the floor, to the left of the Speaker and in front of the Lafayette painting.

Now I hurry back outside the double doors to see if the Supreme Court is ready to travel. Having gotten themselves this far, they are now fully relaxed, jovial and chatting and laughing together. Usually, they even have two former associate justices with them—Justice Stanley Forman Reed of Kentucky, and Justice Tom C. Clark of Texas, and it's a happy reunion. Once a justice, always a justice, but one former justice thought the same should apply to their wives. Former Justice Reed had written Speaker Rayburn so many notes of complaint that Speaker Sam finally put all the blame on me and told him that the Doorkeeper said there was not a single extra seat available for wives. Four raps again. A shove. The pages are ready. Now I call out loudly, "Mr. Speakah, the Chief Justice of the United States and Associate Justices of the Supreme Court."

Then I hurriedly retrace my steps to the door where the cabinet is waiting and go through it all with them. "Mr. Speakah, the members of the President's Cabinet." As has happened with each entrance, there is applause with all members and galleries rising.

As the cabinet seats itself by precedence based on the date on which each department became a member of the executive branch, the electrician is turning on the floodlights and the mikes are being opened. It's time for the main show. Excitement has mounted and tension is high. I go through the door once more.

I am remembering now the last occasion on which it was President Richard M. Nixon who was standing outside the door. I said, "Hello, Mr. President. I'm delighted to see you back looking so good and in one piece." He had just been to Russia. He just looked at me, so I tried again. "I know you have a good report and we have a wonderful crowd assembled."

President Nixon, however, was not in as jovial a mood as I. But he forced himself. Turning to Zeake Johnson, Jr., predecessor to Kenneth Harding, the President said, "Zeake, you're all still letting old Fishbait work here?"

Before Zeake could give his answer, Gerald Ford, who was then Minority Leader and one of the Committee of Escort, jumped in with, "Mr. President, might I remind you, damn it, that Fishbait got here before we were here, and it looks like he's going to be here after we're gone and I just want you to know we better do what he says."

As the laughter subsided, Nixon asked me, "Has that person pointed his finger at you yet?"

My reply was in the negative.

He said, "Fishbait, how's your voice today? Is your throat sore? Is it hurting any?"

I answered, "I haven't had any trouble so far, Mr. President."

He said, "Fishbait, take two steps forward."

He grabbed me by the throat and was choking me. It was a hard grab. I gasped for breath. And then fortunately I saw through my peripheral vision that the TV prompter, who was outside in the hall with us, was giving me the finger—meaning let's go.

So I wrenched myself away, and after what seemed ages but must have been just a few seconds, I said, "Mr. President, let's travel."

As I knocked my four raps on the door, I thought

to myself, "Boy that was close, the poor guy really got rid of a little hostility at my expense."

But with a swallow and a smile, I stalked to the microphone and boomed, as best I could, "Mr. Speakah, the President of the United States."

I hadn't even had a chance to move my right foot to get him down the aisle before I heard him hiss in my ear, "Now let's get this thing over with, I want to get home." As I rushed him down the aisle, double-time as he wanted, I thought, what a terrible letdown this was after all the work and preparation and trouble to welcome him. After all that, all he could manage to say was, "I want to go home."

I didn't realize of course that his days were numbered and soon he'd *really* be home at San Clemente. Even bad as I felt, all my training in helping Hill people when they acted distressed forced me to say softly as I deposited him at the second level of the Speaker's stand in front of the microphone, "God bless you, Mr. President, I'm praying for you."

When I see the new security walk-through X-ray machines, I am glad that even reporters have to be screened before they get to the reception room of the floor. Most people don't know that one of the first cases of violence in the history of the Capitol building resulted in the death of a congressman and involved a newspaper reporter named Charles Kincaid.

In fact, if you enter on the first floor of the House wing of the Capitol and turn right on the marble steps, you can see for yourself on about the third and fourth steps the marks where blood was spattered there back in 1890.

That is the spot where Kentucky Congressman William Taulbee paused in the midst of a heated argument with a reporter and was shot dead by him. All kinds of cleansing agents have been tried to get rid of the blood stains in the porous marble, but they still persist. They remain a mark on the history of the Capitol even till today.

Now there are Capitol police in uniform and plainclothesmen watching everything that goes on in every hall and corner of the Capitol building—and yes, even on the stairs. And to make sure that no one tries to sneak in a window at night, or anytime, there is a special security system underground.

Because of the new threat of letter bombs, all packages and letters are also screened for dangerous material before they even get near the congressmen's or senators' offices. The public doesn't realize it, but when someone takes a little package into a congressional office as a hand-delivered gift, the gift is probably not even opened by the secretary or congressman. It is taken to be X-rayed and opened by security.

Even if someone tried to crawl into the Capitol by way of a sewer, there are alarm systems that would go off.

One thing that shook up the Capitol police and security was the 1973 incident which showed that someone could visit the Capitol and leave behind a little present in the form of a homemade bomb. Fortunately, it had been left in the men's rest room next to the Senate barbershop, and it went off at about 1:30 in the morning. It is hoped that all the devices and watchfulness on all sides will keep a more serious incident from occurring. The final touch in new security has been a $2 million closed-circuit television system that I defy you to find but which even shows who is walking on the Capitol grounds.

The day after the rest-room bomb went off, a call was received at my Doorkeeper's Office which was taken by my assistant. The message was, "Tell Mr. Miller when he gets in that we have one with his name on it and it will be delivered in three or four weeks." I tried to be a little more cautious than usual, but for some time thereafter my assistant would not come to

460

work unless a guard and a Canine Corps dog marched along with him.

The atmosphere of fear on Capitol Hill began in the 1960s when Senator Barry Goldwater ran against LBJ, the year after the Kennedy assassination. Goldwater was so shook that he wanted bulletproof windows in places where he would be, like the Republican National Committee room, and several armed bodyguards went everywhere with him. This was before Secret Service guarded candidates.

I've said it on many occasions that 1972 saw the most mixed up and ridiculous Democratic campaign I've ever witnessed. Even the protection of Senator George McGovern, a really gentle guy, looked like something out of a Keystone Cops comedy. Would you believe it—they got mixed up with a grocery-store robbery that was going on?

McGovern was in Nebraska and suddenly, as he talked, a man came running out of a grocery store with a gun, followed by other men, followed by total chaos with some Secret Servicemen throwing themselves in front of the presidential candidate while others fell over the police who were also chasing the man, and spectators hid wherever they could.

It was over in a few minutes. As it turned out, it was a robber with as bad luck as McGovern's—dare I say he didn't know how to steal a bundle and McGovern didn't know how to steal an election.

Every President has been a headache to protect. With Roosevelt we had orders from the chief of Secret Service, Colonel Starling, on how to keep everyone away from the President. And it wasn't just that wheelchair the President didn't want seen. According to the colonel, Roosevelt was still nervous because of the shooting incident he had been in, a month before he took office, when a bullet fired by Joseph Zangara, a known anarchist, had shot Chicago Mayor Anton Cermak, sitting beside FDR in the car. But a man had been heard to say, "We got him," so maybe the attempt hadn't been against FDR at all. Or so the Hill said.

Truman was not scared of hell itself. Even though he had been shot at when he was staying at Blair House during the renovation of the White House, he continued to have nerves of steel. But he was nervous about speaking at a Joint Session and unlike any other President, he wanted *two* glasses of water every time he came for an address. They weren't even spiked with Bourbon. When he drank so much as he talked, some of the members thought he had a bit of Bourbon in there. I can tell you now that he may have had Bourbon when he arrived, and he usually did, but he drank no Bourbon while giving a speech.

Eisenhower was like Truman in paying little attention to the security measures on the Hill. Having been in the armed forces, he was used to being guarded. What he worried about was how he looked. Ike was the first President to use make-up when he came to the Hill.

Robert Montgomery, the actor, was the man who put Eisenhower into the make-up business. What we did was have a make-up person available on the Hill. He would wait for the President in what we call the "holding room," right off the floor of the House.

I was the only officer of the House to know or see what was going on. The make-up man was from one of the local networks. He would do a good job in applying pancake make-up. Monty, as we called Montgomery, would supervise. What the President was most sensitive about was the baldness on the top and back of his head, and so special care would be taken to put pancake make-up there so that the harsh lights would not bounce off his head.

Ike did not want to wear glasses, so a special stand with a slanting board was made in the carpenter's shop under Monty's supervision. It had to be done in two hours, stained and covered with purple felt. It brought

462

the script closer to the President and at a better angle, but he still needed glasses.

Montgomery had said, "Many Presidents will use this," and he was rather proud of having thought it up. LBJ wanted to improve on it by adding the presidential seal to the front of it, but we turned him down. The Speaker is the law. *He* doesn't have anything saying "Speaker," and the President is merely the *guest* of the House—if he doesn't like it, tough turkey.

The Hill crowd was amused that Eisenhower never made a decision on his own. He always appointed a committee. I heard people speculate that a committee went to the bathroom for Ike. Even when Eisenhower got angry about the squirrels stealing his golf balls and putting them in their nests, he had a committee of White House and Interior people to look into it.

I also remember the time Ike was going to run again in 1956 and he formed a committee of two people from the House and two from the Senate and one from the White House to see if he could change the convention proceedings to make them more to his liking. He wanted to know if they could work it out so that he could receive the nomination by acclamation and not have to stir himself a bit to do anything.

To the best of my knowledge, Kennedy did not wear make-up to make a State of the Union address—just his own suntan. The story was that he spent time at the White House under a sunlamp to keep him looking fresh and sunburned. With Lyndon Johnson, we were back to make-up. It was put on at the White House before he came. They had to put special make-up under his eyes so he wouldn't look so tired.

President Nixon, too, wore pancake make-up, which was applied before he came to the Capitol. I would feel sorry for him, because he would be nervous and the sweat would just pour over his top lip. So as not to draw attention to it, he would lick it off rather than use a handkerchief.

When Jerry Ford became President, he was not going to use make-up but soon he changed his mind and he wore a little.

Kennedy had been used to security all his life. I was told there had been fear of kidnapping once when he was a child, so there was someone with him, even as a congressman, wherever he went. Muggsy, his old bodyguard, used to work with me in the House Post Office.

Kennedy had gotten him the job and Muggsy had told Mr. Scott, our postmaster at the time, that he had to be on call at all times for the congressman. When Jack Kennedy moved to the Senate, Muggsy went to the Senate side, too.

Johnson would make news now and then when run-of-the-mill nuts tried to climb the fence to get in the White House to see him. But Ford, with his usual bad luck, seemed to hit the jackpot security-wise. He had to have a new gate installed when a wild driver tried to crash through. And several times, women with guns tried to take potshots at him. It got so bad that when a woman's flashbulb exploded during the President's visit to Bowling Green State University, the President ducked and the Secret Service jumped on her and wrestled her to the ground.

But with his usual good humor, President Ford had the thoughtfulness to try to make it up to the young photographer, coed Sandy Snyder of Ohio, by sending her a special bracelet with his presidential seal. Sandra's hair and neck had been clawed by spectators as she was dragged away by Secret Servicemen.

What lies in the future? It's hard to say. What it may be coming to in our own lifetime is that presidential candidates will be walking around wearing little bubbletops over their heads like a driver's helmet—but all glass. And bulletproof cloth has been worn on some occasions.

I would rather see bubbletops worn than to have

a situation where a President or presidential candidate would not be seen in public at all, but only on television. That would be like having a Howard Hughes character—you'd never be sure whether he was a real man or a double.

When World War II started, the leadership realized that the Capitol was totally unprotected. We brought in Army men to stand guard inside the Capitol and the office buildings, after House adjournment. And we dreamed up something that seemed quite childish, looking back thirty years later—we mounted fake wooden guns on the Capitol itself and all the office buildings. We also had some things that looked like soldiers kneeling there on the roof. Someone said it was like "scarecrows in a cornfield—it couldn't fool anyone." But among the scarecrows, we did have a few live soldiers up on the Capitol roof.

Almost all the legislators cooperated without a word on the wartime security measure of having to show their passes to get into their office buildings after hours. But Congressman Compton I. White of Idaho was gruff and tough, and he said, "Damned if I'm going to show my pass."

I told him that he had better cooperate because the guards were under orders. It didn't take long for him to have his first and only confrontation. He came back to the Hill to get something at his office and the Army guard wouldn't let him in.

"Get out of my way. I'm Compton I. White of Idaho," he said. But the soldier held him back with the butt of his gun. "I can't let you through until you show me a pass." "Damn it, I don't have to show you anything," Compton said, standing firm. "Get out of my way or you'll be in trouble." Compton was still trying to push his way through.

"Show me your pass or I'll give you the butt of my gun," said the soldier, raising his weapon.

At that Compton caved in and said, "Well, I really

465

believe you mean business. I better show you my pass."

We were lucky that the Nazi planes did not find their way to Washington. But I'm happy to say that now there is much better security on the Hill. But what no security on the Hill can protect us from is the immense amount of bird droppings that bomb the building every year. That is why every spring and fall the fire department of the city of Washington arrives to hose down the building. And every four years the building is painted. On some old sections of the Capitol, there are thirty-two coats of paint.

It became my responsibility to travel on various occasions to represent the House at funerals. To me, the saddest funeral was that of Sam Rayburn. He died on November 16, 1961.

At Bonham, Texas, I not only had to help the undertaker be sure that all of Speaker Sam's wishes were being complied with, but I was responsible for the seating of the members of Congress and for looking after the Presidents who came.

It was a most unusual funeral, with three Presidents —Truman, Eisenhower, and Jack Kennedy—in attendance.

I was almost overcome with grief but I was determined that something good should come of this funeral, so I did something daring. I seated two bitter enemies side by side—Charlie Halleck, Republican of Indiana, the Minority Leader of the House, and Joseph W. Martin, Jr., of Fall River, Massachusetts, Halleck's predecessor, who was still fuming over being replaced by losing to him.

McCormack, who was the Majority Leader, saw what I had done and hissed at me, "You haven't got a damn bit of sense, Bill. You know you're not supposed to put those two together." But later he was forced to admit that I had done a fine thing because eventually they started to talk to each other and they ended up leaving as friends.

After the funeral, there was a small conference in the basement of the Rayburn library between McCormack and Hale Boggs, while I stood guard. That was when the deal was struck that McCormack would succeed Rayburn and Hale would become Majority Leader. They decided exactly how they would work it and who they would get to nominate them.

At the Kennedy funeral that seemed to follow so closely two years later, I had to do some shopping. The instructions had come from the White House on how we were all to dress. I had to buy striped trousers, cutaway coat and vest, ascot tie, high hat and gray gloves.

After I had assisted in all phases of the Hill arrangements that involved the House, I also helped seat the members of Congress at St. Matthews, where the funeral was held. Speaker McCormack sent word to me before the service was over that he wanted me to go with him to the graveside service at Arlington Cemetery.

Never before, in Washington or elsewhere, had I seen such a long funeral procession—over two hundred limousines alone. We had to park far from the place where the eternal flame now burns and after the funeral was over and we were walking back to the car, McCormack and I walked arm in arm and tried to console each other.

Only the sadness of the city over FDR could approach the sadness all around us over the young Jack Kennedy.

When President Lyndon Johnson's body lay in state in the Rotunda of the Capitol, my job was to stand at Lady Bird's ear and whisper the name of each important personage who came by to pay his or her respects. I would say that she was even more poised and in control than Jackie Kennedy had been. We, on the hill, knew that Jackie had taken tranquilizers to help her through, but to my knowledge Lady Bird had no medical aids to stay calm.

Suddenly someone interrupted and Lady Bird told me, after consultation with her little grandaughter, that she had an emergency. Lynda Bird's child wanted a cookie in the worst way. It so happened that I kept my office stocked with everything for my congressmen's snacks, in fact everything but money and whiskey.

I took the little girl to my office, got her cookies and a soft drink and the emergency was over.

When I had finished helping Lady Bird identify all the people who were lined up to see her, the former First Lady said, "Fishbait, I want you to stay up here long enough for my granchildren to grow up and to know everything only you can teach them about— where their granddaddy stood and sat and ate, and everything he did when giving his State of the Union messages."

I'm sorry that I didn't make it for Lady Bird's sake, but I hope she will save a copy of this book for them.

THE ROYAL KNACK

Royalty. Mention royalty and Americans go all atwitter. The British—some of them—from what they told me, regard their royalty like a prize stable of show horses that have to be curried and cared for. And shown off. That I can go for and understand. It's like our Senate and House. But others still believe the British queen was chosen by God. And this, mind you, is three hundred years after Britain disavowed the Divine Right of Kings.

In my job as Doorkeeper, I got a very human look at all the royalty who came to call. I assure you, they are human. But thinking of posterity and all the people who want some link to these demi-god figures, I saved a glass which had been touched by each of these "immortals."

Where are these glasses now? At Ole Miss—the University of Mississippi—in my home state with all my papers and memorabilia. Each time a royal figure, or other world figure like Churchill or de Gaulle, would come to address a Joint Meeting of Congress, I would rush up and get the water glass they had used to clear their throats. I would grab it before anyone else could. I never told anyone about my collection for fear I would have to wrestle them for the glass afterwards. I would take the glass, dump the water and place in it the label of the royal personage whose lips had touched it.

The water needed by the royal person was a headache to get. You just didn't send *anyone* to get a glass of water for a queen. No indeedy.

Any glass of water we served to royalty on the Hill required a retinue of flunkies, plainclothesmen, and very special treatment. State Department security men

469

joined our procession as did a page as we went to the water cooler in the men's room right off the Speaker's lobby. I would stand by with a state department security man as the page took the glass and showed him it had been properly cleaned. Then the security man watched like a hawk as the page drew the water from the water cooler.

I'll never forget the visit of Queen Juliana of the Netherlands because it gave me a mean job to do. She had a hat on and some members were in a tizzy because *someone* was going to have to tell her to take it off. The alternative would be to let her go on the floor of the House with it on. Should we waive our rule for foreign royalty?

Certainly not. "That would hit the newspapers in a most unpleasant way," said Speaker Sam. So naturally, I was selected to give her the bad news.

Queen Juliana had had a full morning that day of April 3, 1952, before she arrived on the Hill with Congresswoman Frances Payne Bolton. Mrs. Bolton had escorted her to Mount Vernon, where the Queen had laid a wreath on the tomb of George Washington.

The two ladies were talking a blue streak and having a lovely time as they arrived at the Speaker's room, when I went to escort Juliana to the floor. I hated to be a sour note that changed their mood, but I would see the wrath of Sam Rayburn if I was remiss in doing my duty.

I decided to be diplomatic that day and not my usual brass self. I told Mrs. Bolton the problem. She turned to Her Royal Highness and said, "This Fishbait of ours, Your Royal Highness, says that you must remove your hat. Of course, he is our unofficial God around here—he's the Doorkeeper—and whatever he says, we've learned we have to do."

Juliana looked startled for a moment—I'm sure she wasn't used to the likes of us—then she laughed and took off her hat. Her hair was very neat and she didn't even have to pat it much. She was very charming looking, and not nearly as heavy as her photos in the newspapers suggested.

What Juliana had come to America to do, was to thank us for the help we had given her in World War II and afterwards. Her way of putting it was quaint. "In this world of ours," she said, "we need cooperation as intimate as that among the cells of one body." I had never thought of that before. Neither had the congressmen, and some of them acted a little startled.

Juliana continued: "You have seen this, and have planned a program for aid to the countries robbed and ruined by totalitarian war—help on such a scale as has never been conceived before. We in the Netherlands were deeply impressed by your great plans and their execution. They enable us to stand once more on our own feet. We shall do so as soon as possible in ever sounder economic circumstances.

"On this occasion again, and in this Hall especially, I want to express the thanks of the Netherlands for this proof of generous friendship, offered by your government and by your people through the voice of Congress and by countless private voices."

Juliana was soundly applauded for her gracious words of gratitude.

"One human race, under the law and the love of one God," she said, as the congressmen and senators applauded.

"Our human legislations seek from afar to follow the divine law. They mostly fail, but they strive on.

"We live in the dawn of a time when we must seek to do this as one human race.

"Mankind should be one kind. A split humanity is like a split personality; it is inclined to go from bad to worse, unless it recovers its unity of purpose, comes to coordinated thinking, and gains sanity and happiness."

People think that foreign dignitaries, such as chiefs

of state, level with us and say very important things before Congress, but that's a crock. They don't stand up in Congress and tell what they are really up to—like that they are seeking money, arms, and whatever else is up for grabs.

When a foreign chief of state makes an official visit to see the President and the secretary of state, Congress, not to be outdone or ignored, invites them to appear before a Joint Meeting. They are not expected to say anything meaningful or state the real purpose of their visit. They certainly don't say, "We've come to get some guns. Give us two hundred tanks." Hell no. They remind us of friendship. The Frenchmen remind us of Lafayette. How we'd have lost the Revolution if it hadn't been for the French. And how Pershing returned the friendship in World War I with his, "Lafayette, we are here."

And India reminds us of that scrawny little peacemaker, Gandhi, whom we loved for his gentleness and admired for his hunger strikes.

Only to the President and secretary of state do royal or VIP "shoppers" let their hair down and come right out with what they are looking for. Through the secretary of state, the President has the sole power to deal with foreign nations. Later, in a luncheon with the Senate Foreign Relations Committee on the Senate side of the Capitol, they might, if asked, let slip something about their problems and hopes for U.S. help.

The routine, which has been underway since the days of Jefferson and Madison and all those old boys, is that the first day of a chief of state's visit, he attends a white-tie-and-tails dinner at the White House (except when some recent Presidents like Kennedy made it merely a black-tie dinner). The morning of the second day, the secretary of state and a protocol officer go to Blair House to have coffee and to escort the foreign dignitary to the Capitol for his speech.

If the President is not present, it is called a Joint

Meeting, but if he is present it is called a Joint Session. Only once that I recall did a President come to the Hill to hear a dignitary's speech, and that was when Truman came up with some gentleman from South America.

After the speech, the foreign dignitary is escorted over to lunch on the Senate side. Present at the luncheon are the guest of honor and the ambassador from the visitor's country, the secretary of state, the hosts of the Senate Foreign Relations Committee and the top echelon of the House Foreign Affairs Committee.

Sometimes even I tagged along. My biggest thrill was when I brought over Prime Minister MacKenzie King of Canada when Prime Minister Winston Churchill of Great Britain, one of my great heroes, was the guest of honor. At this Hill luncheon, there is much good humor and good fellowship and usually a little talk of world conditions in general and that country's problems in particular. That night, many of the same people will see each other again at the white-tie-and-tails dinner at the embassy of the visitor, where he is host. If the embassy is not large enough, we lend the visitor Anderson House, or some other appropriate building.

Knowing that a state visit on Capitol Hill is simply a love-in, I always relaxed and enjoyed it. This got me in trouble, when the British Princess Elizabeth and Prince Philip were there on November 1, 1952. This was just a pure visit. The Princess was not invited to speak before a Joint Meeting.

President Truman himself had directed me to "look after the Princess" and show her around. President Truman had already warned the royal couple at the dinner the night before that they were going to meet "a real character—a Southerner of the old school"— but I didn't learn about that until later. Congress was in session, but some thirty-five members were waiting in the well to be introduced by me to the Princess.

And also, I had obtained permission of Speaker Rayburn to sneak my eight-year-old daughter, Sarah Patsy, and her little friend Judy Meneaugh, whose father was superintendent of the House Radio and Television Gallery, and Mrs. Miller, Sarah's mom, onto the floor of the House. Only members of Congress and certain staff are ever allowed on the floor of the House. So this was a big deal.

It seems that every step of the way I did something wrong, totally confirming Truman's prediction. First, I went out and met the Princess and Prince Philip on the Capitol steps, shaking her hand and saying, "Howdy, ma'am." Then, I took her arm to escort her around. She was my only responsibility because Speaker Sam had directed the clerk of the House, Ralph R. Roberts of Indiana, to look after the Prince.

From the top tier, standing beside the Speaker's desk, I peered upward and saw all the eager aides and secretaries in the galleries above. Trying to make them happy, I pointed them out to Elizabeth and said, "Ma'am, will you just smile and wave a little to our girls and boys in the gallery? They've been waiting a long time to see you." She looked at me a little strangely, but she did so with a very refined little hand wave.

Then I realized that the girls up there were going to hang my hide from the barn door, as LBJ used to say, if I didn't make the Prince wave to them, so I called down to Ralph Roberts, "Hey, pass me up the Prince." The Prince looked a little startled, but he came up to the top of the three-level Speaker's stand where we were. I told him what I wanted him to do and said, "Sir, we people over here in America think you're the most handsome brute in the world. The girls will be thrilled if you just wave up there"—and I pointed at the eager faces.

When I saw Mr. Truman later, the President said,

shaking his head, "Well, Fishbait, I warned them and you sure didn't let me down."

I didn't know how Sarah Patsy had reacted to the Princess' visit until some months later when she was nine and in the fourth grade. The news had come on the air that the King of England had died and Princess Elizabeth was to assume the throne. Suddenly Sarah Patsy burst into tears and in her little voice said, "Sniff, sniff, Mother, just think I now know a real queen. Remember when I got to meet her and Daddy was showing off on the floor and he said, 'Pass me up the Prince,' and you called him down when he got home that night and told him he didn't do right?"

Mable said, "Yes, I remember, dear. Don't cry."

Sarah Patsy, still sniffling a little, said, "I can't help it. It's just because I know a real queen. Mother, would it be all right (sniff, sniff) if I go to school and if they ask what is important to me today—would it be all right if I tell them I know a real live queen—just as long as I don't tell what Daddy said?"

I suppose I shouldn't have been surprised that right after the Princess' visit, the State Department's Office of Protocol sent me to protocol school to learn how to address royalty and all the social amenities that go with it. In fact, the protocol office even took to giving me little cards with instructions of what to say and do on special occasions.

So it came to pass that I had a hand-delivered card given to me when I was about to meet probably the most beautiful foreign lady I had ever feasted my eyes upon on Capitol Hill. Foreign dignitaries do not usually come alone when they speak before the Joint Meeting. Usually they bring their wives, and when I look back at the long parade of glamorous ladies I have seen on these auspicious occasions, I must give the highest mark to the Empress of Iran, Farah Diba. She was a beautiful woman with the mystery of Persia in her eyes.

She arrived with her husband, the Shah, who was going to address Congress.

I would have loved to carry on a little conversation with the dazzling Empress, but I looked at the card, which sounded pretty stern:

INSTRUCTIONS TO FISHBAIT MILLER

Do not touch.

Do not wish her well.

Bow from the waist when you first speak to her, addressing her as Your Imperial Majesty.

Do not grab her arm to direct her onto the floor.

Have two page boys, without your having to direct them, be ready to open the doors.

When you are leading her into the House Chamber to sit in Seat 1, 1st row, bow to her and beckon with your hand to the proper chair.

Then say with a bow, "This is your seat, Your Majesty. Thank you."

That is all. Then you will go immediately to get the Shah, announcing him, saying only this and not a word more.

"MR. SPEAKER, THE SHAH OF IRAN."

I was amused when Elizabeth of England, now a Queen, came back for the Bicentennial celebrations of 1976 and this time it was Vice President Rockefeller who was catching the devil, so to speak, for laying hands on her royal majesty at a congressional luncheon.

As the story went, Rocky "committted a royal breach of etiquette and protocol by giving the Queen an unroyal pat on the back after the luncheon, when he took her to see the copy of the Magna Carta that is on display in the Rotunda."

I was glad that this time it was him not me, but I'll bet they didn't send him to protocol school for seven days and seven nights with no time off for good behavior.

This time, too, the Hill gang learned another idiosyncrasy of a British foreign notable. Queen Elizabeth is sensitive about people watching her eat, so even though President Ford had planned to show the dinner on television, that part of the event was left out.

But worst of all was the boo-boo the President made or let happen when the dancing began. For the first dance, the one at which he was to swing the Queen onto the dance floor, the band played unfortunately, "The Lady Is a Tramp." That really tickled the Democrats.

As someone said, "It's a good thing she doesn't vote here."

By the time Swedish Princess Christina arrived in June 1965, I had at least been browbeaten enough by the protocol office to call her "your royal highness" as I showed her around the hallowed chamber of the House. But when she made a move toward sitting down in the Speaker's chair, I became Mr. Bad Guy again.

I had to stop her and say, "You can't do that in our House of Representatives, Your Highness. Royalty can't sit in the House of Commons in England, either. That's what they told me back in 1952 when I was showing Princess Elizabeth this very room."

Then, maybe I shouldn't have but I told her frankly, "I was instructed by the leadership on what the Princess and her husband Prince Philip could and could not do in this room. They said if the Princess comes, don't you dare let her sit in the Speaker's chair. But we don't care if she sits in the Vice President's chair. That's over in the Other Body, you know, the Senate, Mr. Humphrey's territory."

Princess Christina was very sweet about it and just rolled her eyes a little at the do's and don't's we have, saying she guessed they had a few do's and don't's of their own.

477

Hubert Humphrey, who was Vice President at the time, helped on the tour of the Capitol and even took her in high good humor to see his office. She noticed a carving on his desk of two elephants who are goring each other and asked what it meant. "That represents the unity of the Republican party," the Vice President said, grinning broadly. Then he gave her a little lesson in American symbols of donkeys and elephants, and she laughed as she realized these were the only kind of elephants a Democrat would dare display on his desk.

Then when the Princess became fascinated by the French mirror which hung on his wall, HHH gave another little history lesson telling how the mirror had originally cost $40 and the Senate had been so furious that Dolley Madison had bought an imported mirror that they had ordered a whole investigation of the matter, which had cost $2,000.

But to return to the day the royal personages from Iran came to call, exotic, beautiful Farah sat in the front row to the right of the Speaker when her husband spoke. It was April 12, 1962, and the Shah reminded America of something that most people had forgotten —that Iran had helped on the side of the Allies during World War II and had declared war on the Axis powers. He talked of how oil had been nationalized in Iran in 1950 and how 280 million tons of oil were produced for export to industry in West Europe. Little did I know that more than fifteen years later we would be even more concerned with the oil of Iran.

I looked at the Shahbanou, as she is called, as we call our President's wife, the First Lady. And I thought what a lucky man he was to have all that oil and the jewel of the Persian world besides.

From the Shah's speech, I also learned something I didn't know about the Bible. In fact, as the Shah began speaking, his words had a sound of another world and another time, and I thought it all sounded very

478

poetic. I looked around at our tough legislators and noticed it seemed to cast a spell not just on me:

"I come to you from one of the oldest countries in the world. The ages-old history of Persia, which was once the greatest empire the world has seen, is not, like the chronicle of many vanished empires, an account of conquest, massacre, and injustice. It is the record of a civilization imbued with the spirit of equity and freedom. The text of the Holy Bible bears witness to my statement. In the only eulogy of its kind in so sacred a book, the Bible refers to the King of Kings and the land of Iran as the fount of justice, whence arose the spirit of liberty and respect for the individual.

"The following text was written by order of Darius the King twenty-five centuries ago and is preserved on a bas-relief until this day. It says:

" 'By the will of Ahura Mazda, I am King of Kings. I love justice, I hate iniquity. It is not my pleasure that the lower suffer injustice because of the higher.' "

Other women besides Queen Juliana have also on very rare occasions addressed a Joint Meeting. The first woman to do so was Madame Chiang Kai-shek on February 18, 1943, when, because it was wartime, she voiced China's fear that the Allies viewed the defeat of Japan as "of relative unimportance" and that "Hitler is our first concern." She made the point that "Japan in her occupied areas today has greater resources at her command than Germany," and that "the longer Japan is left in undisputed possession of these resources, the stronger she must become."

What I learned from Madame Chiang Kai-shek was an old adage of Sun-tese, the great Chinese strategist: "It takes little effort to watch the other fellow carry the load."

Yes, indeed, the lady knew how to get a message across.

Though she wasn't royal, Madame Chiang had the

royal knack. Most royal women of the world, in general, could learn one thing from our female movie stars —how to diet—but usually the women have superb posture. And our gals could learn poise from them.

The thing that sets royalty apart from lesser mortals and inspires such deference is their retinue. Because there is a buffer zone of people keeping everyone from their royal personages, the average person gets the feeling they are something special. I remember once the wife of a royal personage had to go to the powder room and I rushed her to it just like I would anyone else. After she came out, she was so grateful that, to stop her outpouring of thanks, I had to give her a little pat in the hand and a peck on the cheek. She acted confused but happy.

The visitors who impressed me most on Capitol Hill were not the royal figures but the non-royal world leaders—men like Winston Churchill and Charles de Gaulle.

To me, de Gaulle was one of God's men chosen to be a leader among men. He was tall and straight and stately as a huge pine tree and he was well-mannerd. But he made one mistake. He made his whole speech before the Joint Meeting without stopping and then it had to be translated into English. He had to stand by the mike and hold on to the lectern while the interpreter translated it all. We told de Gaulle's men to have him give only a sentence or two at a time, and then have it translated, but they wouldn't listen. The congressmen got very bored waiting—except for a very few, including about five from Louisiana, who could understand and speak French fluently.

De Gaulle had come to the U.S. to confer with President Eisenhower in April 1960, on the eve of the summit conference of France, England, Russia and the U.S. on nuclear disarmament.

A little shiver ran through me as I finally heard his warning in English and I wondered if in my lifetime

I would be searching the sky with fear and remembering his words. I still wonder as I read his words again:

"We have reached the last moment when an agreement appears possible. Failing the renunciation of atomic armaments by those states who are provided with them, the French Republic obviously will be obliged to equip itself with such armaments. In consequence, how many others will attempt to do the same?

"In the state of increasing uncertainty in which fear throws the people of the world, the risk grows that, one day, events will escape from the control of those who obey reason and that the worst catastrophes will be unleashed by fanatics, lunatics or men of ambition."

Then he ended his speech with the note of friendship that is obligatory in international relations:

"Three weeks from now, Messrs. Eisenhower, Macmillan, Khrushchev and myself will compare our views after having done so two by two. I do not think that anyone believes that it will be enough that the four of us sit together for problems of such magnitude to be effectively solved. Perhaps we shall, at last, decide on the road to follow, however long and arduous the stages may be. In any event, my country has determined its purposes and its hopes.

"Americans, let me say to you: In the big contest which lies ahead, nothing counts more for France than the wisdom, the resolution, the friendship of the great people of the United States. This is what I came here to tell you." (Applause, the members rising.)

Haile Selassie was a strange little man. Looking at him, it was hard to believe he was the Lion of Judah, addressed as "His Imperial Majesty."

Of the little Emperor of Ethiopia, I used to say to the members, "He's a great American." They would look startled and I'd add, "He's been living on American money for a long time."

I had to admire the way Haile Selassie, unlike de Gaulle, at least read two paragraphs in English before

481

giving up and reading the rest in his native tongue—Amharic. What I learned in the translation was that the U.S. receives some of its finest mocha coffee from his country, as well as goat skins for shoes.

Of the foreign dignitaries I have met on Capitol Hill, Winston Churchill was my pet. I was there right after Pearl Harbor when Churchill came to see us in December 1941 on the problem of coordinating English and American war efforts. Though the mood was serious, he was able to start his speech with a bit that made us feel he was one of us:

"I wish indeed that my mother, whose memory I cherish across the vale of years, could have been here to see. By the way, I cannot help reflecting that if my father had been American and my mother British, instead of the other way round, I might have got here on my own.

"In that case, this would not have been the first time you would have heard my voice. In that case, I should not have needed an invitation; but, if I had, it is hardly likely that it would have been unanimous. (Laughter.)

"So perhaps things are better as they are. I may confess, however, that I do not feel quite like a fish out of water in a legislative assembly where English is spoken. I am a child of the House of Commons. I was brought up in my father's house to believe in democracy. 'Trust the people'—that was his message.

"I used to see him cheered at meetings and in the streets by crowds of workingmen away back in those aristocratic Victorian days when, as Disraeli said, the world was for the few, and for the very few. Therefore I have been in full harmony all my life with the tides which have flowed on both sides of the Atlantic against privilege and monopoly and have steered confidently toward the Gettysburg ideal of 'government of the people, by the people, for the people.'"

At that point he had us in the palm of his hand. In my opinion, he is still the greatest orator of them all. Then he started leading up to the fact that we might be facing a long war and that *he* thought it would be a long war.

"For the best part of twenty years the youth of Germany, Japan, and Italy have been taught that aggressive war is the noblest duty of the citizen, and that it should be begun as soon as the necessary weapons and organization have been made. We have performed the duties and tasks of peace.

"They have plotted and planned for war. This naturally has placed us in Britain, and now places you in the United States, at a disadvantage which only time, courage, and straining, untiring exertions can correct.

"We have, indeed, to be thankful that so much time has been granted to us. If Germany had tried to invade the British Isles after the French collapse in June 1940, and if Japan had declared war on the British Empire and the United States at the same date, no one can say what disasters and agonies might not have been our lot.

"Some people may be startled or momentarily depressed when, like your President, I speak of a long and a hard war. Our people would rather know the truth, somber though it be:

"In the words of the psalmist:

" 'He shall not be afraid of evil tidings; his heart is fixed, trusting in the Lord.'

"Not all the tidings will be evil.

"The boastful Mussolini has crumpled already. He is now but a lackey and serf, the merest utensil of his master's will."

Finally he spoke of what our entering the war meant to the world. And suddenly you could feel the pride swell in that room and a desire of almost all of us to go out there and fight.

"Lastly, if you will forgive me for saying it, to me

the best tiding of all, the United States—united as never before—has drawn the sword for Freedom, and cast away the scabbard.

"All these tremendous facts have led the subjugated peoples of Europe to lift up their heads again in hope. They have put aside forever the shameful temptation of resigning themselves to the conqueror's will.

"Hope has returned. . . .

"In a dozen famous ancient states, now prostrate under the Nazi yoke, the masses of the people, all classes and creeds, await the hour of liberation, when they, too, will . . . strike their blows like men. That hour will strike, and its solemn peal will proclaim that the night is passed and that the dawn has come."

That was Churchill, a man whose patriotism burned so bright that it made everyone around him burn in the same way. I was only a messenger to the Doorkeeper when Churchill came this time, but I was assistant sergeant-at-arms when he returned May 19, 1943, and again addressed the Joint Meeting.

He came at a psychologically important time, a low point in the war—U-boats were sinking our shipping— to whip us into continuing to do our best and keep us from letting down. He praised our air power. He praised our progress. And then again he made us feel that he was one of us, talking of how he used to walk around all over Gettysburg battlefield, before he gave us a final pep talk.

> The enemy is still proud and powerful. He is hard to get at. He still possesses enormous armies, vast resources, and invaluable strategic territories. War is full of surprises. A false step, a wrong direction of strategic effort, discord, or lassitude among the Allies might soon give the common enemy the power to confront us with new and hideous facts.
>
> We have surmounted many serious dangers. But there is one grave danger which will go along with

us until the end. That danger is the undue prolongation of the war. No one can tell what new complications and perils might arise in four or five more years of war. And it is in the dragging out of war at enormous expense till the democracies are tired, or bored, or split that the main hopes of Germany and Japan must now reside.

We must destroy this hope, as we have destroyed so many others; and for that purpose we must beware of every topic, however attractive, and every tendency, however natural, which diverts our minds or energies from the supreme objective of the general victory of the United Nations.

By singleness of purpose, by steadfastness of conduct, by tenacity and endurance, such as we have so far displayed, by these, and only by these, can we discharge our duty to the future of the world and to the destiny of man.

I had escorted Canadian Prime Minister MacKenzie King from the House to the Senate side, but Sol Bloom, chairman of the House Foreign Affairs Committee, wanted me to stand behind him and Churchill as they ate in case they needed anything. Though the luncheon was in the Senate's private dining room and the Senate Foreign Relations Committee chairman, Tom Connally of Texas, was there, the real host this day was the colorful New Yorker, Sol Bloom.

I had the idea Churchill hadn't been fed in at least three weeks, because he devoured the terrible luncheon made up of chicken à la king in patty shell before the others had gotten a good start, and said, "Mr. Chairman, you don't mind my having another?"

Bloom said, "Hell no, if you need another, we'll get Fishbait to get you another." He snapped his fingers and I rushed to get my hero another full plate.

I had brought my own lunch and it was sitting on my desk getting dry. As I watched Churchill clean up

485

that second plate of gummy chicken with the greatest relish I had ever seen on any man, I thought of what I would do to any clown who dared grab my sandwich while I was gone.

"Are you through with me now?" I asked hopefully, since it was getting on toward two o'clock.

"No," said Sol. "Stay planted. I need you because this is going to become a secret meeting on the progress of the war and we don't want anyone barging in here. Why don't you get the cigars?"

He had stashed fresh boxes of three different types of cigars in the next room. I opened the boxes and placed them on a tray and all the men took the kind they preferred. I made another feeble attempt to leave the room, but Sol said, "Forget your stomach. You'll live. This is important. I want you to oversee that the liqueur is properly served." Waiters poured the choice of brandy or chartreuse. Then they were dismissed.

I admired the way Churchill tossed off his brandy. I also admired the way he handled a gold toothpick that he surreptitiously took out of a little case. It was fantastic the way he used it behind a napkin, so adeptly that no one noticed what he was doing.

As Churchill started to light up his cigar. I pulled out my trusty lighter and quickly flipped it to flame. The Prime Minister, who by this time was jolly and calling me by first name, said, "Fishbait, you're wasting petrol. Put that away and I'll show you how we do it." He was brandishing a match that he had taken from a dainty box pulled from his left pocket.

I said, "Mr. Prime Minister, we don't let anybody who is our guest of honor light his own cigar, cigarette or pipe." But I extinguished the lighter and watched as he showed how he used a match. "I take the stem part of the match," he said, "and I shove it into the mouthpiece of the cigar for the wind to come through. And then naturally I would light my cigar with the other end of it, gaining two uses from the same match.

486

But since you have your petrol machine and insist I can't use my match, I will now get three uses out of this match." He carefully put the match back in the box, tucked the box into his pocket and waited for me to do the honors.

That was the end of the frivolities. Suddenly Churchill got very serious and I squirmed as I heard things I had never known about wars and particularly the one in progress. Reports of spies and double agents. I had to listen, but for six months or more I was even afraid I'd talk in my sleep and have to make up something to tell Mable to cover the Allied war plans.

It was four o'clock before I ate my lunch, or tried to. By now the bread was so dry that even memory of the chicken à la king seemed desirable in comparison.

A few years after the war, it was Prime Minister Nehru of India who was the object of all eyes when he came to address the Joint Meeting of Congress. Nehru was a busy visitor that day because he had to give his speech twice. The House and the Senate were meeting in temporary quarters—the Senate in the old Supreme Court chamber and the House in the Ways and Means Committee room of the Longworth House Office Building. So the Prime Minister talked first to the senators and then to the House members. He listened with quiet dignity to the explanation that the braces on each side of our Capitol were discovered to be so weak that we had been afraid we were going to lose our whole membership during the first heavy snowfall. Though I am not sure he understood, a congressman tried to explain that we had been putting spittoons where the heaviest part of the rain would leak through to the House floor.

No wonder men started copying Nehru's high-necked jacket style. He was a picture of the perfect man of distinction, in his beautiful white Nehru jacket against his dark skin. There were whispers that the love of his life was a titled English woman who visited him frequently in India.

All I can say is that the girls in all the House offices swooned for him. They followed him around, leaving their typewriters to grow cold. He had the same sexy appeal that Kennedy did and for days afterwards the girls went around saying, "He looked at me. He looked right through me and I could have died." With Kennedy, women wanted to touch and be touched, but with Nehru they were satisfied with a look from those sad dark eyes.

One of my heroes was Douglas MacArthur. This time, I was in agreement with the minority membership that he was doing a fine job. A few days after President Truman fired MacArthur from his Pacific command for insubordination in the handling of the Korean War, Joe Martin, the Minority Leader, leaned on Speaker Sam a little to arrange for a Joint Meeting so Joe himself could have the honor of bringing over the illustrious controversial leader.

Truman was furious. Joe Martin had sent MacArthur a wire, going over the head of the Commander in Chief—the President—telling MacArthur in effect to do as he damned well pleased because he was conducting the war just fine. So naturally this was one joint meeting that the President did not attend, and Joe Martin was the actual host.

On April 19, 1951, prior to the start of the meeting, it was my good fortune to escort Mrs. Jean MacArthur and her son to the Executive Gallery and see that they got there at the proper time to stimulate the necessary recognition and applause. What I usually did was have some member on the floor ready to start the applause. This day I had Les Arends from Illinois and a few of my staff members on the lookout to start the applause from the first moment that I led her in, which was immediately following the seating of the Diplomatic Corps.

488

That was when MacArthur made his famous remark, "Old soldiers never die, they just fade away." And with that, he made a big bow toward his wife in the Executive Gallery and looked up at her dramatically. Then followed a luncheon hosted by Joe in the Speaker's Dining Room, which he borrowed from Rayburn. I escorted Mrs. MacArthur and her son to be sure they were well taken care of.

Years later, MacArthur was a luncheon guest again at an L. Mendel River quail banquet on the Hill and we reminisced about that historic day and the "old soldiers never die" punch line. He agreed with my recollection, saying, "Yes, as I looked around, there was not a dry eye."

In 1975, when Japanese Emperor Hirohito finally came to the United States and was to be guest of honor at a state dinner at the White House, MacArthur's widow, Jean, refused the invitation. It was very touching that finally it was the old war-time Emperor himself who went to visit Mrs. MacArthur at her home at the Waldorf Towers. I'm sure she was doing exactly what she felt the general would have wanted her to do.

Sometimes it wasn't a personage at all that was the featured attraction around the Hill. Sometimes I found myself announcing the arrival of a messenger from the executive branch, rather than a VIP visitor.

We would frequently receive messages from the White House or bulky documents that were newsmakers in themselves. One was the name of any new appointee to an office and another was the yearly budget. Photographers waited to pounce.

In October 1973, the White House secretary and I had already delivered the unopened brown envelope from President Nixon, containing the message nominating Jerry Ford for Vice President. We had gone through the ceremony of the delivery scene on the House steps, which had been photographed, and the

489

handing of the envelope to Speaker Carl Albert in the Chamber, which had not been photographed.

After Dan Marks, one of the President's secretaries, and I thought we were through, cameramen from two television stations and three still photographers appeared and were furious that they had missed the historic moment. I had to borrow back the empty brown envelope and reenact receiving it on the Capitol steps from Dan Marks.

Photographers were always trying to come up with a new way of showing how much money the President was asking for in the budget. One year they twisted my arm and got me to pose weighing the budget on a kitchen scale. As I recall, the record budget ran to something like eight or ten pounds. The photographers said, as soon as the release date made it possible, that they were going to caption the picture showing how many dollars the budget was worth per ounce.

Back in the 1950s, there was a presidential aide with the same name as mine, Miller, and we used to have a little fun with names when the White House was sending a special message to the Congress, because there was also a third Miller at the Speaker's stand on the floor of the House.

We called it the Miller to Miller to Miller play—it was our version of Tinkers to Evers to Chance. Naturally, the press loved it, as did the photographers, because it gave them a handle for their caption.

The way it worked was that Miller of the White House would call me and I would alert the congressional newsreel guys' still photographers and TV gang that Miller would be there on the steps at 11:45 A.M. for a twelve noon delivery. This allowed us five or six minutes for the press to take their pictures.

The White House Miller would then accompany me to the House Chamber and I would announce that we had a message from the President. The Speaker would nod to me and I would nod to Truman's man who would speak in a mumble so that he could hardly be heard, "Mr. Speaker, I am directed by the President of the United States to deliver to the House of Representatives a message in writing." He would hand me the manila envelope and I would hand it over to the third Miller, the shorthand reporter, who would hand it to Lewis Deschler, the parliamentarian.

I saw a lot of VIP visitors stream through the Capitol from the time of Roosevelt to the days of Jerry Ford. Years after he had been President and was helping the government in reorganization plans called the Hoover Reports, I got to know and like Herbert Hoover. He used to sit around with me for an hour or so after he had attended a luncheon in the Speaker's Dining Room and he would talk of his early days of hardship and his climb to the presidency and how he and his wife would talk Chinese in front of guests at the White House, so no one would know what they were talking about.

It was wonderful to know that underneath that seemingly cold man in the White House I had heard about, who kept his desk as clean and cold as he seemed to be, was a warm-hearted person with sad memories and tender thoughts of the past, just like everyone else.

I got to know two prizefighters too—Jack Dempsey and Gene Tunney. They were such good friends that if you invited one to come to the Hill, you had to invite the other. When they came to the luncheon in the Speaker's Dining Room, they would always square off and take a few jabs at each other, and all the congressmen loved it.

Once Gene Tunney came alone and wanted to see John McCormack on business. Not knowing Hill procedure, he thought he could walk right out on the floor and talk to him. I had to stop him from entering even the lobby of the House. I said, "I'm sorry, Gene, you're not a member of the press and so you can't go in there. You're only the champion of the world." He was amused and very nice about it but the man who was with him, who later became a judge in Boston, was furious. He said that he wanted to remind me that "Folks like you can be bought for a dime a dozen. You shouldn't be so tight with the rules."

I said, "Well, sir, if I'm told I can do something, I go ahead and do it. But if I'm told not to let anyone in, they'd have to go in over my dead body."

I wasn't the only one who was loyal to the job. Most of the men and women on the Hill are loyal, and they will go through any amount of grief and take all kinds of guff from the public to protect their bosses.

One man I met at a VIP luncheon on the Hill long before his name meant anything to the country was George Wallace of Clinton, Alabama. He was a local official and he was the guest of honor mostly because he had been a lightweight boxer. The talk was mostly of sports, and I recall that I was the one who had to say grace, in the absence of an ordained minister. I prayed over George and wished that the Lord might help him rise very high in the field of politics which he had chosen. Years later, when he *had* risen very high, I saw him again and he immediately recognized me and thanked me for what I had said to God.

Then I saw him again a few years later, after a would-be assassin had put him in a wheelchair, and this time he remembered again and said wryly, "It's too bad we can't know all the things we should ask for."

Governor Wallace had the same ability I had. He could go around a room and remember every name. He would go to his hometown of Clinton, Alabama, and all the townsfolk would gather eagerly around him as he called them all by name, recalling little stories about them.

I've met many famous people and gained sidelights on them that the average person would not know. Half of Hollywood has come to the Capitol at one time or another. Jayne Mansfield had a devilish sense of humor. When she was on the Hill having her picture made with some of the good ole boys of Congress, she dipped her shoulder as if by accident and exposed one breast. But it was no accident, because she winked at me to let me know she knew what she was doing. The pictures that resulted from that picture-taking session were prize items around the Hill.

Byron "Whizzer" White, the great Colorado football player who now sits on the Supreme Court, doesn't mind showing his bad temper. He also has a way of shaking hands so forcefully that girls have complained to me about his painful handshake.

I once had to tell him where to sit on an occasion away from the Capitol. On the Hill, he would be with the rest of the Supreme Court justices and there would be no problem about where he sat, but this was a formal occasion and I had my orders from the leadership on where everyone should sit.

When I pointed out his seat, he said, "Damn it, I'm in tuxedo, get lost. You're not telling me where to sit unless I'm in my robes."

I said, "Damn it, Whizzer, I want you in that seat next to that admiral and I want you to take your seat or else." The bullying did the trick, and he went to his seat as meek as a lamb.

I remember when John Glenn came to a Joint Session in triumph after he had become the first astronaut to orbit the earth. The autograph seekers were ten feet deep and the name John Glenn was on everyone's lips. But there was one man with him, the commandant of the Marine Corps, who was afraid that when I hollered out, "Mr. Speakah, the Honorable John Glenn of the Marine Corps," I would not put a heavy enough emphasis on the Marine Corps.

I remember the commandant carried a little stick, a hangover from his rubbing elbows with the British, but he sounded more like LBJ than LBJ when he said,

"Damn it, if you don't holler loud enough, I'm going to have to speak to Rayburn and have him send you back to smell the south end of a northbound mule. And need I remind you that all mules are nothing but oat burners and sometimes the wind is mighty strong." So if anyone wonders what sometimes goes on back of the door when a great man is about to march into the chamber of the House of Representatives, ponder that.

Of course nobody can measure up to Lyndon Johnson's temper. When he was stirred up, he came at you like a steam roller and you did whatever he wanted, just in self-defense. When he had been a messenger to the Doorkeeper in charge of family gallery number three, he had been sweet and helpful and good-natured as all get out. But the more powerful he got, the more irritable and unreasonable he became.

I remember when, as President, he was coming to the Hill to sign the Civil Rights Bill and it was a great occasion. Since there was a shortage of space in the Gold Room, where it would be signed, a certain type of telegram had been sent to those who had witnessed the signing and other invitations went to the larger crowd who would join the President in the Rotunda.

In fact, the President had, himself, selected the place he wanted to stand to make his civil rights speech—between a bust of Abraham Lincoln on one side and a standing likeness of the Great Emancipator on the other.

I was so busy with all my split-second timing on handling the various groups that I didn't realize the President was screaming at me. Finally I heard him yell, "Fishbait, get the hell over here. Take care of some things for me." Since he didn't mind cursing in public, I yelled back that I would be there as soon as I finished a few things. I was busy with committees of escort and ten other things that were in a list in my mind, but I heard that famous finger-snapping again and Lyndon's voice yelling, "I don't give a damn what you're doing, get over here." I did—he *was* the President—and everything and everyone waited as he sent me on an errand, grumbling, "You give such good service to the Speaker, I don't see why I can't get a little of the same for me."

But I forgave Johnson everything that day because he did a very nice thing for my black assistant, Carl E. Sommers, who used to be the headwaiter in the Speaker's Dining Room when LBJ was on the Hill. Johnson sent an invitation by personal messenger to Carl to have him be present at the signing.

FOR SOME SILLY REASON, SOME CONGRESSMEN INSIST ON GETTING THE JOB DONE

I say that tongue in cheek, of course. I'm proud that we have had, and I hope we'll always have, real workhorses in the House of Representatives and the Other Body—men and women who wear themselves out pushing important bills through Congress. The "bulldogs" is what we call them on Capitol Hill.

It's a long and honorable roll, the list of bulldogs who didn't give up. Let me tell you about a few. Eugene Keogh, Democrat of New York, was on the Hill thirty years and he had a dream. The dream was that people who were self-employed be able to have a retirement plan of their own. It took at least six years to achieve, but his name and his place in history is now assured with the Keogh Bill, which made possible the famed Keogh Plan.

Congressman John Dingell, Sr., father of the Social Security Act, worked endless hours for that landmark bill in spite of terrible chest pains. I knew him well and was inspired by him.

The congressman had a son who was also very ambitious, and he became a page back in the days when fathers were still able to do things for their sons without being in trouble for practicing nepotism. John, Jr., was a page from 1938 to 1943, graduated from Georgetown Law School in the nation's capital in 1952, practiced law in Detroit for a while and came back to Congress to fill the vacancy left by the death of his father in

1955. He's been there ever since. He's a conservationist battling to save the wetlands and flyways for birds, and he is deeply involved in the problems of conserving energy.

William Whittington of Mississippi was another congressman who was involved in a different phase of environmental problems—he knew firsthand the terror of floods. He wore himself out working for flood-control legislation, and until he retired in 1951, it took four secretaries working in shifts far into the night to keep up with him.

The more relaxed, easy-does-it guys in Congress, of course, frequently resent the bulldogs and make snide remarks of, "Oh, why doesn't he just shut up?" or "What difference does it make? He's just spitting in the ocean." But the men who try to get things done don't care if they are making it harder for the rest of the go-along guys. They just keep plugging.

Some of them become the watchdogs who jump up and object when they think taxpayers' money is going to be wasted. And some become the only members coming in for every day's session and making it on time to roll calls and votes. And they really go to committee meetings and sometimes they even sit through them after the phoographers have quit taking pictures.

One of the worst watchdogs—meaning best—was Republican H. R. Gross of Iowa. He was always trying to save money, which was hard to do because the Democratic leadership managed to get things done before he could really get started objecting. For example, one year—1972—they ordered the Speaker's Lobby redecorated over an Easter recess to the tune of $160,000. And Gross never forgot.

Even after he retired at the end of 1974, he continued pushing for economy in how Congress operates —especially in the form of a reduction in the $6,500 year stationery account. "When I came to Congress

497

we got something like $2,500 to $3,000 in allowance. That's plenty."

His colleagues were a little startled that the man who was saying this was also the man, you will recall, who collected over $23,000 in back stationery allowance funds after he retired, because they were coming to him.

But then, as they say on the Hill, "Nobody's perfect."

Incidentally, H. R. Gross was not only famous for being the watchdog of the expenditure of tax money, but he was famous for having given Ronald Reagan his first public exposure as an actor. Gross owned a radio station in the old days and he put an aspiring young actor named Reagan to work as a sportscaster at $5 a game. The actor graduated to Hollywood, and just as Gross had graduated into politics, Reagan, too, then followed into politics and became the governor of California. The amusing twist is that after Gross left the Hill and retired, *he* went to work for *Reagan,* helping toward his goal of the presidency.

Politics is full of that kind of twist. They always say, "Be nice to everyone on the way up because if you're lucky, one or two of those you helped will be nice to you when they meet you again on *your* way *down.*"

And if you want another of those great wisdoms the wiseacres say on the Hill—"It's not how you win or lose but how you place the blame."

Going against the tide of the average congressman who hires as many assistants as the law allows— eighteen—and screams for more was Representative William H. Natcher, a Democrat from Kentucky, who actually turned back $166,000 office-staff allowance to the taxpayers.

How did he do it? By hiring only the help he absolutely needed and doing away with such nonessentials as a press aide.

He opened his own mail, dictated his own answers —most mail on the Hill answered completely by staff,

498

with maybe a word of direction from the congressman —and he still found time to have a perfect attendance record on the floor, never missing a vote for twenty years.

Bill Natcher was a special friend of mine because, like me, he was a firm Baptist who didn't drink and whose only vice was popping peppermints.

Natcher, with a regular staff salary allowance of $238,584, chose to hire only eight secretaries—all women. His total payroll in 1975 was $72,318, not even half his allowance.

Lest anyone think he had the option of pocketing the difference, not so, not so. Any unused staff allowance must be turned back at the end of the month. As chairman of the House District Appropriations subcommittee, Bill Natcher's most important job in the Hill, as he saw it, was as watchdog over the cost of the Metro subway system being built in the nation's capital. Unfortunately he could not stem the tide of that spending as he could in setting an example in his own austere office budget. One of the most respected members of the House, Natcher was chosen by the leadership to chair the House debate on Nixon's impeachment.

Even the most liberal men of Capitol Hill were not ready for Congressman Larry Pressler, Republican of South Dakota, who really rocked them back on their heels right after the 1974 election.

At the tender age of thirty-two, he was going to set an example for the whole body by turning back ten percent of his $42,500 congressional salary to Uncle Sam to help stem the recession and inflation.

Larry said, "I'm not going to accept all my salary. I really think this could set an example." Young Larry had a law degree from Harvard but when he went down to the office of the sergeant-at-arms and talked with Kenneth R. Harding, who is responsible for paying the congressmen every month, Larry was informed that, sorry, it just couldn't be done.

Harding cited the law, chapter and verse, but *this* congressman wasn't going to give up that easily. He sat down and wrote his state legislature back home and let them know that he would be sending his state the ten percent of his salary, which he could spare, for use in bettering the conditions of poor people in South Dakota.

Sol Bloom of New York was a dear man. He was there when I arrived on the Hill and he served until 1949. He would drive a beat-up Model-T Ford and he didn't want to give it up for any newer fancy kind of automobile.

Back in the early 1930s, a penny was a coin that bought a big chunk of candy, like a licorice whip. Sol would walk up the steps of the Capitol every morning, strewing pennies, nickels and dimes along his path like Hansel and Gretel had done with crumbs in the fairy tale. He tried to be inconspicuous, but I caught him at it and asked him what he was doing. He said, "Shhhh. Let the little children find them when they come to see the Capitol. In this Depression, someone has to show them that good things can happen."

Dear old Sol Bloom took an interest in me when I was just an ambitious newcomer on the Hill. When he learned that I used to be a puny lad, given very little chance to live to adulthood, he told me a bit of history that made me feel very good.

It seems that Congressman Alexander Stephens of Georgia was such a little guy that, during an argument on the floor of the House, his opponent told him to watch out or he just might get rid of Stephens by swallowing him whole.

The little guy drew himself up and told the bully, "You do and you'll have more brains in your belly than you've ever had in your head."

That was in the 1870s, and exactly one hundred

years later another mighty-mite, Congressman Carl Albert, proved that with hard work even a little guy can rise to the very top of the Capitol Hill hierarchy —to the position of Speaker of the House.

From him, I got this nugget that keeps me, even now, reading and studying every night in my basement hideaway, out of Mable's reach. Carl Albert told me long ago, "Education is what you get from reading the small print. Experience is what you get from not reading it."

He's so right. I've found in life that every time I failed to do my reading, I got my knuckles rapped by life.

For another kind of inspiration, I must pay tribute to a marvelous, unselfish man—Fred Schwengel, a Republican from Iowa—who has dedicated his life to completing the mural decorations of the interior of the Capitol Building. Though Brother Fred was defeated for reelection, he didn't go back home after his term in office but stayed on as president of the U.S. Capitol Historical Society, determined to finish the decoration of the interior of the Capitol, begun over a century ago, in 1855, by that great political exile, Italian muralist Constantine Brumidi.

Schwengel loves to show groups of people what is going on in the decorating and he points out the lone figure of the eighty-year-old artist, Allyn Cox, up on a scaffolding, carefully painting on the plaster of the hall ceilings in a style which is almost a lost art. Cox has been painting the patriotic, historical murals since 1951.

I'm happy to say this is one project that isn't costing the taxpayers a cent. Art lovers and patriotic people around the country have been contributing to the art cost. The Daughters of the American Revolution members, each contributing one dollar, are sponsoring the new $150,000 project.

There are actually four halls and four themes involved. First is the educational motif in the hallway off the Speaker's Dining Room—a hall just completed.

Others will have various themes, including the array of foreign dignitaries who have addressed Joint Meetings. It will end with the final panel of the Bicentennial visitor, King Juan Carlos I of Spain.

Because Cox is not too young, Schwengel worries about who will carry on his work when he is gone. To be safe, Cox will be training an artist to follow in his footsteps.

One day I compared notes with Cox on how he had gotten his Capitol Hill job. We laughed and agreed it was typical bureaucracy. "I applied for the job by sending photos of my work," he said. "And three years later they sent for me."

Barry Goldwater, Jr., a California Republican, deserves a place on the honor roll of bulldogs. Without his "right-to-know" crusade, the federal government could still have damaging material on a person without his being permitted to see it. Now, thanks to Goldwater and his hard and incessant work over several years, any individual can go to the FBI and find out exactly what material is in the files about him.

I'm happy to say that wealth and the "famous-father syndrome" has not affected the son of the presidential candidate. Brother Barry is totally absorbed and dedicated to his various crusades.

Another such man was Frank Chelf. He was a congressman from Lebanon, Kentucky, and he had a dream that children be honored for bravery.

Actually, his own life reflected a little bravery— orphaned at an early age, he was raised in a Masonic orphans' home, yet he managed to attend two colleges and get a law degree, through dogged determination and hard work.

When Frank came to Washington in 1945, at the age of thirty-four, he was the youngest congressman from his district in one hundred years. But what inspired him almost immediately to dare attempt to get

502

legislation passed, though a mere freshman, was the bravery of a little girl in South Carolina who had saved another child from certain death by pulling it from the path of a onrushing train.

Brother Chelf thought it was wrong that there was no national medal for child heroism, like the military gives to honor their brave. So he introduced a bill to give such annual awards, under a program to be administered by the Justice Department. Two times the Congress passed it and two times the Senate killed it.

I remember how upset Chelf was by the rejection, and he would talk very often about the heroic children, building up a large file of such cases. Children had saved adults in fires. They saved other children from being killed by wild animals. They had pulled other children to safety from car wrecks.

"I'm not giving up," he said. "Once I have my mind made up, I'm as persistent as a duck after a June bug." Damned if he didn't introduce the bill again a third time, and this time he made it his personal business to see and pursue every senator who had been against it.

Well, with a one-man army like that, the Senate finally said yes and the bill passed. President Truman signed it into law, and there would be a heart-warming ceremony every year as youngsters came to Washington to be honored for their bravery, with medals given by the Presidents—Truman, Eisenhower, Kennedy, and then Johnson.

But Nixon, for some reason, cared so little for the tradition that he dropped the program, and Chelf, retiring in poor health, was no longer in Congress to fight for it. I hope that someone else will look into the matter and resurrect this most worthy project.

Frank Chelf had a second crusade—to make the congressional term four years instead of two. He did not get too far with it, though he worked very hard, but, again, perhaps someone else will take up the torch. As Chelf saw it, "The vote for congressmen should never fall on the same year as the presidential vote to keep unworthy candidates from riding in on the coat-tails of a President. That's a very poor practice, since we get some mighty bad legislators who just happen to run in a lucky year. So I would hold congressional elections on off-years."

Lest anyone think Chelf was all grim work, let me say he was no mean mouth on a harmonica, and he carried one in his pocket, ever ready.

He was not shy about showing his enthusiasms either. Once, when Kennedy came into the chamber to give his State of the Union Address, there was a big war whoop and what it was was Brother Frank expressing his happiness. Kennedy grinned his famous grin and waved. An historic moment!

Another inspiring freshman, Jerry Litton, was a successful Missouri farmer—a millionaire farmer—and a good businessman. As a Democratic congressman fresh in Washington in 1973, he took an interest in farm problems. In his first year came the consumers' revolt against high prices in the stores—high prices which were being blamed on the farmer.

Litton thought this was untrue and unfair, so he brought many farm groups together to thrash out the problem. The many divergent factions of farmers had always gone their own way. He was the first to organize them. It was thought impossible to get them to work in concert, but Litton, as a freshman congressman, did not know that it could not be done—so he did it. A joint association was formed with ample funds to tell the farmers' story to the angry consumers.

Brother Litton was one of the busiest men on the Hill—always in perpetual motion and the center of activity. He would send out releases on every conceivable subject. So it was not surprising that, though he was only thirty-nine years old, his supporters wanted him to run for the Senate to fill the vacancy that would be created by the retirement of Stuart Symington.

Then, the very day of the primary, Litton was killed —his career cut short by a plane crash. He died on the heels of his upset victory over Congressman Jimmy Symington, who was also running for his father's seat.

I wish we could know what things Jerry would have done had he survived. It is sad and touching that he was taking off in a private plane with his family before the returns were in and he did not even know that he had won.

A woman belongs in this roll of hard workers—I'll call her a bulldog with the jaws of a tiger. She had to be fierce—she was bucking hundreds of men. But let the truth be told, without Martha Wright Griffiths of Missouri, there would have been no ERA—Equal Rights Amendment—pushed through Congress.

That is not only my belief and the belief around the Hill, but the belief held by women's groups around the country, such as ERAmerica.

Let me tell you what she was up against. Manny Celler was chairman of the Judiciary Committee of the House, and he was against the bill to amend the Constitution and give equal rights to women. He wouldn't hold hearings on it to get it out of committee, and it had been bottled up for years. So Martha, in June 1970, filed a discharge position.

That's the one way you can get a bill onto the floor of Congress for a vote, without a committee first reporting it out. It was a very unusual thing to do, and it is also very unusual for a discharge position to be approved. You have to have over half the members of Congress to sign it. Sister Martha not only got half the Congress, but she got the chairman of every other committee, to sign it.

It was a slap at Manny. Martha held on. There was no way to stop her. A lot of debts were owed her and she called all her debts in. She got Wilbur Mills, chairman of Ways and Means Committee to sign it. I knew when he signed, it would go through. But she was taking no chances. Though a Democrat, she got Jerry Ford, a fellow Michigander, the Minority Leader, to get some of his Republican colleagues to sign. So she got it on the floor.

It was debated on the floor and passed overwhelmingly. Then the Senate held hearings on it, under Birch Bayh, chairman of the Constitutional Amendments subcommittee. That was a very tricky move. Sam Ervin, chairman of the full Judiciary Committee, would normally have held the hearing, but he was not a feminist. He would not have let it out of his committee.

So Martha's cohorts went around him—especially helpful was Mike Mansfield, the Majority Leader. He put it on calendar and got it on the floor. However, amendments were put on it that made it unacceptable, so it still died.

I felt sorry for Martha. Everyone but Sam Ervin and a couple hundred other male chauvinists felt sorry for Martha. But Martha didn't feel sorry for Martha.

The next year she was at it again. The House Judiciary Committee did hold hearings—shamed by Martha —they thought they had to. Actually, it was a subcommittee that held the hearings, chaired by Don Edwards, Democrat of California, and it was reported favorably. But the full committee, chaired by Manny Celler, put in amendments that he knew were unacceptable and reported it out that way.

Now, that bulldog, Martha, showed her tiger's teeth. She fought on the floor to get the amendments off, and she won. The floor passed the bill in proper form in October 1971 and sent it to the Senate, where it was passed in March 1972. If Martha hadn't shown her tiger's teeth, they would be wrangling over it yet.

I remember how, after it passed the House, the Hill was amazed that Martha didn't rest but personally phoned or contacted every senator who was home for his Christmas vacation.

That is the story of Sister Martha Griffiths, the Equal

Rights Amendment and one woman's dedication to a cause. When she retired from the Hill, the nation's women lost a great spokesman. She had come to the Hill as a brainy woman, with experience in the state legislature, and retired as a brainier one yet—one of the top women in the country in Social Security, tax matters and government finance.

Martha was a mighty hard worker.

Who worked hardest? Difficult to say.

The best record for answering every roll call vote belongs to Charles E. Bennett, a Democrat from Florida, who went 22 years, 346 days, answering 3,807 votes. Then fate intervened and he missed a call by five minutes, when an unexpected vote on adjournment came up. His record period was June 5, 1951, to February 6, 1974.

Brother Bennett was one of the most dedicated men I knew in many ways. He was author of two books and held a Doctor of Law degree from the University of Florida. He enlisted in World War II from the Florida House of Representatives and served fifty-eight months in the Infantry, including guerilla combat in the Philippines war, elected to Infantry Hall of Fame, and received many medals including the Silver Star.

I just want to mention that, in spite of his record, he was no worrywart. Just a dedicated, hard-working, member of Congress.

When Bennett first came to Congress, he was on crutches. He had every excuse to avoid coming to all those calls of the House. He had been wounded during the war and also had survived a slight case of polio. I rejoiced with him when he switched to canes, which he still uses today.

One of the men I admire most on the Hill is the very dedicated Frank Annunzio, Democrat of Chicago, who is known as "Mr. Ethnic."

He told me, "I don't care that I take a little ribbing among my colleagues for my crusading. I'm proud to

507

be called 'Mr. Ethnic.' I'm proud of every bill I've introduced or campaign I've waged to make up for two centuries of neglect of our great ethnic heroes. It's shocking that it took until 1971 for Columbus—that brave Italian explorer—to have his birthday in October designated a national holiday by law which I authored. I had worked toward that goal for years."

But Columbus is not the only Italian the bulldog congressman has fought to honor. He was also the sponsor of a bill to restore the home of the little-known Italian-American signer of the Declaration of Independence—Governor Paca of Maryland. And a bill to honor the Italian muralist, Constantine Brumidi, by placing a bust of the great man in the very halls of Congress that he spent a lifetime beautifying to the detriment of his health and private fortune.

Brother Annunzio is especially concerned with the public image of Italian-Americans, "not just because I am one of them, but to help counteract the outrageously unfair bias of Hollywood movie makers who persist in portraying Italian ethnic Americans as *the* criminal element of the United States."

It is always easy to know who is working like crazy to climb the ladder on the Hill because they start tackling the leadership of the opposition party, needling them and challenging them in any way. The Republican congressman from Rockford, Illinois, John Anderson, made his move by locking horns with Tip O'Neill, the Majority Leader—a Democrat, of course—over televising the House sessions.

Anderson had been trying to get the House to approve television coverage of House proceedings which have been banned for years. I remember, in fact, when Speaker Sam decided that it would be too humiliating to have television cameras trained on the sleeping members and the empty benches of missing members.

One time, as an experiment, cameramen had been permitted in to take pictures at will on an opening day and, as a result, the pictures that had been published in *Life* magazine of groggy, bored, slouching and snoring members kept the leadership from ever making that mistake again.

But now came Anderson wanting to permit those all-seeing cameras again in the chamber. Tip O'Neill had not gone so daft as to promise an open sesame with all sessions televised if he were to become Speaker and follow the retiring Carl Albert, but he did promise his own personal service. To wit, "I'll go on TV. I'll talk to reporters or I'll do whatever it takes to improve the image of Congress."

Anderson attacked Tip on this point on the floor of the House with devastating sarcasm, "Mr. Speaker, I think it is most gratifying that our distinguished Majority Leader is willing to make the supreme sacrifice of going on TV and even of talking to reporters to help improve the image of Congress. But I would caution the Majority Leader that this will not be enough. He is not the Congress."

But you needn't feel sorry for the subject of Anderson's attack. He's best-known for his own attacks.

Bulldog Tip O'Neill goes down in history as a "Republican fighter," like we used to have "Indian fighters" —but his bullets were words, and if you think that fighting the opposition full-time isn't hard work, you haven't spent much time on the Hill.

Making the bullet easier to take, the Republicans could always count on a little Irish-style humor to accompany the frontal attack of Tip—whose real name was Thomas P. O'Neill, Jr.

As an example of the Tip O'Neill-style, let me share what the Democratic Majority Leader, who started in politics as a friend of Jack Kennedy, said on the morning after President Ford finally announced his candidacy.

Rising and asking for one minute's time to address the House, O'Neill said, "Mr. Speaker, after nine months of announcing that he was going to announce his candidacy, President Ford finally did it yesterday; he announced his candidacy."

Though he was addressing the Speaker, it was obvious that he was really addressing himself to the Republicans for the amusement of his Democratic colleagues. "This Ford campaign took longer to crank up than a Model-T," he continued. "I am sure you gentlemen remember the Model-T, because that is the age in which you are still acting.

"But his campaign strategy is already pretty clear: Do not do anything about unemployment, do not help the consumer, forget about the economy, keep right on blasting Congress and veto everything that provides jobs or stimulates recovery.

"The unemployment rate for June is about the same as May—still nine or ten million unemployed people in this country.

"The administration is still saying that the recession is over, that is, it is all over for all practical purposes. But the President signed into law a bill extending unemployment benefits to sixty-five weeks. That is for the people out of work who have not yet heard that the recession is over.

"Other than that, it must have been a dull recess for the President. He has not had anything to veto for at least a week."

Steve Young, a Democrat from Ohio, was one of the funniest fighters. I had known him first as a congressman, then as a senator. An oddball with a terrible temper—part bulldog, part snapping turtle—he did some great things too besides amuse the Hill. For example, I believe he was the first man on the Hill, in the 1950s, who revealed the complete statement of his wealth—the list of his stocks. He also gave up his law practice back in Ohio completely, as a matter of ethics.

He had no patience with anyone, even constituents,

who didn't agree with him. He would write insulting answers right back to anyone who sent nasty letters or complained about his handling of a bill. Or he would return the letter with a note that said "Some jackass is using your name."

The talk of the Hill was his exchange of letters with a man who resented Young's stand for gun controls. The man called Young a "stupid fool" for wanting to curb private ownership of guns and said, "I am sure you could walk upright under a snake's tail with your hat on and have plenty of head room."

The writer made the mistake of giving the senator his telephone number and of saying, "I would welcome the opportunity to have intercourse with you." This gave Steve Young the perfect opening to write a short, sweet letter:

Sir:
I am in receipt of your most insulting letter.
I note your offer in the final paragraph, 'I welcome the opportunity to have intercourse with you.' No indeed. You go ahead and have intercourse with yourself.

Stephen M. Young

But getting back to the good senator's revealing of his finances, in 1968 the House and Senate followed his lead and set up new standards for their members as a start in his direction.

After Steve Young revealed his financial standing, House side disclosure reforms were led by another bulldog, Charles Halleck, a Republican of Indiana, who worked endlessly with various members on suggestions that went nowhere until John Kyle, Republican of Iowa, came up with the winner. His Code of Ethics, as approved, made it mandatory that House members file a statement of fees received that were over $1,000, the holdings of investments over $5,000 in any firm that does business with the government, and any outside income over $5,000.

Very few men dared come right out and say this was just a drop in the bucket and really amounted to a cover-up of a congressmen's financial statement because it said nothing about what a wife could receive or hold—and everyone knew men like Senator Dirksen kept much of their assets in their wives' names.

On the Senate side, where they set up a Senate Code of Ethics even more lenient than that of the House, only one man got up and blasted it. That was bulldog George Aiken of Vermont, and he said, "I refuse to be a party to perpetrating a fraud upon the American people by making them think that we are trying to purify ourselves, when we are really making ourselves look worse."

Aiken voted against the code—the only dissenting vote in the Senate.

Paul Douglas, the Democratic senator from Illinois, was a hard-working bulldog, known for his liberalism, and a real straight arrow. He accepted no gifts of value over two or three dollars. That made it impossible for any lobbyist to get near him. Nor would he take his disability pension, which he was entitled to, for injuries in World War II.

If he gave a speech to a university, he kept the money. But if it was a speech to some manufacturing group or other commercial group, he gave the money to charity so that he would not be tempted to be influenced in any way.

That was his code, and he lived by it. The irony is, when he eventually lost the election to Charles Percy, it was because voters believed Percy's charge of unfair campaign tactics.

Senator George Aiken was another straight arrow. So careful was he not to permit even a shadow of a thought that he was using his high office for personal advantage, he would not let the road in front of his farm be paved. Instead of living high on the hog, as most Hill men do from their earnings and perks, he lived in a $150-a-month apartment near his office.

And so concerned was he about the ethical quality of the government, he made a dramatic move of self-sacrifice to keep Senator Joseph McCarthy's politics from damaging America's international relations. McCarthy was going to be placed on the Senate Foreign Relations Committee unless someone with more seniority could bump him. Aiken gave up his Senate Labor Relations Committee, on which he had high seniority, to take the lesser post.

Like the liberal Paul Douglas, a conservative senator also set a good example in generosity. That was Strom Thurmond. He gave all his speaking fees to needy students back home—through Winthrop College of South Carolina.

Senator William Fulbright, Democrat of Arkansas, chairman of the Foreign Relations Committee, was one of the most respected and fawned-over men of the Senate. He had a story that he would tell whenever he was embarrassed by a too-laudatory or flowery introduction:

"A farmer was leading a cantankerous calf across a bridge. Halfway over, the calf froze and stood there stiff legged. Nothing would budge it. Finally a car pulled up behind them and stopped, unable to get by.

"The farmer explained the problem, suggested that the driver honk his horn to see if the noise would scare the calf into moving.

"The driver obliged. The horn roared and the calf, terrorized, leoped into the air, plunging over the bridge railing and drowned.

"The farmer turned on the motorist in anger, upbraiding him for overdoing it and killing his calf.

" 'But you asked me to honk,' the driver protested.

" 'Sure,' said the farmer, 'but you didn't have to honk so *big* for such a *little* calf.' "

Back in the days when we had really great orators in the House of Representatives, we Democrats had our big bulldog fighter—Clifton A. Woodrum of Roanoke, Virginia—and the Republicans had their bulldog fighter—Dewey Short of Galena, Missouri, who later became secretary of the army.

Anytime the House had a matter on which they were really divided, Rayburn would line up Woodrum and Joe Martin would line up Dewey Short, giving them a day's notice to get their ammunition ready—and their teeth sharpened.

The big day would arrive and everyone would be tensed up for the fight. Uncle Dewey, as we called Short, would have three snorts before he came on the floor and then he would growl and raise all kinds of hell, without using a note, a map or a chart.

Soon he would have everyone mesmerized. He was a real spellbinder as he ranted from twenty-five to fifty-five minutes. He would have talked longer, but the House runs on an hourly rule.

When he was finished, it would be time for the Democrats to bring on Woodrum, the snorting challenger. He belonged to the old school of the South. He would have been up half the night working with his aides over charts, graphs and statistics. He would come charging in with someone following close behind to carry all his paraphernalia. Cold sober, he needed all that paper to buoy him up, they said.

Dewey would almost foam at the mouth as he berated the Democrats in an emotional approach, but Woodrum would hang on like a true bulldog, insisting on letting the figures speak for themselves.

There is a wonderful follow-up on Dewey Short. Just as strong as he was in battle, so was he strong in friendship. There have been many strange and beautiful pacts on the Hill, but about the most interesting was the friendship pact of Dewey Short, Frank Fellows of Maine and Paul Shafer of Michigan, all Republicans.

They made a drinking buddies' vow that if and when one of them died, the other two would pee on his grave.

So it came to pass that Brother Frank Fellows was the first to meet his Maker. And naturally the other two went to his funeral and they were very sad. In fact, so sad, that when everyone else was leaving the gravesite, they suddenly turned and doubled back and performed the promised ceremony.

I sure miss those fellows. They don't make congressmen like they used to—with originality. But even in this noble hour, there were those detractors who said they were only doing what any bulldog would do.

INDEX

Abernathy, Tom, 172

Abourezk, Jim, 230

Abzug, Bella, 113–114, 117, 127, 128, 277

Abzug, Martin, 116

Adams, Brock, 183–187, 189, 202, 215

Adams, John Quincy, 275, 297

Adams, William, 282

Addonizio, Hugh J., 63, 66

Agnew, Spiro, 179, 322, 433

Aiken, George, 512, 513

Albert, Carl, 73, 82, 132, 152, 172, 174, 175, 176, 178–180, 186, 187, 193, 209, 212, 229, 252, 300, 322–323, 326, 363, 490, 501, 509

All the President's Men, 16

Allen, Leo, 333

American Medical Association, 22

Anderson, Donn, 143

Anderson, Jack, 213, 233, 248, 253

Anderson, John, 508, 509

Anderson, Marian, 257

Andrews, George, 176, 181

Annunzio, Frank, 508

Anti-Semitism, in Congress, 221–224, 225

Archibald, James P., 140

Archibald's (night club), 247

Arends, Leslie, 31, 72, 172, 177, 197

Arlington Cemetery, 467

Auger, Ulysses S., Jr., 142

Ayres, Bill, 294, 336–337, 340

Baker, Bobby 141

Barkley, Alben, 336, 363, 408–409

Barnett, Ross, 379–380

Barry, Rexford G., 210

Bartlett, Charles L., 285

Bartlett, Joe, 174, 180, 181, 186, 193, 202

Bass, Ross, 149

Bassford, Wallace D., 211

Bates, Joe, 65

Battistella, Annabel, *see Fanne Foxe*

Bauman, Robert D., 283

Bayh, Birch, 134, 431, 506

Bean soup, 270, 271, 344, 346

Beckett, John 283

Begich, Nick, 20, 307

Ben-Rubin, 248

Bender, George, 333

Bennett, Charles E., 507, 508

Bentsen, Lloyd, 150

Bevil, Tom, 86

Biffle, Les, 120

Bilbo, Theodore, 301

Black, Ken, 138, 217

Black, Loring, 33

Blanton, Thomas L., 285, 286

Blitch, Iris, 98

Bloom, Sol, 39, 486, 487, 500

"Board of Education Room," 82, 83, 230

Boggs, Corinne, (Lindy), 315

Boggs, Hale, 20, 112, 289, 301, 307, 359, 366, 382–

383, 407
Bolling, Richard, 76
Bolton, Chester, 95
Bolton, Frances, 88, 95, 97, 470
Bolton, Oliver, 94, 95
Borman, Frank, 242
Botzum, Jack, 130
Boykin, Frank, 147, 148
Bradlee, Benjamin, 253
Breckenridge, W.C.P., 284
Brock, Bill, 189, 197
Brokaw, Ann, 100
Brokaw, George, 100
Brown, Gary, 176
Brownlow, Walter Preston, 290
Brumm, James M., 285
Bryan, William Jennings, 33
Bryce, James (quoted) 276
Buckley, James, 117
Bugging, 394, 395
Bull Elephants Club, 137, 217
Burch, John C., 142
Burdick, Quentin, 86
Burke, William, 282
Burke, Yvonne Braithwaite, 281–282, 363
Burnett, Henry C., 286
Burns, John A., 117
Burros, Club, 407
Burton, Philip, 186
Bush, George, 138
Butler, Paul, 367, 373, 374
Butz, Earl, 229
Byrd, Harry Flood, 219
Byrd, Harry Flood, Jr., 252, 254
Byrne, William T., 65, 66
Byrnes, James, 317, 387, 388
Byrns, Joe, Jr., 396

Califano, Joe, 214
Capitol Hill Club, 137

Caraway, Hattie, 92, 93
Carnegie, Dale, 127, 143
Carpenter, Liz, 118–119, 337, 338
Carroll, Charles, 272
Carswell, G. Harrold, 248, 249
Carter, Jimmy, 57–58, 134, 230, 310, 349, 364, 398, 437, 438
Casey, Bob, 360
Cannon, Clarence, 219, 220, 358
Cannon, George, 264
Cannon, Howard, 350
Cannon, Joe, 270, 271, 274, 344, 345
Cederberg, Elford, 191, 307
Celler, Emanuel, 133, 258, 263, 264, 274, 339, 505–506
Cermak, Anton, 462
Challoner, Herschelle, 78
Chalmers, Charles B., 142
Chambers, Whittaker, 64
Chaplain, House of Representatives, 30
Chappaquiddick, 430
Chelf, Frank, 503–504
Chaing Kai-shek, Madame, 479–480
Chiles, Lawton Mainor, Jr., 335
Chisholm, Conrad, 113
Chisholm, Shirley, 89, 111, 113
Chowder and Marching Club, 414
Christina, Princess of Sweden, 477
"Christmas Tree Bill of 1966," 21
Church, Bethine, 134
Church, Frank, 437–438
Churchill, Winston, 473,

518

482–485
Civil Air Patrol, 391–392
Claiborne, William Charles
    Cole, 273–274
Clark, Dick, 230
Clark, James Beauchamp
    (Champ), 210
Clark, John B., 286
Clary, Alla, 314
Clausen, Donald H., 289
Clawson, Carol, 122, 123
Clawson, Ken, 123
Claxton, Thomas, 290
Clay, Henry, 28
Clay, William, 235
Clement, Frank, 364
Cleveland, James, 175, 183
Cochran, John J., 60, 124–
    125
Collins, LeRoy, 365, 368
Colmer, William M., 25, 49,
    52–53, 56, 65, 70, 199,
    221, 265, 394
Conable, Barber Benjamin,
    Jr., 187–188
Congressional Club, 159, 302
Connally, John, 367
Conte, Silvio, 175
Cooley, Harold, 355
Coolidge, Calvin, 320
Cotton, Felix, 349, 350
Cox, Allyn, 501–502
Cox, Edward Eugene, 206
Crane, A.B., 42
Cullinane, Maurice J., 255
Cunningham, Glenn, 339
Curry, Don, 139, 140
Curtis, Charles, 267, 268
Curtis, Thomas B., 241

Dalley, Gifford, 290
Dargens, Louise Maxine, 255
Davis, Mendel J., 141
Dawson, Bill, 257

Day, Edward, 132
De Gaulle, Charles, 480–481
Dellums, Ronald V., 139,
    283, 328
Dempsey, Jack, 491
Derwinski, Edward, 235
Deschler, Lewis, 448, 491
Diggs, Charles C., 76, 77
Dingell, John D., Jr., 141,
    174, 177, 496
Dingell, John, Sr., 141, 496
Dirksen, Everett M., 90, 202,
    235, 376, 420, 425, 440,
    512
DiSalle, Mike, 368
Dodson, Hattie Freeman, 259
Dog Days at the White House
    (Bryant), 336
Dogs, in the White House,
    397
Dole, Elizabeth Hanford, 166
Dole, Robert, 165, 169, 193
Domengeaux, James, 342
Doorkeeper, House of
    Representatives, 15, 16–17,
    62
Doughton, Bob (Muley),
    219, 342
Douglas, Emily Taft, 97
Douglas, Helen Gahagan,
    102–103
Douglas, Paul, 97, 371–372,
    512, 513
Drinan, Robert F., 272
Drinking problems, Congress,
    207–213
Duer, William, 284
Dulles, John Foster, 316–317
Dulski, Thaddeus, 72
Dumphries, Kathryn, 131
Dunn, Edward, 142

Eagleton, Thomas, 113, 382,
    383

Eberharter, Herman P., 211
Edelstein, Morris Michael, 222–223
Edgar, Bob, 27
Edwards, Don, 506
Eisenhower, Dwight D. (Ike), 26, 108, 259–260, 325, 366–370, 401, 403, 413, 462–463, 480
Elizabeth, Queen of England, 474, 475, 477
Embry, Pemmie Lee, 131
Emery, David, 132
ERA (Equal Rights Amendment), 505, 507
Equal-time requirements (FCC), 203
Ervin, Sam, 351, 395, 436–437
Expense accounts, Congress, 73–74
Expulsion from Congress, 286–287

Farah Diba, Empress of Iran, 475, 476, 477
Farbstein, Leonard, 140
Farnsworth, Robert, 43
Farrington, Joseph R., 117
Farrington, Mary Elizabeth, 117
Fascell, Dante, 117
Fauntroy, Walter, 74
Fellows, Frank, 515
Felton, Rebecca Latimer (Mother Felton), 92, 93
Fenwick, Millicent, 277
Filibusters, 169, 203
Fishbait, origin of name, 42
Fitzsimmons, Thomas, 271
"Five Sisters, the," 31
Flanders, Judy, 118
Flood, Catherine, 33
Flood, Dan (Dapper Dan), 33, 34, 79–80
Flores, Yvette Marjorie, 260, 263, 264
Ford, Gerald R., 26, 31, 43, 77, 88, 134, 165, 169, 173, 182, 183, 189, 197, 199, 200, 202, 212, 265, 281, 308, 346, 348–349, 357, 396–399, 413–414, 420, 458, 464, 477, 489, 506, 509
"Fourth branch of government" (lobbyists), 22
Foxe, Fanne, 54, 225, 246
Fraser, Don, 224, 327
Friedesdorf, Max L., 241
Fulbright, J. William, 93, 99, 224
Fulbright, Roberta, 93
Fulton, James, 192, 193, 249–250
Funerals, 466–468

Gann, Dolly, 268
Gardner, Augustus P., 183
Gardner, Colleen, 238–239
Garfield, James, 297
Garner, John Nance, 82, 267–268
Gerry, Elbridge, 275
Gerrymander, 275
Glass, Carter, 28
Glenn, John, 493
Goldwater, Barry, Jr., 94, 138, 502
Goldwater, Barry, Sr., 94, 110, 214, 350, 381, 431, 434
Goodell, Charles, 31
Goodling, Charles, 72
Gore, Albert, 368, 372
Grant, George M., 85
"Grass monkey", 145
Gravel, Mike, 238
Graves, William J., 285

520

Gray, Ken, 238
Green, Bill, Jr., 330
Green, Robert Alexis, 25
Green, Theodore F., 274
Griffiths, Martha, 150, 151,
    505–506
Griswold, Roger, 286–287
Gross, H.R., 73, 76, 77, 126,
    498
Gude, Gilbert, 74
Gunter, Bill, 141
Gurney, Ed, 231

Hackney, Charles W., Jr.,
    173, 180, 181, 193, 197,
    198, 202
Hadley, Jane, 434
Hagen, Harold C., 106
Haile, Selassie, 481
Haley, Jim, 128
Hall, Durward, 172
Halleck, Charles, 466, 511–
    512
Hardwick, Thomas W., 92
Harmon, Randall (Front-
    Porch Harmon), 34–35
Hart, Philip, 127
Hats, ban against in
    Congress, 276–277
Hayden, Carl, 219, 274
Hayes, Brooks, 356, 357
Hays, Wayne, 15, 24, 66, 75,
    78, 122, 127, 128, 139, 149,
    165, 224, 225, 239–240,
    240–245, 262, 300, 307,
    326, 328, 399, 412, 413
Heard, John A., 284
Hébert, F. Edward, 65,
    118, 128, 180, 346
Heflin, Tom, 286
Hennings, Tom, 213
Hepler, Frank M., 449
Herbert, Philemon, 27
Herring, Willie, 66, 67, 68

Hilsman, Roger, 140
Hirohito, Emperor of Japan,
    489
Hiss, Alger, 64
Hoeven, Charles, 341
Holden, Phyllis, 165
Holton, John, 26, 27
Homosexuality, 247, 250
Hoover, Herbert, 385, 396,
    491
Horton, Frank, 210
Hosmer, Craig, 197, 198
Howar, Barbara, 155
Howe, Allan, 251
Howe, Marlene Dee, 252
Hoyt, Ken, 352–353, 357,
    385, 386, 392
Hudnut, Bill, 32, 150
Huff, Corrine, 261
Hughes, Harold, 31
Hull, Merlin, 85
Humphrey, Hubert H.
    (HHH), 57, 110, 169, 170,
    198, 201, 203, 230, 310,
    380, 381, 418, 419, 420,
    421–426, 477–478
Hungate, Bill, 174, 358–359

Ichord, Richard, 86
Ickes, Harold L., 99
Inouye, Daniel Ken, 272

Jackson, Andrew, 274, 275
Jackson, Henry (Scoop), 57,
    231, 354, 430, 439
Jacobs, Andy, 55, 58, 151,
    163
James, Esther, 260, 261
Javits, Jacob (Jake), 57, 157,
    259
Jefferson, Thomas, 28, 279
Jennings, W. Pat, 263
Jim Crow, 256–257
Joelson, Charles, 179

521

Johnson, Earle, 392
Johnson, Jed, Jr., 141
Johnson, Lady Bird, 26, 118, 420, 468
Johnson, Luci, 27
Johnson, Lyndon B. (LBJ), 26, 36–37, 54, 121, 124, 139, 141, 154, 213, 218, 219, 252, 262, 278, 307, 310, 317–318, 322, 348–349, 367–368, 374, 375–376, 378, 380–381, 411–412, 441, 463, 464, 467, 494–495
Johnson, Zeake, 263, 447, 458
Johnson, Olin, 217, 425–426
Jones, Marvin, 311
Juliana, Queen of the Netherlands, 470, 472, 479
Justice, T.T., 41

Karsten, Frank, 60–61, 126
Karth, Joe, 418
Katzenbach, Nicholas, 410
Keating, Kenneth, 334
Keith, Hastings, 81
Kefauver, Estes, 55, 368, 371–372, 373, 426–428
Kennedy, Edward (Ted), 75, 128, 287, 376–377, 430–431
Kennedy, Jacqueline Bouvier, 405–406, 407
Kennedy, John F. (JFK), 16, 27, 107, 148–149, 171, 224, 234, 263, 278, 287, 291, 307, 317, 320–321, 337, 354, 364, 367, 370, 373, 374–379, 393, 405–408, 408, 410, 411, 413, 441, 443, 444, 463, 464, 465
Kennedy, Joseph, Sr., 373
Kennedy, Robert F. (RFK),

27, 287, 372–373, 377
Keogh, Eugene, 496
Keys, Martha, 163, 164
Keys, Samuel Robert, 164
Kimball, Spencer, 251
King, MacKenzie, 473, 485
King, Martin Luther, Jr., 257
Knight, John William, 309
Knutson, Coya, 106–107
Krebs, J. Guy, 50, 52
Kyle, John, 341, 511

La Guardia, Fiorello, 33
Latch, Edward G., 171
Latrobe, Benjamin Henry, 296
Latta, Delbert, 200–201
Laxalt, Paul, 335
Leggett, Robert, 151–152
Legislative Reference Service (Library of Congress), 139–140
L'Enfant, Pierre, 297
Lenthall, John, 296
Levin, Lewis Charles, 272
Lewis, Bill, 107–109
Lewis, Dixon H., 288–289
Library of Congress, 139–140, 295
Lincoln, Abraham (quoted), 336
Litton, Jerry, 506
Lobbyists, 20–23, 235–239
Long, Rose, 95, 98
Long, Huey, 28, 30, 94
Long, Rose, 98, 95
Long, Russell B., 94, 95, 219
Longworth, Alice Roosevelt, 146, 161, 267, 268
Longworth, Nicholas, 145–146, 267, 268
Lowenstein, Allard Kenneth, 133
Lucas, Scott, 333
Luce, Clare Boothe, 98, 99,

522

103, 349, 350, 357
Luce, Henry, 100
Lyon, Matthew, 271, 286–287

MacArthur, Douglas, 391, 401, 402, 488, 489
MacArthur, Jean, 488, 489
McCarran, Pat, 213
McCarthy, Abigail, 135
McCarthy, Eugene, 135, 354–355
McCarthy, Joseph R., 110, 161, 216, 441, 442, 513
McClendon, Sarah, 278, 279
McCloskey, Pete, 244
McCormack, John W., 65, 69, 89, 91, 112, 121, 133, 134, 199–200, 213, 229, 255, 263, 278–279, 299, 303, 310, 314, 321, 323–324, 327, 333, 363, 369–371, 374, 376, 408, 450, 466–467, 491
MacDonald, Torbert, 339
Mace, House of Representatives, 283, 284–285, 286
McFall, John, 235
McGovern, Eleanor, 382
McGovern, George, 111, 112, 383, 461
McGrory, Mary, 214
McKellar, Kenneth, 436
McKinnon, Clinton, 355
McLean, Bill, 137
McPherson, Myra, 152
Madden, Ray, 20, 143, 183, 198, 201
Maddux, Jared, 368
Madison, Dolley, 478
Magnuson, Warren, 366, 367
Mahon, George, 172
Mallett Bakery Shop, 44

Malloy, James T., 233, 306
Mann, James R., 183
Mansfield, Jayne, 492
Mansfield, Maureen, 441
Mansfield, Mike, 74, 440–441, 451–452, 505
Marcantonio, Vito, 221, 330
Martin, Joseph W., Jr., 82, 104, 323, 332, 445, 466, 467, 488, 514
Matsunaga, Sparky, 407
Maverick, Maury, 357
Meade, R.K., 284
Mencken, H.L. (quoted), 82
Mercer, Lucy, 146
Michel, Robert, 235
Miller, Bill, 433
Miller, Clement Woodnut, 289
Miller, George P., 347
Miller, Mable, 16, 59, 400
Miller, Sarah Patsy, 60, 66, 407, 412, 474
Miller, William Mosely (Fishbait), 39–70
Mills, Polly, 245, 247
Mills, Wilbur, 54, 65, 112, 162, 172, 183, 208, 225, 227, 230, 231, 244–246 301, 505
Mineta, Norman Yoshio, 273
Minshall, William E., 72, 212
Mondale, Joan, 32
Mondale, Walter, 32, 128, 135, 310, 438
Monocle (restaurant), 20, 239, 337
Monroe, James, 410
Montgomery, Robert, 462–463
Montgomery, Sonny, 150
Morton, Rogers B., 308
Moss, Frank E., 252, 346
Mundt, Karl, 216

Muskie, Edmund, 151, 382
Muskie, Jane, 157
Musser, B.L., 68–69

Nader, Ralph, 225
Natcher, William H., 498
National Capital Democratic
  Club, 137
National Chili Cookoff
  Contest, 350–351
National Defense Education
  Act, 107
National Press Club, 349
Nehru, Jawaharlal, 487–488
Nepotism, 234–235
Neuberger, Richard L., 369
Nixon-Humphrey campaign
  (1968), 170–171, 202–
  204
Nixon, Patricia, 123
Nixon, Richard M., 16, 26,
  63–64, 102, 115, 117, 122,
  149, 165, 170, 181, 201,
  203, 212, 231, 325, 354,
  356, 381, 394, 395, 408,
  415, 458–459, 463, 489,
  503
Norrell, William F., 245
Norris, George, 213
Norton, Mary Teresa, 281
Nunes, Donnel, 253

O'Brien, Lawrence F., 363
O'Brien, Leo, 129
O'Donnell, Emmett (Rosie),
  109
O'Neill, Dev, 80
O'Neill, Thomas P., Jr.
  (Tip), 78, 230, 252, 508–
  511
Ottinger, Richard L., 283
Owens, Bob, 233

Paddleball Club, 332–333

Pages, Congressional, 140–
  144
Park, Chung Hee, 152
Parr, David L., 230
Pascagoula, Mississippi, 13,
  20, 39, 58–59, 67
Patman, Wright, 237, 395
Patrick, Luther, 84, 357–358
Patten, Harold A. (Porky),
  67
Peak, Pat, 240, 243
Pelham, Bud, 48
Pelly, Tom, 176–177
Pepper, Claude, 304–305
Percy, Charles, 512
Petinaud, Ernest, 244
Philip, Prince, 474
Pocahontas, 28
POETS Club (Piss on
  Everything, Tomorrow's
  Saturday), 136
Powell, Adam Clayton, Jr.,
  75, 227, 244, 255–266,
  286, 326
Prayer Room, House of
  Representatives, 30–31
Press, relationship to
  Congress, 213–214
Pressler, Larry, 498–499
Proxmire, Ellen, 418
Proxmire, William, 346, 416–
  417
Pryor, David H., 141
Pryor, Sam, 385
Pucinski, Roman, 180, 182
"Pumpkin Papers", 63

Quie, Albert, 31
Quinn, Sally, 155

Rainey, Joseph, 271
Ramsay, Dr. Thomas R., 58–
  59
Randolph, Edmund, 410

Randolph, Jennings, 26
Randolph, John, 28
Rangel, Charles, 231
Rankin, Jeanette, 89–92, 281, 440
Rankin, John, 222–224, 256, 386
Rankin, Wellington, 91
Raphall, Morris Jacob, 272
Ray, Elizabeth, 78, 122, 123, 165, 238, 240, 261
Rayburn Conference Room, 278
Rayburn House Office Building, 24, 291–295
Rayburn, Lucinda, 129
Rayburn, Metze Jones, 312–313
Rayburn, Sam, 16, 17, 18, 26, 31, 35, 66, 69, 83, 87, 88, 89, 106, 121, 126, 150, 213, 269, 272, 279, 291–292, 299–300, 302, 303, 309, 310, 319–320, 332, 341, 342–343, 348, 349, 357, 363, 378, 384, 392, 393, 402, 418, 419, 427, 434–435, 445, 446–447, 457, 466, 474, 489, 508, 514
Reagan, Ronald, 498
Reed, Mike, 321
Rees, Edward, 125
Reid, John W., 286
Republican Humor Book, The (Skubik), 229
Rhee, Jhoon, 86
Rhodes, John, 31
Ribicoff, Abraham, 368
Rich, Robert, 85
Riegle, Donald W., Jr., 152
Rivers, L. Mendel, 176–177, 180, 191, 192, 207, 213, 217–218, 354, 488–489

Robertson, Alice Mary, 281
Robertson, Turner, 324
Robinson, Joseph T., 28
Rockefeller, Nelson, 322, 438, 476
Rodino, Peter W., Jr., 63
Rogers, Dillard, 354
Rogers, Edith Nourse, 88, 103, 104, 105, 106
Rogers, John Jacob, 105
Rogers, Will, Jr., 205–206
Rohr, Carl, 48
Roncallo, Angelo, 141
Rooney, John, 72
Roosevelt, Eleanor, 83, 91, 146, 257, 378, 379, 388–389, 393, 396, 405, 444
Roosevelt, Franklin D. (FDR,) 26, 83, 89, 97, 99, 146, 236, 267, 317, 366, 373, 386, 388, 389, 403, 404, 444
Roosevelt, Franklin, Jr., 404
Roosevelt, James, 354, 368, 404
Roosevelt, Theodore, 145
Rosenthal, Benjamin, 225
Ross, Lenny, 364
Rota, Shelva, 131
Rotunda (restaurant), 20, 240, 337
Roybal, Ed, 86
Rumsfeld, Donald, 173, 178, 197
"Runaway Pappy Bill," 400
Russell, Mark, 152
Russell, Richard, 373,
Sabath, Adolph, 333–334
St. George, Katherine, 110
Saund, Dalip Singh, 272
Saylor, John, 192
Schroeder, Pat, 118–119
Schurman, Beatrice, 366
Schwengel, Fred, 501

Scott, Hazel, 256, 258
Scott, Hugh, 74, 439, 440
Scott, William, 213
Secretaries Club, 136
Security precautions, 448, 452, 454, 459, 465
Sedition Act of 1798, 271
Sevilla-Sacasa, Guillermo, 456
Shafer, Paul, 515
Shah of Iran, 478
Sheppard, Harry R., 65
"Shit-ass of the Year Award," 333
Shooting, in House Chamber (1954), 445
Short, Dewey, 131, 514
Shriver, Sargent, 112, 383
Sikes, Robert L.F., 228, 307 368
Siler, Eugene, 341
Silver Slipper (night club), 247
Smathers, George, 305, 369
Smith, Clyde, 107–108
Smith, Ed (Cotton Ed), 216–217
Smith, Howard, 316
Smith, Margaret Chase, 89, 107–110, 281
Smoking, ban against on floor of House, 277
Snyder, Eugene, 27, 165
Snyder, Pat Robertson, 165
Sommers, Carl E., 83, 342, 495
Southwick, George, 285
Sparkman, John, 371
Spence, Floyd, 86
Springer, William, 172
Stanton, James V., 305–306, 399
Stationery fund, Congress, 73
Statuary Hall, 278, 279, 280,

296
Stedman, Charles Manly, 274
Steiger, Bill, 176, 179, 180, 197
Steiger, Sam, 35, 36, 305
Stephens, Alexander, 500
"Sterling Bulletin, The", 24–25
Stevens, Ted, 86
Stevenson, Adlai, 164–165, 259, 325, 368, 369, 371, 377, 379
Stewart, Jimmy, 109
Stokes, Louis, 235
Sumner, Jessie, 88, 103
Swann, Emma, 262
Sweeney, Martin L., 206
Symington, James, 86, 94, 163, 505
Symington, Stuart, 94

Taber, John, 220
Taft, Robert, 359, 385, 387
Taft, Robert, Jr., 174, 180, 184, 190, 193, 197
Taft, William Howard, 288, 354
Teague, Olin, 338
Thomas, Albert, 88, 106, 219
Thompson, Frank, Jr., 122
Thomson, Suzi Park, 152
Thornton, William, 279, 295
Thurmond, Strom, 30, 225, 417, 513
Tierman, Robert O., 141
Tinkham, George, 35
Tower, John, 129, 350–351
Traxler, Bob, 345
Truman, Bess, 257, 456
Truman, Harry, 26, 83, 94, 166, 257–258, 303, 320, 354, 366, 387–390, 392,

401–402, 408, 435–436, 462, 475, 503
Tufty, Esther van Waggoner, 348
Tunney, Gene, 491, 492
Tunney, John, 174
Turner, Charles Henry, 290

Udall, Morris, 305, 306
Udall, Stewart, 234
Ullman, Al, 161
Ullman, Anita, 162

Vineyard, Ann, 131
Vinson, Carl, 85, 274
Voorhis, Jerry, 415

Waldie, Jerome, 232
Wall, Tamara, 201
Wallace, George, 170–171, 177, 181, 492
Wallace, Henry, 99, 388
Walsh, David Ignatious, 247
Washburn brothers, 287
Washington, George, 279, 280, 290, 296, 347
Washington, Isabel, 256
Washington, Walter, 255
Washington Fringe Benefit, The (Ray), 240
Washington Press Club, 438
Watergate, 352–353, 358, 363, 395, 436
"Watergate Follies, The" (poem), 353
Watkins, G. Robert, 169, 198
Watson, Thomas, 92
Webster, Daniel, 426–427

Weiss, Sammy, 223
West, Carolyn, 131–132
West, Milton, 343
White, Byron (Whizzer), 492–493
White, Compton, 66, 141, 465
Whittemore, Benjamin Franklin, 264, 271
Whittington, William, 497
Widnall, William, 72
Willard Hotel, 27
Williams, G. Mennen (Soapy), 347–348
Willkie, Wendell, 385, 386–387
Wilson, Henry, 288
Windsor, Duchess of, 347
Winthrop, Robert C., 284
Wolff, Lester, 188, 202
Woodrow Wilson: American Prophet (Walworth), 248
Woodrum, Clifton A., 85, 514–515
Wright, Jim, 182, 187–188

Yarborough, Ralph, 225
Yates, Sidney, 194
Yatron, Gus, 235
Young, John, 239
Young, Stephen M., 511
Yulee, David Levy, 273

Zahm, Ernest 342
Zangara, Joseph, 462
Zioncheck, Marion, 208–209, 357

WILLIAM "FISHBAIT" MILLER is from Pascagoula, Mississippi. He spent 42 years in Washington, D.C., working for the U.S. Congress, including 28 years as Democratic Doorkeeper of the House of Representatives. He retired in 1975, and now lives in Atlanta, Georgia, with his wife and daughter.

FRANCES SPATZ LEIGHTON is a Washington, D.C., journalist. She has co-authored more than a dozen books including MY LIFE WITH JACQUELINE KENNEDY, by Mary Barelli Gallagher, and DOG DAYS AT THE WHITE HOUSE, by Traphes Bryant. Her magazine articles have appeared in *Ladies' Home Journal, McCalls, Good Housekeeping,* and *Cosmopolitan.*